A
Dictionary
of
Chivalry

Illustrated by Pauline Bayne

A Dictionary of
Chivalry

GRANT UDEN

Thomas Y. Crowell Company
New York

L. C. Card AC 67-10477

First impression 1968
Second impression 1971

ISBN 0 690 23815 0

Printed in Great Britain by
W. S. Cowell Ltd, at the Butter Market, Ipswich, Suffolk

Acknowledgements

The Author and Publishers are grateful for permissions granted by the following:

William Collins & Co., London, and G. P. Putnam's Sons, New York, for extracts from *The Once and Future King* by T. H. White

Blackie & Sons Ltd, Glasgow, for an extract from *The Romance and Legend of Chivalry* by A. R. Hope Moncrieff

The Society of Authors as the Literary Representatives of the Estate of the late John Masefield and the Macmillan Company of New York for a quotation from *The Ballard of Sir Bors*

Eyre & Spottiswoode Ltd, London, for an extract from *A History of Europe* by H. A. L. Fisher

Routledge & Kegan Paul Ltd, London, and the Yale University Press for an extract from *Bertrand of Brittany* by Roger Vercel

Arthur Barker Ltd, London, for extracts from *The Black Mastiff* by M. Coryn

Robert Hale Ltd, London, and the Bertha Klausner Literary Agency, New York, for an extract from *The Splendour of France* by Robert Payne

Miss Collins and Dodd, Mead & Company, New York, for a quotation from *Lepanto* by G. K. Chesterton

The Cambridge University Press and Sir Steven Runciman for an extract from his *History of the Crusades*

George Allen & Unwin Ltd, London, for an extract from *Richard III* by Paul Murray Kendall

Messrs Curtis Brown, London, for an extract from *Simon de Montfort* by Margaret Wade Labarge

Martin Secker & Warburg Ltd, London, for a quotation from *War Song of the Saracens* by James Elroy Flecker

Frederick Warne & Co. Ltd, London, for a quotation from *The Song of Roland* by Hilda Cumings Price

The publishers also gratefully acknowledge the expert advice of J. P. Brooke-Little, Esq., F.S.A., Bluemantle Pursuivant of Arms.

J. E. U.

And, lest we dream too much
 Of great days past,
Tell us great days may always be,
 Even to the last;
That, holding fast the truth,
 Hearts high and free,
Men still may ride abroad
 Armed cap-à-pie.

Abatements of Honour: charges (i.e., designs and figures) placed on coats of arms to show that the bearer had been guilty of some unknightly or dishonourable action. This is the origin of the term still in use today, 'a blot on the 'scutcheon' (escutcheon or shield). Few actual examples are known, probably because men would rather not display arms at all than show their disgrace; and also because the 'blots' were regarded as only temporary and could be erased by some compensating deed of honour. (See *Augmentations of Honour* for opposite.)

Accolade: ceremony of conferring knighthood by an embrace, placing hand on neck, or by a light blow on shoulder or neck with the flat of a sword (from the Latin *collum*, neck).

Accoutrements: equipment and trappings, usually for military service.

Achievement: the complete heraldic composition or picture belonging to a person entitled to bear arms. It consists of the *shield*, carrying the design or 'arms', the *helmet*, the *wreath*, the *crest*, the *mantling* (or *lambrequin*) and the *motto*. (See separate definitions of these words.)

Acton: stuffed or quilted vest or jacket worn under mail and acting as a shock-absorber when blows descended. Later, a jacket protected with mail or plates of armour. (Spelt also *hacqueton*, *aketon*, etc. From the Spanish *alcoton*, *algodon*, cotton.)

Addorsed: set or turned back to back, as of two animals depicted on a shield.

Adoubement: see *Dubbing*.

Agincourt: the village in N. France where Henry V, with about 9,000 men, defeated about 60,000 French, led by D'Albret, Constable of France, on October 24th, 1415 (St. Crispin's Day). The chivalry of France suffered terrible losses. According to one contemporary account 'out of their numbers fell the Dukes of Brabant, Bar and Alençon, five Counts, nearly ninety Barons and standard-bearers; more than 1,500 knights, and between 4,000 and 5,000 other

1

nobles, being nearly all the nobility of the French chivalry.' (Thomas Elmham, monk of Canterbury.) The ground was sodden with rain and the French fought in a confined space which made them an easy target for the merciless flights of arrows from the English longbowmen. A French account describes the French knights as 'so loaded with armour that they could not move. First they were armed in long coats of steel, reaching to their knees, and very heavy, below which was armour for their legs, and above, white harness and basnets with camails, and so heavy was their armour that, together with the softness of the ground, they could with difficulty lift their weapons.' (Jean le Fèvre, Sieur de Remy.) The battle is an example of the armoured knight failing to learn the lessons of warfare, and trying to fight in the old way against new methods and strategy. (For definitions of some words in the accounts above, see *Alwyte Armour, Bascinet, Camail* and *Harness*.)

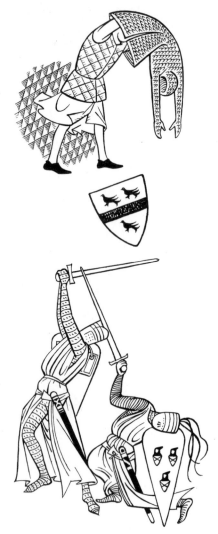

Aketon: See *Acton*.

Allusive (or Canting) Arms: heraldic arms which 'allude', or make reference to, the name or profession of the person entitled to bear them; thus, a man named Martin might show the bird of this name on his shield; an Arundel might choose *hirondelles* (French for 'swallows'); or a member of the Butler family might decide on a wine-cup.

Almain, Almayne or Alman Rivets: kind of light armour, originating in Germany, with plates sliding on rivets, set in slots, so there was great flexibility. *Almain* comes from the early word for German or Germany. In time, this type of armour was made in other countries as well. Henry VIII sent to Milan for 5,000 suits of 'almayne rivets'. The Tower of London records also mention 'almayne corselets'. An armourer from Germany was sometimes called an Almain.

A l'Outrance: to the bitter end, to death. A fight with war-heads to the lances, or other dangerous weapons. Compare *Arms of Courtesy* and *Joust à Plaisance*, and see *Coronel*.

Alwyte Armour: Until the beginning of the 15th century body armour was usually covered by a 'surcoat' (literally, an 'overcoat'). either a long flowing garment gathered in at the waist or, later, a shorter, neatly fitting garment called a 'jupon' or 'gipoun'. Soon after 1400 this outer garment ceased to be worn, and the knight appeared with all his armour uncovered, cased in glittering steel from head to foot. This was 'alwyte' or 'white' armour. See *Surcoat* and *Jupon* for further information on these garments.

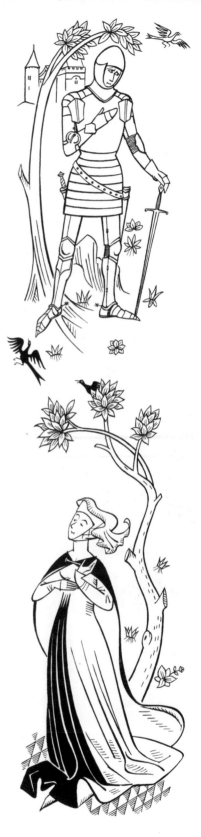

Amadis of Gaul: the hero of one of the greatest and most popular prose romances of chivalry, whose authorship is uncertain. The first four books were written just before 1400, but these were added to by later writers. Just as Arthur is the greatest figure in the chivalric romances of Britain, so Amadis is the central hero in Spanish and Portuguese romances. Amadis was rescued from the sea as a baby by the Scottish knight Gandales, and was in his youth known as the 'Child of the Sea'. Robert Southey (1774–1843) published a good translation of some of the Amadis stories. Interestingly enough, America owes something to them, since California (from the Spanish *Caliente Fornalla*, hot furnace) was named from one of the later Amadis books, written by Ordóñez de Montalvo; and in one Amadis adventure, the scene is set in America – perhaps the only appearance of a mediaeval knight-errant on American soil!

America: See *Amadis of Gaul*.

Angarad of the Golden Hand: the lady at King Arthur's court loved by Sir Peredur, one of the knights of the Round Table. At first she scorns him, and Peredur vows never to speak again till Angarad loves him above all other men. Known thenceforward as 'The Dumb Youth' or 'Young Mute', he performs a long series of heroic deeds until, battered and dispirited, he comes back unrecognized to Arthur's court and makes such an impression on the lady of the Golden Hand that she laments how sad it is that the unknown knight cannot speak, for, if he could, she would love him above all men. This satisfactorily releases Peredur from his vow.

3

Angon: an early type of throwing spear, used by the Franks, with a barbed head and slender iron neck, the whole being about six feet long. One of its most effective methods of use was to hurtle it against an enemy and pierce his shield, dragging it down by the weight of the long shaft. The Frank could then rush in, tread on the down-slanting angon and jerk the shield from the bearer's hand, leaving him defenceless.

Annulet: one of the heraldic *sub-ordinaries*. (See definition of this term.) A ring, larger than a *roundel*, carried as a charge on a shield.

Antique (or Eastern) Crown: one of the eight crest-coronets used in heraldry. It carries an unspecified number of triangular points.

A Plaisance: for pleasure or amusement, as distinct from *à l'outrance* (above). Used to describe a friendly joust, fought with blunted lance-heads. See *coronel* and *lance of courtesy*.

Archalaus the Enchanter: one of the many lusty villains of the old romances of chivalry. A gigantic figure in green armour, he was eventually slain by Esplandian, the son of Amadis of Gaul. The story of Archalaus illustrates one of the most important rules in the code of chivalry – 'Thou shalt never lie, and shalt remain faithful to thy pledged word.' (Léon Gautier.) Amadis of Gaul was walking on the shore with his bride Oriana, when they were confronted by a veiled woman who threw herself at their feet and implored the knight to take pity on her misery and grant her a boon, which easily lay within his power. The gentle Oriana added her plea, and the courteous knight raised the suppliant to her feet, telling her that her wish was already granted. Whereupon, the treacherous lady arose, triumphantly pulled aside her veil and revealed herself as the wife of Archalaus the Enchanter who, at that time, after a life-time of monstrous evil, lay bound in chains, brooding in lonely rage. The Enchanter's wife demanded that Amadis, having pledged his word to grant her wish, should release his enemy; and the knight, scorning to break his promise, even for such an evil pair, ordered his prisoner to be set free, to work further mischief against his

4

deliverer. See *Du Guesclin Bertrand* for a real-life example of the importance attached to the pledged word.

Arçon: raised bow or arch forming front part of saddle; the saddle-bow or pommel. See *Saddle* for the various parts of this important item in a knight's equipment.

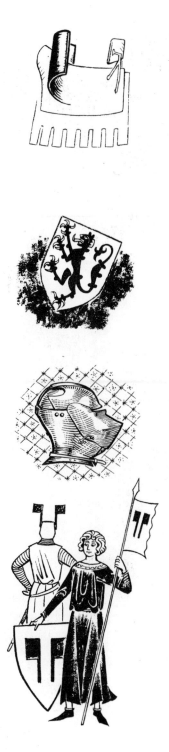

Argent: one of the two 'metals' used in heraldry, deriving its name from the Latin *argentum*, silver. Abbreviated, it should always be written 'arg.'; in painting or drawing it can be represented by white, or by leaving the area blank. See *Metals* and *Hatching*.

Armed: apart from its obvious meaning of equipped with weapons or armour, the word has a special significance in heraldry. Beasts or birds, if their claws, talons, teeth or beaks are of a different colour or 'metal' from their bodies, are described as *armed*.

Armed Cap-a-Pie: armed or accoutred from head to foot; in full harness.

Armet: a type of helmet which appeared not long before 1450, probably originating in Italy and coming to England via Germany, though it was not so popular with Englishmen as it was elsewhere. It was much superior to the earlier *bascinet* (see definition), being lighter to wear and giving better protection; the chief difference between the armet and earlier helmets being that the latter had been put on by lowering them over the head, which carried most of the weight. The lower parts of the armet opened out on hinges, so that the helmet could be closed round the head and the weight transferred via the *gorget* (see definition) to the shoulders.

Armigerous: entitled to display heraldic bearings (from Latin *arma*, arms; *gerere*, to bear). An *armiger* was originally an armour-bearer, an esquire, attending on a knight and slightly below him in rank, but carrying his own armorial device.

Arming Sword: one of the two different sizes of sword used by knights, especially in the 15th

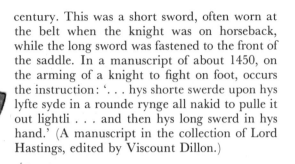

century. This was a short sword, often worn at the belt when the knight was on horseback, while the long sword was fastened to the front of the saddle. In a manuscript of about 1450, on the arming of a knight to fight on foot, occurs the instruction: '. . . hys shorte swerde upon hys lyfte syde in a rounde rynge all nakid to pulle it out lightli . . . and then hys long swerd in hys hand.' (A manuscript in the collection of Lord Hastings, edited by Viscount Dillon.)

Armorial Bearings: the figures, colours, shapes and designs carried on shields, banners, surcoats, etc., belonging to a particular person or family. In cases of dispute, it is the duty of the Heralds to decide who has the just claim to display the bearings. See *Chaucer, Geoffrey* for one of the most famous cases of this.

Armory: the science of heraldry; or, more properly, that branch of heraldry which deals with armorial bearings. See *Armoury*, to distinguish between the two words.

Armour: the defensive covering worn by a fighting man. Usually it was made of iron or steel, but there are records of other tough materials being used; e.g., in a list of armour of Charles VI of France (1411) occurs a set for man and horse made of leather from Syria. So far as England is concerned, the manufacture and wearing of armour falls into four broad periods (a classification given by Charles J. ffoulkes, former Curator of the Tower Armouries):

The Age of Mail (from, roughly, 1000 to 1300)
The Transition from Mail to Plate (1300 to 1400)
The Age of Plate Armour (1400 to 1600)
The Period of Decadence (i.e., loss of excellence) thereafter.

For many centuries the design and manufacture of armour was very much an international affair, and a Spanish or German knight was likely to wear very much the same sort of war-harness as an English or French one. Only after about the middle of the 14th century did more distinct national styles begin to emerge. England was late in developing the manufacture of fine armour, and not till Henry VIII established his workshops within the royal palace at Greenwich

6

in the year 1519 did a recognizably English pattern begin to appear. Even then, it was made by German armourers!

Certain countries, and, within them, certain families, were particularly famous for the manufacture of armour and weapons. Thus, Nuremberg was a great German centre, and another was Augsburg, where the Colman family settled and produced magnificent examples of the armourer's craft. In Italy, the finest armour was made in Milan, where the Negroli family and the Missaglias were the most celebrated manufacturers. The Wolfs of Landshut were equally well-known and worked for Philip II of Spain.

Good armour, like a perfectly-fitting suit, had to be made to measure; and, if armourer and customer could not meet in person, elaborate measurements, or actual models of limbs, were sent from one country to another. It is clear that work-shops were often organized almost on modern factory lines, with a good deal of specialization. In Henry VIII's armouries there were hammer-men to forge steel plates, mill-men to polish them, lock-smiths for the various hinges and fastenings, etc.

One or two special points should be noted about mediaeval armour. The first is that, in its day, no one talked about a 'suit' of armour. This is a comparatively modern term. The knight and the armourer called it 'an armour' or 'harness'. Shakespeare makes Macbeth say: 'Blow wind! Come wrack! At least we'll die with harness on our back'; and in the Bible (1 Kings, 22:34), we read: 'And a certain man drew a bow at venture, and smote the king of Israel between the joints of the harness.' Nowadays, we usually associate harness only with horses. But it is a mistake to think that the common expression 'to die in harness' has anything to do with horses. It really means to die with armour on, i.e., on active duty.

There are many wrong ideas about the weight and flexibility of mediaeval armour. Knights were not the ponderous, slow-moving figures they are often represented as being, helpless unless in the saddle, unable to mount without help. According to one authority (R. Ewart Oakeshott, *A Knight and His Armour*, 1961, and *A Knight and His Horse*, 1962, Lutterworth Press), 'a full plate harness of about 1470 was

no heavier – indeed, it was sometimes lighter – than the full marching kit of a 1914–18 infantryman'; and '. . . at the present day, the full ceremonial uniform and equipment of a trooper in the Household Cavalry weighs a little more than a full armour of 1460.' Mr. Ewart Oakeshott gives the following examples of weights:

COMPLETE ARMOURS

	lb.	oz.
Italian field armour, c.1450 (Scott Collection, Glasgow)	57	0
German field armour, c.1525 (Wallace Collection, London)	41	13½
Field armour, Greenwich, 1590 (Wallace Collection, London)	71	14
Jousting armour, German, 1500 (Wallace Collection, London)	90	1½

MAIL

	lb.	oz.
Long hauberk, 14th century (Royal Scottish Museum)	31	0
Short hauberk, 14th century (Schloss Churburg, Tyrol)	20	11

HELMETS

	lb.	oz.
The Black Prince's helm (Canterbury Cathedral)	7	2
Bascinet (visored) and camail, c.1390 (Schloss Churburg, Tyrol)	12	9
Sallet, German, c.1470 (Wallace Collection, London)	5	0
Jousting helm, English, c.1480 (Tower of London)	23	8

Edward I of England (1239–1307), described by one who knew him as 'of fine figure and tall stature, head and shoulders above the ordinary people', and whose armour would have weighed more than most men's, could leap into the saddle without the aid of stirrups, armed cap-a-pie. A fit man today, even though he has not been trained from his youth upwards as was the knight of chivalry, can do almost as well. At least, tests have been made and filmed in America showing that 20th-century man, though supposedly less tough than his knightly ancestors, can still run and jump in full harness,

8

mount a horse and get off again unaided. The point is that good armour was magnificently made to give the wearer the maximum amount of freedom of movement, and the weight was fairly evenly spread over the whole body.

For some different types of armour see *Alwyte, Damascene, Chain Mail, Fluted, Gothic, Lamellar, Plate, Maximilian, Studded and Splinted, Field Armour, Hosting Harness.*

Armourer's Company: one of the ancient craft guilds of the city of London, established at least as early as the beginning of the· 14th century, and given its charter by Henry VI in 1453. Over the years, it came to incorporate a number of allied crafts, such as the heaumers (makers of helms), the garnishers and repairers, and the blade-smiths. More recently it amalgamated with the Braziers, and is now the Worshipful Company of Armourers and Braziers, with its Hall at the junction of Coleman Street and London Wall. Its surviving records date back to 1413 and show that the Company had the right to examine any weapons or armour exposed for sale in the City and, if the standard of workmanship was approved, to stamp them with their official mark – the letter 'A' and a crown. The Company possesses many treasures, including a harness made by Jacobi Topf of Innsbruck, armourer to the Emperor Maximilian and resident in England 1562–75. It also has the original silver seal used by the Company in the reign of Henry VI, bearing the device of St. George, patron saint of Armourers, on foot and killing a dragon with a spear. A new grant of arms made by Clarenceux King of Arms (see separate entry for this officer) in 1556 was addressed to 'the Fraternitye or Guylde of St. George of the men of the mystery of Armerors.'

Armoury: a place for the storage and safe-keeping of arms; or, particularly in the United States, a workshop for the manufacture of arms and weapons. Cf. *Armory.* The spelling of this group of words is apt to be confusing, since America and England have different ideas about the preservation of the letter 'u'!

Arms: in general, the weapons and fighting equipment of war; in heraldry, the devices and

designs on shields, banners, etc. See *Achievement* and *Kings of Arms*. Oddly enough, in falconry, it can also mean 'legs', i.e., the legs of a hawk from thigh to foot.

Arms of Courtesy: weapons not intended to inflict serious damage. See, e.g., *Lance of Courtesy*.

Arms of England: or Royal Arms. The full story is long and intricate, and the changing arms are a history of England in themselves, faithfully reflecting all the succession of reigning Houses, etc. But the main, unchanging ingredient, from earliest times (heraldically speaking) has been the royal lions or leopards. The first known occurrence of these arms is in a charter of William, son of Geoffrey Plantagenet and brother of Henry II. The charter dates from about 1160 and shows on its seal a mounted knight with a lion rampant both on his shield and on the trappings of his horse. At first the number of lions and their positions seem to have varied; but, on the seal of Richard the Lion Heart, used after his return from Jerusalem, we have the first representation of the three Lions or Leopards which have ever since been regarded as the arms of England.

The only complication is whether they are, in fact, lions or leopards, and experts have indulged in learned arguments on the subject. In the Middle Ages they were almost always called the 'Leopards of England' – though a poet of the reign of Richard I says he knew the king 'by the lions grinning in his shield'. The truth of it seems to be that the two animals, in heraldry, were usually drawn exactly alike, but that when the lion was in the particular position of *passant guardant* (i.e., walking forward with one paw raised, but looking full-faced at the spectator) he was called a leopard! Life is simpler in modern heraldry, with an easily-recognized spotted leopard.

Arms of France: facing the Leopards of England in so many of the wars of the Middle Ages were the Lilies of France. The ancient royal standard of France was called the 'oriflamme' from the Latin words for gold and flame, because the banner was of red silk carried on a gilded lance. The fleur-de-lis (or lys), sometimes known in English as the flower-de-luce, was adopted very early by the French kings as a royal badge, though doubt must be cast on the statement by an early writer that the arms 'were certainli sende by an Aungell from Heaven, that is to say, iij flouris . . . in a field of azure, the which certain armys were giuen to the aforesaid Kyng of Fraunce.' (Dame Juliana Berners, born about 1388, in *The Book of St. Albans*, probably derived from an earlier work written in 1441 by Nicholas Upton.) Since so many English families originally came from France, it is not surprising that the fleur-de-lis is a common device on English shields, and its frequent appearance in the royal arms of England is a record of the claims of various English kings to the throne of France. Originally, on the banner of France, the lilies were 'powdered' (i.e., sprinkled) over the whole surface, but, as in the case of the English leopards, the number was later fixed at three. In heraldry, this is the difference between *France Ancient* and *France Modern*, though the change occurred as early as the 14th century. Edward III of England carried the fleur-de-lis 'powdered', quartered with the leopards of England; whereas Henry V carried only three.

For *Quarterings*, *Quarterly*, *Grand Quarters*, etc., see *Quarters*.

Arrow: for use in heraldry see *Broad Arrow* and *Pheon*.

Arthur, King: the British and Christian hero, real or imaginary, who became the centre and source of much of the greatest legend and romance of chivalry. The opinion that he was a genuine figure of history is based largely on the writings of the Welsh historian Nennius, who was working around 800 A.D., and who credits Arthur with twelve great victories against the Saxons. Another early historian, Gildas, who would have been almost contemporary with Arthur had the king really existed, makes no mention of him. A fairly widely-held view is that Arthur was a real character of early British history, but that he was not a king; only a successful general, whose character and reputation were built up by story-tellers till he reached the status of the ideal champion of the British race.

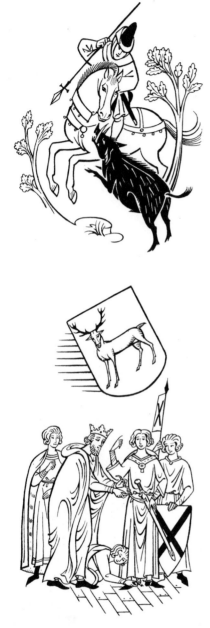

See also *Malory, Sir Thomas; Morte d'Arthur;* and *Round Table.*

Artillery: see *Mediaeval Artillery.*

Arundel: the horse of Bevis of Southampton, the knightly hero of one of the most famous stories of chivalry, which remained popular right on to the 19th century and was constantly reprinted. Bevis was sold as a boy to an Armenian, who presented him to the king. Josian, the king's daughter, obligingly fell in love with him, they were married and Bevis was knighted. It was Josian who presented him with his steed Arundel, 'the best horse in the world', and his great sword Morglay. Bevis's greatest exploits were his destruction of a giant boar, the conquest of Brandamond of Damascus, the slaying of two gigantic serpents in a prison into which he had been thrown, his defeat of the giant Ascapart, who became his slave, and, finally, the annihilation of the terrible dragon of Colein. With this list of achievements to his credit, he returned to England, where he was restored to his lands and titles.

At Gaze: used in heraldry of a deer. Most animals, when they are standing with their four feet on the ground, looking straight at you, are described as 'statant guardant.'. The deer or buck in this position, however, is always termed 'at gaze'.

Athelstane: king of the West-Saxons and Mercians. Lived 895–940. Traditionally, the first man given the accolade of knighthood by his king, using the sword to confer the honour. See *Accolade.* In this case the 'knighter' was Alfred, his grandfather.

Atteints: in tournaments and jousts, points scored by striking the opponent without splintering the lance. The points system was carefully worked out. A hit on the more difficult target of the head, e.g., scored more than a strike on the body.

Audley, Sir James: one of the most famous knights of the Middle Ages who lived 1316(?)–1386, was one of the founder knights of the

Order of the Garter, and fought with the Black Prince in France. Apart from his own exploits, he is best remembered for having four famous squires who fought alongside him in battle – Dutton, Delves, Fulleshurst and Hawkestone. (See these names for further information.) After the victory of Poitiers on September 19th, 1356, Sir James Audley was brought in wounded. In recognition of his gallantry, the Black Prince conferred on him a yearly income of 500 marks. Audley, however, passed it on to his four Cheshire squires. The Prince, when he heard of Audley's chivalrous gesture, doubled the award.

Augmentations of Honour: an addition to a coat-of-arms, especially granted by the Sovereign in recognition of some particularly distinguished deed or service. The Dukes of Norfolk still bear, as part of their arms, the royal shield of Scotland, with a demi-lion pierced through the mouth by an arrow, granted as an honourable Augmentation by Henry VIII after the Battle of Flodden, in which James IV of Scotland was killed.

(See *Abatements of Honour* for opposite.)

Augsburg: see *Armour*.

Austringer: a keeper of hawks or goshawks. See *Falcon* and *Goshawk*.

Aventail: sometimes used of the movable front to a helmet, which the wearer could lift to gulp in some fresh air and cool himself; but, more accurately, the same as the French *camail*. (See separate entry.)

Axe: one of the knightly weapons, subsidiary to the lance and sword, but much used for close fighting and sometimes preferred by individuals above all other weapons. The modern axe-haft still preserves the perfectly-balanced shape of the long-handled battle-axe. See *Battle-Axe, Francisca* and *Pole-Axe*.

3th dren

Stafford

Bourchier

Bowen

Lacy

Wake and Ormonde

Sir Thomas Heneage

Harington

Badge: the distinctive sign, cognizance or decoration worn to show membership of a particular family or household, or allegiance to it; so that, e.g., while the banner and shield of a noble or knight would display his whole arms, his badge would be displayed by his soldiers and servants. Women often adopted badges, too, and the same family, particularly if it were an important one, would sometimes have several. Among the best known are the red rose of Lancaster and the white rose of York; the ostrich feathers of the Prince of Wales; and the thistle and shamrock of Scotland and Ireland.

Here are some typical badges adopted by some of the chief nobles and knights of the reign of Edward IV (1442–1483):

The Duke of Clarence	a black bull
The Duke of Gloucester	a white boar
The Duke of Norfolk	a white lion
The Earl of Northumberland	a silver crescent
The Lord Ferrers	a French wife's hood
The Lord Cobham	a black Saracen's head
Sir Thomas Howard	a silver sallet (helmet)
Sir John Fenys	a silver martin

Among the most popular and curious badges were various types of knot, e.g.:

1 The Stafford knot
2 The Bourchier knot
3 Lacy's knot
4 The Bowen knot
5 The Wake and Ormonde knot
6 Sir Thomas Heneage's knot
7 The Harington knot

Often, these knots were a rough pictorial representation of the wearer's name or initials. Thus, the Stafford knot may be considered as two S's crossed; the Bourchier knot embodies two B's; the Bowen knot is made of bows, or loops; and Lacy's knot is a play on the name, an intricate lacy design.

Bailey: the enclosed courtyard of a castle; often there was both an *inner* and *outer* bailey. See *Motte-and-Bailey*.

Sometimes Bailey could mean the wall enclosing the outer court, and we have an interesting survival of this in the *Old Bailey*, the Central

14

Criminal Court in London, which stands at the outer boundary of the old wall of the City.

Balan, Sir: one of the knights of the Round Table, and brother to Sir Balin, 'two of the most valiant knights the world ever produced.' Their story is told by Sir Thomas Malory (see separate entry) and by Lord Tennyson in the *Idylls of the King*. Balan was the gentler of the two brothers, while Balin, called *le Savage*, was cursed with a black temper that sometimes led him into deeds of violence and earned him the King's displeasure.

On one occasion there came to the court at Camelot 'a damsel the which was sent on message from the great lady Lile of Avelion. And when she came before king Arthur, she told from whom she came, and how she was sent on message unto him for these causes. Then she let her mantle fall that was richly furred; and then was she girt with a noble sword, whereof the king had marvel, and said, Damsel, for what cause are ye girt with that sword?'

The lady explained that she could only be delivered of the sword that encumbered her by 'a passing good man of his hands and of his deeds, and without villainy or treachery, and without treason.' Arthur himself, and a great many of his barons, tried to draw the sword, but failed. In the end it was Sir Balin, recently released from many months in prison for slaying a cousin of the King's, who easily drew the great blade from its sheath; whereupon the damsel asked that it should be returned to her. Balin refused, though the lady warned him that great trouble would come to him if he insisted on keeping the sword. 'Ye are not wise to keep the sword from me, for ye shall slay with the sword the best friend that ye have, and the man that ye love most in the world, and the sword shall be your destruction.'

During a period of banishment from court, Balin, using an unfamiliar shield lent to him for the occasion, rode against another knight, also bearing unfamiliar arms and 'trapped all red and himself in the same colour.' There followed the greatest battle that any of the onlookers had ever seen, till both lay mortally wounded. Balin asked the name of the knight who had fought with him so doughtily. 'My name,' answered the

other, 'is Balan, brother to the good knight Balin.' Thus the damsel's prophecy came true and the two brothers were buried together by Merlin. 'Thus endeth the tale of Balin and Balan, two brethren born in Northumberland, good knights.'

(The quotations are from William Caxton's *The Noble Histories of King Arthur and Certain of his Knights,* completed at his press in Westminster on July 31st, 1485. It was one of the greatest achievements of the first English printer, and certainly the most popular and enduring.)

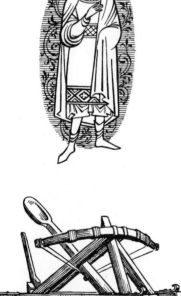

Baldric: a broad belt or girdle, often richly ornamented, passing over one shoulder, across the breast, and under the other, supporting sword, dagger or bugle.

> *The gemmy bridle glitter'd free,*
> *Like to some branch of stars we see*
> *Hung in the golden Galaxy.*
> *The bridle bells rang merrily*
> *As he rode down to Camelot:*
> *And from his blazon'd baldric slung*
> *A mighty silver bugle hung,*
> *And as he rode his armour rung,*
> *Beside remote Shalott.*
> (*The Lady of Shalott:* Lord Tennyson)

Baldwin of Flanders (1058–1118): first King of Jerusalem. During the 1st Crusade (1096–1100), the Crusaders captured Antioch after an eight months' siege (1098) and then went on to occupy the Holy City itself (July 15th, 1099). Godfrey of Bouillon (see separate entry) was in reality the first Christian king of Jerusalem; but he would accept only the title of Count, refusing to wear the golden circle of kingship in the place where his Saviour had once worn a crown of thorns. On his death in 1100, Baldwin succeeded him as the first titular King of Jerusalem.

Balin, Sir: called *le Savage*. See *Balan, Sir.*

Balista: a siege engine which could be adapted to project stones against defences, but which was more often used to hurl great metal shafts and bolts which, for good measure, could carry incendiary material to start fires in the besieged place. The balista was like a great cross-bow, and, working by tension, could throw heavy

missiles with accuracy for a distance of three or
four hundred yards.

Banner: one of the three chief classes of flags
used in the Middle Ages, the other two being the
Pennon and the *Standard*. (See separate entries).
The banner was square or rectangular in shape
and bore the owner's arms over its whole surface,
as though it were his shield. It was normally
carried only by the higher ranks of knights (see
Knight Banneret), peers and princes. The best-
known example today is what is usually called
the Royal Standard, which flies above the royal
residences, or from the masts of ships when the
Sovereign is aboard. But this is, strictly speaking,
an inaccurate term. Heraldically, it is the King's
or the Queen's Banner, bearing the royal arms
blazoned upon it.

> *Farewell the neighing steed and the shrill trump,*
> *The spirit-stirring drum, the ear-piercing fife,*
> *The royal banner, and all quality. . . .*
>
> (*Othello*: William Shakespeare)

Banneret: See *Knight Banneret*.

Bannockburn, Battle of: see Robert I.

Bar: a band horizontally across a shield, usually
occupying about a fifth of it. This makes it
narrower than the *Fess*, which takes the centre
third of a shield. (See separate entry for this).
The bar is never used in the space reserved for
the fess, and is not often found singly. There is a
narrower band called a *barrulet*, about half the
width of the bar; and an even narrower one
which is always one of a pair, called *bars
gemelles*, from the Latin *gemellus*, double. *Barry*
is used to describe a shield divided horizontally
into a number of equal parts, the number being
specified; e.g., *barry of eight*. If there are more
than eight divisions, it is described as *barrulé*
and the exact number of divisions need not be
given.

Barbican: an outwork or fortification built out
in front of a castle to protect the gate-way, one
of the greatest weaknesses in the defences and
therefore elaborately guarded with devices such
as strong towers, drawbridge and portcullis. (See
separate entries for the last two.)

17

Bard: (1) professional poet or singer who composed and sang in camp and hall verses in honour of knightly deeds and high achievements.

(2) defensive armour for a horse, though the word is sometimes also used to describe merely the colourful fabric trappings. Full bards of mail or plate were probably rarely worn owing to their great weight, and very few perfect examples have survived. See *Crinet, Flanchard* and *Peytrel* for some of the chief parts of horse armour. There is a fine bard in the Tower of London armouries, dating from about 1480; and another magnificent specimen in the Wallace Collection, Hertford House, Manchester Square, W.1. This belonged to an Austrian noble named Pancraz von Freyburg and was made about 1475.

Barmkin: the small courtyard in the Pele Towers, built in the border country between England and Scotland during the 15th and 16th centuries as places of refuge for people and cattle. They are miniature fortresses consisting of a strong stone tower and courtyard and were useful during the frequent raids by the reavers (or rievers), the border thieves. See *Pele Tower.*

Barrel Helm: mediaeval helmet so called from its simple barrel shape, often with a flat top. It gave complete covering to the head which, with the aid of a lining and some sort of skull-cap, took the whole weight. Later helmets rested on the shoulders.

Barrulet, Barry and Bars Gemelles: See *Bar*.

Bascinet: a basin-shaped helmet, open at first but later fitted with a visor. It was made in a great variety of shapes. Sometimes the visor was drawn out in a grotesque form to give the *Snout-faced* or *Pig-faced Bascinet.*

Baselard (or Basilard): sharply tapering, two-edged dagger, popular in the 13th and 14th centuries. Though it was sometimes worn with armour, it was more often an accessory of civilian dress and was even carried by ladies, attached to their girdles.

Baston Course: contest fought on horseback

18

with wooden clubs, the object being not to unseat the opponent but to bash his crest to pieces. A baston is a club or cudgel, and is the Old French form of bâton, carried by a field-marshal or wielded by a musical conductor.

Bataille Française: the 'French Battle' or tournament, so called because the mediaeval knightly tournament seems to have evolved in France, some claiming it to have been the invention of Geoffroi de Préville, a knight of Anjou.

Battering-ram: a crude, but highly effective, instrument for making a breach in castle or city walls. A tree or great pole, often with an iron head, was swung to and fro by a team of men working on each side. A variation of the weapon was fitted with an iron spike which hacked away at stone and mortar till whole sections of the masonry could be removed. This was the *Bore*. Often the ram was brought up to the wall or gate-way under cover of a strong timber housing on wheels, which gave temporary cover to the ram-men.

Batters: extra masses of masonry splaying out from towers, etc., to give additional protection against the attacks of battering-rams, etc.

Battle: apart from its usual meaning of an engagement between two hostile armies, this could also mean one division of an army, or the main body as distinct from the van or rear.
> *The French are bravely in their battles set,*
> *And will with all expedience charge on us.*
> (*Henry V:* William Shakespeare)

Battle of the Herrings: an engagement fought on February 12th, 1429, between Sir John Fastolf, at the head of some 2,000 archers and men-at-arms, and 5,000 of the chivalry of France and Scotland under Jean, Count de Dunois, during the siege of Orleans. The Duke of Bedford sent from Paris 300 waggons of munitions and food, chiefly herrings, for the besieging English, who were running short of food, and the convoy was intercepted by the French near Rouvray. Sir John made a barricade of the carts and forced the French com-

mander to retire with heavy losses, leaving the battle-field strewn with herrings. The battle became known in France, perhaps in an attempt to make light of the defeat, as *La journée des harengs*.

Battle of the Spurs: a battle fought under the walls of Courtray in 1302 between the Flemish and the French. The foolhardiness and ill-discipline of the French knights led to a heavy defeat at the hands of the Flemish burghers, and they fled leaving large numbers of gilded spurs (variously estimated at from 700 to 4,000) littering the field. (See also *Guinegate, Battle of*.)

Battle of the Standard: fought on August 22nd, 1138 at Northallerton, Yorkshire, between David of Scotland and Stephen of England. The 'standard' consisted of the consecrated banners of St. Cuthbert of Durham, St. John of Beverley, St. Peter of York and St. Wilfrid of Ripon, mounted on a carriage wheeled into the middle of the battle.

Battle of the Thirty: fought on March 27th, 1351. To settle a dispute over the occupation of a piece of territory, Beaumanoir and Bemborough, the French and English commanders, agreed to a combat between thirty knights on each side. Bemborough was killed and the French were victorious. The French for long had a proverb, as desperate as *le combat des Trentes*, to describe a hard-fought battle.

Battle, Trial by (or Wager of Battle): a method of settling a dispute by letting accuser and defendant fight it out, in the belief that God would defend the right. The practice was probably introduced by the Normans and was largely discontinued when trial by jury became common. But it did not become expressly illegal in England till 1819. (See also *Tournament*.)

Battle-axe: In early centuries it is often difficult to distinguish between the axe as a weapon and as a tool, since it could be put to different uses as occasion required. The battle-axe used by the Franks, however, was essentially a weapon of war. (See *Francisca*.) The Vikings were great axe-men and developed the great broad-bladed, two-handed axe. The great axe was normally used when fighting on foot, but was sometimes wielded by horsemen; more often they chose a much lighter axe, easily swung by one hand.

The axe was not scorned as a knightly weapon and was frequently used in the tournament and joust. When Anthony, Lord Scales, challenged Anthony of Burgundy in 1465 to combat in London, the second 'chapitre' or clause in the regulations drawn up to govern the tournament stated that: 'we shall doo Armes on foote, armyd as it app'teyneth to noble men, and . . . shalbe wepened with speres, axes and daggars: and we shall make but oonly oone caste of the spere, and then we shall fight with the oothir wepens, unto the tyme that oone of us two be borne down or in all poyntis unwepened.' The same chronicle gives a vivid account of what actually happened when the two champions were using their axes in the tournament – fought at Smithfield more than a year after the original challenge was issued. The spelling has been modernized in this longer extract:

'And right as the King of Arms made the cry, the Lord Scales opened his pavilion; and at the second "laissez aller" entered into the field out of his tent . . . and gave countenance that he was ready with hand and foot and axe, inasmuch as he laid his axe upon his shoulder, and eftsoons changed his axe from hand to hand. And then they advanced: and so right afore the King either assailed other in such wise as the Lord Scales . . . with the point of his axe struck through one of the ribs of the Bastard's plates; as the said Bastard showed him after the field. And so they fought together; the Lord Scales with the head of his axe afore, the other with the small end; and smote many cumbrous and thick strokes; till at the last . . . Lord Scales struck him in the side of the visor of his bascinet. Then the King, perceiving the cruel assail, cast his staff, and with high voice cried "Whoo"!'

(For explanation of some words in this passage see *Kings of Arms, Pavilion, Laissez Aller, Visor* and *Bascinet*.)

Bavière: see *Beaver*.

Bayard, Pierre du Terrail (1476?–1524), knight of France: the knight who has come down in history as *sans peur et sans reproche* (without fear and without blame) and whose name became symbolic of the highest ideals of chivalry; so that to be called a Bayard is one of the greatest tributes that can be won. Sir Philip Sidney (see separate entry) is sometimes known as *The British Bayard* and Louis of Nassau, brother of William of Orange, as *The Bayard of the Netherlands.*

The Chevalier Bayard lived in the reigns of Charles VIII, Louis XII, and Francis I of France. Among his greatest exploits was the saving of France from the invading armies of Charles of Austria, who had been elected Charles V, Emperor of the Holy Roman Empire. Charles's army, under the Count of Nassau, was advancing on Mézières to destroy it, when Bayard threw himself into the town. ' "It is not a weak place," cried Bayard, "for men of courage are found there." . . . The imperialists summoned him to surrender. "I need a bridge by which to march out," he answered, "and your bodies have not yet filled the ditch." ' (Victor Duruy's *History of France.*) Bayard was killed in 1524, fighting in Italy.

Beauchamp, Richard, Earl of Warwick (1382–1439): a famous knight and warrior of the Middle Ages, Knight of the Bath and of the Garter; on January 26th, 1403, when just under 21, jousted at the coronation of Joan of Navarre, Queen of Henry IV; obtained leave in 1408 to visit the Holy Sepulchre and on the way was challenged to perform a feat of arms at Verona, where he gained the victory. Having performed his vows at Jerusalem he put up his arms on the north side of the temple; Lord High Steward at Henry V's coronation and held various important commands under him in France; by the king's wish, had care of the infant Henry VI. His effigy in the Beauchamp Chapel, Church of St. Mary, Warwick, is one of the most splendid and important in England. Made of gilt latten, it shows every curve and detail of the knight's armour accurately, both on the upper and under surface. The original armour was probably of Milanese manufacture. (See *Latten.*)

Beaver (Bavière, Beavor, Beevor): the piece of armour that protected the lower part of the face, either forming part of the helmet or fixed to the breast-plate. It could be raised or lowered to allow the wearer to eat or drink.

Beavor: see *Beaver*.

Bedivere, Sir: a knight of King Arthur's Round Table ('Sir Bedivere, the last of all his knights'). It was Bedivere who, with Sir Lucan, carried the mortally wounded king from the last battle-field to a ruined chapel not far from the sea's edge; and it was Bedivere who was commanded by Arthur to take the great sword Excalibur and fling it into the water. The story of the knight's failure, twice repeated, to obey his king, because of the nobility of the great sword, whose 'pommel and haft were all of precious stones', and of its final flight at the third attempt, is one of the most dramatic stories in all the Arthurian legends and, indeed, in all literature. Tennyson, who in this instance follows Sir Thomas Malory's words very closely (see separate entry for *Malory*), described Bedivere's first failure and final obedience thus:

> *There drew he forth the brand Excalibur,*
> *And o'er him, drawing it, the winter moon,*
> *Brightening the skirts of a long cloud, ran forth*
> *And sparkled keen with frost against the hilt:*
> *For all the haft twinkled with diamond sparks,*
> *Myriads of topaz-lights, and jacinth work*
>
> *That both his eyes were dazzled, as he stood,*
> *This way and that dividing the swift mind,*
> *In act to throw: but at the last it seem'd*
> *Better to leave Excalibur conceal'd*
> *There in the many-knotted waterflags,*
> *That whistled stiff and dry about the marge.*
> *So strode he back slow to the wounded King.*
>
> *   *   *
>
> *Then quickly rose Sir Bedivere, and ran,*
> *And, leaping down the ridges lightly, plunged*
> *Among the bulrush-beds, and clutch'd the sword,*
> *And strongly wheel'd and threw it. The great brand*
> *Made lightnings in the splendour of the moon,*
> *And flashing round and round, and whirl'd in an arch,*
> *Shot like a streamer of the northern morn,*
> *Seen where the moving isles of winter shock*

By night, with noises of the northern sea.
So flash'd and fell the brand Excalibur:
But ere he dipt the surface, rose an arm
Clothed in white samite, mystic, wonderful,
And caught him by the hilt, and brandish'd him
Three times, and drew him under in the mere.
And lightly went the other to the King.

Beevor: see *Beaver.*

Behourd: one of the many words used for a tournament or joust; particularly, perhaps, for one not advertised beforehand, but fixed up on the spur of the moment; also called *Burdica.*

Belfry: tall movable tower of timber. used in assaults on castle or town walls. It afforded a measure of shelter for the attackers, and from its height the archers were often able to direct their arrows down on the defenders. Covering the structure with animal hides protected it from fire.

Bells: used in falconry, or hawking, attached to the leg of the bird and particularly useful in helping to trace a lost falcon. The bell, small and usually of brass, is attached to the leg by a leather strap called a *bewit.*

'The darkness became watered with light, with silver radiance, and then it was an eerie sight that dawned upon his vision. Each hawk or falcon stood in the silver upon one leg . . . and each was a motionless statue of a knight in armour. They stood gravely in their plumed helmets, spurred and armed. . . There was a simultaneous tintinnabulation of all the bells, as each graven image lowered its raised foot in distress. They stood on both feet now, disturbed.' (T. H. White, *The Sword in the Stone.*)

Berchlingen, Götz von (1480–1562): known as 'Götz of the Iron Hand.' Berchlingen was a knight of Franconia (part of the ancient German empire) who lost his hand in 1504 in a skirmish under the walls of Landshut, in Silesia. A shot from a cannon smashed his sword hilt in two and drove one half, together with three of his arm-plates, into his right arm. His hand was torn off and his whole arm terribly injured. Despite

24

the pain, he coolly turned his horse and rode back to camp, where they found a surgeon for him. Later, an ingenious armourer forged him an iron hand and, fitted with this, Götz contrived to fight on for another 58 years.

Bernard, Saint, or Bernard of Clairvaux (1090–1153): leader of the Cistercian Order of monks who, towards the end of his life, roused support for the Second Crusade (1147–49) by his preaching and by his letters to influential princes and nobles. Bernard gave a clear picture of chivalry as being both military and Christian – in other words, the true knight was a Christian soldier. In a letter to Duke Wladislaus and the nobles and people of Bohemia, he wrote:

'Safe is the battle in which it is glorious to conquer and a gain to die. Why do you hesitate, you servants of the Cross? Why do you, who want for neither strength nor good, make excuses? . . . I ask and advise you to put the business of Christ before everything else and not to neglect it for what can be done at other times. And so that you may know when, where, and how it is to be done, listen further: The army of the Lord is to set out next Easter, and it has been determined that a large part of it shall pass through Hungary. It has been laid down that no one shall wear any coloured, grey or silk apparel, and the use of gold or silver harness has been forbidden. But those who wish may wear gold or silver when they enter battle, so that the sun may shine upon them and scatter the forces of the enemy with terror.'

And in another letter, to his uncle Andrew, who was a Knight of the Temple, he said:

'Under the sun you fight as a soldier, but for the sake of him who is above the sun.'

Bertrand of Brittany: See *Du Guesclin, Bertrand.*

Besagews: steel discs attached to armour to cover a vulnerable point, e.g., the armpit. They were also sometimes used on such weapons as the pole-axe or cross-hilted sword, to give protection to the user's hand.

Bewits: see *Bells.*

25

c

Bezant: in heraldry, a flat gold disc or roundel. The original bezant, or byzant, was a gold coin struck in Byzantium, or Constantinople.

Birds of the Fist: see *Hawks of the Fist.*

Birds of Prey: see *Falconry.*

Black Monday: April 13th, 1360, during Edward III's campaign in France, which culminated in the Treaty of Bretigny: 'a foul dark day of mist and of hail, so bitter cold that sitting on horseback many died.' A fortnight later, another icy storm, with hailstones as big as pigeons' eggs, swept over the army and it was said that more knights perished that day, struck by lightning, than fell in the battles of Crécy and Poitiers. One chronicler goes so far as to say that it was this experience that caused Edward III to make peace with the French. Raphael Holinshed, writing two hundred years later, said of the year 1360:

'Men and cattle were destroyed in divers places of this realm by lightning and tempest: also houses were set on fire and burnt, and strange and wonderful sights seen. Thousands perished in a storm at Chartres, which fell so hideous in the king's host it seemed the world should have ended; for such unreasonable great stones of hail fell from the sky that men and horses were slain therewith. The storm of tempest, hail, thunder, lightning, and rain was such as the like had never been seen by any of the English people.' (*Chronicles,* 1578.)

Black Prince: see *Edward, Prince of Wales.*

Black Prince's Ruby: the ruby that was given to Edward, the Black Prince in 1367 by Pedro the Cruel of Castile, and that was set in the royal circlet round Henry V's helm at the Battle of Agincourt, 1415. It is now part of the Imperial State Crown of the sovereigns of England, worn on great state occasions such as the coronation of a new monarch.

Blazon: to blazon is to describe a coat of arms in the correct heraldic language and manner. The rules of blazon are strict and fairly complicated; e.g., there is a correct order of blazon

26

to be observed when a description is given:

1. The field, i.e., the surface or background of a shield.
2. The principal charge lying on the field.
3. Other charges on the field, in their order of importance.
4. Charges lying on other charges.
5. Differences, i.e., the small charges added to a shield to identify a particular member of a family, such as the eldest son, or a special branch of a family.

There are others, which special works on heraldry will make clear.

Blot on the 'Scutcheon: see *Abatements of Honour.*

Blue Garter, Order of the: the original name of the order of knighthood now called the Order of the Garter, founded in the middle of the 14th century by Edward III and exceeding 'in majesty, honour, and fame, all chivalrous orders in the world.' It took as its badge a blue garter, symbol of unity, of being joined together in honour and knightly virtue. At their installation the knights, 'the valyantest men of the realm', were exhorted: 'Tie about thy leg for thy renown this noble Garter, wear it as the symbol of the most illustrious Order, never to be forgotten or laid aside, that thereby thou mayest be admonished to be courageous, and, having undertaken a just war . . . that thou mayest stand firm and valiantly and successfully conquer.' The knights wore their insignia for the first time in the New Year of 1348 at the royal palace of Eltham, where many of them jousted before the king.

In its early years, the Order was restricted in number to Edward, the Black Prince, and twenty-four other worthy knights. In theory, the number remains the same today, though in practice it is increased by some extra categories of knights, e.g., foreign princes. The Prince of Wales is always a member, as descendant of the Black Prince. Women have been eligible since earliest times, though none were elected between the reigns of Henry VIII and Edward VII. (See *Chaucer, Alice.*)

The oft-told tale of the founding of the Order and the adoption of its motto is that while the

27

lovely princess Joan of Kent was dancing at a ball in Calais her garter dropped to the ground. Edward III bound it round his knee and reproved the smiles of the court with the words 'Honi soit qui mal y pense' – 'Shame be to him who thinks evil of it' or 'Evil to him who evil thinks.' This has long been considered one of the pleasant, but baseless, legends of history; but recent convincing evidence has been produced that the story is, in fact, true.

Blue-hawk: see *Peregrine.*

Bluemantle Pursuivant: see *Officers of Arms.*

Bohemund of Tarantum or Otranto (1056?– 1111): a Norman crusading knight, one of the leaders of the 1st Crusade (1096–1100). After the capture of Antioch, Bohemund was left in possession as its first Prince.

Bordon: see *Bourdonass.*

Bordure: in heraldry, a frame or edging right round a shield.

Bore: see *Battering-ram.*

Boss: projecting knob in the centre of a shield or ornamental stud on a bridle, etc.

Bouche: notch at or near the right-hand top corner of a shield, to take the lance. In heraldry, a shield of this sort is termed *bouché.*

Bourdonass(e) or Bordon: a light, hollow lance, usually of poplar, made so that it easily shivered to pieces against the opponent's armour. In earlier jousts and tournaments, the main object was to hurl the adversary from his horse, a difficult thing to achieve because of the high projections, back and front, on the saddle. With the bourdonass, honour was satisfied with the splintering of the lance. (See also *Brandon, Charles, 1st Duke of Suffolk.*)

Brandon, Charles, 1st Duke of Suffolk (d. 1545): soldier and Earl Marshal of England; squire of the royal body to Henry VIII and holder of a number of important military commands. Brandon had a considerable reputation for prowess with the lance and in 1514, with the Marquis of Dorset, he appeared as the Champion of England at the tournaments held in Paris to celebrate the marriage of Henry VIII's sister Mary to Louis XII.

He also rode in the jousts at Westminster, held on February 12th and 13th, 1511, in honour of Queen Katherine of Arragon and of the birth of her son, Henry, Duke of Cornwall. Brandon ran eight courses against the King himself. In all, Henry VIII ran 46 courses on the two days, 'acquitting himselfe so worthily that the beholders tooke passing pleasure to see his valiaunte demeanoure in those martiall feates.' (Holinshed's *Chronicles*.) In the possession of the College of Arms is the magnificent original Westminster Tournament Roll, recording in pictorial form the procession to the tournament ground (on the site of the present Horse Guards Parade), the combat and the return to the court. Altogether the roll measures nearly 60 feet and is illuminated in gold, silver and colours.

Another precious survival from the period is a lance in the Armouries of H.M. Tower of London, reputed to have belonged to Brandon of the 'itching horsemanship.' This is an example of the great spear, or *bourdonass*. (See separate entry.) The lance is 14 feet 4 inches in length and weighs 20 lb.

Brass: engraved metal memorial tablet, set in stone, usually attempting to give some sort of pictorial representation of the person commemorated. Often the metal is called 'latten' and one of the plates, 'a latten' (a corruption of the French *laiton*, brass). In fact, the plates are not true brass, but are compounded of about 60–65% copper, 10% lead and tin, and perhaps 30% zinc. Till about 1550, latten was always imported from Flanders and Germany, often coming through Cologne; hence, they were sometimes called 'cullen' plates.

Brasses, though they cannot be relied on for a correct rendering of features, are invaluable and accurate sources for details of contemporary costume and armour. Over 7,000 survive in England, dating from the 13th to the 18th centuries. Originally there were probably at least 150,000 in English churches. The earliest

brasses are often life-size, bold in execution and of thick metal, and usually portray members of the noble and upper classes. From the middle of the 14th century onwards, they include more people of humbler rank and tend to be smaller. From about 1450, the designs become more conventional and less interesting in their craftsmanship and artistry.

While many brasses show civilians, including merchants, judges, priests, etc., the most remarkable and appealing are probably the large number devoted to knights and squires in all the panoply of their armour and weapons. One of the most famous, and perhaps the earliest, is that of Sir John D'Abernon or d'Aubernoun (c. 1277) in the church at Stoke d'Abernon, near Guildford, Surrey. The engraver has worked with such patience and skill that every separate link of the mail is accurately represented, and the rest of the harness and equipment is shown as faithfully. Some other well-known brasses, giving a picture of the development of armour through the centuries, are:

Sir Roger de Trumpington	1289
Trumpington, near Cambridge	
Sir Robert de Bures	1302
Acton, Suffolk	
Sir Robert de Septvans	1306
Chartham, Kent	
Sir John de Argentine	1360
Horsheath, Cambridgeshire	
Sir Robert de Swynbourne	1391
Little Horkesley, Essex	
Thomas de St Quintin	1445
Harpham, Yorkshire	
Sir Robert Staunton	1458
Castle Donnington, Leicestershire	
Sir Thomas Grene	1462
Grene's Norton, Northants	
Sir Humphrey Stanley	1505
Westminster Abbey, London	
Humphrey Brewster	1593
Wrentham, Suffolk	

(See also *Palimpsest Brass*.)

Breach: a break or gap, particularly in fortifications, walls, etc. (See *Battering-ram* and *Mine* for two methods of breaching.)

Brian, Sir Guy de: a founder knight of the Order of the Garter and standard-bearer at the Battle of Crécy, 1346. (See separate entry for this battle.)

'When the troops were all posted, the king rode along the ranks on a small palfrey, carrying a white wand and wearing a crimson surcoat of golden leopards. . . . Beside him was Sir Guy de Brian, bearing the dragon banner of Wessex – the standard under which the English had fought at Hastings . . . His effigy, still coloured in faded Garter blue, can be seen in Tewkesbury abbey.' (Arthur Bryant, *The Age of Chivalry*.)

Bridle: the head-gear of a horse, consisting of the headstall, the bit and the reins. Unlike, e.g., the saddle, the bridle of the mediaeval knight is virtually unchanged today.

(a) The Headstall. Consists altogether of five main pieces, all designed to keep the bit in place: the Head-piece, going across the head behind the horse's ears; the Head-band, in front of the ears; the Throat Lash, under the jaw; the Cheek-bands, lying along the horse's cheeks and attached to the bit at their lower ends; and the Nose-band, going across the face just above the nostrils. Not all these features are found in every head-stall.

(b) The Bit. The iron part of the bridle, inserted in the mouth of the horse. If a horse decides to run away he can catch the bit between his teeth and largely prevent the rider having any control over him; hence the common expression, to 'take the bit between one's teeth', or become unmanageable.

(c) The Reins. Up to about the beginning of Edward I's reign (1272) only a single pair of reins was used; later, a double pair was more common, often consisting of one narrow and one broad strap, the latter with the lower edges cut into elaborate shapes and decorated with embroidery, metal studs or even precious stones.

Brigandine: body armour made of small plates or rings, fastened on to leather or stout

canvas, and often covered with another layer, making a garment that was at the same time very pliable and very resistant to arrow or sword. In a typical example in the Tower of London, the plates are of thin iron, an inch square, with the corners rounded and with a central hole through which the fastening strings pass. In another, the plate is covered with studs that thrust through the outer canvas.

Brigantine: see *Brigandine*.

Broad Arrow: a charge in heraldry. A broad arrow with teeth on the inner edge of the barb is called a *Pheon* by heralds. It seems to have been used by some early tribes as a symbol of holiness or royalty; but was put to baser uses later on as a mark on Government stores, e.g., timber for the dockyards, and then on the coarse garments formerly worn by convicts in England. This seems a far cry from the day when Garter King of Arms, John Smert (d. 1478), was proud to wear the black Broad Arrow as his personal badge.

Brocas Helm: a tilting helm in the Tower of London Armouries, dating from about 1500 and considered by many to be the finest example surviving. It still has its original staples and locking bars, back and front, for fastening it down securely on the shoulder and chest. It weighs 22½ lb.

Bruce, Robert: see *Robert I*.

Buch, the Captal de: the title by which Jean de Grailly, one of the most famous French knights of the 14th century, is usually known, from the manor of Buch, in the Arcachon region, of which he was captal or capitan (= captain or leader). Although he was often little better than a leader of brigands, de Grailly was of noble blood and cousin to the King of Navarre. He fought gallantly at the Battle of Poitiers (1356) against the French; for, often, in the confused politics of the time, with France divided against itself, he brought his mixed army of soldiers and brigands to fight under the banner of England.

One of his greatest exploits was the destruction, in 1358, of *La Jacquerie*, an army of revolted peasants of Picardy, who, some 20,000 strong, roamed the countryside destroying castles and committing acts of the most wanton cruelty against women as well as men. Their leader, Guillaume de Caillet, eventually brought 9,000 of them against the fortress of Meaux, in Brie, where, according to Froissart, 'the duchess of Normandy, the duchess of Orleans, and three hundred other ladies . . . were fled." The Captal de Buch, who had only recently returned from fighting in Prussia, in the true spirit of knight errantry went to their rescue and, with the Duke of Orleans and the Count of Foix, flung his small company against the mob who were swarming through the outer gates. Thousands were slain, and de Caillet was captured and later executed by the French king.

After a life packed with action and fluctuating fortune, he was at length captured by the French king's forces at Soubise and imprisoned in one of the towers of the Temple, in Paris. The king was so delighted at the taking of so redoubtable an enemy that he gave the squire who had captured him 1,200 francs. The English king and his son, the Black Prince, tried hard to secure his freedom and offered several captured French knights in exchange. The French king would only consider releasing his famous prisoner if he would swear never again to bear arms against the crown of France. This the Captal refused to do and languished in close confinement till he died five years later, 'poisoned by homesickness, like a wild beast too old for its cage.'

Buckler: a shield; properly speaking, the small round shield for fighting on foot.

Burdica: see *Behourd*.

Burgonet: an open-faced helmet, with cheek guards, used in the 16th and 17th centuries.

Burgundenses: mercenary soldiers or hand-gun men from Burgundy. They were employed in England during the Wars of the Roses, and the Earl of Warwick had a body of them at the second Battle of St Albans (1461).

Buzzard: a bird of prey of the falcon family, but

33

reckoned very low in the scale for hunting purposes and only suitable for somebody base-born. (See *Hawks*.) It lacks the grace and distinction of the more prized members of the family and is reckoned a hawk 'by courtesy.'

'Of small renown, 'tis true; for, not to lie,
'We call your buzzard "hawk" by courtesy.'
(John Dryden, *The Hind and the Panther*, 1687)

There is a curious and impolite survival of the contempt for this bird in the occasional description of a rather stupid and bumbling character as a 'stupid old buzzard!'

Byrnie: a mail shirt, reaching almost to the knee, worn in the 12th and 13th centuries. Over much of Europe it was also known as a *hauberk*.

Caballero: (from the Spanish *caballo,* horse). A Spanish knight or gentleman; one of the many European words indicating how much the horse was an essential part of knightly equipment. See also *Chevalier and Cavalliere.*

Cabasset: type of helmet or morion worn by pikemen in the 16th century.

Cadency, marks of: in heraldry, marks used to distinguish between the arms of various brothers in the same family, or the families of different brothers. Thus, in a family of nine sons, they would all carry the family coat-of-arms. but each would be distinguished by a particular mark according to his seniority:

Eldest son:	a Label (a rectangular strip)
Second son:	a Crescent
Third son:	a Mullet (five-point star)
Fourth son:	a Martlet (swallow-like bird, with legs cut off)
Fifth son:	an Annulet (a ring)
Sixth son:	a Fleur-de-Lys (a lily, as in the French royal arms)
Seventh son:	a Rose
Eighth son:	a Cross Moline (see *Cross*)
Ninth son:	a Double Quatrefoil (eight-leaved clover)

'Caen, Crécy, Calais': the motto of the Radclyffe family, celebrating the part played by one of the knights of the Hundred Years' War, Sir John Radclyffe, in Edward III's French campaign of 1346–47. The motto commemorates the sacking of Caen, the immortal victory of Crécy (see separate entry), and the 11-month siege of Calais, after which the King spared the lives of John de Vienne, captain of the town, and the other chief burgesses, when his Queen, Philippa, knelt before him to beg mercy for them.

Caerleon-upon-Usk: the place in Wales which tradition says was the chief royal residence of King Arthur and where he held his court, or Round Table, at Whitsuntide.

Calatrava, Red Cross Knights of: an order of knighthood instituted by Sancho III of Castile in 1158 and named after the city in Spain where it was founded. Their badge is a red cross formed

of lilies, carried on the left breast of a white surcoat.

Calvary Cross: in heraldry, a Latin cross (i.e. the type usually carried by crusaders on their surcoats) mounted on three steps.

Calveley, Sir Hugh (d. 1393): a distinguished soldier from Cheshire, who saw long years of service as a captain of freebooters and mercenaries. He was one of the champions of England in the Battle of the Thirty (see separate entry) and fought under the banner of the Black Prince. It is some indication of the muddle of mediaeval warfare that he captured the great Bertrand du Guesclin at Juigné bridge, holding him to ransom for thirty thousand crowns, then, a little while afterwards, served under him in Spain, vowing: 'Myself will keep you in good company. By God who created the world, I will go everywhere it may please you to go. I will fight against the whole world, on this side and on the other side of the sea, except the Prince of Wales, to whom I have pledged allegiance.' (Roger Vercel, *Bertrand of Brittany*). Before long, they were on opposite sides again, quite properly, according to the accepted practice of war.

Calveley was a red-haired giant of a man, with long teeth and a vast appetite. He plundered mercilessly but, it is said, showed his devoutness by having all the booty sprinkled with holy water. With some of the proceeds won from the wars he founded the collegiate church at Bunbury, Cheshire, where his armoured effigy can still be seen.

Camail: a curtain or cape of mail, hanging from the bottom of the helmet and covering chin, neck and shoulders.

Camelot: the name imperishably celebrated in poetry and romance as King Arthur's chief seat of government, though its exact whereabouts, like all the cherished places of legend, remains mercifully mysterious. Winchester, the early capital of England, has the best claim, conceded by, among others, Sir Thomas Malory. 'Also Merlin let make by his subtilty that Balin's sword was put in a marble stone standing upright as great as a millstone, and the stone hoved always above the water, and did many years, and so by adventure it swam down the stream to the city of Camelot, that is in English Winchester.' (1470)

Camisarde: a night attack; so named from the *camise*, or peasant's smock worn over armour and serving the double purpose of concealing the gleam of metal in the darkness and helping the attackers to more easily recognize their fellows if the fighting became confused. (Also known as a *camisado*.)

Camp-followers: civilians accompanying an army, e.g., servants, tradesmen selling food, wine, etc. to the soldiers. On at least one occasion they helped to defeat the chivalry of England. At the battle of Bannockburn (June 24th, 1314) between Edward II and Robert the Bruce of Scotland, when the English knights were reeling from the sudden onslaught of Bruce's reserves, they saw another force, with raised banners, emerging from the woods. This completed the rout of the disorganized English ranks; though the 'force' was the camp-followers, intent on getting their share of the plunder from the battle-field. The 'banners' were blankets hung on young trees and branches.

Canterbury: see *Edward, Prince of Wales*.

Canting Arms: see *Allusive Arms*.

Canton: a division of a shield, rather smaller than a quarter (strictly speaking it should be about a third of the chief) nearly always occupying the dexter chief, i.e., the top left-hand corner from the onlooker's point of view.

Caparison: a rich, ornamental covering, usually for a horse. Some caparisons from a Smithfield tournament of 1467 may be taken as good examples. The English knight (Anthony, Lord Scales) had a retinue of nine horses, trapped or dressed as follows:

1st horse: White cloth of gold, with a cross of St. George of crimson velvet, bordered with a fringe of gold six inches deep.

2nd horse: Tawny velvet ornamented with many great bells.

3rd horse: Russet damask down to the hooves, powdered with the knight's initials couched in goldsmiths' work.

4th horse: Purple damask, rich with goldsmiths' work and bordered with blue cloth of gold.

5th horse: Blue velvet reaching to the hooves, with pleats of crimson satin and bordered with green velvet shot with gold.

6th horse: Crimson cloth of gold, bordered with a foot and a half of fine sable furs.

7th horse: Green damask to the feet, decorated with goldsmiths' work and bordered with six inches of russet cloth of gold.

8th horse: Tawny damask.

9th horse: Ermines, bordered with crimson velvet and with tassels of gold.

Cap-a-pie: Old French, meaning head-to-foot; i.e., fully armed or accoutred.

Cap, Arming: a thick pad covering the head, acting as a shock absorber when blows landed and taking some of the weight of the helm.

Captain, the Great: the name given to Gonzalo de Córdoba (1453–1515), the Spanish general who was largely responsible for reorganizing that country's infantry and turning it into one of the finest fighting forces of the 16th century. Its efficiency attracted many foreigners into the service of Spain and, in the early 17th century, of 39 units of about 6,000 men each, only seven were Spanish, the rest being made up of Italians, Walloons, Burgundians, Swiss, Irish and Germans.

Caracol(e): a half-turn or wheel made by a horseman. The name is also applied to a manoeuvre in early warfare when hand-guns had come into use. The front rank of a galloping troop fired its pistols and peeled off to right and left, leaving the field of fire clear for the second rank who, in turn, veered off to let the third rank ride to the fore.

Carpet Knight: a stay-at-home soldier; one who has not won his title on the field of battle; a knight of the drawing room and boudoir.

Carrick Pursuivant: one of the Officers of Arms attached to the Court of the Lord Lyon, the Scottish Court of Chivalry.

Castellan: the governor or warden of a castle.

Castle: fortress or fortified building which was also usually the private residence of its lord and his household. It is this that distinguishes it from the earlier types of fort. In England the castle is almost unknown before the Norman Conquest of 1066. Domesday Book (1086) mentions 49, some 30 of which were built by the Conqueror himself. In the troubled reign of Stephen (1135–1154), when law and order were largely forgotten, the great barons built hundreds of illegal or 'adulterine' castles which Henry II, who succeeded him, had to fight to bring back under the royal control. A monk of Peterborough, recording the events of his time, wrote:

> 'When King Stephen came to England he held an assembly at Oxford. . . . When the traitors perceived that he was a mild man, and a soft and good, and that he did not enforce justice, they did all wonder. They had done homage to him and sworn oaths, but they no faith kept; all became forsworn, and broke their allegiance, for every rich man built his castles, and defended them against him, and they filled the land full of castles. They greatly oppressed the wretched people by making them work at these castles, and when the castles were finished they filled them with devils and evil men. Then they took those whom they suspected to have any goods, by night and by day, seizing both men and women, and they put them in prison for their gold and silver, and tortured them with pains unspeakable, for never were any martyrs tortured as these were. They hung some up by their feet, and smoked them with foul smoke; some by their thumbs, or by the head, and

39

they hung burning things on their feet. They put a knotted string about their heads, and twisted it till it went into the brain. They put them into dungeons, wherein were adders and snakes and toads, and thus wore them out. Some they put into a crucet-house – that is, into a chest that was short and narrow, and not deep – and they put sharp stones in it, and crushed the man therein so that they broke all his limbs. There were hateful and grim things called rachenteges in many of the castles, and which two or three men had enough to do to carry. The rachentege was made thus: it was fastened to a beam, having a sharp iron to go around a man's throat and neck, so that he might no ways sit, nor lie, nor sleep, but that he must bear all the iron. Many thousands they exhausted with hunger. I cannot and I may not tell of all the wounds and all the tortures that they inflicted upon the wretched men of this land.'

After this period of anarchy it became the policy of the Crown to keep down the number of castles and to exercise control over their custodians.

The earliest castles in England (from 1066 for about the next hundred years) were not made of stone, but were simple constructions of strong timber and earth works.

The next period saw the development of the stone castle, able to withstand the always-improving skill of armies laying siege to them. Often the stone castles were raised on the site of the earlier fortifications of earth and timber. The century and a half from, roughly, 1150–1200, was a great age of castle building; the next 150 years saw ever-increasing mastery of the art of military architecture and such splendid structures as Conway, Caernarvon and Beaumaris. After that, for a variety of reasons, the power and importance of the castle begin to decline, and the great buildings that had seen so much of strife and hardihood, heroism and terror, the ceaseless pitting of the craft and cunning of the besieger against the strength and obduracy of the besieged, gradually change (where they are not permitted to fall into desolate ruin) into comfortable homes or are put to other usages of peace.

For some types of castle, and some special

40

features, see *Concentric, Crusader, Edwardian, Motte-and-Bailey.*

Castle Dangerous: the castle of Douglas in Scotland, which Sir Walter Scott celebrated in his novel *Castle Dangerous* (1832). It was so called because, when it was garrisoned by the English, Sir James Douglas (1286?–1330), called 'the Good', three times attacked and destroyed his own castle, 1306–7. On Palm Sunday, March 19th, he attacked the garrison while they were in church, slew the soldiers remaining in the castle and then set fire to it. When it had been restored and re-garrisoned, Douglas disguised his followers as drovers of cattle and tempted the captain of the castle to sally forth to steal the herds. The 'drovers' turned on the attackers, defeated them, and again captured the Douglas stronghold. On the third occasion, to their shame, the English fell again for more-or-less the same trick. This time the Douglas followers were disguised as country-folk carrying corn and grass to market. Once again an attempt was made to plunder them, but Sir John de Walton, who had sworn to hold the castle for a year and a day, was killed and the marauding garrison over-powered.

Douglas was knighted on the field of Bannock-burn for his valour. He was thus described by the Scots poet John Barbour in about 1375:

> *In visage he was some deal gray,*
> *And had black hair, as I heard say,*
> *But then of limbs he was well made,*
> *With bones great, and shoulders braid . . .*
> *When he was blyth, he was lovely*
> *And meek, and sweet in company;*
> *But who in battle might him see,*
> *Another countenance had he . . .*

See also *Douglas, Sir James.*

Castle in Spain: a dream, an unreal or impracticable project or plan; the French have the phrase *Châteaux en Espagne.* A 'castle in the air' means much the same thing, a fanciful thing without real foundation.

Cat: a type of mediaeval siege-engine; a long, movable shelter made of timber and tough hides, used to give protection to soldiers while they built a causeway across the moat or ditch sur-

rounding a town or castle, and then burrowed into the wall to set their mines.

Catapult: one of the group of missile-throwing engines used in siege warfare. It was commonly employed for projecting smaller stones, darts and lighted brands to start fires in the besieged place. For engines throwing larger missiles see *Perrier, Mangon* and *Balista*.

Cavalliere: another of the European words for knight, this time Italian, from the word for horse, showing how the two are inseparable.

Caxton, William (1422?–1491): the first English printer, and a great lover of the deeds and stories of chivalry. Among the books printed by him were *The Order of Chivalry or Knighthood* (1483–85); *The Fayts of Arms of Chivalry* (1489); and, most important, *The Noble Histories of King Arthur and of Certain of His Knights* (1485). The last, a noble folio of 432 leaves, is in many ways the peak of Caxton's achievement. He worked from a manuscript by a Warwickshire knight named Sir Thomas Malory (see separate entry) and produced a book of stories that have never lost their hold and are still, in one form or another, frequently reprinted. Though his career as a merchant and, later, as a printer, gave him no opportunity for deeds of arms, he always cherished the ideals of knighthood, which he expressed in various ways; e.g., 'Do after the good and leave the evil, and it shall bring you to good fame and renown.'

Another great book of knighthood printed by him was *The History of Godfrey of Boloyne: or the Conquest of Jerusalem* (1481), which contains the words:

> The hye couragyous faytes And valyaunt actes of noble Illustrous and vertuous personnes ben digne to be recounted, put in memorye, and wreton, to thende that ther may be gyven to them name Inmortal by soverayn laude and preysyng.

(The high, courageous deeds and valiant acts of noble, illustrious and virtuous persons are worthy to be recounted, put in memory, and written, to the end that there may be given to them a name immortal by sovereign [i.e., the highest] praise).

42

The paragraph above is set in a type very similar to those used by Caxton in his books. There is a splendid MS. copy of the book on Godfrey of Bouillon (see separate entry) in the British Museum, richly illuminated, and this is probably the copy from which Caxton worked.

Caxton's chief patron in England was one of the best-known of 15th century knights, Anthony Woodville, 2nd Earl Rivers, who fought a celebrated joust with Anthony of Burgundy. (See *Woodville*.)

Celestial Crown: in heraldry, a crown with a number of long, narrow points, each tipped with a small star.

Chain Mail: see *Mail*.

Châlus (or Châluz): the castle in the Limousin district of France before which Richard-Coeur-de Lion was killed (1199), when he was besieging it in order to seize a newly-found treasure, a rare ornament of gold, representing an emperor and his family seated at a table. The king was struck in the shoulder by the bolt from a cross-bow and the wound became infected. Richard, in knightly fashion, forgave the archer who shot the fatal bolt. So the king who had survived so many great battles fell before an obscure castle defended by a handful of knights, so short of weapons that one used a frying-pan as a shield.

Champion of England: an office thought to have been created by William the Conqueror, and held for a long time by the Marmion family. In the region of Richard II the title came to their descendant, Sir John Dymoke, and has continued in the family, as an hereditary right, ever since. When the Champion carried out his duties in full panoply, he rode into Westminster Hall armed cap-a-pie during the banquet following the coronation of a new sovereign, and publicly challenged to combat anyone who dared dispute the king or queen's title to the throne. Unhappily, the ceremony has not been carried out since the reign of George IV – perhaps because we came to the conclusion that kings of his calibre were hardly worth fighting for.

As a reminder of this chivalric office, the head of the Dymoke family quarters with his own arms a silver sword on a black shield. The motto, too, *Rege dimico*, 'I fight for the King', cleverly combines a play on the surname and the office held by the family for so many centuries. Earlier Dymokes went even further in the desire to illustrate their name on their coat of arms by bearing as a crest two donkeys or 'mokes.' Later members apparently became sensitive on the point, and the mokes were metamorphosed into hares.

Chandos, Sir John (d. 1370): one of the most famous knights and soldiers of the Middle Ages, and perhaps the most beloved on either side in the wars with France. He fought at Crécy and, some three years afterwards, became a Knight of the Garter. At Poitiers, in 1356, he was by the Black Prince's side and urged him on with a stirring speech recorded by Froissart:

'Sir John Chandos said to the prince, "Sir, Sir, now push forward, for the day is ours. God will this day put it in your hand. Let us make for our adversary the king of France, for where he is will lie the main stress of the business. I well know that his valour will not let him fly, and he will remain with us, if it please God and St. George; but he must be well fought with, and you have before said that you would show yourself this day a good knight." The prince replied, "John, get forward. You shall not see me turn my back this day, but I will always be among the foremost." He then said to Sir Walter Woodland, his banner-bearer, "Banner, advance! in the name of God and St. George." '

After over thirty years of tough fighting and great valour, Chandos met his end, not in the press of battle, but by an unfortunate accident, which the same chronicler relates thus:

'Sir John Chandos, who was a strong and bold knight, and cool in all his undertakings, had his banner advanced before him [at Mortemer, 1370] surrounded by his men, with the scutcheon above his arms. He himself was dressed in a large robe which fell to the ground, blazoned with his arms on white sarcenet, argent a pile gules, one on his breast and the other on his back; so that he appeared

44

resolved on some adventurous undertaking and in this state, with sword in hand, he advanced on foot towards the enemy.

'This morning there had been a hoar frost, which made the ground slippery; so that, as he marched, he entangled his legs with his robe, which was of the longest and made a stumble; during which time a squire called James de St. Martin (a strong expert man) made a thrust at him with his lance, which hit him in the face, below the eye, between the nose and forehead. Sir John Chandos did not see the aim of the stroke, for he had lost the eye on that side five years ago, on the heaths of Bordeaux, at the chase of a stag. What added to this misfortune, Sir John had not put down his vizor, so that, in stumbling, he bore upon the lance, and helped it to enter into him . . . That gallant knight only survived one day and night. God have mercy on his soul! For never since a hundred years did there exist among the English one more courteous, nor fuller of every virtue and good quality than him.'

Chanson de Roland: see *Roland, Song of.*

Chansons de Geste: the old national epics, chanted and sung in France and other countries of Europe by wandering minstrels or *jongleurs* in inn, market place and castle. See *Roland, Song of* for one of the most famous. The stories, told in swinging metre that made them more easily remembered, were handed down by word of mouth and were added to as the years went on.

'Chanted to rhythmical numbers, the songs which celebrated the early valour of the fathers of the tribe become its war-cry in battle, and men march to conflict hymning the praises and the deeds of some real or supposed pre-cursor who had marshalled their fathers in the path of victory. No reader can have for-gotten that, when the decisive battle of Hastings commenced, a Norman minstrel, Taillefer, advanced on horseback before the invading host, and gave the signal for onset, by singing the Song of Roland, that renowned nephew of Clarlemagne, of whom romance speaks so much, and history so little.' – (Sir Walter Scott)

Chappe: semi-circular flap, often highly decorated, covering the centre part of the crossguard of a sword.

Charlemagne (742–814), otherwise Charles the Great or Charles I: the great king of France and Emperor of the West, who performed many courageous deeds in real life, including 53 campaigns in defence of the Christians of the west, and around whom has gathered such a volume of legend and story, that it is difficult to disentangle fact and fancy.

'To his Frankish warriors he was the ideal chief, tall and stout, animated and commanding, with flashing blue eyes and aquiline nose, a mighty hunter before the Lord. That he loved the old Frankish songs, used Frankish speech, and affected the traditional costume of his race – the high-laced boots, the crossgartered scarlet hose, the linen tunic, and square mantle of white or blue – that he was simple in his needs, and sparing in food and drink, were ingratiating features in a rich and wholesome character.' – (H. A. L. Fisher)

He was king of France for 46 years and Emperor of the West for the last 14. It is a sign of his great reputation as a warrior and defender of the Christian faith that the Patriarch of Jerusalem sent him the keys of the Holy Places, relying on him for their proper defence. He fought against Avars, Danes, Dalmatians, Lombards, Saxons, Slavs and Spaniards, and made central Europe safe for the Church. But he was much more than a soldier. He used his immense power and prestige to bring learning and literature to the continent of Europe, and attracted great scholars to his Court, chief among them the Englishman Alcuin, from Northumbria.

By one of the ironies of history, Charlemagne is best remembered, not for his long series of victories, but what was virtually his only defeat – a defeat which, in the centuries that followed, gathered more glory round it than all his splendid achievements. This was the reverse he suffered in 778 when, on his return from Spain, the rear-guard of his army was wiped out by the Moors in the pass of Roncesvalles. Among those who fell was Charlemagne's nephew, Count Roland, one of the king's famous Twelve Paladins (see next entry). The story of Roland in the pass of Roncesvalles, enriched and embroidered by countless minstrels and troubadours, became the most famous story of the Middle Ages and is still loved today.

> *Charles' army sleeps. The world is very still,*
> *Soft silvered by a radiant moon that sails*
> *Across a velvet sky of darkened blue;*
> *So silently she moves, her face so calm,*
> *Most wonderful the beauty of the night.*
> *But Charles looks up, his eyes all dimmed with tears.*
> *He cannot sleep, too heavy is his heart,*
> *As thinks he of brave Roland and his peers*
> *Who fought to hold the pass at Roncevaux.*
>
> (From a modern translation of the Song of
> Roland by Hilda Cumings Price)

Charlemagne's Paladins (or Peers): the twelve heroes – not always the same twelve – who, according to a great volume of legend, were the Emperor's closest companions and most trusted warriors. Few have any basis in history. The most famous was Roland (see separate entry) called Orlando in Italian romance. Among the rest of the brotherhood were Archbishop Turpin, who is supposed to have chronicled their exploits; Ogier the Dane, who became a national hero of Denmark; Oliver, who, with Roland, was the most famous of the Paladins; Ganelon the traitor; and Naymes, the wise counsellor.

Château Gaillard: a castle standing on a cliff 300 ft. above the River Seine, and built by Richard Coeur-de-Lion on the model of some of the great fortresses in the Holy Land. It has three baileys in a line, with deep moats between each. In 1203–4, the Château was the scene of a bitter siege, when Roger de Lacy, holding the castle for King John, was beleaguered by Philip II of France.

Chatelaine: the wife of the castellan, the mistress of a castle or château. A pleasant reminder of her responsibilities survived until very recently in the ornamental clasp and chain – known as a châtelaine – which hung from a lady's waist, with keys and trinkets attached.

Chaucer, Alice: grand-daughter of Geoffrey

Chaucer (see below). She married successively Sir John Phelip (killed at Harfleur, 1415); Thomas, fourth Earl of Salisbury (killed in France after the siege of Orleans, 1428); and, while still only 24, to William, first Duke of Suffolk (beheaded at sea, 1450). She was one of the first women members of the Order of the Garter; and her magnificent tomb in the church of St. Mary the Virgin, Ewelme, Oxfordshire, shows her wearing the Garter on her left forearm.

Chaucer, Geoffrey (1340?–1400): the poet of chivalry, who gave us, among other well-known portraits of mediaeval society, the famous descriptions of the Knight and the Squire. Probably Chaucer had real characters in mind when he wrote. Some scholars have, in fact, suggested that, in his account of the Squire, the poet was recalling his own youth. The italic lines give a modern translation, without any attempt to preserve the verse form.

A KNYGHT ther was and that a worthy man
A knight there was – a distinguished man
That fro the tymë that he first bigan
Who, from the time that he first began
To riden out, he loved chivalrie,
To ride out, loved chivalry,
Trouthe and honour, fredom and curteisie.
Truth and honour, freedom and courtesy.
Ful worthy was he in his lordës werre,
Most worthy was he in the King's wars,
And therto hadde he riden, no man ferre,
And no man had ridden further in them,
As wel in cristendom as in hethënesse,
Both in Christendom and in heathen lands,
And evere honoured for his worthynesse.
And was always honoured for his worth.

* * * * *

At mortal batailles hadde he been fiftene,
He had been in fifteen mortal battles,
And foughten for oure feith at Tramyssene
And had fought for the faith at Tremissen*
In lystës thries, and ay slayn his foo.
Three times in the lists, and each time killed his foe.
This ilke worthy knight hadde been also
This same worthy knight had also been

* i.e., Tlemçen, in Algeria, N. Africa.

48

Sometyme with the lord of Palatie
At one time with the Lord of Palathia
Agayn another hethen in Turkye;
Against another heathen in Turkey;
And everemoore he hadde a sovereyn prys,
And always he had won the highest reputation,
And though that he were worthy, he was wys,
And though he was so brave, he was prudent,
And of his port as meeke as is a mayde.
And as modest in his demeanour as a maid.
He nevere yet no vileynye ne sayde
He had never done any evil
In al his lyf unto no maner wight
In all his life, to any class of person.
He was a verray parfit gentil knyght.
He was a true and perfect noble knight.

*   *   *   *   *

With hym ther was his sone, a yong Squier,
With him was his son, a young Squire,
A lovyere and a lusty bacheler,
A lover and a lusty candidate for knighthood,
With lokkes crulle, as they were leyd in presse.
With locks as curly as if set that way.
Of twenty yeer of age he was, I gesse.
He was about twenty years of age, I suppose.
Of his stature he was of evene lengthe,
In stature he was well-proportioned,
And wonderly delyvere and of greet strengthe;
Wonderfully active and of great strength;
And he hadde been somtyme in chyvachie,
And he had recently been on a knightly expedition,
In Flaundres, Artoys and Pycardie,
In Flanders, Artois and Picardy,
And born hym weel, as of so litel space,
*And had borne himself well considering his short
    experience,*
In hope to stonden in his lady grace.
In hope of standing in his lady's favour.
Embrouded was he, as it were a meede,
His clothes were embroidered like a meadow
Al ful of fresshe floures whyte and reede;
Full of fresh flowers, white and red;
Syngynge he was or floytynge al the day;
He was singing or whistling all day;
He was as fressh as is the monthe of May.
He was as fresh as is the month of May.
Short was his gowne, with sleves longe and
    wyde;
His gown was short, with long wide sleeves;

49

Wel koude he sitte on hors, and faire ryde;
He could sit a horse well and ride gracefully.
He koude songes make and wel endite,
He could make songs and compose the words,
Juste and eek daunce and weel purtreye and write.
Joust, dance, draw, and write.
So hoote he lovede that by nyghtertale,
So fervently he loved that at night-time
He sleep namoore than dooth a nyghtyngale.
He could no more sleep than does a nightingale.
Curteis he was, lowely and servysable,
He was courteous, modest and obliging,
And carf biforn his fader at the table
And carved before his father at the table.

Chaucer served as a soldier himself, was taken prisoner in Brittany and was ransomed by Edward III in 1360. He was also called as a witness in a famous dispute about the right to bear a particular coat-of-arms. In 1375, Sir Richard Scrope and Sir Robert Grosvenor were both using the same arms, a golden bend on a blue field, and the case was brought before a court of chivalry, which decided that Scrope had the best right to the coat-of-arms, but allowed Grosvenor to bear them also, with a silver border for difference. This was not satisfactory, since it seemed to imply that Grosvenor was a junior member of the Scrope family, whereas there was no relationship. An appeal was made to the king (Richard II) and he ordered Grosvenor to give up the golden bend altogether and to carry on his blue shield a 'garb' or sheaf of grain. The Duke of Westminster, who is descended from Sir Robert, still bears in one part of his complicated shield, nearly 600 years afterwards, a golden wheatsheaf, and the Scropes still carry a golden bend on a blue field – reminders of this ancient quarrel and of the shield-of-arms as a mark of personal honour, not to be disgraced or lightly relinquished.

Chaucer's own coat is described as party per pale, argent and gules a bend counterchanged.

Chausses: leg and foot armour, like long stockings of mail.

Checky (or Checquy): in heraldry, the pattern made on a shield by drawing transverse perpendicular and horizontal lines, making a large number of small squares. The coat-of-arms would be described as, e.g., checky or and azure (gold and blue).

Chevalier: a knight or horseman (French *cheval*, a horse); a member of some foreign orders of knighthood.

Chief: the upper part of a shield, a broad horizontal stripe occupying the top third.

Childe: a title of honour, given in early days to a member of a noble family before he attained knighthood. Childe Roland, Childe Arthur, etc., are examples. In Anglo-Saxon, the word *cniht* means both 'knight' and 'child'.

Children's Crusade: the disastrous expeditions begun in 1212 by thousands of children in France and Germany in a pathetic effort to rescue the Holy Land from the infidels where their elders had failed. In France, the crusade was preached by Stephen, a twelve-year-old shepherd boy with an extraordinary gift of eloquence. He promised his followers that the seas would dry up before them, as they did before the Israelites, when they marched to the delivery of Christendom. Towards the end of June, 1212, many thousands of children (witnesses spoke of 30,000, twelve years old or less) gathered at Vendôme from all over France. Noble and simple, boys and girls, accompanied by a few priests and older people, started on the straggling expedition southward, with Stephen, as leader, travelling in a cart covered by a canopy to shelter him from the sun.

In a blazing summer, short of water and dependent on charity for food, many dropped by the road or turned round and tried to struggle home again. At Marseilles, the remaining young crusaders were disappointed and indignant when the seas remained obstinately impassable. After some time, two merchants, apparently in the goodness of their hearts, hired seven ships to take them free of charge to the Holy Land. They sailed; and a curtain of silence fell for nearly twenty years. Then, at last, the dismal news filtered through to castle and cottage all over France. Two of the ships had been

wrecked in a storm off Sardinia; the remaining five, by prior arrangement, were soon surrounded by a Saracen squadron, and the children were taken off and sold into slavery on the coasts of Algeria. According to the priest who brought back the news, there were still about 700 living in 1230.

Soon after Stephen had preached the Crusade in France, Nicholas, a German boy, followed his lead in Cologne. Soon another army, slightly older than the French expedition, set out for Italy. Its fate was almost as dismal. One division, according to some chroniclers numbering about 20,000, tried to cross the Alps by the Mont Cenis pass. Only a remnant of the original army struggled through to Genoa, where a number settled down and became Genoese citizens. Some of the more valiant struggled on and one party, led by Nicholas himself, reached Rome, much to the embarrassment of the Pope, who advised them to go home and leave their struggle against the infidel till they were older.

The other division of children went through the Saint Gothard pass and, after heavy losses, reached the sea. A few managed to find ships to take them to the Holy Land, the rest straggled back along the long road to home, which only a handful ever saw again.

In all the annals of chivalry, there is no more tragic story than that of these hundreds of thousands of aspirants to the knighthood of the Cross, doomed before their ragged march began.

Chivalry: the general term for the knightly system of the Middle Ages and for the virtues and qualities that inspired it. It can also mean the actual knightly ranks of an army, e.g., 'the chivalry of France', 'the English king and all his chivalry', etc. See *Code of Chivalry* and *Court of Chivalry*.

Christendom: the portion of the world where Christianity was recognized, as distinct from the lands of the infidel.

Cid, The: or Cid Campeador, meaning 'the lord champion'; the name given to Ruy, or Rodrigo, Díaz de Bivar, a great Castilian hero (1040–99) who won glory against the Moors. His name has gathered round it a whole body of legend, so that it is difficult, as with other mediaeval heroes, to disentangle truth and fiction.

Cinquefoil: in heraldry, a sort of clover with five rounded petals. Coats-of-arms can also be found with the *trefoil* (three petals), *quatrefoil* (four), *sixfoil* (six), *octofoil* or *double quatrefoil* (8), etc.

Citadel: a castle, or a strongly fortified place commanding a city and intended as a final defence or place of retreat. The word means 'little city'.

Clarenceux King of Arms: see *Officers of Arms*.

Clisson, Sir Oliver de: a famous Breton knight, friend of *Bertrand du Guesclin* (see separate entry) and successor to him as Constable of France. On one occasion, in the early hours of the morning, he had a fortunate escape on his way to his lodging, when, riding with eight unarmed squires, he was set upon by an enemy, Sir Peter de Craon. De Clisson had only a short sword, about two feet long, but managed to stay on his horse and parry the murderous attack till he was 'villainously struck on the back part of the head' and fell stunned from the saddle. Fortunately he fell right against the door of a baker, who was up in the small hours of the morning baking his bread. Hearing the sounds of strife in the cobbled street, the baker half opened the door and Sir Oliver, striking it heavily in his fall, burst it open and rolled into the shop where, because of the smallness of the entrance, those on horseback could not follow. As Froissart says: 'It must be owned for truth, that God shewed great favour to the Constable.'

Close Helmet: type of helmet very popular in the 16th and 17th centuries, deriving from the great bascinet, and fitting much more closely to the natural shape of the head.

Coat-armour: heraldic device or escutcheon of a person or family; derived from the surcoat worn by knights over their armour and decorated by devices to distinguish one from the other.

53

Hence, 'a gentleman of coat-armour' is one entitled to bear to display a coat-of-arms.

Coat-of-arms: closely connected with *coat-armour* (see above); the complete heraldic achievement of a person entitled to bear arms. See *Achievement*.

Coat of Plates: sleeveless coat of overlapping iron plates fastened down on to strong material beneath.

Cockatrice: a fabulous beast, half bird, half serpent, sometimes found in heraldry. It has barbed wings, a cock's head, spurs on its legs and a spiked tail.

Codrington, John: Henry V's standard bearer at the Battle of Agincourt (see separate entry). As arms, he bore, on a silver field, three red lions and a red fess (the centre third of a shield). Later, as a reward for his good services as a soldier and knight, he was permitted to show the fess 'embattled', i.e., looking like the crenellated top of a castle wall.

Code of Chivalry: While it is difficult to find precise rules laid down for the conduct of a knight, it is clear that a code comes to be recognized, even though, in the stern tests of day-to-day life, it was rarely faithfully lived up to; and since, as a German philosopher has said, 'ideals cherished in the minds of men enter into the character of their actions', amid all the treachery, greed and cruelty there are to be found shining examples of unselfish courage, gentleness and mercy inspired by those rules that only a perfect man could keep perfectly.

Some seventy years ago, Léon Gautier, a French scholar who had devoted his life to the study of the literature of chivalry, worked out what he called the Decalogue, or Ten Commandments governing the conduct of a knight. They required:

1. Unswerving belief in the Church and obedience to her teachings.
2. Willingness to defend the Church.
3. Respect and pity for all weakness and steadfastness in defending them.
4. Love of country.

5. Refusal to retreat before the enemy.
6. Unceasing and merciless war against the infidel.
7. Strict obedience to the feudal overlord, so long as those duties did not conflict with duty to God.
8. Loyalty to truth and to the pledged word.
9. Generosity in giving.
10. Championship of the right and the good, in every place and at all times, against the forces of evil.

The picture of the true knight as a Christian soldier emerges clearly. Military glory and prowess were not enough. They must be gained and displayed in the service of the Church and of worthy ends. 'It is not without reason,' wrote St. Bernard to the Knights of the Temple, 'that the soldier of Christ carries a sword; it is for the chastisement of the wicked and for the glory of the good.'

Carved in the stone of Chartres Cathedral is a knightly prayer:

'Most Holy Lord, Almighty Father . . . thou who hast permitted on earth the use of the sword to repress the malice of the wicked and defend justice . . . cause thy servant here before thee, by disposing his heart to goodness, never to use this sword or another to injure anyone unjustly; but let him use it always to defend the just and right.'

Examples of observance of all the ten rules can be found scattered throughout this book. Not the least remarkable are those which illustrate the importance attached to keeping the pledged word. See, e.g., entries for *Du Guesclin, Bertrand* and *John the Good*, king of France.

Among other attempts to define the rules of chivalry, perhaps Lord Tennyson's was the shortest and neatest: 'Live pure, speak true, right wrong, follow the Christ, the King.'

Collar of SS.: a collar made of a series of letter S's in gold, either intertwined or set closely together. It occurs in many records and pictures of noble costume and is worn by Kings of Arms and heralds. Its origin and significance are uncertain.

College of Arms: the headquarters of the

English Officers of Arms, who exercise jurisdiction over all heraldic matters, including the granting of arms, the recording of pedigrees, the preservation of records, validity of descent, etc. They also perform special functions at great ceremonies of State.

The present building in Queen Victoria Street, London, is on the site originally granted to the Heralds by Queen Mary in July, 1554, 'to the end that the Officers of the College might be enabled to assemble together and consult and agree among themselves for the good of their faculty, and that the Records and Rolls might be more safely and conveniently deposited.' The building was destroyed in the Fire of London (1666) though, fortunately, the records were saved. Rebuilding took place soon after, probably under the guidance of Sir Christopher Wren.

The collection of rolls and other genealogical records is the finest in the world. An Officer of Arms is always on duty to deal with enquiries. See *Officers of Arms*.

Colours: see *Tinctures*.

Combat à l'outrance: see *à l'Outrance*.

Concentric Castle: type of late 13th and early 14th century fortress with an outer and inner ring of defences. There are fine examples at Beaumaris, Harlech and Caerphilly.

Condottiere: (from the Italian, meaning captain). A soldier of fortune in the 14th and 15th centuries who sold his services and those of his followers to anyone who would pay their wages. It must not be thought that this was reckoned a shameful pastime. Many condottieri were distinguished soldiers, and there were English equivalents such as Sir John Hawkwood (see separate entry) who took his company of free lances to some notable campaigns in Italy. See *Calveley, Sir Hugh* for another famous commander of free lances.

Conjoined: in heraldry, linked together.

Consecrator: one name given to the man capable of creating another a knight. See *Parrain* for a fuller account of this office.

56

Constable: a word which really means 'count of the stable' and which has held a variety of meanings through the centuries. It was often used in connection with high military commands; and from about the time of Stephen there was a Lord High Constable in England for many centuries – an office that has been described as that of 'quarter-master general of the court and army.' At times he had responsibilities for the king's household accounts, at others for the management of the feudal army – summoning, billeting, organizing and controlling it by martial law. He was also, at times, one of the presiding officers of the *Court of Chivalry*. (See separate entry.)

In France also, the *connétable* wielded great powers as the first officer of the Crown, the chief commander of the army and the controller of all matters connected with chivalry. The most famous Constable of France was Bertrand du Guesclin (see *Du Guesclin*) who held the office from 1370–80. He took it with great reluctance. 'He who had always fought untrammelled must in future go into battle weighted down, hampered, by this tremendous responsibility. A lost battle would not mean a Breton knight defeated, but the Kingdom of France defeated. He who had governed his life by his own honour must now be governed by another, and an overpowering honour.' (M. Coryn.) When he knew he was dying, he sent back the Constable's great sword, with its hilt of gold, enamelled with *fleurs-de-lis*, to Charles V. 'Take it, and return it into the keeping of the king – and do you tell him that never have I betrayed him or it.'

Constantine's Cross: the cross that Constantine the Great (272–337), claimed to have seen in the sky during the march to Rome in the year 312 when he wiped out his rival Maxentius under the walls of the city. The cross, which was a monogram of the first letters in the Greek name for Christ, was accompanied by the motto 'By this sign thou shalt conquer'.

Constantine adopted the badge and became the champion of Christianity to the extent that he granted it complete toleration. He did not, however, accept baptism as a Christian himself for another quarter of a century, in his last illness.

There are a number of other stories of crosses

appearing at critical moments; e.g., the Cross of St. Andrew that appeared to the King of the Scots before his battle with Athelstan; the fiery cross which gave Waldemar of Denmark victory over the Esthonians in 1219, and the one which heralded Alfonso of Leon's defeat of the Moors some eighty years before at the battle of Ourique, at which five Saracen kings are said to have fought. Alfonso adopted as his shield-of-arms five blue escutcheons on a silver field, each escutcheon charged with five *bezants* (see separate entry) in memory of the five wounds of Christ; all five escutcheons being so arranged as to form a cross themselves.

Conyers Falchion: see *Falchion.*

Cordova: an ancient city in southern Spain, famous for its leather throughout Europe. The English word 'cordwainer', meaning a shoe-maker, really means a worker in Cordovan leather.

Córdoba, Gonzalo de: see *Captain, the Great.*

Corduroy: a popular modern material, with princely origins. The word probably comes from the French *cord du roy*, (king's cord), the corded fabric worn by the kings of France while hunting.

Coronel or Cronel: iron head of a tilting lance, roughly heart-shaped and with several blunt points. This was to prevent damage to combatants, as distinct from the war spear. (See also *Lance of Courtesy.*)

Cote-hardi: a tight-fitting tunic, much worn in the Middle Ages by both men and women. It seems they were often used as gifts; the chronicler Sir John Froissart, e.g., was given a handsome cote-hardi by Amadeus, Count of Savoy in 1368, together with twenty florins of gold.

Coudières: special plates of metal or hardened leather, of various shapes and sizes, to protect the elbow in a suit of armour. The terms 'butterfly' and 'fan-shaped' indicate two patterns. Coudières for right and left arms some-

58

times varied in style. When the shield was discarded as a means of defence, the left arm became much more important than the right for warding off blows, and the coudière on that side was often made larger and stronger.

Council of Troyes: the Council, held in 1228, at which the Knights Templars (see separate entry) were recognized as an Order, and rules drawn up for their governance.

Council of Westminster: a Council summoned by Anselm in 1102. One of its decisions was that bishops and abbots should no longer have the power to make knights. See *Parrain*.

Course: method of combat in joust and tournament during the Middle Ages. Many varieties can be found; for some of the chief see *Baston Course*, *Free Course*, *German Course* and *Italian Course*.

Courser: literally, a running or swift horse; almost always, in the days of chivalry, the warhorse, though the word was sometimes used less precisely for a jousting or tournament horse.

Court of Chivalry: sometimes known as the Court of the Constable and Marshal, this emerged during the 13th and 14th centuries to adjudicate in cases arising from deeds of arms outside the kingdom, and those within it that could not be settled at Common Law. It also heard disputes connected with the bearing of arms, and, for this reason, the heralds and Officers of Arms came to play an important part because of their vast knowledge of pedigrees, coats-of-arms, etc.

Court of Love: one of the frolicsome Courts held in Provence at the time of the troubadours (see separate entry) to decide knotty problems of the heart. In a typical case, the Court was asked to decide which man was really the favoured suitor if a lady listened to one, squeezed the hand of another and touched the foot of a third with her toe. Often the tribunal consisted of ladies.

Courtesy: as well as its familiar meaning of politeness and civility, the word in early cen-

turies meant particularly the accepted manners of the court and courtly society, which aspirants to knighthood were most anxious to acquire. They were often attached for the purpose to some great household. Books were compiled to help the young in this strict period of training. Two of the most famous of these 'courtesy books' were Hugh Rhodes's *Boke of Nurture* (1450) and *The Babees' Boke* (1475), 'a lytyl reporte of how young people should behave.' Caxton printed *The Book of Courtesy* very early in his career, for the benefit of 'lytyl John' in his 'tendre enfancye.' Typical instructions (some, at least, of which will have a faintly familiar ring to young members of 20th century households) were:

> Burnish no bones with thy teeth, for that is unseemly.
>
> Rend not thy meat asunder, for that swerves from courtesy.
>
> Scratch not thy head with thy fingers when thou art at meat.
>
> Fill not thy mouth too full, lest thou perhaps of force must speak; nor blow out thy crumbs when thou doest eat.
>
> Blow not thy pottage nor drink, for it is not commendable.

Courtesy titles: titles not having any legal value, but which are used as part of social customs that have developed through the centuries.

Courtrai (Courtray), Battle of: see *Battle of the Spurs.*

Couvre-chef de mercy: the scarf or kerchief carried by one of the tournament officials at the head of his lance, for the purpose of touching a knight seen to be in serious difficulties and thus signalling that no further attack was to be made on him.

Coward or Cowed: term used in heraldry to describe an animal with his tail between his legs.

Crakeys (or crakys) of war: name given to a type of cannon used by Edward III.

Creanse: a fine line, fastened to a hawk's leash when it is first lured. (See *leash* and *lure.*)

Crécy, Battle of: one of the most celebrated victories in English history, won on August 26th–27th, 1346, when the chivalry of France, under Philip VI, attacked the defensive position held by the English on the low ridge, facing south-west, between the villages of Crécy and Wadicourt, with woods to the right and behind. The French forces probably numbered something over 40,000, the English 13,000, of whom about 3,000 were knights and men at arms and most of the rest archers.

Because of the indiscipline of the French knights, in striking contrast to the behaviour of the English army, the battle began when the sun was already lowering in the sky instead of awaiting, as Philip intended, the dawn of another day.

The contemporary accounts of the engagement are full of memorable scenes; among them, the preliminary attack by the Genoese crossbowmen who, to intimidate the waiting English host, yelled and leapt in the air three times as they advanced. They were greeted with silence. Then, having at last come within bow-shot, the Genoese began to fire fiercely – and the English line suddenly came to life. The longbowmen took a step forward and, firing four or five times faster than their opponents, literally shot them from the field, the shafts flying 'with such force and quickness that it seemed as if it snowed.'

The French knights, cursing the despised Genoese, rode through shattered ranks, trampling the stricken men. To the chorus of the wounded, it must have been an awesome sight – the close-ranked knights of France, riding knee to knee in the setting sun with the sacred oriflame and thousands of banners blowing above them.

They met the same reception – the same unwavering line of archers, the step forward, the ruthless whistling arrows aimed chiefly at the horses. The resulting confusion was indescribable, the slaughter terrible.

The battle ended soon after midnight. The French who survived wandered hopelessly off in the darkness; the exhausted English flung themselves down where they lay, and slept through the rest of the short summer night.

In the morning could be seen the most pitiful sight of the whole battle – the English heralds

and clerks, at the command of the king, moving slowly and steadily through the fallen host of France, identifying the nobles and knights from the dimmed colours of their coats-of-arms – immediately recognizable to the officers of arms – and carefully listing their names.

The record still survives; and the valley below the ridge is still called *La Vallée aux Clercs*, the Valley of Clerks.

It was a humiliating day for the gallant but disorganized knighthood of France. Armoured and horsed, with centuries of proud deeds behind them, they had been defeated by the lowly bowmen and, though the knights were slow to learn the lesson (see *Agincourt*), mediaeval warfare was never the same again.

The French losses have been variously estimated, from the lowest, 1,500 knights and 10,000 common soldiers (Sir Arthur Bryant) to 'eighty banners, the bodies of eleven princes, twelve hundred knights and about thirty thousand common men' (Sir John Froissart). Incredibly, the English seem to have lost less than 50.

(For other incidents and figures in the battle see *Edward, Prince of Wales* and *John, king of Bohemia*.)

Crécy Window: the great window in Gloucester Cathedral, at the east end, seventy feet high and nearly forty wide, containing the coats-of arms and faces of many of the commanders at the Battle of Crécy, chief among them Edward III and the Black Prince. It was erected soon after the battle and is the largest window in Europe.

Crenellation: the provision of battlements, with notches or indentations, along the top of the wall of a castle or other building. Each embrasure is a *crenel* or *crenelle*.

Crescent: a popular charge in heraldry. Properly speaking, the half-moon is described as a crescent only when the points and the opening face upwards. If the opening faces the onlooker's left it is an *increscent*; facing the onlooker's right it is a *decrescent*. See also *Cadency*.

The crescent has also come to be commonly accepted, in such phrases as 'Cross versus Crescent', as the badge of the infidel or the

Saracen, as compared with the insignia of the Christian knight.

Crest: see *Achievement*. The figure, often of an animal or part of an animal, surmounting a knight's helmet. In France, the knights were sometimes called 'the crested helmets', as distinct from the more lowly men-at-arms.

Crested Armour: a type of ridged and fluted armour developed at the end of the 15th century.

Crinet: protective armour for a horse's neck, often of over-lapping plates to allow free movement.

Cross: the foremost emblem of the Holy Wars and of the Christian knight. It was used before the time of the First Crusade, but it was Pope Urban II, at the Council of Clermont in 1095, who gave it as the standard symbol in the fight against the pagan:

> 'The Cross of Christ is the symbol of your salvation. Wear it, a red, a bloody cross, on your breasts and shoulders, as a token that His help will never fail you; as the pledge of a vow which can never be recalled.'

Nearly five hundred years later, Spenser, in *The Faerie Queene*, echoes the words in his description of the Red Cross Knight:

> *And on his brest a bloodie Crosse he bore,*
> *The deare remembrance of his dying Lord,*
> *For whose swete sake that glorious badge he wore,*
> *And dead, as living, ever him ador'd:*
> *Upon his shield the like was also scor'd,*
> *For soveraine hope which in his helpe he had.*
> *Right faithfull true he was in deede and word . . .*

In heraldry, there are a great many varieties of cross, some of the most interesting in design being the *Cross Crosslet, Cross Fleury, Cross Moline, Cross Patée* and *Cross Potent*. See also *St. Andrew's Cross, St. Patrick's Cross, St. George's Cross* and *Maltese Cross*.

Cross-bow: a type of weapon known from very early centuries but not, at least in Europe, recognized as a fitting weapon for warfare till the 12th century. Pope Innocent II, in 1139, placed it under an interdict as unfit for Christians to fight with, and Innocent III took the same

view. Christian kings, however, developed other views, and Richard I of England and Philip Augustus of France encouraged its use on the Third Crusade. King John paid his cross-bowmen threepence a day on foot, sevenpence halfpenny mounted (if the bowman had one horse) and double that amount if he boasted two.

In England, the cross-bow had a short life and was soon replaced by the more formidable and efficient long-bow. (See separate entry.) On the Continent it was used over a much longer period. Cross-bowmen usually fought in the front, and on the wings, of a battle, where their bolts or 'quarrels' discouraged the oncoming enemy cavalry. They were often in an unfortunate position since, whether they were successful or whether they broke, the accompanying knights did not hesitate to ride through them, either despising them for their lack of prowess or insisting on sharing whatever glory was going. (See, e.g., *Crécy, Battle of.*)

Cross-bows were of several kinds, ranging from the simple type drawn by the hands alone to those operated by levers, wheels, rachets and pulleys. Some could throw stones and balls of lead; but the usual missile was a bolt terminating in a four-sided, pyramid-shaped head. The range of a 15th century cross-bow seems to have been from 370–400 yards. But greater distances were possible. In 1901, Sir Ralph Payne-Gallwey, using a steel cross-bow of the 15th century, shot several bolts across the Menai Straits – a distance of about 450 yards.

Crown: various types of crown are used in heraldry, often as part of the crest. They do not indicate rank. Among them are the *Naval Crown*; *The Eastern,* or *Antique Crown*; the *Celestial Crown*; *Vallery, Crown*; *Pallisado, Crown*; and the *Mural Crown*. See separate definitions.

Crupper: leather loop, passing under the tail of a horse and round its hindquarters and fastened to the saddle to keep it from slipping forwards.

Crusader Castles: the great fortresses raised in Syria and Palestine by the various crusading armies and by the military orders of knights who established bases there. The first that can be dated accurately is the castle raised by Raymond, Count of Toulouse at Mount Pilgrim in 1104, when he was besieging Tripoli. Some of the most famous were Krak des Chevaliers, the great fortress of the Knights Hospitallers; Kerak of Moab; Beaufort; and Sahyun, in northern Syria, where an artificial chasm 100 feet deep was carved in the solid rock to serve as a moat.

The Crusaders learnt much about military architecture from the east and introduced many Byzantine ideas into Europe. See *Château Gaillard* for an example.

Crusaders' Colours: At certain periods different colours were adopted to distinguish the soldiers of one country from another. On the Third Crusade, the English wore a white cross, the French red and the Flemings green. The English, however, soon took over the red cross of St. George as their own, following the institution of the Order of the Garter by Edward III, who 'appoynted his Souldiers to wear white Coats or Jackets, with a red Crosse before and behinde over their Armour.' This is doubtless the origin of the 'red coats' retained by the British army till very recently, and still worn ceremonially by some regiments.

Crusades: or Wars of the Cross; the military expeditions carried out by the Christian countries in the 11th–13th centuries for the recovery of the Holy Land from the hands of the Saracens. It is customary to distinguish eight crusades, the first, from 1096–1100, under Godfrey of Bouillon, Raymond of Toulouse and Bohemund of Tarantum; the last, that led by St. Louis, King of France (1270–72). The most important from the English point of view, though its success was slight, was the 3rd Crusade (1189–92), because of the participation of Richard Coeur de Lion and his encounters with the famous Salah-ad-Din-Yusuf, better known as Saladin.

For some of the great figures in the Crusades see *Baldwin of Flanders, Bohemund of Tarantum, Montferrat, Conrad of, Godfrey of Bouillon, Louis IX, Richard I, Saladin.*

Two opinions of the Crusades:

(i) 'The Crusades are not, in my mind, either the popular delusions that our cheap literature has determined them to be, nor

Papal conspiracies against kings and peoples . . . nor the savage outbreaks of savage expiring barbarism thirsting for blood and plunder, nor volcanic explosions of religious intolerance. I believe them to have been, in their deep sources, and in the minds of their best champions, and in the main tendency of their results, capable of ample justification. They were the first great effort of mediaeval life to go beyond the pursuit of selfish and isolated ambitions; they were the trial-feat of the young world, essaying to use, to the glory of God and the benefit of man, the arms of its new knighthood." – (Bishop Stubbs.)

(ii) 'The historian as he gazes back across the centuries at their gallant story must find his admiration overcast by sorrow at the witness it bears to the limitations of human nature. There was so much courage and so little honour, so much devotion and so little understanding. High ideals were besmirched by cruelty and greed, enterprise and endurance by a blind and narrow self-righteousness; and the Holy War itself was nothing more than a long act of intolerance in the name of God . . .' – (Steven Runciman.)

Crusillée (or Crusilly): used to describe a shield scattered over with crosses. Unless another type of cross is specified, the crosses are *cross-crosslets*, i.e., crosses each arm of which is in the form of a cross.

Cuirass: armour for the body, breast and back, buckled or strapped together.

Cuir Bouilli: literally, 'leather (or hide) boiled'; tough leather, moulded to shape, and much used in early times as armour in its own right, or to reinforce plate and mail.

Cuishes (or cuisses): defensive armour for thighs. Sometimes, e.g., during certain types of jousts, they were fastened to the saddle of the horse, to prevent damage to the riders when horses collided.

Cullen Plate: see *Brass.*

Curtain Wall: the exterior defensive wall

running round a castle. These walls were often built with deep plinths (see *Batters*), for greater strength and for protection against mining operations by attackers. Curtain walls were from 20 feet to 30 feet high and of great thickness. Those of Conway are nearly 11 feet; those of Beaumont, Anglesey, 15 feet.

Curtana: the Sword of Mercy, sometimes called 'Edward the Confessor's Sword', which has for centuries been carried at the coronation of English kings and queens. It is square-ended, having its end blunted in token of mercy. The sword is first mentioned by name at the coronation of Queen Eleanor, wife of Henry II, in 1236. It is also named in an inventory of the reign of Edward III. As an example of history repeating itself, Henry, fourth Earl of Northumberland carried Curtana at the coronation of Richard III, July 6th, 1483; 470 years later, his descendant Hugh, tenth Duke of Northumberland, bore the sword at the coronation of Queen Elizabeth II, June 2nd, 1953.

During the Commonwealth, under Oliver Cromwell, Curtana was sold or destroyed with the rest of the royal regalia. A new sword was made by order of Charles II, from drawings of one given to Henry VIII by the Pope. The blade is 32 inches long and 2 inches wide.

D

D'Abernon (D'Aubernon or D'Aubernoun), Sir John: the subject of what is now generally recognized as being the oldest surviving brass in England. (See *Brass*.) It is set in the floor of the chancel in the church of St. Mary, Stoke d'Abernon, Surrey. Measuring all of six feet in length, it is a wonderful example of craftsmanship, showing the knight in mail, with his lance and great two-handed sword. The blue enamel still glows on his shield (or, a chevron azure). Round the edge of the brass is carved in stone: SIRE: JOHANN: DAUBERNOUN: CHIVALER: GIST: ICI: DEV: DE: SA: ALME: EYT: MERCY. (*Sir John D'Aubernoun, knight, lies here. God on his soul have mercy.*)

Next to him lies his son, the second Sir John. His brass, fifty years later, shows clearly the development in armour, since he is clad, not in mail like his father, but in half plate.

Stoke d'Abernon has other claims to fame. In 1189, a young knight who was to become a famous soldier and Regent of England, married the heiress of the Earl of Pembroke and spent his honeymoon in the old manor by the church. The knight was William Marshal (see separate entry) and the honeymoon is the first actually recorded in English history. The poetical biography of William Marshal, *L'Histoire de Guillaume le Maréchal*, a work of 19,000 lines written in early French and finished only six years after his death, contains the words:

> Quant les noces bien faites furent
> E richement, si comme els durent,
> La dame emmena, ce savon,
> Chies sire Angeran d'Abernon
> A Estokes, en liu paisable
> E aesie e delitable –

which, putting it simply, means that after her wedding the lady was taken to the home of Sir Engerrand D'Abernon at Stoke, a peaceful, comfortable and delightful place. Confirmation of the wedding occurs in the documents known as the Pipe Rolls, or Great Rolls of the Exchequer, for 1189, where the cost of the bride's trousseau is given as £9 12s. 1d.

Dagger: a weapon in the Middle Ages, growing in popularity with the knightly class from the 13th century onwards. Though it is usually thought of as a sort of short sword, tapering and double-edged, there were some types with a single edge, more like a modern carving knife. They could reach such a length, between eighteen inches and two feet, that it is sometimes difficult to distinguish them from swords. (See *Baselard, Kidney Dagger, Main-Gauche, Miséricorde* and *Rondel Dagger*.)

Dagonet: in the legendary history of King Arthur, the king's fool, who was knighted by Arthur himself. 'King Arthur loved sir Dagonet passing well, and made him knight with his own hands; and at every tournament he made king Arthur laugh.'

Damascene: to ornament, often by inlaying with gold and silver, in the manner of Damascus, which had an especial reputation for this type of work in the Middle Ages. It was used with particular effect on armour.

Damoiseau: a young man of gentle birth, aspiring to knighthood, but not yet admitted to the order of chivalry. Often, as the next step up, he became squire to an established knight. (See *Knight*.)

Dapple: the name of the donkey ridden by Sancho Panza, squire to Don Quixote, Knight of La Mancha, in the mock-romance written by Miguel de Cervantes (1547–1616). Dappled, from an Icelandic word for spot, means spotted or mottled; hence, a dapple-grey is a horse of a variegated light and dark grey colour.

D'Argentine, Sir Giles (d. 1314): one of the most famous knights at the Battle of Bannockburn, June 24th, 1314, when the chivalry of England, under Edward II, were disastrously defeated near Stirling by Robert Bruce. With the archers cut to pieces, and the horsemen floundering hopelessly in the burn and peat bogs where they had been relentlessly driven, the English king was hustled out of the fight by a company of knights and set galloping on the road to Stirling and safety. Then, having guarded the king thus far, Sir Giles D'Argentine, turned back to die, with the words: 'I am not of custom to fly; nor shall I do so now. God keep you!'

Deer: 'I have gone rownde aboute Crystendome, and overthwarte Crystendome, and a thousande or two and more myles out of Crystendome, yet there is not so moche pleasure for harte and hynde, bucke and doo, and for roo bucke and doo as in England.' The words, written by Andrew Boorde, an early 16th century traveller and physician, commemorate vividly what was for centuries one of the favourite pastimes of English kings, nobles and the knightly classes. 'In the forests,' wrote Richard Fitz-Neale (or Fitz-Nigel), Treasurer of England and Bishop of London, at the end of the 12th century, 'are the secret places of the kings and their great delight. To them they go for hunting, having put off their cares, so that they may enjoy a little quiet. There away from the continuous turmoil of the court, they can for a little time breathe in the grace of natural liberty. . . The king's forest is the safe dwelling place of wild beasts, not of every sort, but of the sort that dwell in woodlands, not in any sort of place, but in certain places suitable for the purpose.'

Fierce laws were made to protect the royal forests. Poachers and illegal hunters could suffer the lash, blinding, mutilation or even execution. In time, as the result of grants by various kings, great stretches of forest, usually known as 'chases', came under the control of other land-owners, whose laws were often as a harsh as the king's.

Great hatred existed between the country folk and the foresters, or verderers, employed to guard the forests; and history is full of vivid descriptions of cases of arrest (and of battles of wit to preserve poachers from punishment). A typical 'inquest' held in 1248 about an incident in Huntingdon-shire, records that at midnight on August 2nd the foresters 'met a red greyhound worrying a doe. They called the greyhound and took it. After-wards twelve men came . . . one of them with an axe in his hand, another with a long stick, and the other ten with bows and arrows. And they led three greyhounds in a leash, of which one was white, another speckled with black and white, and of what colour the third was they know not. The foresters called the men, who shot six arrows at them . . . and the foresters shot at the men, who entered the wood, and on account of the thickness of the wood and the darkness of the night the foresters know not what became of them.'

The wild boar and the deer were the most prized objects of the chase. Lesser animals, such as the wolf, the fox, the hare and the wild cat, were also hunted; but often because they were regarded as the enemies of the nobler beasts. The largest of the English deer was the stag, or red deer. Others frequently met in history and literature are the fallow deer, so called from its pale colour, and spotted white in summer; and the little roebuck, agile and graceful, preferring the high ground.

Defender (or Advocate) of the Holy Sepulchre: the title taken by Godfrey of Bouillon (see separate entry), one of the greatest knights of chivalry, who refused the title of King of Jerusalem when it was taken by the crusaders in 1099, preferring the humbler name.

Delves of Doddington: one of the four famous Cheshire squires of Sir James Audley (see separate entry), who fought with him at the Battle of Poitiers, September 19th, 1356, and who were given by Sir James the pension of 500 marks bestowed on him for his gallantry by the Black Prince. Froissart records how Audley sent for his four squires and said to a company of assembled witnesses:

'Gentlemen, it has pleased my lord the prince to give me five hundred marks as a yearly inheritance; for which gift I have done him very trifling bodily service. You see here these four squires, who have always served me most loyally, and especially in this day's engagement. What glory I have gained has been through their means, and by their valour: on which account I wish to reward them. I therefore give and resign into their hands the gift of five hundred marks, which my lord the prince has been pleased to bestow me, in the same form and manner that it has been presented to me. I disinherit myself of it, and give it to them simply, and without a possibility of revoking it.'

Delves, along with the other squires, was also granted an heraldic honour by his master. Sir James's arms were gold frets (narrow interlacing bands) on red; and Delves, in addition to the three black billets he carried on a silver shield,

was given a red chevron fretted with gold. (See also *Dutton, Fulleshurst* and *Hawkestone.*)

Demi-greaves: light metal armour protecting the front of the legs. 'Closed greaves' guarded both front and back and were hinged on the outside.

Denys (or Denis), Saint: Bishop of Paris and Patron Saint of France. French armies often fought under his banner, and his name was as familiar a battlecry as St. George was for England.

Destrier: the Great Horse, or most powerful and knightly of the steeds used in the Middle Ages, carefully bred and highly trained, and ridden chiefly in joust and tournament. *Destrier* derives from the Latin *dextra*, right hand; and the explanation is often given that the horse was led by a squire on the knight's right hand. Some expert horsemen, however, believe the name came from the fact that the jousting horse was always trained to lead with the right leg so that, if he had to swerve, he did so away to the right and not into the opposing horse.

Dexter: in heraldry, the right-hand side of the shield; *but,* from the point of view of the onlooker, the left-hand. The shield is always described from the position of the man holding it and standing behind it.

Dieu et mon Droit: the English royal motto, meaning 'God and my Right', adopted by Edward III in 1340. The 'Right' may have been taken to refer to his claim to the throne of France; but the motto is much older and is reputed to have been used by Richard I at the Battle of Gisors, September or October 1198, as a declaration that he was not the vassal of France, but owed his kingdom to God.

Divisional Signs: signs used to identify various army groups and divisions. The early, and basic, use of heraldry as a means of recognizing an individual and all his supporters and retainers, has been revived in modern warfare; and many ancient devices have gone into battle again. In the Second World War, the badge of the First Army was the red cross of St. George and, on it, a golden sword. The Second Army wore the golden crusader's sword on a blue cross. The 43rd (Wessex) Division carried the ancient dragon of Wessex, a gold wyvern on blue – the mythical beast that fluttered above the heads of soldiers at Hastings, Crécy and Agincourt. (See also *Dragon*.)

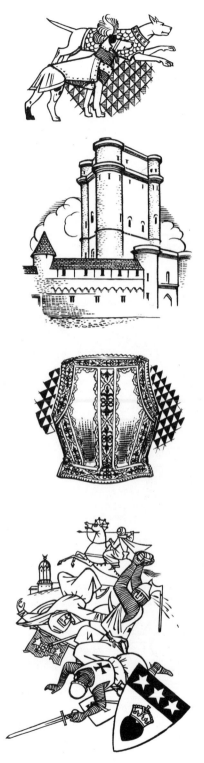

Dog Armour: light armour occasionally manufactured in parts of Europe for the protection of hunting dogs.

Donjon: the great central tower or keep of a mediaeval castle. The lowest storey was often used as a prison – hence 'dungeon', a variation of the same word.

Double Knot Decoration: a type of etched decoration frequently found on 16th century armour, used in Milan and then adapted by English armourers. There are good examples in the Metropolitan Museum, New York, and in the Tower of London.

Douglas, Sir James (1286?–1330), called 'The Good': one of the most famous and valiant of Scottish knights. (See also *Castle Dangerous*.) After the death of King Robert the Bruce in June, 1329, Douglas was entrusted with the heart of the king, enshrined in a silver casket, to convey it to the Holy Land, thus enabling Bruce to fulfil the crusader's vow he had not lived long enough to carry out.

Douglas was well on the journey when he was tempted by the King of Castile to join in a fight against the Moors of Granada. Mortally wounded, and knowing his pilgrimage was ended, he flung the heart of his king into the thick of the infidel host, shouting 'Go first, as thou wert wont to go!' Thus Bruce, as he had always wished, led an army against the Saracen. The heart was rescued and brought back to Melrose Abbey in Scotland.

The old shield of Douglas was silver, with three silver stars on a blue chief. To it was added, to commemorate this last gallant exploit of a great knight, the red heart of Bruce, later surmounted by a royal crown.

Douglas, James, second Earl (1358?–1388): best known for his end, leading an invading force from Scotland against an English army headed

by the Percies, including the famous Hotspur (see separate entry). Part of the Scottish army was set upon at Otterburn where, though the English were defeated and Hotspur was taken prisoner, the Earl of Douglas was killed.

The story of the battle has been much confused by the popular ballad of Chevy Chase, which was based on the Otterburn incident, but distorted the facts. In the 15th century song, for instance, Hotspur is killed along with Douglas. It begins:

> The Perse owt of Northomberlande,
> And a vowe to God mayde he,
> That he wolde hunte in the mountayns
> Off Chyviat [Cheviot] within dayes thre,
> In the mauger [in spite] of doughte Dogles,
> And all that ever with him be.

Sir Philip Sidney, soldier and poet of Elizabeth I's reign, wrote of this poem: 'I never heard the old Song of Percie & Douglas, that I found not my heart moved more than with a Trumpet.'

Dragon: one of the most ancient symbols of power and leadership, and the standard of many early English kings. Harold fought under it at Hastings, and it is represented twice in the Bayeux Tapestry. A document of 1244 records an order of King Henry III for the standard of a dragon to be placed in the Church of St. Peter, Westminster: 'And also to cause a dragon to be made in the fashion of a standard, of red silk sparkling all over with gold, the tongue of which should be made to resemble burning fire, and appear to be continually moving, and the eyes of sapphires or other suitable stones; and to place it in the Church of St. Peter, Westminster, against the King's coming there.' 'The terrible standard of the dragon' was borne on Richard Coeur de Lion's crusade, and the 'unconquered standard of the Dragon Gules' fluttered at Crécy.

There is some difficulty in distinguishing between the dragon and the wyvern, another fabulous beast. Strictly speaking, the dragon should be represented as four-legged, covered in scales, with webbed claws, wings like a bat, a barbed tail and a barbed tongue. The wyvern has only two legs and a curious crest to its head. But in early pictures the two are often indistinguishable, and the Bayeux Tapestry dragon has, in fact, only two legs.

Drawbridge: the bridge across the castle moat which could be drawn up or away, often by counterbalanced beams, as a protection against attack.

Dubbing: the act of conferring knighthood, often by a blow from hand or sword on shoulder or neck. (See also *Accolade*.)

Du Guesclin, Bertrand (1320–1380): one of France's greatest captains of the Middle Ages, and the best loved. The son of a Breton nobleman and his beautiful Norman wife, he was an ugly and neglected child and grew into an immensely strong, squat, wry-necked, swarthy man. The arts of battle he first learnt in the fields and woods about his home, organizing and drilling the peasant lads in mock warfare. Some of them followed him for the rest of his life. While staying with an aunt at Rennes, when he was seventeen years old, he wrestled in the market square and overthrew the champion, coming home with the prize of a hood worked in gold and silver – an exploit which, because of his gentle birth, so shocked his aunt that he promised never to fight again without knightly weapon in his hands. Shortly after, incognito and in borrowed armour, he broke fifteen lances in his first joust and only refused battle when at last his father, not knowing it was the despised Bertrand, rode out against him. Thereafter, perceiving his mettle, his father saw to it that he was properly equipped with his own armour and horses.

After being little more than a captain of free-booters and brigands for some years, he received the dignity of knighthood at the hands of Charles of Blois, swore the ancient vows of chivalry and took as his battle cry 'Notre-Dame-Guesclin!' (Our Lady and Guesclin). At the age of fifty, after thirty years unremitting soldiering in France and Spain, he reluctantly accepted the highest honour the crown could offer – that of Constable of France. Ten years later he died while besieging for the crown the Chateauneuf-de-Randon, held by a mixed garrison of English and Gascons. When du Guesclin demanded his surrender, the English captain of the garrison gave his promise to do so if help and supplies had not reached him by July 12th. On July 13th, after a short illness, the great Constable died in his tent, and the

commander of the garrison, by the convention of war, was freed from his oath. But he kept his word. Not only because of his promise, but in honour of a valiant captain who might otherwise go with his last mission unfulfilled, the English leader, accompanied by his officers, came from the fortress and placed its keys in the hands of the Constable of France.

On his tomb in Paris the simple inscription was cut: 'Here lies the noble man, Messire Bertrand du Guesclin, Count of Longueville and Constable of France, who died at the castle of Randan in Givaudan, in the seneschalry of Beaucaire, on July 13, MCCCLXXX. Pray to God for him.'

Apart from his own physical toughness, Bertrand's greatest strength probably lay in his easy power of leadership, his sway over the hearts of the common people, whom he always understood, loved and defended. His last words, when he lay dying, were a plea to his officers to remember that their business was only with those carrying arms like themselves; that churchmen, poor folk, women and children, were not their enemies.

As one of his biographers (M. Coryn) has written:

'He was Seigneur of Broons, Seigneur of la Roche Derrien, Seigneur of la Roche-Tesson; he was Count of Longueville, Duke of Trastamara, Duke of Molina. He was Chamberlain to the King, Marshal of Normandy, Connétable of Castile, and Connétable of France. And yet, during his lifetime he was always written of and spoken to in the simple fashion that is used for a peasant – or a king – by his first name alone. *Cilz connestables fust Bertran appelez.*'

Du Terrail, Pierre: see *Bayard.*

Dutton of Dutton: one of the four famous squires of Sir James Audley (1316?–1386) who fought by his side at the Battle of Poitiers, 1356, and who were rewarded by him in such knightly fashion. (See *Audley, Sir James.*)

Dymoke: see *Champion of England.*

Earl Marshal: See *Officers of Arms* and *Marshal*.

Eastern Crown: See *Antique Crown*.

Edward I (1239–1307): one of the greatest warrior kings of England, described by one of his contemporaries as 'of fine figure and tall stature, head and shoulders above the ordinary people . . . None were more suited, by reason of their sinewy vigour, than his supple arms, proportionate in length to the rest of his body, to the wielding of the sword . . . His great length of leg gave him a sure seat on noble horses, running or jumping.'

He was 6 ft 2 in. tall – much above the average of his time – and the length of leg referred to by the chronicler earned him his nick-name of 'Longshanks.'

He was famous as jouster, hunter and wrestler; and, at the same time, enjoyed music, poetry, fine building and chess. In 1271 he sailed to the Holy Land as a crusader, defeated the Saracens at Haifa and made a ten-year truce. He was accompanied by his wife Eleanor of Castile, herself the daughter of a crusading king. When Edward was struck down by a poisoned Saracen dagger, she saved his life by her devoted nursing, even, it is said, herself sucking the poison from the wound. Her sculptured head still looks down serenely in Westminster Abbey. (See *Eleanor of Castile*.)

An interesting document has survived showing how Edward (then Prince Edward) was financed on his crusade. His uncle, Louis IX (St. Louis) had appealed for help in the various courts of Christendom, and Edward sailed for France in August, 1269. But he had to explain to Louis that, eager though he was to join the fight against the infidel, he could not provide the necessary funds to equip an army. The French king was so keen to secure the services of the young soldier that he lent him 70,000 *livres turnois*, probably equal to about £17,500 sterling in English money. In return, Edward had to promise to repay the money by sums of 5,000 *livres* each year in March and July; to prevent his troops from doing any damage while passing through the dominions of the French king and his allies; and to put himself under the orders of Louis for the duration of the crusade. In the original agreement, which Edward sealed, Louis required Edward to send

one of his sons as a hostage or pledge of good faith; but, in fact, he let his nephew off this requirement.

Edward had a raven-black horse called 'Ferraunt' and, with his great frame topped by flaxen-silver hair, must have looked in the saddle the ideal of the mediaeval knight.

Edward III (1312–1377): grandson of Edward I and, like him, a redoubtable warrior, though not such a great king. Among the memorable events of his reign were the battles of *Crécy* and *Poitiers*, and the founding of the *Order of the Garter*. (See separate entries for each of these.) He was a great lover of the display and trappings of chivalry, and a promoter of many tournaments. In a typically-colourful event at Cheapside, his knights arrayed themselves as infidel warriors from Tartary and paced their gaily-caparisoned horses through the streets of London leading in silver chains a number of court ladies clothed in ruby velvet and challenging any man to come to their rescue. But Edward was far from being a mere playboy king and, indeed, was sometimes prepared to shed his royal dignity and to fight as a nameless knight. We read in the chronicles of Froissart, for instance, how, in 1348, he fought incognito under the banner of Sir Walter Manny (see separate entry) outside Calais, and singled out one of the most redoubtable of the French knights, Sir Eustace de Ribeaumont, who twice beat the king to his knees, but was eventually compelled to surrender his sword. Not till the fight was over did the French know that the king of England had been in Manny's ranks. As ever, the captured knights received great hospitality and were waited on at supper by the Prince of Wales himself. When the meal was done, the tables were removed and Edward III stood amidst the knights of both countries with only a chaplet of fine pearls round his forehead to mark his rank. When he came to Sir Eustace de Ribeaumont he smiled and said:

'Sir Eustace, you are the most valiant knight in Christendom that I ever saw attack his enemy or defend himself. I never yet found anyone in battle who, body to body, had given me so much to do as you have done this day.'

With the words, Edward took off his chaplet of pearls, placed it on the head of Sir Eustace in tribute to his valour, and set him free without ransom. Thus were war and play, hardihood and courtly pleasantry, mixed.

Edward IV (1442–1483): though a brilliant commander in his early manhood, this Plantagenet is not usually thought of as one of the most knightly of English kings; but he performed one great service to chivalry in replacing the ruinous Chapel of the Knights of the Garter, instituted by Edward III, with the magnificent new building of St. George's Chapel, Windsor, begun about 1478. (See *Garter, Order of the* and *St. George's Chapel.*)

Edward, Prince of Wales (1330–1376): known as the Black Prince and one of the greatest heroes of English chivalry. Among his achievements were his command of the van at Crécy, 1346, while still only 16; the rout of the French at Poitiers, 1356; and the defeat, at the Battle of Najera in Spain, of Henry of Trastamara, 1367. Though a gallant soldier and a great exponent of knightly courtesies due to men of rank, he was sometimes ruthless and cruel in his campaigning, e.g. in the sack of the town of Limoges, 1370, when all the inhabitants were massacred without regard to age or sex.

'The chief flower of chivalry of all the world', as the chronicler Froissart called him, lies buried in Canterbury Cathedral in one of the most impressive tombs in the world, and one of the greatest examples of mediaeval craftsmanship. The effigy of the Prince, in gilt latten that glows like gold, is in full plate armour. For centuries there hung above the recumbent figure, the mailed hands touching as though in prayer, his great helm, gauntlets, scabbard – from which the sword disappeared three hundred years ago – surcoat and wooden shield with leather covering. These precious survivals from the age of chivalry are now preserved in a glass case near the tomb, which has exact replicas above it. The surcoat, embroidered with the leopards of England and the lilies of France, is probably the only 14th century example surviving in England.

Among the other interesting features of the tomb are the shields running round it, showing the Black Prince's 'shield for war' and 'shield for peace'. The 'shield for war' bears the royal arms

of England, with a silver label of three points to show that he was the king's eldest son. His 'shield for peace' shows the famous three ostrich feathers, which we now always associate with the Prince of Wales, along with the motto *Ich Diene* ('I serve').

There are two picturesque traditions associated with the Black Prince that seem to have little basis in fact. The first is in connection with the three feathers which, it is commonly said, were adopted by the Prince from the arms of King John of Bohemia, who was slain at Crécy (see separate entry). It is much more likely that, as some other princes did, he took as his 'shield for peace' one of his mother's devices; and Philippa of Hainault, Edward III's queen, is believed to have included silver ostrich feathers among her personal insignia.

The other cherished and universally accepted story is that Edward was called the Black Prince from the colour of his armour. But there seems no evidence that he ever, in fact, wore black armour; though there are representations of him in gilt and in silver. He may have worn a black surcoat with the silver feathers; or, as one chronicler suggests, he was 'styled black by the terror of his arms.' Shakespeare seems to use the term in this way in *Henry V*, when he makes the French king refer to 'that black name, Edward, Black Prince of Wales.'

Edwardian Castle: the name sometimes given to the type of great castle raised in the reign of Edward I (1272–1307), marking great advances in military architecture. Conway and Caernarvon are good examples, having no massive central keep as in earlier types, but using the contours of their terrain and relying for their strength on the skilful arrangement of walls and towers. Sometimes, as at Beaumaris and Harlech, a concentric pattern is used.

Eglington Tournament: the farcical affair of 1839, when Archibald William Montgomerie, 13th Earl of Eglington, tried to revive the splendours of the days of chivalry by staging a tournament at Eglington Castle, Ayrshire, complete with a 'Queen of Beauty' and various guests impersonating famous knights from the past. The tournament is described in Disraeli's

Endymion and, very fully, in a modern book, *The Knight and the Umbrella* (Ian Anstruther).

Elbow-cops: metal plates protecting the knight's elbows. (See *Coudières*.)

Eleanor of Castile (d. 1290): the queen of Edward I who accompanied him on his crusade to the Holy Land in 1271, and is credited with having saved his life after an attack by an assassin with a poisoned dagger. What is certain is that she was a virtuous and greatly-loved queen. When she died at Harby in Nottinghamshire in November, 1290, Edward, whose guiding star she had been, had her brought to Westminster in easy stages. Wherever the procession halted a richly-carved cross was erected in her honour. Opinions vary as to whether there were in all thirteen, fourteen or fifteen. Three survive, at Geddington, Northampton and Waltham. The last was near the site of the present Charing Cross Station, and is commemorated in the name. This was demolished in the 17th century, but a replica stands in front of the station.

The old manor house and chapel at Harby have gone; but in a niche above the tower doorway of the newer church stands the little crowned figure of Eleanor of Castile, Queen of England, surrounded by the shields of Castile, Leon, England and Ponthieu.

Eltham Palace: formerly in Kent and now part of the London Borough of Greenwich; a royal palace originally built by Antony Bek (d. 1310), the warrior prince-bishop of Durham. It was the scene of more than one parliament and of many brilliant feasts and tournaments. It was here that the newly-constituted knights of the Garter, including the young Black Prince, first wore their insignia in 1348 at one of the nineteen tournaments organized about that time in various parts of the country.

Embattled: (i) arrayed, as with an army, in order of battle; (ii) furnished, as with a castle, with battlements; (iii) on a shield, a line of division or partition drawn like the battlements of a castle. In heraldry, there are rules governing the use of this particular line; e.g., the *bend* and *fess* (see definitions) should be embattled only

on their top edges. If for some special reason the bottom edges are embattled too, the chevron or other figure is described as *embattled-counter-embattled*!

Emblazon: as with *blazon*, to describe a coat-of-arms in the correct heraldic manner; or, more generally, to decorate in brilliant colours.

Enarmes: the rear looped straps by which the mediaeval shield was held by the bearer. There were usually three, arranged at intervals and of different sizes, so that one could be gripped by the fingers, one held the wrist, and the third took the full thickness of the mailed forearm thrust through it.

Engrailed: divided (on a shield) by a line made up of small concave curves, like tiny waves. If the curves are the other way, i.e., convex, the line is *invected*.

Enid: in the Arthurian legends, the wife of Sir Geraint and the personification of purity and wifely devotion.

Epaule de Mouton: literally, *shoulder of mutton*, from its shape. A special piece of armour, attached to the right vambrace (see separate entry) to give special protection to the bend of the arm against lance thrusts. The term, in course of time, was corrupted to *Polder* or *Polder Mitten*.

Ermine: (i) a fur much used in the decoration of royal and noble garments, made of, or imitating, the fur of an animal of the weasel family which, in winter, is snowy white except for the black tip of its tail. When used on robes, the black tips are arranged at regular intervals in the white. (ii) in heraldry, black spots, which can be of various patterns, on a white ground.

Ermines: in heraldry, much like ermine, but consisting of white spots on a black ground.

Erminois: allied to *ermine* and *ermines*, but, this time, black spots on a gold ground. See also *Pean*.

Erpingham, Sir Thomas (1357–1428): a famous soldier of the Hundred Years' War, who saw service in Spain, Lithuania, Ireland and France. His part in the battle of Agincourt (see separate entry) is celebrated by Shakespeare in *The Life of King Henry V*. At one point the king says:

> *Good morrow, old Sir Thomas Erpingham:*
> *A good soft pillow for that good white head*
> *Were better than a churlish turf of France.*

To which Erpingham makes valiant reply:

> *Not so, my liege: this lodging likes me better,*
> *Since I may say 'Now lie I like a king.'*

Escalade: one of the methods of close assault on castles, by means of scaling-ladders.

Escutcheon: the technical name in heraldry for a shield. See *blot on the 'scutcheon* in *Abatements of Honour* entry.

Esquire: a courtesy term now given to all men, particularly when addressing envelopes, etc., to them; but really denoting a rank immediately below that of knight. *Esquire* and *squire* both derive from the Latin word for shield, thus indicating their early duty as shield-bearer to, or attendant on, a knight.

Etched Decoration (on armour): a system of decoration of armour by means of acid biting into a surface otherwise protected by wax. The earliest example dates from the end of the 15th century; so that the armourers were using this technique before the first printing on paper from etched plates; and, as Sir James Mann has written, 'it is stimulating to reflect that Rembrandt and Whistler and other great practitioners of the art of etching owe the use of their medium to the anonymous decorators of armour in the late fifteenth century.' As time went on, certain patterns became well-established and can be traced with fair certainty to some of the great centres of armour making, and even to a particular workshop and artist.

Three standard patterns were the *Running Vine*, *Strapwork Arabesque* and *Double-knot*.

Eu, Count of: See *Holland, Thomas*.

Excalibur: the great sword of King Arthur that 'gave light like thirty torches'. In the Arthurian

stories, the name is given to two different swords – the one that the young king pulled from the anvil set in the stone before the church, and so proved his right to the kingship; and the other which the king took from the arm that rose above the surface of the lake, 'clothed in white samite, mystic, wonderful' and which eventually received back the sword when Arthur was dying.

Here is the taking of the sword from the stone from the most famous modern re-telling of the ancient story:

'He turned his mount and cantered off the street. There was a quiet churchyard at the end of it, with a kind of square in front of the church door. In the middle of the square there was a heavy stone with an anvil on it, and a fine new sword was stuck through the anvil. . . . He tied his reins round a post of the lych-gate, strode up the gravel path, and took hold of the sword. . . .

"Come, sword," said the Wart.

He took hold of the handles with both hands, and strained against the stone. There was a melodious consort on the recorders, but nothing moved.

The Wart let go of the handles, when they were beginning to bite into the palms of his hands, and stepped back, seeing stars . . . He took hold of it again and pulled with all his might. The music played more strongly, and the light all about the churchyard glowed like amethysts; but the sword still stuck.

"Oh, Merlyn," cried the Wart, "help me to get this weapon."

There was a kind of rushing noise, and a long chord played along with it. All round the churchyard there were hundreds of old friends . . . there were badgers and nightingales and vulgar crows and hares and wild geese and falcons and fishes and dogs and dainty unicorns and solitary wasps and corkindrills and hedgehogs and griffins and the thousand other animals he had met. . . . Some of them had come from the banners in the church, where they were painted in heraldry, some from the waters and the sky and the fields about – but all, down to the smallest shrew mouse, had come to help on account of love. . . .

The Wart walked up to the great sword for the third time. He put out his right hand softly and drew it out as gently as from a scabbard.' (T. H. White, *The Once and Future King*.)

Tennyson's words describing the end of the other sword Excalibur will be found under the entry for *Sir Bedivere*.

Eyas (Eyass): an unfledged hawk; one from the nest, not yet trained and able to seek its prey.

Falchion: type of sword used throughout the Middle Ages, mainly by archers and foot-soldiers, but sometimes also by knights. Usually shorter than the long-sword, it varied in design, but in nearly all examples had one convex cutting edge. Some widened considerably towards the point, as in the famous 'Conyers Falchion', exhibited in the library of Durham Cathedral. This reputedly dates from about 1175, but may be a replacement of 150 years later. The ancient manor of Sockham was held from the Bishop of Durham on a tenure which required the lord of the manor to present a falchion to any new Bishop of Durham when he first entered the diocese from the south. The 'Conyers Falchion' is one presented in this way. The blade measures approximately 1½ inches at the top and 4 inches at the bottom.

Falcon: properly speaking, a member of the 'long-wing' group of the birds of prey trained to hunt game. The chief long-wings are the *Gerfalcon* (Gyrfalcon), *Peregrine, Kestrel, Merlin* and *Hobby.* (See separate entries for all these.) The long-wings are known as True Falcons, and also as Hawks of the Lure, because most of them are trained to return to the *Lure* (see separate entry), rather than to the fist. See also *Hawk.*

The long-wings are recognizable by their brown eyes and the 'tooth' or notch on both sides of the upper beak.

Falconry, or Hawking, one of the earliest and most popular sports, was known in England at least 1,000 years ago. According to the size and weight of the hawk, ranging from a few ounces to a stone, a great variety of game could be taken, from young rabbits and game-birds upwards. The great eagles could be flown at foxes, deer, ante-lope, and even wild boar and wolves.

The birds were so prized that many laws were passed to protect them and their eggs, e.g., Edward III directed that stray hawks should be taken to the sheriff, and made it a serious crime to steal either bird or egg. There were even strong efforts to institute a social order among hawks, and to match their power and dignity with various ranks of society. Thus, Dame Juliana Berners (born *c.* 1388), who became prioress of Sopwell nunnery, though in her youth she had known court life and the popular pastimes, wrote a book which contained a treatise on Hawking

86

and gave the following order of precedence:

Gerfalcon for a king.
Falcon Gentle and *Tercel Gentle* for a prince.
Falcon of the Rock for a duke.
Falcon peregrine for an earl.
Bastard hawk for a baron.
Saker or *Sakeret* for a knight.
Lanner and *Lanneret* for a squire.
Merlin for a lady.
Hobby for a young man.
Goshawk for a yeoman.
Tercel for a poor man.
Sparrowhawk for a priest.
Kestrel for a servant.

(See separate entries for many of these types of hawk.)

Falconry is now one of the rarest of sports, followed by only a handful of enthusiasts, for various reasons – among them the expense, the difficulty of obtaining birds and the shortage of places where hawks can still be flown at live game. Many people will not regret this, though the falcon is undoubtedly a noble and beautiful bird. It cruises in the air at anything up to 800 feet and when it 'stoops' or dives is thought to reach a speed of nearly 100 m.p.h.

Recently a new use has been found for falcons. On certain Air Force bases, such as the Royal Naval Air Station at Lossiemouth, Scotland, so much damage has been done by gulls striking aircraft, that peregrine falcons have been flown at them by trained service men.

Falcon (and Falconet): early types of light cannon. The names of several types of mediaeval artillery (see also *Saker*) were taken from falconry, perhaps because of the plunging flight of the shot.

Falcon Gentle: the female or young goshawk.

Fald (or Fauld): type of protective armour for the stomach, often consisting of overlapping half-hoops of metal reaching from waist to thigh.

Falkirk, Battle of: the decisive battle fought on July 22nd, 1298, between the Scots under Sir William Wallace (see separate entry) and Edward I of England. Wallace had very few cavalry, and relied for his chief force on four densely-

packed 'schiltrons' (shield-troops), bristling with long spears, triple-banked at three different levels, made by the men crouching, kneeling and standing. The English knights failed to break these fearsome blocks of infantry, but they mopped up the Scottish cavalry and rode down the bowmen; so that, when Edward threw in his longbowmen, the schiltrons were sitting targets. Ruthlessly the English bowmen sent their rain of arrows against each in turn; then the armoured cavalry reformed and this time smashed through in triumph. Wallace escaped, but the flower of his army had perished, and for his remaining years he was little more than a hunted fugitive.

Fastolf, Sir John (1378?–1459): a famous soldier of the reigns of Henry V and Henry VI. He distinguished himself at Agincourt, Verneuil (where he captured the Duke of Alençon) and the 'Battle of the Herrings'. (See separate entry.) The College of Heralds possesses a wonderful manuscript *Chronicle of the Wars in France*, from 1415–1429, written for Sir John by Peter Basset and Christopher Hanson. This is the only contemporary account from an English pen.

A number of letters by him, and about him, are included in the Paston Letters, a famous collection of over a thousand letters concerning a Norfolk family, and covering the reigns of Henry VI, Edward IV, Richard III and Henry VII. In one document Sir John lists the debts of the Crown to him, totalling £14,066 3*s*. 6*d*. One item declares:

> the said Fastolf is yet owing for his portion and part for the recompense and reward that should grow and be due to him for the taking of John, calling himself Duke of Alancon, at the battle of Verneuil, which that paid for his ransom 40,000 marks (26,666*l* 13*s*. 4*d*.)

Sir John's share of the spoil was 4,000 marks (£2,666 13*s*. 4*d*.).

Despite the similarity of name and period, it is unlikely that there is any connection between this Norfolk soldier and the famous character of Sir John Falstaff, created by Shakespeare.

Ferrers: See *Oakham*.

Fess: in heraldry, a wide band going horizontally across the middle of the shield and occupy-

ing a third of it. The *fess point* is the middle of the
shield.

Field: (1) a place where a battle is fought; or
the battle itself, e.g., Flodden Field for the
Battle of Flodden.
(2) The whole surface of a shield or escutcheon.
When a shield is described or blazoned (see
Blazon), the field is named first, as the background
to all the rest; e.g. *az., a lion rampant arg* means an
azure, or blue, shield with a silver lion rampant.

Field Armour: good practicable armour intended for use on the battlefield, rather than
more highly decorated harness for display and
public occasions. *Hosting harness* means the same
thing.

Field of the Cloth of Gold: the name given to
the meeting, in June, 1520, between Henry VIII
of England and Francis I of France at Guisnes.
It was so called from the splendour and magnificence of the occasion. Aged less than 30, Henry
was at the peak of his manhood and was described
by a Venetian observer as 'much handsomer than
any other sovereign in Europe; a great deal
handsomer than the King of France . . . On hearing that Francis I wore a beard, he allowed his
own to grow, and as it is reddish, he now has a
beard that looks like gold. He is very accomplished, a good musician, composes well, is a
most capital horseman, a fine jouster . . .'
Francis I was three years younger, and the two
monarchs vied with each other in the richness of
their retinues and the lavishness of their hospitality. 2,800 tents were needed for the two
companies. A temporary palace was erected
especially for the reception of Henry, with fountains spouting wine playing in front of it.
A week was given over to tournaments, except
for a day of high wind. The lists, pitched between
Guisnes and Ardres, were 900 feet by 320 feet.
A fosse, or ditch, was dug all round to keep back
the crowds. A remarkable feature was the 'per-
ron' or Tree of Nobility, on which were hung the
shields of the challenging and the answering
knights, with, above the rest, the shields of the
two royal contestants, for both Henry and Francis
took the field with their knights. The trunk of the
tree was of cloth of gold, the foliage was green

silk, the flowers and fruits of silver and Venetian gold; and beneath the glittering branches were grouped the heralds, their resplendent tabards a shifting pattern of azure and argent, or and gules, sable and vert.

Fimbriated: heraldic term meaning 'edged with'; so that *a cross vert fimbriated or* means a green cross edged with gold.

Fire-pot: type of burning pot hurled against buildings or into the opposing ranks, filled with mixtures of sulphur, nitre and naphtha. It is supposed to have been invented by the Greeks and is often called 'Greek Fire'.

Fitchée: in heraldry, used to describe a cross whose base arm is pointed.

Flag: see *banner, pennon* and *standard.*

Flail: a cruel weapon of the Middle Ages, very like the hinged country flail used for threshing corn, but with the shorter arm having instead a chain with a spiked ball on the end. With the grim sort of humour of the soldier, it was sometimes called a 'holy water sprinkler'.

Flamberge: two-handed sword with wavy edges.

Flanchard: a piece of armour for the thigh. In horse armour, a piece covering the flank.

Flanders: the north-eastern part of the kingdom of France, from the 9th–14th centuries, governed by Counts who were subject to the king. It was a very wealthy and densely-populated area, with the great cloth cities of Ghent, Bruges, Ypres and Douai. On occasion, the burghers and clothworkers turned themselves into redoubtable fighters, as at Courtrai, often called the *Battle of the Spurs* (see separate entry). It also produced many famous crusading knights, such as the various Counts of Flanders who went to the Holy Land. *Baldwin* (1058–1118) was one of them. (See separate entry.)

Flanking Towers: towers set at intervals in a castle wall, and projecting outwards, so that defenders could fire down and along the intervening wall, particularly at attackers trying to make a breach at the base.

Fleur-de-lys: the emblem of the kings of France from about the reign of Louis VII (1120–1180). Various accounts have been given of its origin, e.g., from a spear-head, but the most generally accepted is that it is based on the iris flower. (See *Arms of France* for other details.)

Flodden, Battle of (September 9th, 1513): the battle in Northumberland, known as Flodden Field, between James IV of Scotland and the English under Thomas Howard, Earl of Surrey. The heavy losses of the Scots – between 11,000 and 12,000 men – and the low casualty list of less than 2,000 on the English side, do not accurately reflect the balance of the battle, which could easily have been an English defeat if their opponents had made better use of their chances. At one point, the English right wing was completely defeated. As on so many occasions, the shattering onslaught of the English longbowmen proved a critical factor.

The most splendid and tragic episode was the heroic resistance against tremendous odds put up by the Scottish centre in defence of their king, who was himself slain surrounded by the flower of his chivalry. The College of Arms possesses precious relics, presented to it by in 1681 by Henry, Duke of Norfolk, as 'the very Sword and dagger and a gold ring set with a Turquoise Stone which his Ancestor the Duke of Norfolk took from James IVth, King of Scotland, at the Battle of Flodden Field, where the said King was slain.' Modern expert opinion, however, puts the fine falcon-headed Spanish blade about 50 years later than Flodden; though the ring is undoubtedly authentic and was given to James IV by Anne of Brittany, Queen of France.

Several poems tell the story of Flodden, one of the earliest of which is the 17th century ballad beginning:

> *King Jamie hath made a vow,*
> *Keep it well if he may!*
> *That he will be at lovely London*
> *Upon Saint James his day.*
> *'Upon Saint James his day at noon,*
> *At fair London will I be,*

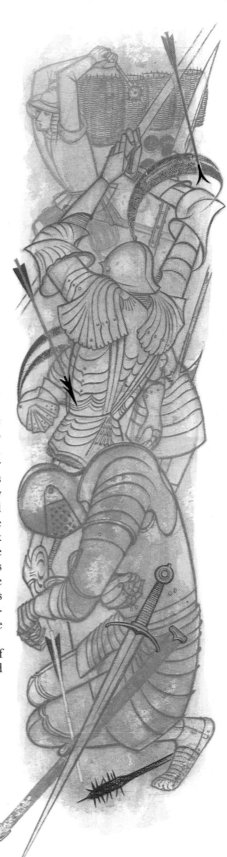

And all the lords in merry Scotland,
    They shall dine there with me.'
But perhaps the one that best recaptures some of the drama and tragedy of the long-ago battle is the old poem by William E. Aytoun which tells how one of the Scottish knights, Randolph Murray, preserved the royal banner by bringing it back alone to the Provost and the City Fathers of Edinburgh. This is part of the poem:

Right bitter was the agony
    That wrung that soldier proud,
Thrice did he strive to answer
    And thrice he groaned aloud.
Then he gave the riven banner
    To the old man's shaking hand
Saying: 'That is all I bring ye
    From the bravest of the land.
Aye! ye make look upon it,
    It was guarded well and long
By your brothers and your children,
    By the valiant and the strong.
One by one they fell around it
    As the archers laid them low,
Grimly dying, still unconquered,
    With their faces to the foe.
Aye! ye may well look upon it,
    There is more than honour there,
Else, be sure, I had not brought it
    From the field of dark despair
Never yet was royal banner
    Steeped in such a costly dye,
It has lain upon a bosom
    Where no other shroud shall lie.
Sirs! I charge you, keep it holy,
    Keep it as a sacred thing,
For the stain ye see upon it
    Is the life-blood of your King!'

Flower of Souvenance: a flower to serve as a reminder, a keepsake; sometimes a real flower, but sometimes an artificial one, made of jewels, to serve as an encouragement to, or the badge of, some knightly enterprise. One of the most famous examples is related by Anthony Woodville, 2nd Earl Rivers. On Wednesday, April 15th, 1465, after he had been to high mass, he approached his sister Elizabeth, wife of Edward IV, to discuss some matter with her.

'I drew me to the Queen of England and of France and Lady of Ireland, my sovereign

92

lady, to which I am right humble subject. And as I spake to her ladyship on knee, the bonnet from mine head, as me ought . . . the ladies of her company arrived about me; and they of their benevolence tied about my right thigh a collar of gold garnished with pearls . . . And to that Collar was tied a noble flower of souvenance, enamelled, and in a manner of an emprise.'

In his bonnet, Anthony found a small parchment, sealed and tied round with a gold thread, which he took to the king, along with the flower of souvenance; for he knew that, by this little ceremony, he had been charged by the ladies of the court to perform some knightly exploit, and the king's consent must be secured. The outcome of this particular incident was a two-day tournament at Smithfield (June, 1467), between Anthony Woodville and Anthony of Burgundy, a famous knight who was brother to Duke Charles of Burgundy and a Knight of the Golden Fleece. For some details of this tournament, see *Woodville, Anthony*.

Fluted Armour: armour made with its surface in ridges or channels, which made it very effective as a defence against lance and sword. This is one of the chief features of *Maximilian Armour* (see separate entry).

Fork (Military): a popular weapon for foot soldiers from the 12th century onwards and based, like some other mediaeval arms, on homely implements of the countryside. It was usually two or three-pronged, sometimes with the prongs of unequal length. Some had hooks as well, for pulling a rider from his horse, or defenders from battlements.

Formigny, Battle of (April 18th, 1450): the battle of Normandy in which the Constable of Richemont defeated an English army of, according to one estimate, 6,000 men, about two-thirds of whom were killed. This finally put an end to the long-fought English claims on France. Artillery played a vital part in the battle. According to H. A. L. Fisher 'although the English brought artillery upon the field of Creçy, it was not until the battle of Formigny 104 years later that the French were able to produce a

culverin which outranged the flight of the English arrow.'

Fosse: a ditch or moat round a fortress.

France Ancient: See *Arms of France*.

France Modern: See *Arms of France*.

Francisca: the throwing axe of the Franks (see next entry).

Franks: the West German tribes who conquered Gaul in the 5th century and founded the mediaeval kingdom of France, with Paris as its capital. In the deeds and customs of these warriors can be traced some of the origins of chivalry. An eye-witness, who was on a visit to Lyons in A.D. 470 has left us a vivid description of their appearance and favourite weapons:

> ... they wore high, tight, and many-coloured garments which hardly reached down to their bare thighs; their sleeves only covered their upper arms; their cloaks were green, embroidered with red. Their swords hung down from their shoulders on baldricks, and round their waists they wore a belt of fur adorned with bosses ... In their right hands they held barbed lances and throwing axes, and in their left shields, on which the light shone, white on the circuit and red on the boss, displaying both opulence and craftsmanship.

Frederick I (called 'Barbarossa' or 'red-bearded'): the emperor who ruled Germany from 1155–1189. 'All the qualities most generally admired in the age of chivalry, courage, energy, good cheer, joy in battle, and love of adventure, the rough justice that goes with hearty common sense, and the geniality which accompanies superb physical health, belonged to Frederick. No German sovereign since Charlemagne possessed qualities so well fitted for the governance of the German people. He could both frighten and charm. Churchmen, nobles, peasants, were prepared to regard him as the perfect knight.' (H. A. L. Fisher).

The end of this restless and action-filled life came when he took the Cross and joined the Third Crusade with Philip II of France and

Richard Coeur de Lion. He set out in May 1189 from Ratisbon with the largest single army ever to leave for the Holy Land, numbering, according to one estimate 50,000 horsemen and 100,000 foot soldiers. On June 10th the army came to the river Calycadnus, which had to be crossed for the crusaders to enter the city of Seleucia. The 63-year-old Emperor was ahead with his bodyguard. By the time the main army came up their heroic leader was lying dead on the bank. Either he had fallen from his horse and gone down with the weight of his armour; or he had unwisely plunged into the water to refresh himself and been swept away by a strong current. The news destroyed his great army, which lost all cohesion and broke up.

Free Companies: military adventurers who collected under some enterprising captain and hired themselves out to whatever country needed their services. This was a recognized and honourable profession in the Middle Ages, and some notable Englishmen were among the Captains of Free Companies. (See, e.g., *Calveley, Sir Hugh* and *Hawkwood, Sir John*.) See also *Condottiere* for the Italian equivalent. In France they were called *Compagnies Grandes*, or Great Companies. One of the best-known was *La Blanche Compagnie*, about which Conan Doyle wrote a fine historical novel, 'The White Company'.

There was little nonsense about the Free Companies, although they had their own strange code of loyalties. 'If they have terrified people and history, it is because they were in every sense of the word men of war. They practised war with a terrible sincerity. They divested it of all vain ornament; they displayed it in its frightful reality, in its bestial nudity. They had the only qualities that war requires, bravery and discipline . . . That is why even their enemies . . . sometimes admired these handsome, brutal soldiers. The pope called them *doctiores in excitione armorum,* doctors of arms . . . Men make war only to take what they can. Those who do not covet do not make war; they endure it. Repudiating all hypocrisy, the Great Companies always proclaimed this primordial aim. Their enemy was he who owned what they wanted. They pillaged with a fierce impudence in every

camp. They did not trouble themselves with excuses, they did not cloak themselves with flags or principles . . . As for the other virtues that are held up to men of war – magnanimity, respect of property and persons – the bandits rejected them either as nonsense or betrayal.' (Roger Vercel, *Bertrand of Brittany*).

Free Course: one of the methods of combat in the tournament, much like the Italian Course (see separate entry), but run without the central barrier. The chief object, at least in the later period, was not so much to unhorse one's opponent, as to shiver one's lance. The knight's score was, in fact, often measured by the number of lances he broke. For this purpose, the heavy lance gave way to a lighter weapon, usually made of poplar, which would easily break, rather than strike the opponent from the saddle. (See *Bourdonass* and *Brandon, Charles*.)

Froissart, Sir John: the greatest of the chroniclers of the Middle Ages, who recorded for all time many of the most famous exploits and personalities of the age of chivalry. Much about him is obscure, including his dates, but he lived from about 1338–1410. He travelled widely and was three times in England, at one period acting as secretary to Queen Philippa, wife of Edward III. He seized every opportunity to talk with eye-witnesses of events, was poet as well as historian, and knew Geoffrey Chaucer.

His Chronicles are best known in two translations, the first, published 1523–25, by John Bourchier, second Baron Berners, who was himself a soldier and was present at the Field of the Cloth of Gold (see separate entry). The second, published in 1803–5, is by Thomas Johnes. His translation begins:

'That the honourable enterprises, noble adventures, and deeds of arms, performed in the wars between England and France, may be properly related, and held in perpetual remembrance – to the end that brave men taking example from them may be encouraged in their well-doing, I sit down to record a history deserving great praise.'

This is the task Froissart set himself and accomplished with such success.

Fulleshurst, Sir Robert: better known as Fulleshurst of Barthomley; one of the four Cheshire squires who fought by Sir James Audley's side at the Battle of Poitiers, 1356. (See *Audley, Sir James*. For the other three squires see *Dutton of Dutton*, *Delves of Doddington* and *Hawkestone of Wrinehill*.)

Furs: one of the three main groups of heraldic 'tinctures' or colours. In all, there are nine different furs, some of which are very rarely found. For definitions of five of them see *Ermine*, *Ermines*, *Erminois*, *Pean* and *Vair*.

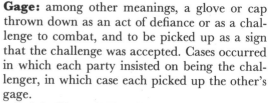

Gage: among other meanings, a glove or cap thrown down as an act of defiance or as a challenge to combat, and to be picked up as a sign that the challenge was accepted. Cases occurred in which each party insisted on being the challenger, in which case each picked up the other's gage.

Leigh Hunt (1784–1859), perhaps using a story from earlier centuries, wrote a popular poem about a lady at the court of Francis I of France (1515–1547) who used the device of the challenge to satisfy her vanity, with unexpected results. The king was watching a pack of hungry lions fighting in a sanded pit. Among the company were the Count de Lorge and the lady he hoped to make his bride. She, to prove de Lorge's love before the king and all his court, dropped her glove in the lion pit.

> She dropped her glove to prove his love:
>   then looked on him and smiled;
> He bowed, and in a moment leaped
>   among the lions wild:
> The leap was quick, return was quick;
>   he soon regained his place;
> Then threw the glove, but not with love,
>   right in the lady's face!
> 'In truth!' said Francis, 'rightly done!'
>   and he rose from where he sat:
> 'No love,' quoth he, 'but vanity, sets
>   love a task like that!'

Galahad, Sir: in the Arthurian legends, the son of Sir Lancelot and the purest of all the knights; the only one who could sit in the *Siege Perilous* (see separate entry) without peril of his life, and one of the few who achieved the quest of the *Holy Grail* (see separate entry). The last verse of Lord Tennyson's well-known poem on Sir Galahad is:

> The clouds are broken in the sky,
>   And thro' the mountain-walls
> A rolling organ-harmony
>   Swells up, and shakes and falls.
> Then move the trees, the copses nod,
>   Wings flutter, voices hover clear:
> 'O just and faithful knight of God!
>   Ride on! the prize is near.'
> So pass I hostel, hall, and grange;
>   By bridge and ford, by park and pale,
> All-arm'd I ride, whate'er betide,
>   Until I find the holy Grail.

98

Gambeson: quilted and stuffed tunic or long garment worn under armour to lessen the shock of blows and prevent chafing. Worn by itself, without chain mail or plate, it was still useful as a defence against sword-cuts or long-range arrows.

Garde-de-bras: piece of armour introduced in the 15th century to protect the inside bend of the left arm. It was particularly useful in tilting.

Garrison: a body of troops stationed in a castle or fortified place; or the stronghold itself.

Garter King of Arms: see *Officers of Arms*.

Garter, Order of the: see *Blue Garter*.

Gasconade: a piece of boasting or bravado; from the province of S.W. France, whose inhabitants were proverbially given to this sort of weakness. An old example is the Gascon who, to prove how noble and valorous his family was, declared that the only fuel they used on the fires in his father's house were the bâtons [i.e. staffs of office] of his ancestors who had been marshals in the armies of France. But Gascony produced many great knights, and its territory was some of the most fought over in the Hundred Years' War. At one period Gascony belonged to the King of England, when he was Duke of Aquitaine.

Gate-house: strong defensive structure guarding a castle entrance.

Gauntlets: armoured gloves, often formed of a single plate for the back of the hand fastened to leather, and smaller overlapping plates for the fingers to enable them to move easily. With some types, spikes of iron called 'gadlings' were fixed to knuckles and joints, thus converting the gauntlet into a formidable weapon of offence, failing any other. The most magnificent examples of gauntlets that have survived are probably those of Charles V (1516–1568) in the Royal Armoury at Madrid.
  A particularly interesting type of gauntlet was the so-called 'forbidden gauntlet', invented in the 16th century to prevent the weapon being

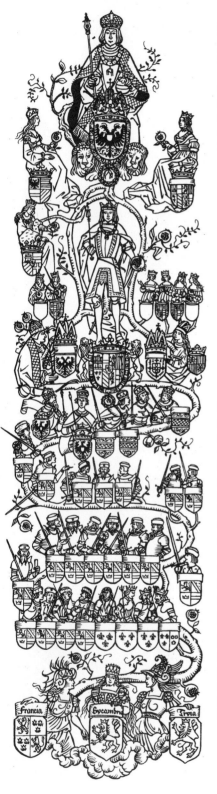

knocked or forced out of the user's grip. A plate projecting over the fingers could be locked, by means of a hole, to a metal knob on the wrist.

Gawaine (or Gawayne), Sir: the second-made of King Arthur's knights, and one of the bravest and most courteous. One of his most celebrated encounters was with the Green Knight, who rode into Arthur's hall on New Year's Day.

'He was the tallest man anyone there had ever beheld, and the strangest in guise and looks. His face was as fierce as his limbs were stalwart; his red eyes glowed out of a shock of bristly hair; and over his broad breast hung a beard as big as a bush. From head to foot he was dressed in green, coat, hood and hose, only his spurs being of bright gold. His horse, too, was as green as grass, its mane knotted with gold threads, its tail tied with a jewelled green band, its green trappings hung with golden bells. He wore no armour, and bore neither spear nor shield, but in one hand a green holly bough, in the other a huge axe, sharp as a razor, its handle and head richly chased in gold and green.' (A. R. Hope Moncrieff.)

Gaze, at: used, in heraldry, to describe a stag or a buck which is standing and gazing at the onlooker. (See also *Statant guardant* under *Lion*).

Genealogy: the history, investigation and description of the descent of families in the natural order of successive generations. English families can try to trace their ancestors and descent by various methods, including the consultation of records at Somerset House, London (for births, marriages, etc., since 1837), registers of parish churches, and the records and library of the Society of Genealogists. With families that bear, or have borne, a coat of arms, the College of Arms is the best place to seek information. Though people may have the same surname, this is not often safe evidence that they had a common ancestor or belong to the same families. But if people bear similar arms, there is a strong likelihood that they share a common ancestor or have some other close connection, even though it may be hundreds of years ago.

William Sidney = Anne, daughter of
of Penshurst, Kent,   Hugh Pagenham,
Chamberlain and   or Packenham
Steward to Henry VIII
A commander at Flodden
1515

Sir Henry Sidney = Mary, eldest   Mary = Sir Wm. Doymer,   Lucy = Sir Jas.   Ann = Sir William   Frances =   Thomas
Knight of the Gar-   daughter of   knight of   Harrington,   FitzWilliam,   Radclif, Earl of
ter, lord deputy   John Dudley,   Ascot in Bucks.   knight   knight, of   Sussex
of Ireland and   Duke of North-   Milton, Northants.
president of Wales   umberland
d. 1586

Sir Philip Sidney, =   Frances,   Sir Robert Sidney, =   Barbara,   Thomas Sidney = Margaret,   Mary = Henry,
knight, born   daughter of   knight,   daughter and   daughter and   Earl of
24 Nov. 1554,   Sir Francis   Lord Sidney of   heir of Sir   heir of   Pembroke,
killed at   Walsingham;   Penshurst,   Thomas Gamage,   Arthur Dakins   Knight of
Zutphen   married (2)   Viscount Lisle   of Coyly, in   the Garter
16 Oct. 1586   Robert Devereux,   and first Earl   Glamorganshire
    Earl of Essex   of Leicester
    (3) Richard,   d. 1626
    Earl of
    Clanricard

Elizabeth = Roger Manners,
    Earl of Rutland

N.B.   The = sign means 'married'. All the
children of a marriage are shown on
the same straight line beginning with
the eldest on the left; e.g., Sir Philip
Sidney was the eldest child of Sir
Henry and Mary Sidney, and Thomas
was his youngest brother.
    The table also shows, e.g., that
William Sidney was Elizabeth, Countess of Rutland's great-grandfather.
(Not all the marriages and children
are shown.)

The descent, or pedigree, of a family is often drawn in the form of a *genealogical table* or *tree*, showing the successive generations, their marriages, children, etc. A true 'tree', as the name implies, pictures the family growing upwards from the roots and spreading out into various branches; thus, the College of Heralds has a vellum roll, showing the pedigree of Elizabeth I in the form of a tree, with William the Conqueror at the foot of the trunk and a crowned Tudor Rose flowering at the top. But it is more usual, and much easier, to invert it. Here is a small part of the pedigree of the family of Sidney, showing the descent of Sir Philip Sidney (see separate entry), the English 'Flower of Chivalry.'

The arms show the Pheon of the Sidneys, a broad arrow, with teeth on the inner edge of the barb.

A full family pedigree can stretch to an enormous size, particularly with some of the more absurd ones, which attempt to trace an ancestry back to mythological and Biblical characters; e.g., the College of Heralds has a 24-foot vellum roll which shows, among other things, the ancestry of Henry VI back through the Saxon kings to Woden and Adam. Almost equally absurd, if not so elongated, are the thousands of claims to prove Norman descent and from a knightly ancestor who fought in William's company at Hastings. Probably less than half-a-dozen families in England can prove direct descent from a participant in the battle. Among them are the Giffards of Chillington, Staffordshire, whose ancestor was William the Conqueror's standard-bearer in Normandy, but who asked to be excused duty on the Hastings expedition because of his age. Two of his sons were present at the battle, and from one of them came the present family, which has been settled at Chillington since about 1178.

The Mallets of Somerset descend from the Norman knight who, it is said, was sent out by the Conqueror after the battle to search for the body of Harold, the defeated king of the English.

Genouillières: (from French, *genou*, knee); armour for the knees, knee-caps. In early times, they were often of leather or *cuir bouilli* (see definition); later, they were made of metal in a wide variety of patterns, and were often richly ornamented.

102

Geoffrey of Monmouth (1100?–1154): bishop of St Asaph and chronicler. His most famous work was *Historia Regum Britanniae*, 'The History of the Kings of Britain', which is not really a reliable chronicle, but a romance of early British history, including a good deal of material about King Arthur which became a permanent part of English literature. Here is his description of the amusements following the crowning of Arthur at Whitsuntide, at the high court of Caerleon:

'Refreshed by their banqueting, they go forth into the fields without the city, and sundry among them fall to playing at sundry manner games. Presently the knights engage in a game on horseback, making show of fighting a battle whilst the dames and damsels looking on from the top of the walls, for whose sake the courtly knights make believe to be fighting, do cheer them on for the sake of seeing the better sport. Others elsewhere spend the rest of the day in shooting arrows, some in tilting with spears, some in flinging heavy stones, some in putting the weight; others again in playing at the dice or in a diversity of other games, but all without wrangling; and whosoever had done best in his own game was presented by Arthur with a boon of price.'

George, Saint: the patron saint of England and hero of one of the most famous legends of the Middle Ages. The real Saint George – George of Cappadocia – was a Christian soldier who was martyred in A.D. 303, after imprisonment and torture in defence of his faith. The chief legend attached to his name is that he came to Silene, in Libya, and found that a dragon was terrorising the inhabitants and could be appeased only by human sacrifice. George arrived when a young and beautiful princess was about to be devoured, and immediately attacked the monster, which was killed on the spot after a ferocious struggle, or, in another version of the story, was led captive into Silene on the girdle of the princess.

In England, the Council of Oxford, in the year 1222, ordered that April 23rd should be kept as a national festival in honour of St. George, the day observed ever since. Just over 100 years later, Edward III nominated him as the Patron Saint of England. The red cross of St. George is incor-

porated in the Union Flag, and the representation of his slaying of the dragon will be found in many places, including the jewel suspended from the ribbon of the Knights of the Garter.

St. George is also the patron saint of other groups of people in other countries, including the Greek army, Greek shepherds and the province of Aragon in Spain. His day is often celebrated in much more spectacular fashion than in England – with athletic contests, processions, mock battles and solemn services.

'Saint George!' was long the battle-cry of English kings and knights.

(See also *St. George's Chapel* and *St. Michael and St. George, Order of.*)

Geraint, Sir: one of the knights of the Round Table, married to Enid. Through a misunderstanding, he believed her to be unfaithful to him and treated her with great harshness; but, after she had nursed him with uncomplaining tenderness and devotion when he was seriously wounded, he could no longer doubt her and they lived in great happiness.

Gerfalcon (Gyrfalcon): sometimes just called the Gyr. One of the greatest and noblest of the falcons, at one time reckoned as the proper bird for a king to fly (see *Falcon*). 'Paramount in battle ... peerless of flight', the gerfalcon is relentless in pursuit, but one of the most difficult to train.

German Course: a method of combat between knights, particularly in the early Middle Ages. The aim was to splinter the lance or unhorse the opponent, and a target for the lance was often provided in the shape of a small shield, not carried by the left arm, but simply hanging from straps. One of these shields in the Wallace Collection is made of oak, more than an inch thick and 14 inches wide.

Geste: an old word for exploit, adventure, a tale of achievements, particularly as told in mediaeval ballads and metrical romances.

Giants: one of the favourite targets of knights and heroes of romance, who carried out a regular slaughter of these unwieldly folk, any one of whom might be anything up to 300 feet high, muster as many as a hundred heads, place his feet on two mountains, or cover nine acres of land with his body. In real life, giants have not been so spectacular and have rarely grown to more than 7 or 8 feet, though one or two seem to have reached 10 feet.

Gipoun: see *Jupon*.

Gisors, Battle of (1198): Richard Coeur de Lion's last pitched battle, in which he is said to have unhorsed three knights at a single charge and made them prisoners. It was on this occasion, too, that Richard is credited with having first used what became the royal motto, *Dieu et mon Droit*. ('Not I, but God and our right have vanquished France.')

Glaive: sometimes used to mean a broadsword or falchion; but, properly speaking, a blade fixed on the end of a pole, often with the cutting edge on the outside curve.

Gloucester, Humphrey, Duke of (1391–1447): called 'The Good Duke Humphrey' because of his patronage of men of letters and his services as a soldier; commanded one of the English divisions at Agincourt and was wounded; a Knight of the Garter and Great Chamberlain of England. As well as being an accomplished soldier he was a scholar, and gave the University of Oxford its first library of books.

Godfrey of Bouillon (1508?–1100): one of the most famous of crusading knights and a leader of the First Crusade. He was in reality the first King of Jerusalem, but refused the title because he would not wear the golden circle of kingship where Jesus had worn a crown of thorns. (See *Defender of the Holy Sepulchre*.) Godfrey's sword and spurs are preserved in the Latin Sacristy of the Church of the Holy Sepulchre at Jerusalem. William of Malmesbury called him 'that brilliant mirror of Christian nobility, in which, as a splendid ceiling, the lustre of every virtue was reflected.'

Goedendag: see *Mace*.

Golden Eagle: one of the 'short-wing' hawks.

(See *Hawk* and *Hawks of the Fist.*) The most power-ful of the birds of prey, with the strongest grip and the heaviest beak, but not one of the most popular with falconers because of its fierce temper and weight on the wrist. 'When an eagle pushes down to take off from your fist she knocks it to knee-level. At the same moment her great wings may smack you across the head, and a Golden Eagle's beating wings have about them something like the power of her grip.' (Frank Illingworth).

The Golden Eagle is not often seen in the British Isles, except in north Scotland, where it still breeds. Its colour is dark brown, with its charac-teristic golden shade on the head and back of the neck.

Golden Fleece: after the Order of the Garter, the most famous order of knighthood in Europe. It was founded in 1430 by Philip the Good, Duke of Burgundy. It took its name either from the fleece or sheep-wool that was the foundation of the wealth of Burgundy, or from the old legend of Jason and the Golden Fleece. William Caxton saw the great chamber of the Castle of Hesdyn, where Philip had ordered the legend to be vividly illustrated, and where a 'subtil engyn' could reproduce thunder, lightning, rain and snow.

Gonfalon (or Gonfanon): type of flag, probably deriving its name from the Norse *gunn-fane* or 'war-flag.' With the Normans it had a square body with three or more tails. Later, it became particularly associated with some of the Italian republics.

> *Ten thousand thousand ensigns high advanced,*
> *Standards and gonfalons, 'twixt van and rear*
> *Stream in the air. . . .*
>
> (John Milton: *Paradise Lost*)

The most famous early illustrations of the gonfalon occur on the Bayeux Tapestry, where there are at least 25 examples, with a varying number of tails, from two to four. One is shown much bigger than the rest, its long tails straight in the wind. This probably represents the con-secrated flag specially sent by Pope Alexander to Duke William. The tapestry shows it being car-ried by a Norman knight, Eustace of Boulogne, who, at a critical moment in the battle, when a rumour is spreading through the panic-stricken troops that the Duke has fallen, lifts the great gonfalon high in the air and points with his other hand to the face of the leader, who has tilted back his helmet for all to see.

An early mention of the famous flag of Venice, the Gonfalon of St. Mark, occurs in Geoffroy de Villehardouin's Chronicle of the Fourth Crusade, when the famous Doge of Venice, Enrico Dandolo, over ninety years old and nearly blind, led the galleys of the Crusaders against the walls of Constantinople. Dandolo moved into the attack standing in the bow with the gonfalon displayed before him. It was still with him, an encouragement and a call to battle, when the old man struggled ashore.

'And when the Venetians saw the Gonfanon of St. Mark on land and the galley of their leader which had been beached in front of them, then each man felt himself shamed, and all approached the land, and those in the huissiers [horse transports] leapt out and went on shore, and those in the great ships got into barges and got to the shore as quickly as each one could.'

The Venetian flag was the golden winged lion of St. Mark.

Gorged: in heraldry, used to describe an animal which is 'collared' round its neck, often with a crown. (See *Crown* for various types.) Examples: (Annaly) 'an Irish wolfhound, gorged with an antique crown', (Stafford) 'a swan argent ducally gorged', (Sondes) 'a bear gorged with a belt argent', (Saumarez) 'a unicorn arg. the tail cowed navally gorged azure.'

Gorget: close-fitting armour, of mail or plate, to protect the throat and upper part of the chest. Often, it was accompanied with a back-plate. The word was also used for a type of ruff or wimple worn by women.

Goshawk: (see also *Falcon* and *Shortwings*). One of the largest and most powerful of the hawks, weighing up to two-and-a-half pounds, and with a particularly fierce grip; sometimes known as 'the cook's hawk.'

Gothic Armour: term often used to describe the splendid armour made in Germany in the late 15th century because, in its fine lines and delicate

decoration, it recalls the beauty of Gothic architecture. There are good examples in Vienna and in the Wallace Collection, London. (See *Beauchamp, Richard, Earl of Warwick* for an effigy in England which portrays the characteristics of this type of armour). It was intended more for display and ceremonial purposes than hard fighting in the field.

Götz of the Iron Hand: see *Berchlingen, Götz von*.

Grail, The (also called the Holy Grail, Saint Grail and Sangreal): one of the most complicated of the long series of stories and legends that make up the Arthurian romance, changing its nature and meaning as it develops. One of the earliest heroes engaged in the Quest for the Grail was Sir Percival (see separate entry). His adventures were in search of a number of talismans, or magical charms, among them a bleeding lance, a sword and a 'Grail' which, according to different versions of the story, was a wonder-working stone or curious vessel.

Later, the chief figure in the Quest becomes Sir Galahad (see separate entry) and the story takes on a more strictly religious form, with the Grail becoming the Cup used in the Last Supper, in which Joseph of Arimathea treasured the blood that flowed from the wounds of Christ on the Cross. This meaning is often symbolized by the mystic Rose, as in John Masefield's poem, 'The Ballad of Sir Bors'. Two verses are:

> *Would I could see it, the rose, when the light begins*
> *to fail,*
> *And a lone white star in the West is glimmering on*
> *the mail;*
> *The red, red passionate rose of the sacred blood of*
> *the Christ,*
> *In the shining chalice of God, the cup of the Holy*
> *Grail.*
> *The dusk comes gathering grey, and the darkness*
> *dims the West,*
> *The oxen low to the byre, and all bells ring to rest;*
> *But I ride over the moors, for the dusk still bides*
> *and waits,*
> *That brims my soul with the glow of the rose that*
> *ends the Quest.*

Granada: the small hill-kingdom of Spain for

long held by the Moors and the scene of many crusading exploits. It was here that the heart of Robert the Bruce was flung into battle to lead the Christian army (see *Douglas, Sir James*, 1286?– 1330). Oddly enough, it was a Moor of Granada, Ibn Jubayr, who gives us one of the loveliest surviving pictures of an essential part of the code of chivalry – the honour and respect due to womanhood. On his travels in Christian lands, he witnessed, in the filth and stink of battle-ravaged Acre, a marriage ceremony, where the formidable men of war walked in courtesy as a guard of honour. He wrote:

> 'Proud she was, walking with steps of half a span, like a dove or in the manner of a wisp of cloud.'

Grand Champion of England: See *Champion of England*.

Grand Quarters: the name given to the original four large quarters of a shield, when one or more of them has been divided into smaller quarters. (See *Quarters*.)

Grant of Arms: official permission, given by one of the Officers of Arms, to bear and display a shield of arms.

In England, the supreme jurisdiction is exercised by the College of Arms, London, of which the hereditary head is the Earl Marshal, the Duke of Norfolk, who nominates the Officers, though they hold their appointments by special Letters Patent under the Great Seal of England.

In Scotland, grants are made by the Lyon Office, in Edinburgh, under the Lord Lyon King of Arms. It is interesting evidence of his authority and of Scotland's proud history that the royal arms, as displayed in England, are not accepted north of the border. On the Scottish shield, the royal lion of Scotland (*or, a lion rampant within a double tressure flory counter-flory gules*) takes pride of place in the first and fourth quarters instead of the three English lions, or leopards, passant-guardant; and the two supporters (see separate entry) change places, with the unicorn on the dexter side (the shield-bearer's right) and the lion on the sinister, or left, side.

In Ireland, the position is complicated by the division of the country. Grants of arms for the six

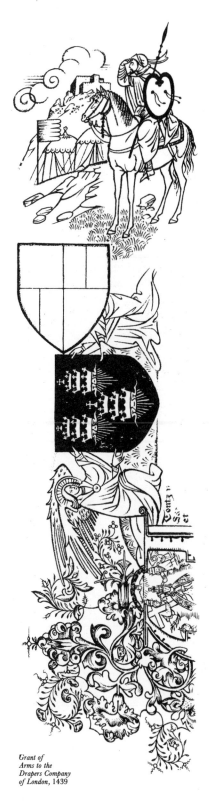

Grant of Arms to the Drapers Company of London, 1439

northern counties come under the control of the English College of Arms in the person of one of its chief heralds, Norroy and Ulster King of Arms. The chief authority in the rest of the country is held by the Chief Herald of Ireland, based on the Irish Genealogical Office in Dublin.

Great Companies: see *Free Companies.*

Great Horse: see *Destrier.*

Greaves: armour for the legs or shins. *Demi-greaves* protected the front of the legs only. *Closed greaves* fastened right round in two sections. Other names for armour of this kind were *jambs* and *jambarts.*

Greek Fire: see *Fire-pot.*

Greenwich Armour: armour from the royal workshops at Greenwich, in south-east London, established by Henry VIII in 1519, using chiefly German armourers. They succeeded in giving English armour a rather better reputation than it had enjoyed before. Though a good deal of armour was made in England in the Middle Ages, it was common, clumsy stuff of not very good quality, and all the finest harness, especially that worn by the upper classes, was imported. Most of the early armours in the world's great collections are German, Italian and Spanish, especially the first.

The first great house at Greenwich was built by Humphrey, Duke of Gloucester (1391–1447), who commanded one of the English divisions at Agincourt and saw other service in France. This house, Bella Court, was developed by Margaret of Anjou, Queen of Henry VI, into the Palace of Pleasaunce, or Placentia, and it remained a royal palace for some two hundred years. The Tudor monarchs in particular spent a great deal of time there. Henry VIII, who hunted and hawked in the park, staged great jousts and tournaments in the tilt-yard and developed the armoury. One visitor was the Emperor Charles V, who arrived with a retinue of 2,000 and needed fodder for 1,000 horses.

The site is now occupied by the Royal Naval College, in a splendid procession of buildings dating from 1664–1789. The only surviving part of the old palace is under the Queen Anne block (1697–1731). The finest examples of Greenwich armour are to be seen in the Tower of London.

Grey Goose Feather (or Wing): the English arrow, flighted with goose feathers, used by the longbowmen. Another term used was the 'cloth-yard shaft', from its length. (See also *Long-bow*.)

> *No warring guns were then in use*
> *They dreamt of no such thing;*
> *Our Englishmen in fight did use*
> *The gallant grey-goose wing*
> *(Early Ballad)*
> *With Spanish yew so strong,*
> *Arrows a cloth-yard long,*
> *That like to serpents stung,*
> *Piercing the weather;*
> *None from his fellow starts,*
> *But playing manly parts,*
> *And like true English hearts,*
> *Stuck close together.*
> (Michael Drayton:
> *Agincourt*)

Grey, Thomas, second Marquis of Dorset (1477–1530): a courtier of Henry VIII's who rose to high favour because of his skill in the tournament, one of the king's favourite sports. Dorset rode as one of the Champions of England at the Paris tournaments of 1514, when Henry VIII's sister Mary was married to Louis XII, and was also present at the Field of the Cloth of Gold. (See separate entry.)

Grid-iron Helmet: type of helmet developed in the 15th century with the face protected by a grid or lattice-work. It was designed, not for use against lance and spear, which would have easily penetrated the grid, but for tournaments with maces and clubs as weapons. (See *Baston Course*.)

Griffin: heraldic animal with the forepart of an eagle, with upturned ears, and the hindquarters of a lion. Sometimes it is shown without wings but with spikes protruding from it, in which case it is called a *Male Griffin*. Other spellings are Griffon, Griffen, and Gryphon. It was the legendary guardian of gold-mines and hidden treasure.

It will be recalled that Alice in Wonderland

encountered a Gryphon, lying fast asleep in the sun, who later said to the Mock Turtle: 'This here young lady, she wants for to know your history, she do.'

Grosvenor-v-Scrope Controversy: see *Chaucer, Geoffrey*.

Guidon (spelt also Geton, Gytton, Guidehomme, etc.): a small swallow-tailed flag.

Guige (spelt also Gige): the main strap by which the knight's shield was slung across the shoulder or round his neck.

Guildford, Sir Henry (1489–1532): master of the horse and comptroller of the household under Henry VIII; fought against the Moors and was knighted by Ferdinand of Castile; standard-bearer in the French campaign of 1513, in which the English won the Battle of Guinegate (see separate entry); accompanied the king to the Field of the Cloth of Gold. His father, Sir Richard, was a Knight of the Garter and died on pilgrimage to Jerusalem.

Guillim, John (1565–1621): one of the best-known early writers on heraldry, who produced, in 'A Display of Heraldry' (1610), the first serious and methodical treatment in English of the subject. He held the office of Rouge Dragon Poursuivant (see *Officers of Arms*).

Guinegate, Battle of (August 16, 1513): victory gained by Henry VIII against the French. Like the Battle of Courtrai, over 200 years earlier, it is known as the Battle of the Spurs (see separate entry under this heading), because the French used their spurs more than their swords. It is said that this was caused by the French pretending to give way, in an effort to decoy the English cavalry into a rash attack, and thereby bringing about a panic-stricken stampede in their own ranks.

Guinivere (or Guinevere, Genever, etc.) wife of King Arthur. The popular modern Christian name Jennifer, and the surname Gaynor, derive from it.

Guisarme (or Gisarme): type of large pike, a cross between a spear and a scythe, used by foot-soldiers throughout the Middle Ages, and taking on many forms and accessory features, so that it is often difficult to distinguish it from other common weapons, such as the glaive and partisan. (See separate entries for these.)

Gules: heraldic name for red, one of the five chief colours, and usually abbreviated 'gu.' when blazoning. When the shield is uncoloured, gules can be represented by vertical shading lines.

Guy of Warwick: one of the most popular heroes of mediaeval romance, and accepted as a genuine historical figure by a number of early chroniclers. In the stories surrounding him, he served as a page to one of the Earls of Warwick, and married his daughter Felice after demonstrating his prowess by fighting against the Saracens and slaying a dragon in Northumberland. He made pilgrimage to the Holy Land and, on his return, vanquished the Danish giant Colbrand outside the city of Winchester. By this time Felice had given up all hope of seeing her knight again, and devoted herself to good works, building churches, clothing and feeding the hungry. Guy himself, travel-stained and in the garb of a pilgrim, came to his own castle gate and received alms from her. Rather than disturb her life of peace and charity, he resolved not to reveal himself, but stole away to a wooded cliff near Warwick, where he built himself a hermitage and lived the rest of his life in penance for his former pride of possessions and knightly power.

Only on his death-bed did he send Felice the ring that she had given him on his departure for the Holy Land, and the lovers were at last re-united, Felice going on hunger-strike and dying of a broken heart. It might be thought from all this that Guy had more knightly courage than plain common-sense; but the story won all hearts for centuries. The French romancers have sometimes been so base as to claim that he originated in France as Guido of Tours.

Gyrons: triangular segments of a shield, formed by sub-dividing the 'quarters'. It is possible to

have as many as twelve gyrons. (See illustration for the various arrangements, which can be described as a gyronny of eight, twelve, etc.).

Hackney: an ordinary sort of horse, of no particular quality, for everyday purposes. The word is at least as old as Chaucer, and comes from a French word meaning 'an ambling horse.'

Hacqueton: see *Acton*.

Halberd (or Halbert): long-handled weapon, of many different forms and designs, but consisting essentially of a spike at the head and an axe-blade, either square or curved, convex or concave. For pageant and parade purposes richly decorated examples with very long handles were sometimes made; but the war-weapon, used by the foot-soldier, was only five or six feet in length. See *Battle of the Spurs* (1302), for an occasion when this type of weapon was used with terrible effect against the armoured knight. The most advanced types could hook, trip and pierce, as well as cut.

Hammer: see *War Hammer*.

Harlech Castle: in Merioneth, Wales; one of the chain of castles built by Edward I at strategic points. In 1285, about £205 was spent in hewing out the ditch from the rock in front of the castle, and from 1286–1290 nearly £8,000 went on masonry. In the course of its troubled history it withstood several sieges, but in 1404 was taken over by the famous Welsh rebel leader Owen Glendower (Owain Glyndwr), who made the castle his capital and summoned a Parliament there. In 1460, it sheltered Queen Margaret for some months after the capture of Henry VI at the Battle of Northampton. By the end of the 15th century the castle was falling into disuse and it is now a roofless ruin.

Harness: a common mediaeval term for armour. (See *Armour* for examples, and also *Hosting Harness*).

Hatching: system of indicating, by means of shading, the heraldic colours and metals when for some reason proper colours cannot be used.

Gules (Red) is indicated by fine vertical lines.
Azure (Blue) is indicated by fine horizontal lines.
Sable (Black) is indicated by cross vertical and horizontal lines.

Vert (Green) is indicated by fine diagonal lines drawn left down to right.

Purpure (Purple) is indicated by fine diagonal lines, drawn right down to left.

Or (Gold) is indicated by tiny dots all over the surface.

Argent (Silver) is indicated by leaving the surface plain.

(See *Tinctures* for the standard abbreviations often used for these colours and metals.)

Haubergeon (Habergeon): properly speaking, a short hauberk (see below); a short coat of mail, sometimes sleeveless.

Hauberk: long coat of mail, almost knee-length, the short sleeves becoming, in time, long and close-fitting and terminating in 'mufflers', i.e., mittens of mail with a separate thumb-stall. (See also *Byrnie*). Though, to be accurate, there is a difference between the hauberk and haubergeon, in early writings the two words are often used to mean the same thing. Usually it was the outermost garment, with the well-stuffed *acton* or *gambeson* beneath (see separate entries); but the knight later covered it with his surcoat, with his arms displayed or a special device such as the crusaders' cross.

By an odd coincidence, one of the best illustrations of the hauberk is on the brass of Sir Nicholas Hawberk (1407) in the church at Cobham, Kent. He is shown with hands touching in prayer, sword and dagger at side, hauberk of banded mail showing beneath the jupon, under a magnificent canopy enshrining the Trinity, Madonna and Child, and St. George killing the dragon.

Hawk: name applied generally to the birds of prey used in falconry, including the falcon; but properly speaking, the 'shortwings', among them the eagle, goshawk, sparrowhawk and buzzard. They differ from the true falcons in lacking the characteristic notch or 'tooth' in the beak and in having shorter, less pointed, wings. Their eyes are yellow rather than brown.

Hawks of the Fist: the 'shortwings'.

Hawks of the Lure: the 'longwings'.

116

Hawkestone of Wrinehill, Sir John: one of the four famous Cheshire squires of Sir James Audley (see separate entry) who distinguished themselves at the Battle of Poitiers.

Hawkwood, Sir John (d. 1394): known as 'Needle John', because he began life as a tailor. Tiring of his sedentary life he took to soldiering and became one of the most famous leaders of his time, leading his 'free lances' in many campaigns, chiefly in the wars between the various factions and states in Italy, first on one side, then the other, as was the way with mercenaries. (See *Free Companies*.) The well-known White Brotherhood or White Company served under Hawkwood, who reached such a position of repute that he acted as ambassador for England at Rome, Florence and Naples.

Headstall: see *Bridle*.

Heater Shield: the type of shield that followed the kite-shaped variety used by the Normans; rather like the bottom of a long flat-iron, but curved to the body.

Heaume: another form of *Helm* (see below). *Heaumers* were makers of helms.

Helm: complete covering for the head, usually made of four or five iron plates riveted together, and often worn right over other protective coverings beneath, e.g. the mail coif surrounding the face and iron cap. Earlier types were flat topped, later ones rounded or pointed. After about 1420, helms, instead of being supported by the head, came down on to the shoulders and were securely fastened to the chest and back. The great jousting helms, with their narrow eye-slit and the jutting lower half slightly overlapping the upper, look almost impossible to see out of. But an English authority, Mr. Ewart Oakeshott, who has had the rare privilege (and ability) to try it with an authentic early helm, says: 'You can see through the eye-slit very well so long as you hunch your shoulders and bend your head, as you would do when charging with a lance . . . You have to raise your head at the moment when you and your adversary run together. You can't see anything then, but for the vital moment that is not import-

ant. The great thing is that you are fully protected.' (*A Knight and His Armour*.) Fine examples which have survived are those that belonged to the Black Prince (Canterbury Cathedral) and Henry V (Westminster Abbey). The Brocas Helm (see entry) has already been illustrated in this book.

Some of these narrow-slitted helms look so peculiarly frog-like that they have become commonly known as 'frog-mouthed' helms. For other types see *Barrel Helm, Grid-iron Helm*.

Helmet: for various types, as distinct from the great Helm, see *bascinet, cabasset, close, kettle-hat, morion, salade* and *sallet*.

Henry II of France (1519–1559): an undistinguished king, with few gifts but those of strength and physical prowess which, in the end, brought about his downfall. In 1559, in order to celebrate the double marriage of his sister and daughter, the king arranged a series of splendid fêtes and tournaments, before the two princesses departed to their future husbands. Right at the end, Henry II, who had carried himself well, said he would run a final course with Count Montmorency, the Captain of the royal guard. The two lances struck each other, but Montmorency was unable to lower his in time, and it pierced the king's visor. He died eleven days later.

Henry V (1387–1422): king of England, and one of the most famous of her warriors. His greatest victory was that of Agincourt in 1415. (See separate entry.) He was the hero of one of the most spirited and martial of Shakespeare's plays, which contains some of the best-known passages in English literature, including the rousing speech before Harfleur and, most of all, the one delivered in the English camp before Agincourt:

> *This day is call'd the feast of Crispian:*
> *He that outlives this day and comes safe home*
> *Will stand a tip-toe when this day is named,*
> *And rouse him at the name of Crispian.*
> *He that shall live this day, and see old age,*
> *Will yearly on the vigil feast his neighbours,*
> *And say, 'To-morrow is Saint Crispian.'*
> *Then will he strip his sleeve and show his scars,*
> *And say, 'These wounds I had on Crispin's day.'*

118

Old men forget; yet all shall be forgot,
But he'll remember with advantages
What feats he did that day. Then shall our names,
Familiar in his mouth as household words,
Harry the king, Bedford and Exeter,
Warwick and Talbot, Salisbury and Gloucester,
Be in their flowing cups freshly remember'd.
This story shall the good man teach his son;
And Crispin Crispian shall ne'er go by,
From this day to the ending of the world,
But we in it shall be remembered –
We few, we happy few, we band of brothers.

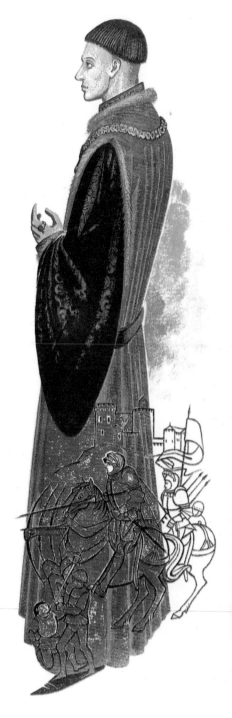

An early writer, who was familiar with Henry's appearance, describes him as having thick brown hair, evenly cut. 'He has a straight nose, and wide, handsome features . . . His eyes sparkle brightly, having a reddish tinge when wide open. In peace they resemble those of a dove, but in rage are like a lion's. His teeth are snowy, strong and even . . . He has a cleft chin and his neck is everywhere evenly thick . . . His limbs are well-formed and strong with bone and sinew.' Another said: 'He outstripped all his equals in age at running and jumping . . . in so much that, with two chosen companions, he frequently, by sheer speed of running and without help of whatever kind, killed the swiftest fallow deer driven out into the plain from the woodland shades.'

But he was not just brawn and battle-hungry. He was a patron of poets and was renowned for his justice and religious spirit; so that, in his best moments, he came closer than most kings to the ideal of the Christian knight. His tomb and chantry chapel are in Westminster Abbey. On an oak beam hang his great helm, his shield and saddle. The royal arms on the front of the shield have worn away, but the back is covered with blue silk powdered with fleurs-de-lys. The padded wooden saddle, more than 500 years old like the rest, is the only one of its kind known in this country. On the walls of the chantry chapel are two splendid representations of Henry in armour and in full career on his war-horse. Here is a good place to remember the last words of the prayer Shakespeare put into his mouth before his greatest martial exploit:

. . . all that I can do is nothing worth,
Since that my penitence comes after all,
Imploring pardon.

Henry VII's Chapel: in Westminster Abbey, and 'one of the most perfect buildings ever erected in England.' André Horault, Ambassador from Henry IV of France to Queen Elizabeth I of England, saw it about 70 years after it had been finished by the brother master-masons William and Robert Vertue, and described it as:

'. . . of marvellous workmanship, and one cannot see nor speak of anything fairer . . . nor do I think that anywhere in the world can the like be seen, nor one so fairly adorned.'

Henry VII, who planned the chapel, directed that it should be 'garnished and adorned with our arms, badges and cognisants . . . in as goodly and rich manner as such work requireth', and the royal beasts – leopards, greyhounds, dragons and the like – stare down from the canopies of saints, and peer half-hidden from the vaulting. The great bronze gates also carry his badges.

The Chapel is brave with the coloured banners of the Knights of the Bath (see also *Knight*), hanging over their stalls. It is here that the installation takes place of new knights of this ancient order of chivalry.

Henry VIII (1491–1547): see *Brandon, Charles; Field of the Cloth of Gold; Greenwich;* and *Tower of London.*

Henry of Lancaster, Duke of Lancaster, Earl of Derby and Earl of Lincoln (1299?–1361): Edward III's trusted counsellor, a famous soldier and a knight held in high honour throughout Christendom; courageous, courteous, learned for the times in which he lived, and pious. He soldiered for nearly 50 years in Scotland, France, Cyprus, Prussia and Granada. Among his exploits, he defeated Sir William Douglas, knight of Liddesdale, in a tournament; bluffed his way into taking the strongest fortress on the Garonne by pretending to the governor and the garrison that the walls had been mined by his engineers, whereas the soldiers, despite all their efforts, had found them too strongly built; and fought, not only in all the land campaigns, including Poitiers, but in the two most important sea battles of the century – Sluys (1340) and Espagnols-sur-Mer (1350). In the latter, against a strong Spanish convoy (the name given to the battle literally means 'The Spaniards on the Sea'), he rescued the Black Prince in the nick of time, when his ship was sinking under him:

'The young prince of Wales and his division were engaged apart: his ship was grappled by a great Spaniard, when he and his knights suffered much; for she had so many holes that the water came in very abundantly, and they could not by any means stop the leaks... During this danger of the prince, the duke of Lancaster came near, and, as he approached, saw he had the worst of the engagement, and that his crew had too much on their hands, for they were baling out water. He therefore fell on the other side of the Spanish vessel, with which he grappled, shouting, 'Derby to the rescue!' The engagement was now very warm, but did not last long, for the ship was taken, and all the crew thrown overboard, not one being saved. The prince, with his men, instantly embarked on board the Spaniard; and scarcely had they done so when his own vessel sunk, which convinced them of the imminent danger they had been in.' (Sir John Froissart.)

Henry was a founder member of the Order of the Garter. It is a measure of his many-sided ability that he wrote two widely read devotional works, in one of which, called 'Mercy Gramercy', he sought forgiveness for all the sins he had committed and gave thanks for all the mercies he had received.

He was one of the most valiant knights of his age and many of the noblest young squires of England, France and Spain tried to serve under his banner as the best training-school in Europe in the arts of war and of chivalry.

Heralds: see *Officers of Arms.*

Heralds' College: see *College of Arms.*

Hobby: a small type of falcon, weighing only about six ounces, but valued because of her accurate flight, her intelligence and readiness to learn.

Holland, Thomas, 1st Earl of Kent (d. 1360): provides a good example of the importance of capturing the right sort of prisoner in the Middle Ages. Holland was of modest origins, with few assets but skill in the tournament. At the storming of Caen in 1346, he took prisoner the wealthy Count of Eu and won a large fortune in ransom money almost overnight. To provide the perfect story book ending, though he did not live happily ever after, he married a princess, Joan of Kent, and became Earl of Kent.

Holy Land, The: for Christians, Palestine, the birth-place of their religion and the most highly-regarded place of pilgrimage, whether for the crusading soldier or the civilian. Hazardous though the journey was, it did not prevent numbers of women endeavouring to make it. When Isabel Parewastel came back home to Bridgwater, Somerset, in 1366, she had a sad story to tell of misadventure, culminating in being taken by the Saracens, placed head downwards on the rack, and beaten. Of all places in Palestine, the most venerated was Jerusalem and, within that city, the Church of the Holy Sepulchre, much enlarged and rebuilt by the Crusaders, 1114–1130.

Holy Company: the name once enjoyed by the far-from-holy free-lances of Sir John Hawkwood, when they were in the service of the Pope. (See *Hawkwood* and *Free Companies*).

Holy Grail, The: see *Grail*.

Holy Water Sprinkler: see *Flail*.

Honi Soit qui Mal y Pense: 'shame be to him who thinks evil of it'; or 'evil to him who evil thinks'; the motto of the Knights of the Garter since their founding by Edward III just before 1350. For comment on the adoption of the motto, see *Blue Garter, Order of*.

Honour Point: One of the nine points on a shield used to indicate the position of the various charges and the dividing lines. They are:

A. Dexter Chief Point
B. Middle Chief Point
C. Sinister Chief Point
D. Honour Point
E. Fess Point
F. Nombril Point
G. Dexter Base Point
H. Middle Base Point
I. Sinister Base Point.

See accompanying illustration for position of these. It should be remembered that 'dexter' is right, 'sinister' left, and that positions are always described *not* from the onlooker's point of view, but from that of the man behind the shield.

Honours of War: sign of respect to a defeated, but honoured, foe; e.g., allowing them to march out of a surrendered town armed, with drums beating and colours flying.

Hood: part of the 'furniture' used in hawking and falconry, particularly in 'manning' or training, and serving much the same purpose as horse blinkers. It prevents the bird being startled and, slipped on at time of fear and restlessness, calms it. See *Bells* for a vivid description of hooded hawks.

Horse: for various types, see *Courser, Destrier, Hackney, Jennet, Palfrey* and *Rounsey*; an indispensable part of the knight's equipment, as essential as his armour and weapons. Though he might sometimes fight on foot, he belonged on the back of his horse and took great pride in its breeding, training and accomplishments. In many stories, the horse is almost as well-known as the owner. Thus, in the realm of romance, Orlando had his Brigliadoro ('golden bridle') and Don Quixote his Rosinante ('once a hack'); in history, the Earl of Warwick rode his famous Black Saladin and the Cid his Babiéca (meaning 'simpleton') – the explanation of the latter being that when, as a young man, he was choosing his horse, he ignored all the fine-looking specimens and chose a rough-looking colt; whereupon his godfather called the youngster a simpleton and the future 'lord champion' (see *Cid*) transferred the epithet to his horse.

A late 15th-century writer said a good horse should have fifteen qualities – three of a man, three of a woman, three of a fox, three of a hare and three of an ass: e.g., the boldness and hardihood of a man, the ease of movement of a woman, the short ears and good trot of a fox, the great eye of a hare, and the flat leg and good hoof of an ass.

The horse was an ancient symbol of power and kingship, so that many very early coins bear this device in one form or another; some of the

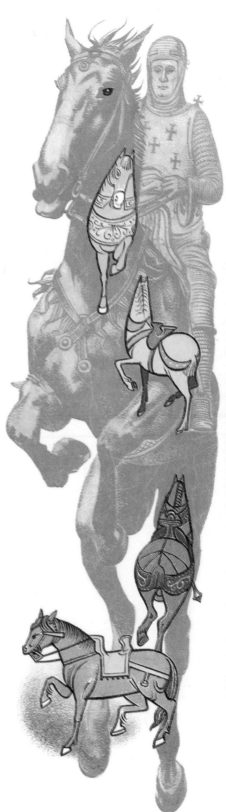

Saxon chiefs used the 'white horse as their standard; and cut in the chalk downs of Berkshire is a white horse, 374 feet long, marking the victory of Alfred over the Danes in 871.

And it fell in the days of Alfred,
  In the days of his repose,
That as old customs in his sight
  Were a straight road and a steady light,
He bade them keep the White Horse white
  As the first plume of the snows.

And right to the red torchlight,
  From the trouble of morning grey,
They stripped the White Horse of the grass
  As they strip it to this day.
                    from *The Ballad of the White
                    Horse*: G. K. Chesterton

Horse Armour: protective covering for horses, made of leather, mail or, later on, plate. The magnificent 'bards' (see separate entry) of plate-armour were probably only made for the very wealthy and powerful, not for the ordinary knight, whose horse was provided with lighter and cheaper defences. (See *crinet, flanchard* and *peytrel* for some pieces of horse armour.)

The records of the Tower of London contain some interesting items of horse armour in their store inventories, e.g.:

'Horse Armour Cappape [i.e. cap-à-pie = head-to-foot] white and plain wth Gauntlett made for Charles Brandon Duke of Suffolk y^e Horse furniture being a Shaffron [chauffron], brestplate and buttock of ye same, a Sadle [saddle] plate guilt [gilt] with Sadle, Bitt and Bridle.'

'Compleat Armour Cappape engraven wth y^e Ragged Staff wth a main guard and pass-guard made for ye Earle of Leicester ye horse furniture being a Shaffron, Crinett and Brest-plate of ye same Sadle, Bitt and Raynes.'

Hospitallers: See *Knights of St. John of Jerusalem.*

Hosting Harness: see *Field Armour.* 'Hosting' meant a battle or encounter, so that a hosting harness meant armour suitable for battle.

124

Hotspur: the familiar name of Sir Henry Percy (1364–1403), eldest son of Sir Henry Percy, 1st Earl of Northumberland. Some say it was given him because of his fiery temper; others that it dates from an occasion when, with his brother Ralph, he was waiting at Yarmouth with 600 lances and 300 men-at-arms for an invading French force; until, too impatient to delay longer, he commandeered every vessel in Yarmouth harbour, packed his men aboard and made a series of surprise raids on the French coast, bringing off a good deal of rich booty. He saw his first actions, even if he did not participate, at the age of about twelve; was knighted at the age of thirteen, at Richard II's coronation; and, when still only about fourteen, led the final assault on the garrison of Berwick after a nine-day siege. He rebelled against Henry IV and was killed at the battle of Shrewsbury, 1403. Shakespeare falsifies history in *Henry IV, Part I* by making Hotspur and Prince Henry, later Henry V, contemporaries, whereas Hotspur was more than twice his age.

Howel-y-Fwyall, Sir (fl. 1356): 'Was a noble warrior, and was in the battle of Poictiers with the Black Prince, when the French King was taken prisoner: where, with his pole-ax, he behaved himself so valiantly, that the prince made him a knight, and allowed a mess of meat to be served before his ax or partisan for ever, to perpetuate the memory of his good service: which mess of meat, after his death, was carried down to be given to the poor of his soul's sake; and the said mess had eight yeoman-attendants found at the king's charge, which were afterwards called Yeomen of the Crown, who had eightpence a day of standing wages, and lasted till the beginning of the reign of Elizabeth.' (Thomas Pennant, 1796).

Sir Howel-y-Fwyall's arms also commemorated his gallantry – *sable, between three flower-de-luces a pole-axe argent.*

Howell of the Horse Shoes: Sir Howel-y-Pedolau (born *c.* 1284), a Welsh knight who was foster-brother to Edward II and stood high in favour with him. He was of such great strength that he could break or straighten horse-shoes with his bare hands. His arms were *gules, between*

three lioncels rampant a chevron or. The old heralds, if there several lions on a shield, sometimes called them 'lioncels' – 'little lions.'

Hugo of Tabarie, Sir: the hero of one of the many stories told about the great infidel leader Salah ad-Din Yusuf, commonly known as Saladin, for whom many Christian knights and romancers seem to have entertained a good deal of respect and affection. One popular tale relates how Saladin had long 'afflicted the true faith, and made Christian blood to flow like water upon the soil of the Holy Land, where the knights of Christendom had joined to make a struggle against him. From all countries they came in arms, lords and heroes of renown, and if courage could have given victory the Sultan would have been overthrown. But heaven willed it otherwise; for in a great battle the best of the Christian champions were slain or taken captive.' (Hope Moncrieff.)

One of the prisoners was Hugo of Tabarie, upon whom Saladin fixed a ransom of a hundred thousand gold bezants and, when the knight protested that the sale of all his lands would not bring half that sum, gave him leave to seek help from his friends on condition that he returned to captivity on a fixed day. If the ransom were not paid, Sir Hugo must lose his head.

The knight gave his parole and travelled round Palestine trying to raise the ransom, but failed. On the appointed day he returned to Saladin's camp, prepared to die. The infidel leader was greatly impressed by the good faith of a knight who would yield up his life rather than break his word, and desired to know more of Christian knighthood and its vows.

Sir Hugo of Tabarie told Saladin how he had progressed from page to squire and how the great day came when, after preparation by vigil, fast and prayer, he went through the solemn and beautiful ceremony and received his arms and armour.

'From then on,' he explained, 'I was bound to honour the Church, to obey my king, to speak the truth and disdain a lie, to practice courtesy to all ladies, to strive against wrong in all the world, to help the oppressed, to keep my word, to fear no man and nothing save dishonour.'

Saladin sat deep in thought, faced with the

126

dilemma of keeping his own oath, sworn by the Prophet, that the knight should pay with his life if he could not produce his ransom, and his wish to spare so gallant a foe. At length he rose and led his captive into a hall crowded with his chiefs and captains.

'Here is a noble foe who will die because he kept his word and because he cannot find his ransom. Will you give of your treasure to buy his life?'

The Saracens, confronted with this challenge from their great leader, cast their gold till the whole ransom was piled in a shining heap. Saladin smiled and turned to Sir Hugo.

'Behold! your debt is paid. Take your freedom, and the money with it, as a proof that there are noble knights in the host of Saladin as well as in the Christian array.'

Sir Hugo of Tabarie thanked him courteously as one knight to another, but begged another boon – that the gold should be used to ransom some other captive crusaders.

'Take them,' said Saladin. 'Since no amount of gold is enough for such a man as thou art, take them. They are all free.'

And, laden with gifts and honourably escorted by their enemies, they came back joyfully to the Christian camp.

(See also *Saladin*.)

Hundred Years War: the long period of almost uninterrupted bickering and warfare between England and France in the 14th and 15th centuries. Various dates are given for its starting and finishing points, but 1338–1453 may be accepted as a fair compromise; i.e., from the time Edward III's first expedition set out to the time when the valiant Sir John Talbot was killed in the Battle of Castillon, and, of all the English possessions in France, only Calais remained. (See *Talbot, Sir John*.)

The war saw some of the greatest martial exploits in English history, among them the land battles of Crécy, Poitiers and Agincourt; and the sea-fights of Sluys and Les-Espagnols-sur-Mer. (See separate entries for all these.) Some of the greatest and most colourful figures in the history of chivalry come and go – Edward III, the Black Prince, Henry V, du Guesclin, Joan of Arc, Manny, Chandos, blind John of Bohemia,

Froissart – the long roll is inexhaustible. It was a breeding-ground of courage, honour, and of splendid gestures; but also of much cruelty, avarice and misery. 'Barren glory chequered with disgrace' was one summary; though perhaps glory is not entirely barren if, centuries later, it can still lift men's hearts and stir to admiration or even emulation.

Ibn Jubayr: see *Granada*.

Ice-brook temper: Othello, in Shakespeare's play, says:

I have another weapon in this chamber;
It is a sword of Spain, the ice-brook's temper.

This is a reference to the custom of some of the Spanish sword-makers of plunging weapons red-hot from the forge into an ice-cold brook, particularly one called Salo or Xalon. To temper a blade is to bring it to a proper degree of hardness; and if it was of 'ice-brook temper', it was supposed to be of the finest possible quality.

Ich Dien (or Diene): the centuries-old motto of the heir-apparent to the throne of Britain. It appears on the Black Prince's tomb in Canterbury Cathedral. (See *Edward, Prince of Wales*.) It has been claimed that the words are Welsh, 'Eich dyn', meaning 'Here is the man', and date from the occasion when Edward I, having promised the Welsh people a prince who could speak no English, displayed his new-born son, Edward of Carnarvon. But since that story is highly suspect, the alternative and generally accepted interpretation – that it is German in origin and means 'I serve' – is probably the right one.

Idylls of the King: the long series of poems, written over a period of nearly 30 years by Alfred, Lord Tennyson (1809–1892), based on the ancient stories of King Arthur and his knights of the Round Table. Though he took many liberties with the legends, he brought to them much new beauty and a highly-polished craftsmanship; so that many of the lines are among the best-known in English literature. See, e.g., the *Oxford Dictionary of Quotations*, which lists more than 80 well-known quotations from the *Idylls*, including Tennyson's close rendering of the code of the knight of chivalry:

To reverence the King, as if he were
Their conscience, and their conscience as their King,
To break the heathen and uphold the Christ,
To ride abroad redressing human wrongs,
To speak no slander, no, nor listen to it,
To honour his own word as if his God's.

Imperial State Crown: one of the two most important crowns in the royal regalia of England, its platinum frame set with more than 3,000 precious stones, chiefly diamonds and pearls. The most important and historic of these stones is the *Black Prince's Ruby*, set in the cross at the front. (See further details under this entry.)

Increscent: in heraldry, a crescent with its opening facing to the right (dexter) of the shield-bearer, and the left (sinister) of the person facing the shield. (See also *Crescent.*)

Inescutcheon: in heraldry, a small shield charged within another shield and placed at its centre.

Infantry: foot-soldiers, usually carrying small-arms. The word derives from the old one meaning a child or youth; and, in default of any better explanation, it may be true that the name was first applied 'to a body of men collected by the *Infante* or heir-apparent of Spain for the purpose of rescuing his father from the Moors.' (Dr. Cobham Brewer.)

Infidel: literally, one who is unfaithful or does not hold the faith. The term is frequently met with in the story of the Crusades, meaning a Saracen or follower of Mahomet. But the Christians borrowed the word from the Mohammedans, so that an infidel was a Christian or a non-Christian, according to which side you were on.

Inn Signs: are constant reminders of the great days of chivalry. The *Trip to Jerusalem* and the numerous *Saracen's* and *Turk's Heads* bring back the crowded and colourful canvas of the Crusades; the dust and sweat of war is in the *Castle* and the *Five Arrows*; heroes ride again in the sign of the *Black Prince*, the *George and Dragon* and the *Great White Horse*; great families live on in the arms of *Luttrell*, *Talbot*, *Chandos*, *Grosvenor*, *Sidney* and a thousand more; ancient royal badges and standards flaunt again in all the *Golden Lions*, *Dragons*, *White Harts*, *Rising Suns*, *Fleurs-de-Lys* and *Crowns*.

Invected: see *Engrailed.*

Inverted: in heraldry, term describing a bird whose wings are pointing downwards.

Inverurie, Battle of (1308): the battle in which Robert Bruce defeated the Earl of Buchan, who had acknowledged the overlordship of the English kings, and began Bruce's series of successful campaigns of liberation, which included the devastating victory over Edward II's forces at Bannockburn in 1314. (See Robert I.) At the opening of the campaign, Bruce was so stricken with illness that he could not mount his horse unaided; but, stirred into action by the news that Buchan's forces were on the move, showed the iron resolution and courage that made him a great leader of men, by taking command supported by two men on each side of the saddle.

Investiture: the ceremony of conferring rank or office, as in the making of a knight. See *Ordain.*

Iron Crown of Lombardy: the ancient crown of the kings of Lombardy, in northern Italy, dating from the 6th century. The jewelled exterior was added in about 1100; but inside is the original iron band, about three-eighths of an inch wide and a tenth of an inch thick, said to have been forged from one of the nails of the Cross. It was used at the coronation of all the Lombard kings, and the Holy Roman Emperors who were also kings of Lombardy, including Charlemagne. (Napoleon, with typical arrogance, also had himself crowned with it.)

Ironside, Edmund (981?–1016): king, son of Æthelred the Unready. Famous for his great physical strength and courage; but perhaps receiving his nick-name, as well, for the iron armour he wore.

Iron Hand (or the Iron-hander): see *Berchlingen, Götz von.*

Isabella (Isabel or Isabelle): a popular name among the ladies of the Middle Ages; but, more remarkably, the name given to a brownish-yellow colour following an incident involving either Isabel of Austria or Isabel of Castile. The former, it is related, vowed not to change her

linen till Granada fell; the latter, not to put on a clean shift till Ostend was taken. Since the siege of Ostend lasted three years (1601–1604), the colour of the garment when the town fell at last to the Spaniards can be well imagined. Horses of dun-yellow colour were often described as 'isabelle' or 'isabel'.

Islam: the followers of Mahomet, or the countries in which they live; the foes of the Crusaders.

Isumbras (spelt also Isenbras and Ysambras, etc.): a favourite hero of mediaeval romance; an over-proud and arrogant knight who learnt humility through adversity and so came to true knighthood. Sir John Millais painted a famous picture 'Sir Isumbras at the Ford' in 1857, showing the ageing knight crossing a river with the two children of a poor woodman on his saddle.

Italian Armour: at its best, among the finest ever made. By the 15th century Milan had become the greatest centre of armour making in Europe and manufactured harness for the kings and nobility of France, Spain and Italy – and for their enemies as well, if required. The two greatest families of armourers were the Negroli and the Missaglia. It is some indication of the prestige they attained that Tomasso Missaglia, having made armour for so many knights, was himself knighted in 1435.

The Milanese armourers put on a particularly splendid display in 1491 on the occasion of the marriage of Lodovico Sforza, Duke of Milan (called *Il Moro*, The Moor). The chief street of the armourers was lined with glittering effigies of mounted knights, clad cap-à-pie in mail and damascened steel.

With the manufacture of armour went also the gayer trappings of the tournament and the procession, all the fluttering bunting and ribbons and 'favours'. This is why we still call a seller of such wares a milliner, or Milaner.

Interesting details of trade in ready-to-wear armour (as distinct from the tailor-made harnesses of the rich and noble) have survived in the accounts of a merchant, Francesco Datini, trading in Avignon in 1350–1383. He did a brisk business with the knights of the Papal Court and with the various Free Companies, including Bertrand du Guesclin's (see separate entry). An inventory of Datini's stock in 1367 listed 25 bascinets, 3 'iron hats', 10 rimless low iron hats, 60 breastplates, 20 cuirasses, 12 coats of mail and 23 pairs of gauntlets. His goods came mainly from Milan and were sent by mule-train across the Alps in canvas bales stuffed with straw.

As well, he made up some of his own goods and employed a Belgian armourer. Among the merchandise that came to his busy workshops were sword-blades, hilts and scabbards, sheet metal, wire, and metal studs for shields, gauntlets, etc.

Datini was also prepared to run a hire-service for noblemen and knights who had fallen on hard times; as in 1369, when the Sieur de Courcy rented a bascinet and a pair of gauntlets.

(Details from Iris Origo, *The Merchant of Prato*, based on the vast collection of Francesco Datini's letters and documents preserved in Prato, Tuscany.)

Italian Course: called also *Uber die Pallia* ('over the barriers'). A form of tournament run with a central barrier. This was of wood, about five feet high. The lance usually had a coronel head (see separate entry), and the knights rode on either side of the barrier, left hand inwards. Special suits of armour were worn, one feature of which was often the *manteau d'armes*, a special concave shield, fixed to the breast-plate by screws, and protecting the left side of the body, arm and shoulder. Originally the object was to unhorse the opponent, but later the combatants were content to shiver their lances, using the light-weight *bourdonasse* (see separate entry).

Ivanhoe: the hero of the novel of that name, by Sir Walter Scott (1771–1832), the greatest of the 19th century stories of chivalry, set in the reign of Richard Coeur-de-Lion.

The title of the novel came from Scott's chance recollection of an old rhyme about a quarrel between the Black Prince and one of the ancestors of the famous John Hampden, during a game of tennis. The Black Prince was struck with a racket, and Hampden was punished by having to forfeit three of his manors, Tring, Wing and Ivanhoe.

Tring, Wing, and Ivanhoe,
For striking of a blow
Hampden did forgo,
And glad he could escape so.

Some of the most vivid and exciting chapters are concerned with the tournament, when Ivanhoe appears incognito as the *Desdichado*, or 'Disinherited Knight'; and the archery contest, in which the outlaw Robin Hood, under the name of Locksley, matches his skill against the best archers of the day. Two passages must serve as samples:

'At length, as the Saracenic music of the challengers concluded one of those long and high flourishes with which they had broken the silence of the lists, it was answered by a solitary trumpet, which breathed a note of defiance from the northern extremity. All eyes were turned to see the new champion which these sounds announced, and no sooner were the barriers opened than he paced into the lists. As far as could be judged of a man sheathed in armour, the new adventurer did not greatly exceed the middle size, and seemed to be rather slender than strongly made. His suit of armour was formed of steel, richly inlaid with gold, and the device on his shield was a young oak-tree pulled up by the roots, with the Spanish word *Desdichado*, signifying Disinherited. He was mounted on a gallant black horse, and as he passed through the lists he gracefully saluted the Prince and the ladies by lowering his lance. The dexterity with which he managed his steed, and something of the youthful grace which he displayed in his manner won him the favour of the multitude, which some of the lower classes expressed by calling out, "Touch Ralph de Vipont's shield – touch the Hospitaller's shield; he has the least sure seat, he is your cheapest bargain."

The champion, moving onward amid these well-meant hints, ascended the platform by the sloping alley which led from it to the lists, and, to the astonishment of all present, riding straight up to the central pavilion, struck with the sharp end of his spear the shield of Brian de Bois-Guilbert until it rang again.'

*　　*　　*　　*　　*

'. . . Hubert resumed his place, and not

neglecting the caution which he had received from his adversary, he made the necessary allowance for a very light air of wind, which had just arisen, and shot so successfully that his arrow alighted in the very centre of the target.

"A Hubert! a Hubert!" shouted the populace, more interested in a known person than in a stranger. "In the clout! – in the clout! – a Hubert for ever!"

"Thou canst not mend that shot, Locksley," said the Prince, with an insulting smile.

"I will notch his shaft for him, however," replied Locksley. And letting fly his arrow with a little more precaution than before, it lighted right upon that of his competitor, which it split to shivers.'

Another memorable episode is when King Richard, returned secretly from the Holy Land and, also riding incognito, takes part in the tournament before his rascally brother Prince John, acting as his regent. The theme of Coeur-de-Lion wandering unrecognized about his realm was a favourite and irresistible one with mediaeval story-tellers.

Scott was not greatly concerned with historical accuracy, and some of his long passages are tedious to modern readers. But all the panoply and colour of chivalry are here. '*Amo* Locksley, *Amo* the Templar,' wrote Thackeray; and we can perhaps all share a little Scott's own feeling: 'God only knows how delighted I was to find myself in such society.'

Ivry, Battle of (March 14, 1590): fought in the religious wars between Catholics and Protestants in France. Henry IV (of Navarre), an able and likeable soldier despite great faults, heavily defeated the Catholic League, headed by the Duke of Mayenne, on the plain of St. André, near Ivry. The League had some 16,000 men, including 4,000 horsemen with a brave display of lances. Henry had about 8,000 infantry and 3,000 cavalry.

'Friends, keep your ranks well,' said Henry. 'If you lose your companies, cornets or guides, the white band on my arm shall serve to guide you while I have a drop of blood. Follow it; you will find it always in the path of honour and glory.' (Victor Duruy's *History of France*.)

Lord Macaulay (1800–1859) devoted one of his spirited poems to the Battle of Ivry. It includes the lines:

Hurrah! the foes are moving. Hark to the
   mingled din
Of fife, and steed, and trump, and drum, and
   roaring culverin!
The fiery Duke is pricking fast across St André's
   plain,
With all the hireling chivalry of Guelders and
   Almayne.
Now by the lips of those we love, fair gentlemen
   of France,
Charge for the Golden Lilies – upon them with the
   lance!
A thousand spurs are striking deep, a thousand
   spears in rest,
A thousand knights are pressing close behind the
   snow-white crest;
And in they burst, and on they rush'd, while, like
   a guiding star,
Amidst the thickest carnage blazed the helmet of
   Navarre.
   *   *   *   *   *

Ho! gallant nobles of the League, look that your
   arms be bright;
Ho! burghers of St. Genevieve, keep watch and
   ward to-night;
For our God hath crush'd the tyrant, our God hath
   raised the slave,
And mock'd the council of the wise, and the valour
   of the brave.
Then glory to His holy name, from whom all
   glories are;
And glory to our Sovereign Lord, King Henry of
   Navarre!

Jack: among its many meanings, a cheap-quality defensive coat of mail or leather.

Jack of Newbury: the nickname of John Winchcomb, of Newbury, Berkshire, the greatest cloth merchant of his day, who is said to have run a hundred looms in his own house and to have sent, at his own expense, the same number of his own men, fully equipped, to fight for the king at Flodden Field. (See separate entry.)

Jaffa: one of the principal ports of the Holy Land, much used by crusaders and pilgrims, and much fought over during the wars. It was the scene of Richard Coeur-de-Lion's last, and most spectacular, victory. In July, 1192, Saladin swooped on Jaffa and captured it after a three-day siege. When the news was brought to Richard, in Acre, he immediately sent his army by land and himself took to sea and arrived with a fleet of 50 galleys. Beaching his ships, he waded ashore at the head of his small force and flung himself at the citadel, while the beaten Christian garrison again seized arms and joined in. Coeur-de-Lion recaptured Jaffa with only about 80 knights, with three horses among them, 400 bowmen and some 2,000 Pisan and Genoese marines.

Meanwhile, the king's overland army was still advancing overland, and Saladin determined to strike again before they could link up. The formidable Moslem cavalry hurled themselves against the camp outside the walls of the citadel in seven great waves of 1,000 horsemen each. Richard met the attacks with his men in pairs, their shields set as a solid fence, their spears stuck in the ground and angled outwards. An archer stood behind each pair. The Saracens charged, wheeled and charged again, hour after hour, their horses growing more and more tired, without breaking that inflexible wall. Then, at the critical moment, Richard suddenly changed his tactics. The archers stepped to the front, sent a shattering volley of arrows into the oncoming horsemen, then retreated again. As the Saracen host checked, Coeur-de-Lion suddenly charged at the head of his small force of horsemen. In the end, the Saracens pulled out and retreated to Jerusalem.

It is a measure of the chivalrous conduct of which Saladin was capable that, when Richard was unhorsed in the thick of the battle, the

Saracen leader sent him two fresh horses in recognition of his bravery.

One of the crusader-chroniclers, Jean, Sire de Joinville, gives us a colourful picture of Jaffa when it was defended by a relative of his, the Count of Jaffa:

'When the Count of Jaffa saw that the king was coming, he prepared his castle in such wise that it seemed to be a town well capable of defence; for at each of the battlements – of which there were full five hundred – he set a shield, with his arms, and a pennon; and this thing was fair to see, for his arms were *or* with a cross of gules *patée*.'

The Count of Jaffa (whose French title was the Count of Brienne) was fond of displaying his arms in this way. When he first landed in Palestine he came with 'his galley all painted, within and without, with escutcheons of his arms, which arms are *or* with a cross of gules *patée*. He had at least three hundred rowers in his galley, and for each rower there was a targe with the count's arms thereon, and to each targe was a pennon attached with his arms wrought in gold.'

(For another note on Jaffa, see *Wey, William*.)

Jamb: leg-armour, made up of *cuishes, greaves* and *poleyns*. (See separate entries.)

James IV of Scotland (1473–1513): one of the most famous of Scottish kings and 'the most chivalrous prince of his day in Europe.' While he had many faults, he endeared himself to his people by his sense of justice and by his affability to all those, of whatever class and degree, with whom he came in contact. 'He excelled in all warlike exercises and manly accomplishments; in music, horsemanship, and the use of sword and spear'; and he took a delight in splendid tournaments, in which he often participated in person. 'One of the rules of these encounters was that the victor should be put in possession of his opponent's weapon; but when this was a spear, a purse of gold, a gift from the king, was attached to the point of it.'

A contemporary poet wrote of him:

And ye Christian princes, whosoever ye be,
If ye be destitute of a noble captayne,
Take James of Scotland for his audacitie
And proved manhood, if ye will laude attayne. . .

Yet this his manhood increaseth not his pride,
But ever sheweth he meknes and humilitie,
In word or dede, to hye and low degree.
(*laud* = praise, *meknes* = meekness, modesty)
(For the end of James IV, see *Flodden, Battle of.*)

James of Compostella, Saint: the saint whose
shrine in Galicia, north-east Spain, was one of
the greatest places of pilgrimage in the Middle
Ages and one visited, not only by countless poor
pilgrims, but by archbishops, kings, nobles,
knights and soldiers. Among them were a number
of people mentioned in this book, including The
Great Captain, Don John of Austria and Anthony
Woodville, 2nd Earl Rivers (see separate entries).
The special badge of Compostella was the scallop
shell, which is common along the Galician coast
and which often occurs in mediaeval pictures and
literature.

The road to Compostella from the passes in
the Pyrenees at Somport or Roncesvalles is one
of the most historic in Europe and has carried the
traffic of peaceful pilgrimage, the march of
armies, cavalcades of horsemen and the burdens
of merchandise for a thousand years. The earliest
travellers' guide book, produced by a Frenchman
in the Middle Ages, gives information about the
road and includes a vivid description of Compostella.

James of St. George, Master: chief castle-
builder to Edward I (1239–1307) and builder of
some of the finest examples known to military
architecture, including the great concentric
castles of Conway, Caernarvon and Beaumaris.

Jeanne d'Arc: see *Joan of Arc.*

Jehan de Saintré, le Petit: the hero of a
popular story, which may have had some foundation in fact, of the late Middle Ages. He found
favour as a page at the court of France, and also
with a beautiful young princess, the Dame des
Belles-Cousines. After an involved courtship, and
being dubbed knight by the king, Jehan set out
to win glory in the East. When he returned, he
found he had been supplanted in his lady's
affections by the abbot of a rich monastery, an
athletic, hard-riding type who devoted little time
to his duties as a churchman.

At a banquet in the abbey, the monk mocked at the world of knights and chivalric enterprise, saying that Jehan and his like were only courageous when they were inside a suit of armour with weapons in their hands; and, encouraged by the derisive laughter of the Dame des Belles-Cousines, he defied the knight to wrestle with him. Though this was an unfamiliar sport to Jehan de Saintré, he could not stomach the monk's insolence, and accepted the challenge. The company moved to a nearby meadow, where the well-practised abbot made short work of the knight, who was thrown time and time again, amidst the applause of the onlookers and the jeers of Jehan's lady-love.

De Saintré, hiding his shame and anger as best he could, invited the whole company to dine with him next day in his castle. The abbot came with the rest, and they partook merrily of the rich repast offered them. Afterwards, they admired some of the knightly appointments of the castle, the banners, weapons and glittering armour. Jehan pointed out a particularly large armour which he had stripped from a vanquished Saracen with his own hands, and remarked that only a man of great strength and stature, like the abbot, could wear it. Deceived by this cunning flattery, and persuaded by the Dame des Belles-Cousines, the vainglorious monk put on the Saracen harness, willingly helped by de Saintré. When the monk was well and truly encased and was strutting up and down before the company, the knight slipped into an adjoining chamber where his squire awaited him, and came back armed head-to-toe, followed by a herald carrying two shields and a selection of weapons.

'Yesterday,' said Jehan de Saintré, 'you challenged me to a combat in which you were experienced and I was not. Now the position is reversed and you can prove your strength and valour with my weapons.'

The rascally abbot, turned suddenly coward, tried hard to avoid the combat; but, cornered beyond escape, chose battle-axe and dagger as being most likely to suit his great strength. In a few minutes he had crashed to the ground, and de Saintré's axe was poised above his head while the Dame des Belles-Cousines implored the knight for mercy.

De Saintré spared the abbot, saying his blood was too base to be shed by one of knightly degree;

but, to prevent any further insults to those who followed the code of chivalry, slit his opponent's tongue with his dagger.

Jennet: a small horse, popular with ladies in the Middle Ages; sometimes used as a fighting horse in Spain, where the word originated.

> *A courser for the warrior,*
> *A rounsey for the squire,*
> *A sumpter for the baggage-train,*
> *A screwbald for the friar;*
>> *But I will braid the jennet*
>> *And shine the bridle-rein*
>> *For the riding of my lady*
>> *When she is home again.*

> *A destrier for jousting,*
> *A hackney for the maid,*
> *A palfrey for the princely one*
> *Who preens it on parade;*
>> *But I will gloss the jennet*
>> *That is cosy in the hay*
>> *For the riding of my lady*
>> *In the merry month of May.*

Jerusalem: the capital of the Latin kingdom of Jerusalem, and the city whose rescue from the hands of the infidel inspired the crusades, though the efforts to capture and hold it were strangely spasmodic and inefficient. More than once, the enemy offered to yield it up on certain conditions; in 1219, for example, the Sultan al-Kamil, nephew of Saladin, sent two captured knights with the proposal that, if the Christian armies would evacuate Egypt, they could occupy Jerusalem, Galilee and all central Palestine, as well as receiving back the True Cross. It is amazing that, for various reasons and amidst conflicting views from various sections of Christendom, the offer was refused.

Richard twice came within striking distance of the Holy City during the Third Crusade but, for reasons which had nothing to do with courage, withdrew. The chronicler Joinville gives a graphic picture of one occasion:

'While they were speaking . . . one of his knights cried:

"Sire, sire, come so far hither, and I will show you Jerusalem!"

And when the king heard this he threw his

Arms of Jerusalem

coat-armour [i.e., probably his shield] before his eyes, all in tears, and said to our Saviour: "Fair Lord God, I pray Thee suffer me not to see Thy Holy City since I cannot deliver it from the hands of Thine enemies!" '

In 1192, Richard made a treaty with Saladin which gave the coastal cities of Palestine as far south as Jaffa to the Christian armies and allowed crusaders and pilgrims to visit the Holy Places unarmed. Richard himself would not go. Jerusalem was temporarily recovered in 1229 and finally lost 15 years later. It was nearly seven hundred years before the city was entered again by a Christian army.

The arms of the Kingdom of Jerusalem consisted of five crosses – a large central cross potent surrounded by four plain crosses. The crosses are gold on a silver field – a rare example of one of the fixed rules of heraldry being broken, i.e., that metal may not be placed on metal. (See *Metal*.)

Jerusalem Chamber: the Chapter House of Westminster Abbey, London. It is said that Henry IV of England (1367–1413) was told he would die in Jerusalem. He did, in fact, go on pilgrimage to Jerusalem in 1392–3 and lived to tell the tale; but the ancient prophecy was fulfilled twenty years later when he died in the Jerusalem Chamber of the Abbey. In *Henry IV Part 2, IV, iv*, Shakespeare sets the scene near this Chamber and makes the king say:

Laud be to God! even there my life must end.
It hath been prophesied to me these many years
I should not die but in Jerusalem,
Which vainly I suppos'd the Holy Land.
But bear me to that chamber; there I'll lie:
In that Jerusalem shall Harry die.

So the king met his end in the same surroundings where, thirteen years before, he had come for his coronation with 'round his neck the order of the king of France . . . in a jacket . . . of cloth of gold, mounted on a white courser, with a blue garter on his left leg'; and where, in the nearby hall, the King's Champion had ridden, as they sat at dinner, 'completely armed, and mounted on a handsome steed, richly barded with crimson housings', to deliver the traditional challenge to any who would deny that Henry was the rightful sovereign.

Jesses: strips of leather, one to each leg, used to hold the falcon on the falconer's wrist.

Joan of Arc (Jeanne d'Arc): known as The Maid of Orleans (La Pucelle d'Orleans) or just The Maid (1412–1431) France's best-known figure of the Hundred Years' War, who appeared from the village of Domrémy at the age of 16, claiming a divine mission to lead the armies of France to victory. The chroniclers have given us the immortal story of how, when she was taken to meet the king for the first time, he put on common garb and hid himself among his brilliantly attired courtiers; and how, ascending the eighteen steps that led into the hall, the Maid unhesitatingly singled him out, fell on her knees 'the length of a lance' away and said, 'Dieu vous donne bonne vie, gentil Roi.' ('God give you good life, noble King.') In the face of the doubts with which she was received, she pleaded: 'Why do you not believe me? I tell you that God has pity on you, your kingdom and your people, for St. Louis and St. Charlemagne are on their knees before Him praying for you. If you will lend me men I will raise the siege of Orleans and I will lead you to be consecrated at Rheims, for it is the will of God that his enemies, the English, shall go back to their land and that the kingdom shall remain to you.'

In the end, her simplicity, directness and burning sincerity overcame the doubters and questioners. The king gave her a military entourage, including her two younger brothers, two noble pages, Louis de Contes and Raimond, and her personal squire, John d'Aulon. On April 27th, 1429, Joan left Blois to keep her promise and raise the siege of Orleans. It was a strongly fortified place, which had been besieged by the English for many months and was reaching a desperate condition for lack of supplies. The English army, under the Duke of Bedford, was itself in poor shape, worn down by a winter siege and weakened by desertion. Their troops were largely dispersed in some dozen siege towers outside the walls.

Joan began by sending a strange and unorthodox letter to the Duke of Bedford:

'In the name of Jesus and Mary – You, King of England; and you, Duke of Bedford, who call yourself Regent of France; you, William

de la Pole; you, Earl of Suffolk; you, John Lord Talbot; and you, Thomas Lord Scales, who call yourselves Lieutenants of the said Bedford, in the name of the King of Heaven, render the keys of all the good towns which you have taken and violated in France, to the Maid sent hither by the King of Heaven. She is ready to make peace if you will consent to return and pay for what you have taken. And all of you, soldiers, and archers, and men-at-arms, now before Orleans, return to your country, in God's name. If this is not done, King of England, I, as a leader in war, whenever I shall meet with your people in France, will oblige them to go whether they be willing or not; and if they go not, they will perish; but if they depart I will pardon them. I have come from the King of Heaven to drive you out of France. . . . If you will not obey, we shall make such a stir as hath not happened these thousand years in France. The Maid and her soldiers will have the victory.'

It is hardly surprising that the document was received with scorn and amusement. But Joan soon removed the smiles. On April 29th, having crossed a flooded river and accompanied by a light force of about 200 lances, she rode triumphantly through the streets of Orleans, with the delirious crowds hailing her and clinging to her knees and feet. Provisions, corn and cattle had been successfully brought through the English lines, and half the battle was won. But the English were still outside the walls, and must be dealt with.

The French were by this time in so much better heart that one of their leaders, Dunois, said that, whereas it had previously needed only 200 Englishmen to put 800 of the French to flight, now 500 Frenchmen were prepared to take on the whole English army.

By May 8th, after a series of skirmishes and engagements, the English were pulling out. Joan had not gone unscathed. In the course of one six-hour attack, when she had herself helped raise one of the scaling-ladders, she was seriously wounded between shoulder and neck by a bolt from a cross-bow and had to be carried from the fight. But, hearing that a French retreat might be ordered, she rallied her reserves of strength, insisted on remounting her horse, and flung herself again into the battle, not resting till darkness had fallen and victory was assured.

When the news of the deliverance of Orleans reached Paris on May 10th, a clerk noted the event in his official register and, in the margin, made a little sketch of a woman in armour, holding in one hand a banner and in the other a sword. It is still treasured among the national archives of France.

Joan had three banners. The largest carried a representation of God enthroned in Heaven, holding in one hand a globe, and flanked by two kneeling angels with golden fleurs-de-lys in their hands. A smaller triangular standard showed the Annunciation, and a third small banner was emblazoned with the Crucifixion. The Maid treasured her banners, she said, forty times more than her sword, for with the former she could wound no-one. There is, in fact, no record that, in all her fighting, she ever herself shed blood.

Records of her appearance are very scanty. Her esquire, Jean d'Aulon, described her as 'a beautiful and well-formed girl.' Another French knight, Guy de Laval, wrote a letter to his mother on June 8th, 1429, describing how he saw her mount 'all in white armour but unhelmeted, a small steel sperth [a little battle-axe] in her hand. She had a great black horse, which plunged at the door of her house, and would not permit her to mount. "Lead him to the Cross!" she cried. It stands in front of the church. There he stood as fast as if he were bound with cords, and she mounted and, turning towards the church gate, she said in a sweet womanly voice, "Ye priests and churchmen, go in processions and pray to God!" '

Most pictures show Joan as fair-haired, but she was probably dark. This is stated by one chronicler and, in one letter she wrote, embedded in the seal, perhaps intentionally, is a black hair.

Her wonderful career was short. After fulfilling her two-fold mission, to relieve Orleans and have the king crowned in Rheims, she had some other successes, including the Battle of Patay, in 1429. She was captured on May 25th, 1430 and, a little over a year later, burnt as a witch at Rouen. She was just over 19 years old, and her military career lasted thirteen months.

Joan of Kent (1328–1385): 'The Fair Maid of

Kent', daughter of Edmund of Woodstock, Earl of Kent, and reckoned one of the most beautiful women of her age. She married, as her second husband, Edward the Black Prince. (See separate entry.) It was her garter, dropped by accident at a ball in Calais, that was bound round his knee by Edward III and taken as the badge of the Order of the Garter. (See *Blue Garter, Order of*). As Countess of Salisbury, she had been present at the Battle of Neville's Cross, 1346, and it was probably her Froissart describes as moving among the king's forces, 'desiring them to do their devoir to defend the honour of her lord the king of England and, in the name of God, every man to be of good heart and courage.' (See also *Edward, Prince of Wales; Blue Garter, Order of;* and *Neville's Cross, Battle of.*)

Jockey of Norfolk: Sir John Howard, 1st Duke of Norfolk (1430?–1485), Knight of the Garter and Earl Marshal of England. (See *Norfolk, Dukes of* for further particulars of this family.)

Sir John was a faithful adherent of the ill-starred Richard III and, before the Battle of Bosworth in 1485, which ended the Yorkist line and brought the Tudors to the throne of England, found a warning note in his tent:

Jockey of Norfolk, be not too bold,
For Dickon thy master is bought and sold.

Howard disregarded the advice, and fell in the battle along with his king. 'Jockey' at that time had nothing like its modern associations, but was a diminutive form of 'John'. 'Dickon' was a nickname for Richard.

John of Bohemia, King (d. 1346): one of the bravest knights of his age and the hero of one of the most moving episodes in the wars between France and England. The king was blind, but refused to sit at home while his peers were fighting. He came with the rest of Europe's chivalry to the Battle of Crécy (see separate entry) having already predicted that he would fall in battle, fighting against the bravest knights in the world.

John said to his companions: 'Gentlemen, you are all my people, my friends and brethren at arms this day: therefore, as I am blind, I request of you to lead me so far into the engagement that I may strike one stroke with my sword.'

His gallant company said they would lead him

forward and, to avoid losing him in the press of men, they fastened all their reins together and rode into battle, the king at their head. The next day they were found as they had fallen, the reins still joined. Edward III and the Black Prince attended in person the burial of this valiant enemy.

John II of France (1319–1364): called 'the Good', but not because of any sterling worth of character. He was a violent, courageous and extravagant man who is said, at one period of great national need, to have given 50,000 crowns to one of his knights.

He was the chief captive at the Battle of Poitiers in 1356 (see separate entry) and was treated with the greatest honour, the Black Prince waiting on him at table and refusing to sit with him, saying he 'was not worthy of such an honour, nor did it appertain to him to seat himself at the table of so great a king, or of so valiant a man as he had shewn himself by his actions that day.'

There was confusion and some undignified squabbling about the king's capture, two of the Gascon squires who had fought on the side of the English, Denys de Morbeque and Bernard de Trouttes, declaring an equal right to him. They had got to the stage of arranging to fight each other when the Prince arrested them to let them cool down. King John himself supported the claim of de Morbeque, so the Prince ordered that 2,000 nobles (gold coins worth about 6s. 8d. each) should be paid him privately 'in order to enable him the better to support his rank.' Much more serious trouble threatened from the Gascon barons when they learnt that the Prince proposed to take his royal prisoner to London, where Edward III was anxious to see him. Eventually a payment of 100,000 gold florins, to be divided amongst them, seems to have quieted them.

With an escort of 500 men at arms and 2,000 archers, John was brought across the Channel and, after eleven days and nights at sea, landed at Sandwich. Elaborate preparations were made in London, and the French king rode through the streets of a richly caparisoned white horse, with the Black Prince beside him on a 'little black hackney.' Even the choice of steeds was a chivalric compliment to the high rank and reputation of the prisoner. His captivity must

John of
Austria

have been one of the most easy and luxurious on record. In every place he was lodged he was royally entertained and pursued any sport and entertainment he fancied. His son Philip accompanied him, and they were often visited by the French lords who had also been brought to England. But in the end he tired of it all, and arranged to pay as his personal ransom the sum of 4,000,000 crowns and to give up half France to the English king. But Paris would have none of this treaty, declaring that John would have to remain in England and that God, when He saw fit, would provide a remedy.

The ransom was later reduced to 3,000,000 gold crowns and a rather smaller slice of France; and, as a guarantee, the French king left a number of important hostages in England, including his son, the Duke of Anjou. John made a last grand gesture, more worthy than some of his acts. After his return to France, he heard that the Duke of Anjou had broken his parole and escaped. Holding himself dishonoured by this action, King John voluntarily came back to London in his son's place. A French historian says the subsequent fêtes and banquets killed him. He died in London in 1364.

As well as the two Gascon squires mentioned above, many others claimed some share in the king's capture, including at least two Englishmen, Sir John Pelham and Sir Roger de la Warre. Pelham's descendants, the Duke of Newcastle, the Earl of Chichester and the Earl of Yarborough, still bear as part of their arms King John II's sword-buckle and belt. Burke's Peerage records that Sir Roger de la Warre 'had, in commemoration of so valiant an exploit, the crampet, or chape, of the captive prince's sword.' He took this as a badge, with the letter 'r' for 'rex'. Though this badge, displayed by Sir Roger, no longer seems to figure in the arms of Earl de la Warr, the motto *Jour de ma vie*, in celebration of Roger's great day, still survives.

John of Austria, Don (1547–1578): Spanish soldier, brother to King Philip II of Spain. In the biggest naval battle of the century in the Mediterranean, he overwhelmingly defeated a great fleet of Turkish galleys, releasing thereby hundreds of Christian captives used as slaves at the oars. G. K. Chesterton, in his great battle-

148

poem 'Lepanto', calls Don John 'the last knight of Europe.'

> *Dim drums throbbing on the hills half heard*
> *Where only on a nameless throne a crownless*
> *   prince has stirred,*
> *Where, risen from a doubtful seat and half*
> *   attainted stall,*
> *The last knight of Europe takes weapons from*
> *   the wall,*
> *The last and lingering troubadour to whom the*
> *   bird has sung,*
> *That once went singing southward when all the*
> *   world was young.*
> *In that enormous silence, tiny and unafraid,*
> *Comes up along a winding road the noise of the*
> *   Crusade.*
> *Strong gongs groaning as the guns boom far,*
> *Don John of Austria is going to the war,*
> *Stiff flags straining in the night-blasts cold,*
> *In the gloom black-purple, in the glint old-gold,*
> *Torchlight crimson on the copper kettle-drums,*
> *Then the tuckets, then the trumpets, then the*
> *   cannon, and he comes –*
> *Don John laughing in the brave beard curled,*
> *Spurning of his stirrups like the thrones of all*
> *   the world,*
> *Holding his head up for a flag of all the free,*
> *Love-light of Spain – hurrah!*
> *Death-light of Africa!*
> *Don John of Austria*
> *Is riding to the sea.*

John of Gaunt, Duke of Lancaster (1340–1399): so called from his birth-place, Ghent. The fourth son of Edward III, he won some early distinction as a soldier, serving with the Black Prince. But he is probably most remembered, not so much for his chequered career, but for the famous speech Shakespeare puts into his mouth in *Richard the Second*. The twenty lines beginning 'This royal throne of kings, this scepter'd isle' are among the best known in literature. They include:

> *This blessed plot, this earth, this realm,*
> *   this England,*
> *This nurse, this teeming womb of royal kings,*
> *Fear'd by their breed and famous by their birth,*
> *Renowned for their deeds as far from home –*

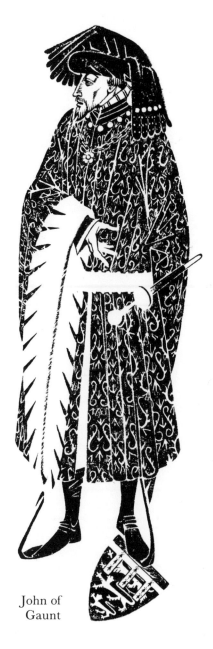

John of
Gaunt

For Christian service and true chivalry –
As is the sepulchre in stubborn Jewry
Of the world's ransom, blessed Mary's son.

Joinville, Jean de (1225–1317): a French chronicler, of noble family, who took part in the First Crusade and wrote down his recollections of it in his old age. He gives a vivid picture of how he set out for the Holy Land:

'At Easter, in the year of grace that stood at 1248, I summoned my men, and all who held fiefs from me, to Joinville . . . All that week we feasted and danced, and my brother, the Lord of Vaucouleurs, and the other rich men who were there, gave feasts on the Monday, the Tuesday, the Wednesday and the Thursday.

'On the Friday I said to them: "Lords, I am going oversea, and I know not whether I shall ever return. Now come forward; if I have done you any wrong, I will make it good, as I have been used to do. . . ." Because I did not wish to take away with me any penny wrongly gotten, therefore I went to Metz, in Lorraine, and placed in pawn the greater part of my land. And you must know that on the day when I left our country to go to the Holy Land, I did not hold more than one thousand livres a year in land [perhaps about £800], for my lady mother was still alive; and yet I went, taking with me nine knights and being the first of three knights-banneret. . . .

'The Abbot of Cheminon gave me my scarf and staff of pilgrimage; and then I departed from Joinville on foot, barefoot, in my shirt – not to re-enter the castle till my return . . . And never . . . would I turn my eyes towards Joinville for fear my heart should melt within me at the thought of the fair castle I was leaving behind, and my two children.'

Joinville was six years in the Holy Land. His great hero was Louis IX of France, afterwards St. Louis, in whose company he spent most of his time as a crusader. Fifteen or sixteen years after Joinville's return from Palestine Louis and the King of Navarre pressed him to take the Cross again; but he refused on the grounds that it would be more pleasing to God for him to stay at home and defend his own impoverished people, who had suffered greatly during his former absence.

Jongleurs: wandering minstrels and tellers of stories in the Middle Ages, especially in northern France. They were welcome guests at the feast and at entertainments in the great hall of the castle. Singing, reciting or, later, just reading, their subjects were the warlike deeds, the adventures and loves of old-time heroes. They also spread the current news and political gossip.

When Margaret of France married Edward I of England in 1299, £40 were distributed to the English minstrels and £60 to the French. John Mautravers, who harped before Edward on the Feast of the Epiphany, 1305, received 20 shillings, probably equivalent to at least fifteen times that amount in modern money. There are numbers of recorded payments of twice that amount, which is some indication of the high value put on their services. Many of these minstrels were professionals in the train of some noble, and casual wanderers would not expect to do quite as well.

Joust: properly speaking, single combat between knights or squires. (See *Free Course, Italian Course, Joust à l'Outrance. Joust à Plaisance, Tilt, Tourney* and *Tournament.*)

Joust à l'Outrance: a joust to the bitter end, i.e., till the opponent was forced to surrender, wounded or killed. It was fought with the sharp lance or spear. (See *Joust à Plaisance* and *Coronel.*)

Joust à Plaisance: course run 'for the fun of it', with a blunted lance or one fitted with a special head. (See *Coronel.*)

Jousting Cheques: strips of paper or parchment on which points scored by combatants were recorded by the officials controlling the jousts. The score was kept by pricks or by short marks rather like those used in a cricket score-book. Few have survived, but the College of Arms, in London, has an interesting collection. The earliest of these date from 1501 and were kept at the celebrations attending the marriage of Prince Arthur, eldest son of Henry VII, to Katherine of Aragon.

Joyous Gard (Joyeuse-Garde or Garde-Joyeuse): Sir Launcelot's (or Lancelot's) favourite castle; according to different versions of

the Arthurian stories, 'won with his own hands' or given to him as a reward by King Arthur. Some early writers identified it with Alnwick Castle, or Bamborough Castle, both in Northumberland.

Jugglers: like minstrels, though on a lower level, favourite entertainers in the Middle Ages, at castle, court and fairground.

Jupon: sleeveless outer garment, popular till about 1410–20, worn over armour and to be seen on countless brasses and knightly effigies. It was fairly close-fitting and reached from the neck to the thighs. Made of several thicknesses of material, the outer layer was often of some rich material such as velvet or silk, worked with the arms of the wearer.

Kay, Sir: in the Arthurian stories, the son of Sir Ector and foster-brother of King Arthur, who made him his seneschal or chief steward. Kay pretended he had plucked the sword from the stone in the churchyard (see *Excalibur*) and thereby claimed the kingship, but was soon forced to confess that he had it from Arthur.

'And therewithal Sir Ector kneeled down to the earth, and Sir Kay . . .

"Sir," said Ector unto Arthur, "will ye be my good and gracious lord when ye are king?"

"Else were I to blame," said Arthur, "for ye are the man in the world that I am most beholding to . . . And if ever it be God's will that I be king, as ye say, ye shall desire of me what I may do, and I shall not fail you."

"Sir," said Sir Ector, "I will ask of you no more but that you will make my son, your foster-brother, Sir Kay, seneschal of all your lands." '

Keep: the main tower or stronghold of the mediaeval castle, with walls of great thickness. At Dover, for example, they are up to 24 feet thick. A good early example is the Keep or Great Tower of the Tower of London, which is the earliest part of the building and which gave its name to the whole structure. The chief architect was Gundulf, a monk of Bec, in Normandy, who afterwards became Bishop of Rochester, where he also exercised his skill as a builder.

The keep was usually the chief residence of the castle, as well as the main fortress, and was often divided into several floors, providing storage space, offices for the administration of business, private apartments, sleeping quarters and a chapel. It also guarded the well that was the main water supply. Many of the finest keeps are square, but, to make it more difficult for sappers to undermine the corner stones, later builders developed the round or cylindrical keep. One of the best examples of this is at Pembroke.

Kenilworth Castle: a 12th century castle in Warwickshire, now largely ruined. Unlike some of the more elaborate examples (see above), its strong tower keep had only one floor above the basement. In the 14th century, the castle became more of a princely palace than a plain fortress, and John of Gaunt added a great banqueting

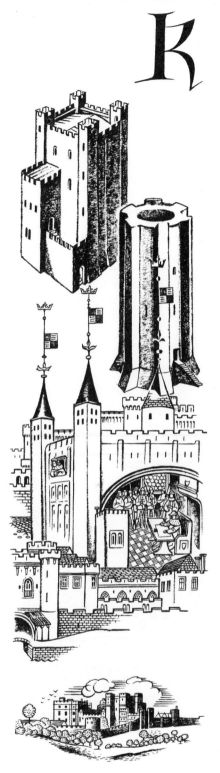

L

hall. Another famous owner, mentioned in this book, was Simon de Montfort. The castle was the scene of a magnificent entertainment given in 1575 to Queen Elizabeth by Robert Dudley, Earl of Leicester.

In the Birmingham City Museum and Art Gallery are six bronze horse terrets (or small 'turrets' of bells which jingled above their heads) engraved and enamelled with the arms of Henry, Earl of Lancaster (1281?–1345), grandson of Henry III. They were dug up at Kenilworth in the 19th century and are a striking reminder of troublous times more than 600 years ago, when Henry of Lancaster had charge of the captured Edward II at Kenilworth Castle.

Kestrel: a small species of hawk or falcon, the commonest in England. It is one of the *long-wings* or *hawks of the lure* and was popular with falconers because of its friendliness and ease of training. It is often called the 'Hover Hawk' because of its remarkable skill in remaining suspended in the air with only its wing-tips quivering.

Kettle-hat: plain iron hat with a broad brim, popular in Europe up to the middle of the 15th century.

Kidney dagger: type of dagger in use over a long period, so-called from the kidney-shaped lobes at the base of the handle.

Kildare, John FitzThomas, 1st Earl of (d. 1316): an Irish soldier who served Edward I in the Scottish wars. Some of his descendants, e.g., the Dukes of Leinster, carry a chained ape as a crest and similar animals as supporters to their shield of arms. The long-established tradition is that when FitzThomas was an infant in the Castle of Woodstock, near Athy, in County Kildare, a serious fire broke out. In the confusion, the baby was overlooked and, when the panic-stricken servants came to look for him, they found the chamber burnt out and in ruins. Then they heard a strange sound from one of the castle towers and, looking up, saw an ape, which was usually kept chained in the household, high up with the infant safely in his arms. When he grew to manhood, the earl adopted an ape for his crest in gratitude.

Kildare, Thomas, 10th Earl of (1513–1537): known as 'Silken Thomas', from the silk fringes on the helmets of his retainers. He packed a lifetime of action and adventure into his short 24 years. He threw off his allegiance to Henry VIII and for a time outwitted all attempts to capture him. When he finally surrendered in Ireland, he was brought to London with the promise that he would receive a full pardon; instead of which he was executed at Tyburn with five of his uncles.

Kilhwch: a cousin of King Arthur's in an early Welsh version of the stories. (See *Mabinogion.*) The poetic description of him tells how he rode forth on:

'. . . a steed with head dappled grey, of four winters old, firm of limb, with shell-formed hoofs, having a bridle of linked gold on his head, and upon him a saddle of costly gold. And in the youth's hand were two spears of silver, sharp, well-tempered, headed with steel, three ells in length, of an edge to wound the wind, and cause blood to flow, and swifter than the fall of the dew-drop from the blade of reed-grass upon the earth when the dew of June is at the heaviest. A gold-hilted sword was upon his thigh, the blade of which was of gold, bearing a cross of inlaid gold of the hue of the lightning of heaven; his war-horn was of ivory. Before him were two brindled white-breasted greyhounds, having strong collars of rubies about their necks, reaching from the shoulder to the ear. And the one that was on the left bounded across to the right side, and the one on the right to the left, and like two sea-swallows sported around him. And his courser cast up four sods with his four hoofs, like four swallows in the air, about his head, now above, now below.'

In the course of time, Kilhwch met Olwen, who was destined to be his faithful bride, and was a fitting match in appearance:

'The maiden was clothed in a robe of flame-coloured silk, and about her neck was a collar of ruddy gold, on which were precious emeralds and rubies. More yellow was her head than the flower of the broom, and her skin was whiter than the foam of the wave, and fairer were her hands and her fingers than the blossoms of the wood anemone amidst the spray of the meadow

fountain. The eye of the trained hawk, the glance of the three-mewed falcon was not brighter than hers... Four white trefoils sprung up wherever she trod.'

King Cole: the 'merry old soul' of the nursery rhyme. Traditionally, the father of the Empress Helena, who was credited with having discovered the True Cross in the Holy Land. The legends are enshrined in the arms of Colchester, Essex – a ragged silver cross and three gold crowns on a red field.

King-maker, the: see *Neville, Richard, Earl of Warwick.*

Kings of Arms: the three officers who, under the Earl Marshal, exercise supreme authority in English heraldry. Their responsibilities are divided thus:

Garter King of Arms: presides over the College of Arms.

Clarenceux King of Arms: heraldic affairs south of the River Trent.

Norroy King of Arms: heraldic affairs north of the River Trent.

The office of Garter King of Arms was instituted by Henry V. Previously, Clarenceux seems to have been the principal officer, taking his name from the Duke of Clarence, third son of Edward III. The title Norroy means 'North Roy' or 'North King' and dates from the same period.

In Scotland, the chief heraldic authority is the Lord Lyon King of Arms.

(For other officers, see *Officers of Arms.*)

Kite-shaped Shield: early form of the knightly shield, used by the Norman cavalry and throughout the Norman period. It was more serviceable than the round shield in that it guarded the upper part of the body with the widest part, and tapered downward to protect the left leg. It was normally of wood, covered with leather or parchment, and sometimes with metal reinforcements.

Knee-cops (or caps): see *Genouillières.*

Knevynton, Sir Ralph de: the subject of a well-known brass (date 1370) in the church at Avely, Essex. It has many unusual features, including an unconventional pose for the figure of the knight, a long pointed hauberk, and a misericorde of extraordinary length. (See *Hauberk* and *Misericorde*.)

Knight: usually, one who had served an apprenticeship as page and squire and then been admitted to an honourable degree of military rank, often by means of a special ceremony. (See *Accolade, Damoiseau, Dubbing, Ordaining* and *Parrain*.)

The young boy spent much of his early years with nurses and the womenfolk. But he was soon given a pony and brought to look upon the horse as an indispensable part of his life and education. At about the age of ten or twelve, the boy of noble birth reached the first important milestone in his career, when he was sent to join the household of some great lord to receive a thorough training in the ways of courtly behaviour and the management of horse and weapons. For those with enough influence, the king's court was the highest 'school' of all; but famous knights who had proved their worth and valour were much sought-after. (See, e.g., *Henry of Lancaster*.)

After a short period, if he made satisfactory progress, the aspirant to knighthood became a squire, and put on silver spurs. He would be assigned to a knight as master and would become virtually an all-round servant, waiting on him at the table, tending his armour and weapons, dressing him, leading his horses, fighting at his side in battle and supplying him with fresh arms if need be. It was a hard and thorough training and some squires won a great reputation. (See e.g., the four squires of *Sir James Audley*.)

About the age of seventeen to twenty came the great day when the silver spurs were exchanged for the golden, or gilded, spurs of knighthood. The knighting ceremony could take place in the peaceful, holiday atmosphere of the castle greensward, witnessed by a colourful crowd of womenfolk and other squires and knights; or in the grimmer, more practical surroundings of the field of battle. In the most elaborate ceremonies, the rite was shared, one man girding on the sword, another the spurs, while the knighter gave the squire a cuff on the neck or a blow with the sword. There was also a picturesque ecclesiastic form of knighting, when the squire laid his arms

on the church altar and kept his vigil there all night. A ceremonial bath was sometimes taken as symbolic of the purity of the vows the knight was taking. This is the origin of the name of the Order of the Bath. The ceremony could take place in the church itself, with a bishop acting as parrain, or knighter. It is not always realized that every knight had the right of making knights.

Most squires and knights were of gentle birth, and the criticism is often levelled at the system of chivalry that it was restricted to a select class. But it was not, in fact, exclusive. Peasants, tradesmen and common soldiers could climb the ladder to knighthood. The entry on *Italian Armour* shows that a famous armourer became a knight. Sir John Hawkwood, the famous captain of free-lances who became ambassador for England in several Italian states, began life as a tailor. Sir Robert Knollys was another who rose from the ranks (see *Hawkwood* and *Knollys*).

It is important to realize the difference between the personal honour of knighthood and holding land by 'knight service.' In early times the tenant paid for his land by fighting, when required, for his overlord or for the king; but by a later arrangement he could pay in cash instead of going to the war (see *Scutage*). As soon as this system arose, it was possible for a man to render 'knight service' who was not a knight at all in the chivalric sense and had no thought of ever becoming one. Indeed, there were often occasions when gentlemen wondered whether, despite all the show and glamour, it was worth being made a knight. For it became an increasingly expensive business to equip oneself properly with armour and horses and to maintain a suitable show.

It was, however, to the king's advantage to be able to put as many well-equipped knights as possible into the field. This is probably why they thought up, from time to time, splendid attractions like new orders of knighthood, sometimes held mass knightings, and even occasionally bore the expenses themselves. In 1252, when Henry III's daughter Margaret married Alexander III of Scotland, the English king knighted Alexander and 20 other young men at the same time. The same king, on another occasion, knighted more than 50 English and foreign nobles. Edward I, when he knighted the 22-year-old Prince of Wales in 1306, proclaimed that any who wished to receive this honour with the prince should present themselves in London, and that the king would pay for the ceremony. As a result, 267 squires turned up with their own horses and armour, and Edward I supplied their knightly robes and a glittering feast into the bargain.

Knight Bachelor: the oldest class of knight, a member of 'the bachelery of England'; usually a landless knight who had won his spurs but was not a member of any order of chivalry; or a young knight following the banner of another.

In modern times it means a man given the honour of knighthood for some service to the crown or the community, but whose title does not descend to other members of his family. There is an Imperial Society of Knights Bachelor which, in 1965, established in the ancient church of St. Bartholomew-the-Great, Smithfield – the oldest of London's parish churches – a special shrine as a 'spiritual home to be a symbol of the inspiration of the Chivalry from which knighthood itself derives.'

Knight Banneret: sometimes a knight of high standing who led others to war under his own banner; but also a knight created on the field of battle, in which case the king or knighter often cut off the tail of the long pennon to make it a square banner as a symbol of the new rank.

Knight-errant: a wandering knight, seeking romantic adventure and the opportunity to display his prowess.

Knight of the Leopard: one of the chief characters of Sir Walter Scott's novel *The Talisman*, which deals with Richard Coeur-de-Lion, Saladin and the Third Crusade. In this romance, the Knight of the Leopard is David, Earl of Huntingdon, prince royal of Scotland, who accompanies Richard disguised and under an assumed name. (See *Talisman*.)

Scott was following a favourite custom of the writers of early romances in giving this sort of fanciful name to a knight. Examples are:

The Knight of the Ebon Spear
   (Britomart in *The Faerie Queene*)
The Knight of the Invincible Sword
   (Amadis of Gaul)

The Knight of the Silver Keys
  (Pierre of Provence)
The Knight of the Sun
  (Almanzoe, Prince of Tunis)
The Knight of Two Swords
  (Sir Balin, in Malory's *King Arthur*)
The Knight of the White Moon
  (Samson Carrasco, in *Don Quixote*)

Knight of the Tower: see *La Tour Landry, Geffroi de.*

Knight's Fee: a portion of land held by a knight in return for military service to his overlord. As is pointed out in the entry for *Knight* this is a different thing from the knighthood of chivalry, which has nothing to do with the ownership of land or legal service due to an overlord. Under William the Conqueror, the land was parcelled out among his followers, who could sub-let pieces of their estates into perhaps 6,000 or 7,000 knight's fees, all of which were bound to supply a fixed number of knights and men for the wars.

Knighthood, Degradation from: the severest punishment that could be inflicted on a knight and one resorted to only in extreme cases. Few examples, therefore, have survived. In 1464, Sir Ralph Grey, for his part in a rebellion against Edward IV, was sentenced by the Constable of England to be degraded. His coat of arms was torn from his back and another, with his arms reversed, put in its place. The reversal of a coat of arms was an accepted sign of disgrace.

In 1621, Sir Giles Mompesson and Sir Francis Mitchell were tried before the House of Lords for the political offence of exercising harsh 'monopolies' over the licensing of inns and the manufacture of gold and silver thread. Both were degraded.

'Sir Francis's sword and gilt spurs, being the ornaments of Knighthood, were taken from him, broken and defaced, thus indicating that the reputation he held thereby, together with the honourable title of Knight, should be no more used. One of the Knight Marshal's men . . .cut the belt whereby the culprit's sword hung, and so let it fall to the ground. Next the spurs were hewn off his heels and thrown, one one way, the other the other.

After that, the Marshal's attendant drew Mitchell's sword from the scabbard and broke it over his head, doing with the fragments as with the spurs.' (Sir Bernard Burke, Ulster King of Arms.)

In the case of members of knightly orders, such as the Garter, the banner and stall-plate are removed from the Chapel.

Knighthood, Orders of: see *Blue Garter, Golden Fleece, St. Michael & St. George, Thistle.* For Order of the Bath, see *Henry VII's Chapel* and *Knight.*

Knights Hospitallers: see *Knights of St. John of Jerusalem.*

Knights of Malta: see *Knights of St. John of Jerusalem.*

Knights of Rhodes: see *Knights of St. John of Jerusalem.*

Knights of St. John of Jerusalem: one of the great monastic orders of knighthood, which gradually took on more of a military character, particularly as a result of the Crusades. They have a bewildering series of names, owing to their changes of headquarters, beginning as the Hospitallers or Knights Hospitallers, because their chief duty was to guard and entertain pilgrims to the Holy Sepulchre. It is recorded that in 1112 their Hospital or monastery could accommodate 2,000 guests as well as providing for the sick. The monastery was dedicated to St. John the Baptist, so that, from about 1120–1314, they were known as the Knights of St. John of Jerusalem. When they were dispossessed there, they took the Island of Rhodes as headquarters and with it their next name, the Knights of Rhodes. Finally, they moved to Malta in 1530 and became known as the Knights of Malta.

The knights took monastic vows, followed the rule of St. Augustine and wore a black habit with a white cross. At the height of their power, especially in the East, they were a magnificent organization, building great castles (see e.g., *Krak des Chevaliers*), barracks for their knights and soldiers, hospitals for sick and aged knights, rest houses and recruiting stations. They enlisted many noble-minded men and offered a hard life

161

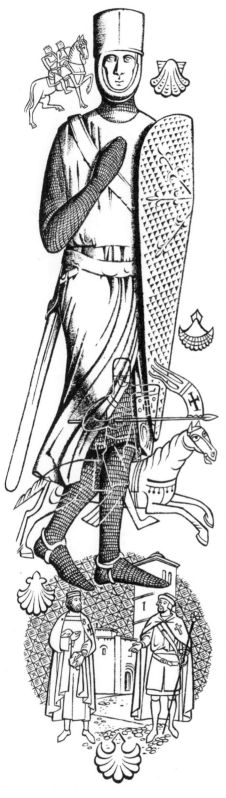

of genuine endeavour, as compared with many of the orders of knighthood associated with courts, socially brilliant but with little of spartan discipline and self-denial about them.

The Hospitallers established communities in various European countries, including England, where they arrived in about 1100. Each manor or commandery was under a preceptor, who was answerable to the Prior of the Order, who lived at Clerkenwell in great state and ranked as a baron of the realm. In the middle of the 14th century there were three main classes in the English commanderies – the knights, the chaplains and the esquires, or serjeants-at-arms.

Hospitality, in accordance with its origins, was always one of the first obligations of the Order. The accounts of the Prior's establishment at Clerkenwell for the year 1338 include as a general item:

'. . . much expenditure which cannot be given in detail, caused by the hospitality offered to strangers, members of the royal family, and to other grandees of the realm who stay at Clerkenwell and remain there at the cost of the house.'

The account closes: 'Thus the expenditure exceeds the receipts by twenty-one pounds, eleven shillings and fourpence'!

The total membership in England was only about 120. The Order was suppressed by order of Henry VIII in about 1540. In May, 1888, under a royal charter from Queen Victoria, the Order of the Hospital of St. John of Jerusalem was constituted as a restoration of the old religious and military order. The knight's mantle is still of black silk with, on the left side, a Maltese cross of white linen. The Order is closely connected with hospital and ambulance work, and it issues a Life-Saving Medal. (See also end of next entry.)

Knights Templars: the second (see above) of the great religious-military orders founded in the early 12th century for the protection of pilgrims and the defence of the Holy Sepulchre. The knights adopted the monastic rule of the Benedictines and wore a white mantle with a red cross. Like the Hospitallers, they rose to considerable power and established houses in many countries. Their headquarters in England were first in Holborn and then, from 1185, in Fleet Street.

162

The superior officer was called the Master of the Temple and was often summoned to Parliament. Their great Church, circular in form like the Church of the Holy Sepulchre and containing fine Crusader brasses such as that of William Mareschal, or Marshal (see separate entry) and Sir Geoffrey de Magnaville, was severely damaged by bombing in the second World War. Its restoration was completed in 1958.

The Order adopted much the same sort of organization as that of the Hospitallers, but it seems to have earned much greater envy and enmity, because of its greed and its activities as banker and money-lender. By the beginning of the 14th century, accusations of corruption, vice and heresy in the Order were widespread.

In October, 1307, Philip of France had all members of the Order in France arrested and put on trial. Within a few months Pope Clement V gave orders for the same action in every country where the Templars had property. The subsequent proceedings against an Order which, whatever its later faults, had fought valiantly for the Cross and faithfully supported the Pope, were a disgrace to Christendom. Members were put to the torture and burnt at the stake. Among those who suffered the extreme penalty was the Grand Master, Jacques de Bourg-Moulay, who was roasted on the island of the Seine 'in the light of the setting sun.' 45 Templars were burnt in one day in Paris.

In England, the Order was suppressed without these barbaric cruelties. The property of the Order was handed over to the Hospitallers, and many of the knights entered monasteries.

The main problem of the great military Orders was that, with the passing of the Crusades, their usefulness was outlived and their energies could become misdirected; so that, with their great wealth and military strength, particularly if they chose to unite, they could prove a menace to the nations of Europe. This is why rulers chose to strip them of their power and influence; and why they became a shadow of their former selves, both in their ideals and in their strength to achieve them. But the old flame could still burn.

Writing in the last century, Sir Edward Strachey said:

'The last expiring token of the old spirit in the old forms which I have found, is in the

records of the Knights of Malta – the Knights Hospitallers of St. John of Jerusalem – when the news of the great earthquake in Sicily, in 1783, arrived at Malta. Then those poor feeble-minded sybarites remembered for a moment their manhood and their knighthood, and their vows as Hospitallers; they manned their galleys, and, with food and clothing and medicines, and the consolations of their faith, were speedily seen, in their half-military, half-priestly garb – the armour covered by the black robe with the white cross – at the bed-sides of the wounded and the dying, as they lay amid the still tottering ruins of their devastated houses.'

Knights, Teutonic: the Knights of the Virgin Mary, or Teutonic Knights of the Hospital of St. Mary the Virgin. A third important religious-military Order, founded at the Siege of Acre in 1190. As its name implies, it was German in origin. Its knights wore a white mantle with a black cross. They took the vow of poverty, chastity and obedience and were originally con-cerned with the care and protection of German pilgrims. In the 13th century they turned their energies from the Holy Land to the conquest of the heathen Prussians and conquered the terri-tory between the Vistula and the Memel, ruling it from great castles. The headquarters of the Grand Master was, at various times, in Venice, Marienburg and Königsberg. With terrible irony, the Order received a virtual death-blow in a battle against Christian forces, when its knights were smashed by the Poles and Lithuanians at Tannenberg in 1410. It struggled on till its re-maining possessions were seized by Napoleon in 1809.

Knights, Various Orders of: It would be impossible to list, let alone give details of, all the Orders of Knighthood which have been estab-lished for one purpose or another, most of them eminently worthy, through the centuries. They include such curiosities as the Dog and Cock, the Palm and Alligator, the Fools, the Bee, the Scarf and the Broom Flowers, the Slaves of Virtue and Neighbourly Love; and such colour-fully named organizations as the Angelic Knights, the Dove of Castile, the Golden Shield, the Lily

164

of Navarre, the Palatine Lion, the Thistle of Bourbon, the White Falcon and the Wing of St. Michael. There have been a number of female Orders, the first woman knights being, it is said, those who defended Tortosa (province of Tarragona, Spain) against the Moors in 1149.

Knollys (Knolles), Sir Robert (d. 1407): one of the most distinguished knights and commanders of the 14th century. Two of the great soldiers he served with were Edward, the Black Prince and Henry of Lancaster, and he had the distinction of capturing the famous Bertrand du Guesclin in 1359. (See separate entries for all these names.) He seems to have been of humble origin and served as an ordinary soldier, then rose to be a captain of free lances 'who conquered every town and castle he came to' and gained a great fortune from plunder. Froissart records how the Black Prince, out of love for him and as a reward for his valour, 'appointed him captain of the knights and squires of his household. . . He ordered them to pay Sir Robert the same obedience as to himself, which they promised willingly to do.'

He later spent much of his wealth on charitable works, including 'a goodly fair bridge' over the River Medway at Rochester, with a chapel and chantry at the eastern end, and a hospital at Rome for English travellers and pilgrims.

(See also *Knollys' Mitres.*)

Knollys' Mitres: 'Being sent general of an army into France, in despite of their power, he [Sir Robert Knollys] drove the people before him like sheep, destroying towns, castles, and cities in such manner and number that, long after, in memory of this act, the sharp points and gable ends of overthrown houses and minsters were called Knolles' Mitres,' (John Weever, 1631.)

Knyvet, Sir Thomas: one of the three knights who, with the king himself, held the lists at the great Westminster Tournament of February, 1511, staged to celebrate the birth of a son, Henry, Duke of Cornwall, to Queen Katherine of Aragon. The Westminster Tournament Roll (see separate entry) calls Knyvet *Vaillant Desir* (Gallant or Valiant Desire) and shows him in jousting armour of plate, entering the lists beneath a canopy striped red and blue and sprinkled with golden 'K's.

Krak des Chevaliers: the great castle of the Knights Hospitallers, some 25 miles inland, north-east of Tripoli. It defied all Saladin's efforts to reduce it but fell to another sultan, Baibars, in 1271. Krak was built in a dominating position, high on solid rock. Of all the crusader castles it is reckoned to have had the loveliest Great Hall; and within the grim fortifications were other beautiful features, more characteristic of church or palace than fortress, such as the Grand Master's chamber, with ribbed vaulting, slender columns and frieze of five-petalled flowers carved in stone. It has been called 'the best preserved and most wholly admirable castle in the world'; with 'its cold stone in such good order that the steel-clad garrison could move in again tomorrow.'

Label: (see also *Cadency, Marks of*). One of the devices or marks used on a shield, either for distinguishing between the brothers of one family or the families of different brothers. The eldest son and heir takes a label of three points – a narrow strip with three strips pointing downwards, making a letter 'E' standing on its arms. Reference to the illustration of the arms, in Canterbury Cathedral, of Edward, the Black Prince will show the label he carried as Edward III's eldest son and heir apparent. Labels can sometimes be found as an ordinary charge on a shield, and not necessarily with three points.

La Hire: the common name, meaning 'the growler', of Etienne de Vignolles (1387–1442), a rough, freebooting Gascon captain who became one of Joan of Arc's devoted adherents. It is said that, under the Maid's influence, he strove hard to give up swearing blasphemous oaths, but that, to give him some means of venting his hot temper, she allowed him to swear by his stick.

A remarkable prayer of La Hire's has also been recorded. On his way to a fight he met a priest and asked him for absolution from his sins. 'Confess them first,' said the priest. 'I've no time for that,' answered the soldier, 'I have to fall upon the English. But I have done all that a man of war is accustomed to do.' The chaplain therefore gave him absolution, whereupon La Hire fell on his knees and prayed:

'God, I pray thee that to-day thou wilt do for La Hire that which thou wouldst have La Hire do for thee, if he were God and thou wert La Hire.'

Another version is:

'I pray my God to do for La Hire what La Hire would do for Him, if He were Captain and La Hire was God.'

'Laissez aller!': 'Let go!' – the cry of the heralds at joust and tournament, as the signal for the knights to charge.

'The Constable comaundid an harauld to crye *Lessez aler*. And then they ranne a cours coragiousely, seekyng toon the toodir [the one the other].' (From a 1471 account of a tournament at Smithfield.)

Lamboys: skirt of rich material such as velvet

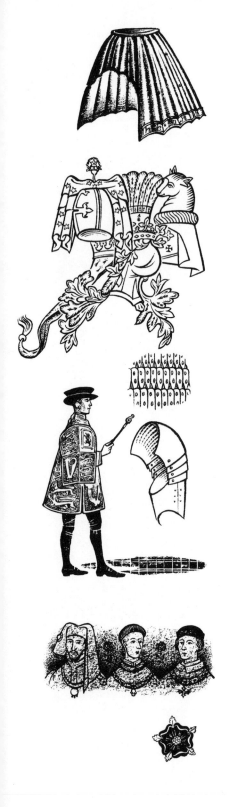

or brocade, and sometimes imitated in steel, hanging in folds from the waist over the thighs. The finest example of the latter is probably the armour in the Tower presented by Maximilian I to Henry VIII in 1514. The steel lamboys flares out in curved folds like a giant lamp-shade, the bottom edge decorated in brass with the initials 'H' and 'K'.

Lambrequin (Lambriquin): a protective covering of cloth, fastened to the knight's helmet and hanging down over his shoulders to shield him from the hot sun. Soldiers in France's famous Foreign Legion wore much the same sort of thing in the desert.

It is depicted, in heraldry, as part of a full 'achievement' (see separate entry) hanging behind the helmet; as one well-known modern herald remarks: 'looking like a heavy fall of seaweed, sometimes like a blanket hung up behind the shield on pegs, and sometimes more like the mantling of reality.' *Mantling* is another common term for the same thing.

Lamellar Armour: early armour was often made of small metal scales sewn or riveted to a backing of stout leather or cloth. In lamellar armour these small plates were pierced along the edges and laced together, giving greater flexibility.

Lames: the small metal plates used in the manufacture of armour.

Lancaster, Henry of: see *Henry of Lancaster.*

Lancaster Herald: see *Officers of Arms.*

Lancaster, House of: the family of English kings that ruled for just over 60 years towards the end of the age of chivalry. Its great figure was Henry V (see separate entry). The kings were:

Henry IV	1399–1413
Henry V	1413–1422
Henry VI	1422–1461

Lancaster, John, Duke of: see *John of Gaunt.*

Lancaster, Rose of: the red rose that is the best-known badge of the Lancastrian kings, though they used a number of others, including the white swan, the columbine flower and the crowned panther.

The old story has it that the origin of the red rose of Lancaster and the white rose of York (see *York, House of* and *Rose of*) lies in the quarrel that sparked off the Wars of the Roses, when the representatives of the rival families each snatched roses of different colours to serve as their distinctive badges. But, whether the quarrel took place or not, the red and white roses had been used as family badges long before. The golden rose appears with Eleanor of Provence, Queen of Henry III. It was used by many of her descendants, including Edward I, II, III and the Black Prince. The red rose came of the same stock, so to speak; for Edmund Crouchback, second son of Henry III and Eleanor, changed the colour of the rose from gold to red for 'difference.'

Edmund, incidentally, seems to have been called Crouchback or Crossback, not because of any deformity, but because he had taken the Cross and been on crusade in 1271.

Lance: the chief knightly weapon and, though other arms were employed, the one most used in joust and tournament. For hundreds of years, though there were many local variations of pattern, the lance was little more than a tapering pole up to a dozen feet in length, with a small metal head. A later refinement was the *Vamplate* (see separate entry). Some war-lances were much longer, if one can accept the statement that, at the Battle of Poitiers, the French knights, fighting without their horses, had cut down their lances from twenty feet to six in length.

In the 15th century a special bracket was bolted to the breastplate (right side), to take the butt of the lance and so transfer part of the weight to the armour. The long lance was never held straight out, but slanted across the body from right to left, to the left of the horse's neck. Many pictures of jousts between knights go astray on this point. (See *Bourdonass* for a later type of tournament lance.)

'Lance' was also a term used for a fighting unit of several men, so that a captain riding 'with thirty lances' could, in fact, be leading a hundred and fifty men. A 'lance' might be made up of a leader, a couple of archers and two or three other armed men. This is the origin of our modern army

169

'lance corporal' and the small unit of men often assigned to him for various duties.

Lance of Courtesy: the tournament lance fitted with a special blunted head, to prevent serious damage. (See *Coronel*.)

Lancelot: see *Launcelot*.

Langued: in heraldry, 'tongued', i.e., with tongue protruding. Used of beasts and birds of prey; e.g., a lion *rampant, argent, armed and langued azure* is a silver lion in the 'rampant' position with blue claws and tongue.

Lanner: type of long-tailed falcon; according to Dame Julia Berners (see *Falcon*), coming half-way down the scale of precedence and being suitable for use by a squire.

Lannoy, Gilbert de (1386–1462): a knight employed by Henry V, who entertained dreams of going on crusade like his ancestors, to write an accurate description of the places through which an army might successfully be led against the infidel. In 'A Survey of Egypt and Syria undertaken in the year 1422 by Sir Gilbert de Lannoy, Kt.' (the original MS. is in French), Lannoy gives an eye-witness account of towns, walls, fortifications, along with suitable ports, sources for provisions and water, etc.

La Tour Landry, Geoffroi de: a French knight who, in about 1371, wrote a book for the instruction of his three daughters. He tells us:

'In the beginning of April, in the year of our Lord thirteen hundred and seventy-one, I was in my garden, in the shade, all sad and pensive; or, if I was a little comforted, it was at the carolings and the chirpings of the wild young broods, with all their quaint notes – the merle, the tit and the throstle – which were welcoming in the spring, so gay and sprightly . . . and as I looked before me, I saw my daughters coming, and to whom my soul's desire was, that all honour and advantage might be theirs; for they were but young, and small . . . And so . . . I thought that I would make a book, wherein they might see how to carry themselves in the world, and have set before them the good and the evil which had passed in it, and, thus, the better be able to judge of the present.'

He set to work with two priests and two clerks in his household to read and extract from all the books he had, such as the Bible, the Chronicles of France, England and Greece, the Gestes, or achievements, of kings and princes. Having assembled his materials he proceeded to lay down the law, in the nicest possible way, on a multiplicity of topics, including how women ought to fast, how they should avoid eating tit-bits in the absence of their lords, how they should be courteous and avoid twisting their heads right and left.

'And if, at any time, you have occasion to look on one side, turn face and body together. And this will give you the reputation of being straightforward and to be depended upon. For those will ever be esteemed but light who go twinging and twisting themselves about.'

There were also stern words about women who take half a day to dress themselves and who take too much delight in tournaments and fêtes.

Whether the daughters really appreciated all this, and dutifully followed father's advice, is as doubtful as it ever was or will be. But perhaps La Tour Landry who 'used to go caracoling about the world, in Poitou and other parts' found this a way of making up for his own mis-spent youth.

Caxton thought highly of the book and, when he printed it at Westminster in 1484, advised 'every gentleman or woman having children, desiring them to be virtuously brought forth, to get and have this book, to the end that they may learn to govern them virtuously in this present life.'

Latten: see *Brass.*

Latticed Helmet: see *Grid-iron Helmet.*

Launcelot (Lancelot): the strongest and most valiant of the Knights of the Round Table and the hero of innumerable stories; though, in the end, his love for Queen Guinevere brought about the destruction of the Round Table and its noble achievements. With the king and most of the fellowship dead, Launcelot turned monk and lived out the rest of his life in repentance.

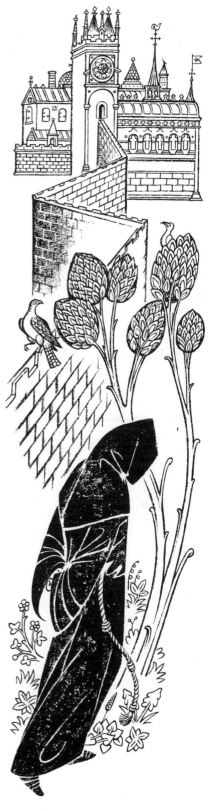

Tennyson gives one sort of picture of him in such lines as:

His broad clear brow in sunlight glow'd;
On burnished hooves his war-horse trode;
From underneath his helmet flow'd
His coal-black curls as on he rode,
        As he rode down to Camelot.

T. H. White, the greatest modern chronicler of Arthur, describes Launcelot as small, twisted-faced and ugly.

'Lancelot's [profile] the old ugly man's, was the outline of a gargoyle. It might have looked in hideous meditation from Nôtre Dame, his contemporary church. But, in its maturity, it was nobler than before. The lines of ugliness had sunk to rest as lines of strength. Like the bull-dog, which is one of the most betrayed of dogs, Lancelot had grown a face which people could trust.' (*The Once and Future King*.)

The knights of romance are almost invariably handsome beyond belief. The knights of history come in as many shapes and sizes as ordinary men and, like White's Launcelot, and history's Bertrand du Guesclin (see separate entry), could be misshapen and ugly. Chivalry has never had much connection with good looks.

Laws of Chivalry: see *Code of Chivalry*.

Leash: used to tether a hawk to its perch or block.

Leg-Armour: see *Cuishes, Greaves, Genouillières, Jambs, Knee-cops* and *Poleyns*.

Leicester, Earl of: see *Montfort, Simon de, Earl of Leicester*.

Leopard, and Leopards of England: see *Arms of England*.

Les Espagnols-sur-Mer: literally, 'the Spaniards on the Sea'; a great sea-fight, in which many knights were involved, in August 1350. It was, in fact, not a naval action in any modern sense, but the king's host fighting on ships instead of on land. The English had long been troubled by Spanish pirates and took advantage of a lull in the fighting with the French to strike a blow in return, on a rich Spanish convoy.

Froissart's account is typically vivid, and includes a picture of the great Sir John Chandos in unfamiliar guise – being made, by Edward III, to sing with the minstrels. It is not recorded whether this was a subtle means of intimidating the Spaniards.

'The king posted himself in the fore part of his own ship. He was dressed in a black velvet jacket, and wore on his head a small hat of beaver, which became him much. He was that day, as I was told by those who were present, as joyous as he ever was in his life, and ordered his minstrels to play before him a German dance which Sir John Chandos had lately introduced. For his amusement, he made the same knight sing with his minstrels, which delighted him greatly.

From time to time he looked up to the castle on his mast, where he had placed a watch to inform him when the Spaniards were in sight. Whilst the king was thus amusing himself with his knights, who were happy in seeing him so gay, the watch, who had observed a fleet, cried out:

"Ho! I spy a ship, and it appears to me to be a Spaniard."

The minstrels then were silenced; and he was asked if there were more than one. Soon after he replied:

"Yes, I see two . . . three . . . four – and so many that, God help me, I cannot count them!"

The king and his knights then knew they must be the Spaniards. The trumpets were ordered to sound, and the ships to form a line of battle for the combat . . . The king ordered wine to be brought, which he and his knights drank; when each fixed their helmets on their heads. . . .

When the king of England saw from his ship their order of battle, he ordered the person who managed his vessel, saying:

"Lay me alongside the Spaniard who is bearing down on us; for I will have a tilt with him." ' [Note how the king uses an essentially land term in a sea-fight.]

An account of the Black Prince's adventure in this battle, when his ship almost sank under him, will be found in the entry for *Henry of Lancaster*. An act of particular gallantry was performed by

a soldier called Hanequin (Hannekin), when an English ship, firmly grappled by a Spaniard with all sails set, was being towed out into the gathering darkness. Hannekin managed to scramble aboard the Spanish ship and, before he was overpowered, hacked through the halliards of the mainsail, so that the vessel became unmanageable and lost way. While her crew struggled in the tangle of fallen sail and slashed rigging, she was boarded and the English ship saved.

The Spaniards lost at least fourteen ships. The royal fleet came triumphantly into Rye and Winchelsea, 'when the king, the prince of Wales, the Duke of Lancaster, the earl of Richmond and other barons disembarked, took horses in the town, and rode to the mansion where the queen was, scarcely two English leagues distant'. The court had had, in fact, a grandstand view, for the battle had been fought in mid-channel in clear summer weather, with the queen's attendants watching from the high land near the coast.

Letters of Protection: were often issued to knights going on crusade or travelling to take part in a tournament in a foreign country. These served as a passport or safe-conduct. Thus, Henry III issued letters of protection to some hundreds of knights and squires in 1270, so that they might accompany Prince Edward to the Holy Land. When Anthony of Burgundy fought at Smithfield with Anthony, Lord Scales, in 1467 (see *Woodville, Anthony* and *Flower of Souvenance*), the latter had to obtain a safe-conduct for his opponent to come into England.

Lewes, Battle of (May 12th, 1264): fought between Henry III and the rebellious barons under Simon de Montfort. (See *Montfort.*) The future Edward I, then Prince Edward, opened the battle by breaking through de Montfort's right and pursuing the disorganized troops for many miles in undisciplined triumph. He at length galloped back to find the royalist right and centre completely defeated and the king captured. Though Edward cut his way back into the baronial host in a last desperate effort, he, too, was forced to surrender.

Leybourne (or Leyburn), William de (d. 1309): a baron of Edward I's reign and a distinguished soldier. In one record he is described as 'Vaillans homs sans *mes* et sans *si*' – 'a brave man without *but* and *if*'; i.e., he didn't dither or procrastinate, but was a man of direct action.

At least two episodes in his career are worth remembering. In October, 1301, the castle of Montgomery in Wales was entrusted to his charge, and the indenture in the British Museum gives a list of the armour and weapons in the castle. They included 'Balistas' – cross-bows and quarrels (see *Crossbow*), an unusual feature being that they were apparently made of horn instead of steel; a number of shields; five hauberks with hoods attached and five without; and a set of chains for the drawbridge.

In 1294, Edward I was preparing a fleet to sail for the invasion of Gascony and, to reinforce the existing fleet, ordered his foresters to find timber for 200 more ships. To command them he appointed officers known for the first time in English history as 'admirals' (the original word comes from Arabic); and de Leybourne was designated 'admiral of the King of England's seas'.

Liber Regalis: the magnificent manuscript, dating from the reign of Richard II and now in the possession of Westminster Abbey, giving the form and order of the coronation of English kings. This was probably used as a handbook at all the coronations from 1399–1558. (For some entries connected with coronations see *Black Prince's Ruby, Champion of England* and *Curtana*.)

Lilies of France: see *Arms of France*.

Lincoln, The Fair of: a strange affair in 1217, with the unusual spectacle of a French army fighting in the streets of an English city. The castle of Lincoln was being besieged by the adherents of Louis of France, who had landed at the invitation of the barons of England, in revolt against King John. The French were defeated by William Marshall, 1st Earl of Pembroke (see separate entry).

Lindsay (or Lyndsay), Sir David (1490–1555): Scottish poet and Lyon King of Arms. He completed a valuable Register of the Arms of the Scottish Nobility and Gentry, the most notable source for early Scottish heraldry. As a poet he

was extremely popular, both at the court and with the common people, for his broad humour and his satires directed against various abuses. On one occasion he attacked some of the princes of the Church, in the king's presence, by mockingly asking for the position of master tailor to his majesty.

' "I have," said me, "servit your grace lang, and luik to be rewardit as others are; and now your maister taylor, at the pleasure of God is departit, wherefore I wald desire of your Grace to bestow this little benefite upon me."

The king replied that he was amazed at such a request from a man who could neither shape nor sew.

"Sir," rejoined the poet, "that maks nae matter, for you have given bishopricks and benefices to mony standing here about you, and yet they can nouther teach nor preach. And why not I as weill be your taylor, though I can nouther shape nor sew?" '

Lion: the most important and kingly of the heraldic animals. (See *Arms of England* for part of its complicated history.) One great heraldic authority (A. C. Fox-Davies) has said 'no figure plays such an important and or such an extensive part in armory as the lion, in one or other of its various positions.'

Here are twenty of those positions, some fairly modern in origin and some rarely met with. They do not exhaust the possibilities:

combattant	said of two lions facing each other in the rampant position.
couchant	lying down with the head erect and in profile.
coward	with the tail between the legs.
dormant	lying down with the head resting on the fore-paws and the eyes closed.
passant	walking, with the right fore-paw raised.
passant guardant	as in passant, with the head turned to face the onlooker. (The Lions of England are in this position.)
passant regardant	as in passant, with the head turned round to look behind.

rampant	balanced on the left hind-paw, the right fore-paw high in the air.
rampant guardant	as in rampant, with the head turned to face the onlooker.
rampant regardant	as in rampant, with the head turned round to look behind.
salient	in a springing position, with both hind-legs on the ground and both fore-paws high, close together.
salient guardant	as in salient, with the head turned to face the onlooker.
salient regardant	as in salient, with the head turned round to look behind.
sejant	sitting on the haunches, with both fore-paws on the ground. (He can be *sejant guardant* and *sejant regardant*, as in the other examples.)
statant	standing, with all four paws on the ground, the two front ones usually together. (He can be *statant guardant* and *statant regardant*, as in the other examples.)

Two lions facing each other, not *combattant,* but merely *passant,* are said to be *respecting each other* or *regarding each other.*

Lions can have many tricks played with their tails, e.g., elevated and turned over the head, or extended horizontally (as with the Percy lion in the Duke of Northumberland's crest). If it has two tails, it is *double-queued.* If the tail is forked, it is *queue-fourché.*

Most heraldic beasts and monsters can take on the same positions described for the lion; but there are one or two exceptions, e.g., for beasts of the chase. A stag, buck or deer is not described as *statant guardant,* but *at gaze;* and he is not *passant,* but *trippant.*

Lioncels: occasionally found in descriptions of arms (e.g., the town of Warrington, Lancashire); but indistinguishable from lions. They date from the ancient controversy about lions and leopards, and, at one time, if there were more than two

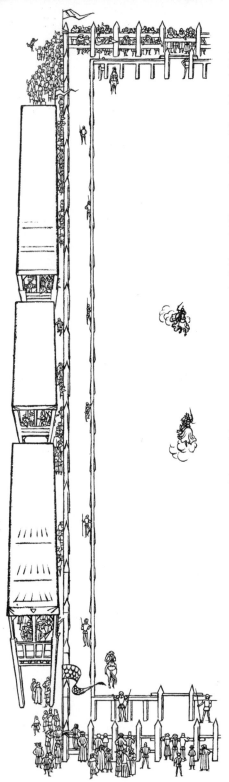

lions on the same shield, they were called lioncels.

Lions of England: see *Arms of England*.

Lists: the enclosed area of land where jousts and tournaments were held. At a celebrated tournament at Smithfield, London, in 1467, the Constable ordered that the lists should be 90 yards long and 80 yards wide, surrounded by posts 7½ feet high joined by heavy bars. This was for a contest between only two knights. When large numbers were involved, the lists could be much bigger. At the Field of the Cloth of Gold in 1520 (see separate entry), they measured 300 yards by over 100, and a ditch was dug all round to keep back the spectators.

Some idea of these areas can be gained by remembering that the regulation size for a modern Association Football Field is, at most, about 130 yards long and 100 yards wide; i.e., the lists at the Field of the Cloth of Gold were nearly three times as big. With the dust rising in clouds, one wonders how much the mass of onlookers, apart from the privileged few in the grandstands, could really see. Most modern artists' pictures of lists obviously show them as much too limited in area.

Liveries: distinctive uniforms or costumes worn by the servants of knights and barons in the Middle Ages. These bodies of retainers, bearing the colours and devices of their chiefs, amounted to private armies and often acted as though they were above the law. There were frequent protests about, e.g., 'officers of great men that weareth their liveries, the which . . . robbeth and despoileth the poor'; and 'hats and liveries . . .' by the granting of which a lord could induce his neighbours to 'maintain him in all his quarrels, whether reasonable or not.' Livery really means something delivered or given.

The liveries and badges of great commanders were well known, and the sight of them on the battlefield could alter the course of events by encouraging, or putting fear into, the combatants. There was at least one case of a disastrous mistake being made. At Easter, 1471, Edward IV and the Earl of Warwick met in their final battle at Barnet, about fourteen miles north of London.

At first Warwick's Lancastrian troops were successful, with his brother, Lord Montague, and the Earl of Oxford putting the Yorkist left to flight. But it was a morning of clinging fog and this changed triumph to disaster. The badge of the Earl of Oxford was a silver star, one of Edward IV's was a rising sun. As Oxford's soldiers came back through the thick mist after their pursuit, some of their comrades mistook the star for the rising sun and sent a shower of arrows into their own forces. There were angry shouts of 'Treason!', and out of the resulting confusion Edward IV was able to turn the tide of battle and win the day.

Livery and Maintenance, Statutes of (1495 and 1504): statutes passed by Henry VII to curb the power of the barons and restrict the number of retainers wearing their colours. The king set up the famous Court of Star Chamber to enforce the statutes.

The best-known case arising from Henry's determination to break the system was that of John de Vere, Earl of Oxford. In his *History of Henry VII*, Lord Bacon tells us that the king was entertained by the earl at Castle Hedingham. When he left, 'the earl's servants stood, in a seemly manner, in their livery-coats, with cognisances, ranged on both sides, and made the king a lane. The king called the earl unto him and said, "My lord, I have heard much of your hospitality, but I see that it is greater than the speech. . . . By my faith, my lord, I thank you for my good cheer, but I may not endure to have my laws broken in my sight; my attorney must speak with you." ' Though Oxford stood high in Henry's favour, he is reported to have been fined 15,000 marks for his offence.

Livery Colours: in heraldry, a family's livery colours are the principal colour and metal (see *Tincture* and *Metal*) of their arms; or, what is almost the same thing, the colour of the field and of the principal charge; since the Queen of England carries golden lions on a red field as the principal charge, her livery colours are red and gold. These have dated from the accession of the Stuarts in 1603.

There is a tradition that this is the origin of the 'pink' worn on the hunting field. In earlier times,

no man could hunt without licence from the Crown. He was, therefore, enjoying a royal sport and wore the royal livery colour.

Lobster-tail helmet: name given to a late kind of helmet (mid 17th century), deriving from a mediaeval type. The tail-piece, extending over the neck, looks like a lobster's scales.

Lombardy, Crown of: see *Iron Crown of Lombardy*.

Long-bow: (see also *Grey Goose Feather*). The long-bow, as particularly developed in England, was much superior to the cross-bow (see separate entry). It was lighter, more rapid in fire, a plentiful supply of arrows could easily be carried, and the archers, standing virtually shoulder to shoulder, needed much less room than the cross-bowmen. It seems to have been peculiarly fitted to English physique and strength, and Continental nations did not succeed in copying their prowess. There is evidence of the formidable accuracy of the English archers as early as the 12th century, when Richard of Devizes tells us that, at the siege of Messina by Richard Coeur-de-Lion, the Sicilians left the walls unmanned 'because no one could look abroad but he would have an arrow in his eye before he could shut it.' Richard I himself, and other knights, used the bow in battle. But it was in the course of the Hundred Years' War, under such leaders as Edward III, that the use of the long-bow was brought to such a pitch of perfection.

Ash or elm could be used, but yew proved to be the finest wood. The bows were from five to six feet tall, and the arrows a cloth-yard long, tipped with steel. Not merely the arm, but the strength of the whole frame went into drawing the bow. In a famous sermon preached before Henry VIII, Bishop Latimer described how he had been taught in his youth:

'My father was as diligent to teach me to shoot as to teach me any other thing. He taught me how to draw, how to lay my body in my bow, and not to draw with strength of arms, as other nations do, but with the strength of the body. I had my bows bought me, according to my age and strength, for men shoot never so well except they be brought up in it; it is a goodly art, a wholesome kind of exercise . . .'

The effective range of the long-bow has been a matter for much argument. According to one writer, 'a first rate English archer who in a single minute was unable to draw and discharge his bow twelve times with a range of 240 yards, and who in these twelve shots once missed his man, was very lightly esteemed.' At the same distance, the archer is said to have been able to drive an arrow-point through an inch-thick plank. Shakespeare uses this 240-yard figure in *Henry IV Part* 2, when Justice Shallow, commenting on the skill of an old archer, says:

> ". . .'a drew a good bow . . . 'a would have clapped in the clout at twelve score."

He goes on to say that, with a 'fore-hand shaft', i.e., one aimed no higher than the eye could sight along, the archer's arrow would have carried 290 feet. Presumably, therefore, with the arrow angled upwards, it would have gone considerably farther. Legendary heroes like Robin Hood were credited with 800 yards, but this is clearly on a level with many of his other fictional exploits. In 1929, a very strongly built American, using a 5-foot bow from a standing position, flighted an arrow nearly 392 yards. But, whatever the maximum flight the long-bowman could achieve, the *effective* range, as a fighting weapon, was probably a furlong (220 yards) or a little more.

An instance is recorded of a Welsh archer, in the reign of Henry II (1133–1189), driving an arrow through a knight's armoured thigh and saddle, and pinning him to his horse's flank. But in the days of armour's perfection, with its immensely hard, glass-smooth surface, not even the long-bowman could penetrate plate. That is why, with the ruthless logic of war, he often shot at the horse instead of the rider and so sowed confusion in the ranks of knights; and why, to counteract such moves, the knights often left their horses in the rear and came forward to fight it out hand to hand.

The early archers were only lightly armed; but, after they had demonstrated their supreme effectiveness as fighting men, were often themselves mounted and given a certain amount of armour, so that they could range far and wide.

Long-wings: the so-called True Falcons, which

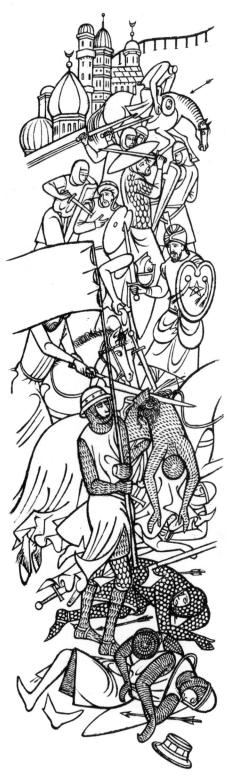

include the *Gerfalcon, Peregrine, Kestrel* and *Merlin*. (See separate entries.)

Longespée, William: see *Longsword, William*.

Longsword, William (1212?–1250): eldest son of the Earl of Salisbury, and sometimes called by that title himself, though he never succeeded to the earldom. Knighted when he was about twenty-one, he went twice to the Crusades, and met his end in most valiant manner in the castle of Mansourah or Massoura, Egypt.

St. Louis of France (see *Louis IX*) had landed in Egypt in 1249 and occupied Damietta. Longsword joined him there in October, with 200 English knights, and the army advanced on Cairo. There was a preliminary skirmish, as a result of which the Egyptian army was routed and the majority of them took refuge in Mansourah.

There was then a sharp division of opinion among the Christian knights as to the next move. The headstrong Frenchman Robert of Artois wished to attack Mansourah immediately. William de Sonnac, Grand Master of the Knights Templars, who would have preferred to wait till Louis's main army caught up with them, counselled caution, and William Longsword agreed with him. Artois thereupon denounced them as cowards and stung the English knight into replying:

'Count Robert! I will go so far in danger today, that you shall not even dare to touch the tail of my horse.'

With wiser counsels flung to the winds, the English and French knights buckled on their harness again and flung themselves into the town with no special plan and little discipline. As soon as they were inside, the Egyptians closed the gates and the Crusaders were cut off from their supporting army.

Desperate fighting took place in the streets and the Christian knights were gradually broken and borne down, selling their lives dearly. The fate of Artois, who had provoked the whole sorry attack, is unknown. The Templar de Sonnac died from a poisoned arrow. But the grimmest struggle of all took place where Sir William Longsword and his loyal companions determined on a last stand. Sir Richard de Guise, his standard-bearer, lost his left hand and somehow contrived to keep the banner flying with the stump. Unable to dislodge Longsword from the saddle, the Saracens cut off his left foot, whereupon he struggled down from the saddle and, supporting himself on the shoulder of Richard de Ascalon, continued to swing his sword and do great execution. Offered protection if he surrendered, he refused defiantly and battled on, still gripping de Ascalon's shoulder. A Saracen sword cut off his right arm and, tottering now without support, he took his sword in his left hand and swung at an enemy whose last blow took off that hand, too.

Only then did Longsword fall to the ground, and was hacked to pieces. The gallant de Ascalon fell across him, followed by the banner-bearer de Guise, who did not care to survive his lord. It is some measure of the disaster that, of the 290 Templars alone, only five survived.

There is a long contemporary poem, in French though perhaps written by an Englishman, in the British Museum, describing the assault on Mansourah. This is a translation of some of the last lines:

'The brave warrior Brother Richard de Ascalon fell wounded and bleeding upon the Earl, not for all the land of France would he have gone away . . . Sir Richard de Guise, who carried his banner, when he saw his lord die . . . without more delay fell upon his lord and suffered himself to be cut to pieces. The Earl and his Bannerer, and his Bachelors, and Sir Rauf de Henfeld the bold and brave, and Sir Robert Widele, who loved him right dearly, all five good knights were slain – all five were thus slain together. Their souls are with Jesus in Paradise.' (*Excerpta Historica*.)

Lord Chamberlain: the chief officer of the royal household, a peer, a privy councillor and a member of the government. He is responsible for the administration of the various departments of the household and the chapels royal, and for the supervision of great state ceremonies. An early 19th century *Manual of Rank and Nobility* gives a more detailed list:

'He has the oversight of the King's chaplains, although he is a layman; also of the officers of the standing and removing wardrobes, beds, tents, revels, music, comedians, etc.; of all physicians, apothecaries, surgeons,

barbers, messengers, trumpeters, drummers, tradesmen, and artisans, retained in his Majesty's service . . . He carries a white staff in his hand, as a badge of his office, and wears a gold key tied with a blue ribbon above his pocket.'

Lord Great Chamberlain: an office to be carefully distinguished from that of the *Lord Chamberlain* (above). This is a much older office, probably the only one that can be traced back directly to the Norman period. Originally he was the chief financial officer and was in charge of the king's chamber; but his duties have for long now been mainly ceremonial. He is in charge of the Palace of Westminster, supervises the arrangements for the State Opening of Parliament, etc. At coronation ceremonies, he touches the king's heels with the golden spurs in token of his knighthood; with a queen, he may merely proffer them to be touched before they are returned to the altar where they have been lying.

Lord Lyon: see *Grant of Arms* and *Officers of Arms*.

Lose-Coat Field, Battle of (1470): battle fought near Empingham, Rutlandshire, between the forces of Edward IV and an army of insurgents under Sir Robert Welles. The latter were heavily defeated and, to hamper their flight as little as possible, threw away their outer coats.

Louis IX (1226–1270): king of France; canonized for his devotion as a Crusader. A French historian describes him as 'the true hero of the Middle Ages, a prince as pious as he was brave . . . who reverenced the Church, and who could, when necessary, resist its head; who respected all rights, but above all followed the course of justice; who had a frank and gentle spirit, a loving heart filled with Christian charity.'

During a serious illness in 1244, he made a vow to take the Cross and, four years later, led a crusade which took him away from France for six years – years which saw little but trouble, including fever and dysentery, the tragic affair of Mansourah (see *Longsword, William*) and a period of captivity for the king. Sixteen years later, he set out again, and died of plague beneath the walls of Tunis with a great part of his army. His greatest admirer and chronicler was Jean de Joinville, who refused to accompany him on his second crusade (see *Joinville*).

Steven Runciman, the great modern historian of the Crusades, thus summarises the career of St. Louis:

'King Louis had been a great and good King of France, but to Palestine, which he had loved even more dearly, he had brought little but disappointment and sorrow. As he lay dying he thought of the Holy City which he had never seen and for whose deliverance his labours had been fruitless. His last words were "Jerusalem, Jerusalem." '

Lower Cannon: part of the armour for the arms – the plates enclosing the forearm. The pair enclosing the part above the elbow were the 'upper cannon.'

Lozenge: a diamond-shaped figure on a shield. A shield whose surface is divided into small diamond shapes is described as 'lozengy'. A figure rather larger than a lozenge, longer but narrower, is called a 'fusil'.

Lucy: heraldic term for a pike, i.e., the fish.

Ludlow: in Shropshire, was one of the chief strongholds on the Welsh borders, and the scene of many changes of fortune during the wars of the Middle Ages. Its castle was built in the 12th century. Some of its history is recalled in its coat of arms, a white lion *couchant guardant* (see *Lion*) and three white roses, all on a blue field. These are Yorkist badges, a reminder of the time when, in the Wars of the Roses, it was a rallying point for the Yorkist leaders.

Lure: a dummy bird used by the falconer to bring the hawk back at the end of the day's sport or to entice it down from a tree.

Luttrell (Luterel), Sir Geoffrey: a 14th century knight, best known to history because of the magnificent psalter, known as the Luttrell Psalter, written for him in about 1345. Its pages, apart from its orthodox contents for use in prayers and church services, abound in delight-

185

fully-drawn and amusing animals, and in faithful scenes of mediaeval life, particularly of work in the fields. But the most famous picture is that of Sir Geoffrey himself, a dazzling figure setting off for the tournament. His lady is handing up his triangular pennon and his great helm, while her companion holds his shield. His surcoat, his shoulder defences (ailettes), the horse's sumptuous bard, his crest, his banner, even the ladies' trailing gowns, all carry the Luttrell arms, *or, a bend between six martlets sable*.

Lymphad: the heraldic ship, usually in the form of a mediaeval galley.

Lyon, the Lord: see *Grant of Arms* and *Kings of Arms*.

Lyonesse: the legendary land from which King Arthur came, between Land's End and the Scilly Isles, now deep beneath the sea; described by Tennyson as:

A land of old upheaven from the abyss
By fire, to sink into the abyss again;
Where fragments of forgotten peoples dwelt,
And the long mountains ended in a coast
Of ever-shifting sand, and far away
The phantom circle of a moaning sea.

It was, too, the scene of the last great battle in the west, when:

. . . all day long the noise of battle roll'd
Among the mountains by the winter sea;
Until King Arthur's table, man by man,
Had fallen in Lyonesse about their Lord.

(See also *Bedivere, Sir*.)

Lys, Du: the surname granted to Joan of Arc's family in honour of her exploits.

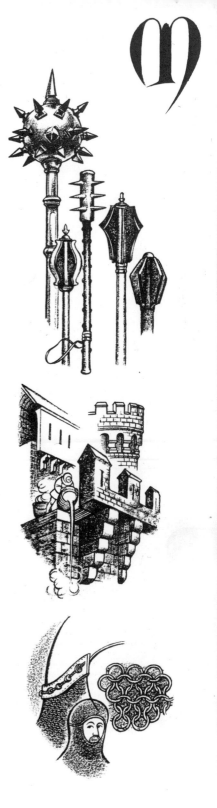

Mabinogion, The: a collection of very early Welsh stories, five of which are concerned with King Arthur. (See *Kilhwch* for an extract.) They were translated (1838–49) by Lady Charlotte Guest from a manuscript known as the Red Book of Hergest. *Mabinogion* means, roughly, tales for the young.

Mace: a club-like weapon, popular through many centuries. Shapes and patterns varied a great deal, but one of the commonest had a flanged head with sharp edges and points. They were grim weapons, but were sometimes given fanciful names, such as 'Morning Star' (*Morgenstern*) and 'Good-day!' (*Goedendag*). Another example of this sort of humour is found with the 'Holy Water Sprinkler' (see *Flail*). Maces were favourite weapons with soldier-churchmen like Odo, the warrior-bishop who fought at Hastings and went on crusade in 1096. Since the mace was only a crushing and bruising weapon (though capable of inflicting terrible damage) they were able to argue that they were not shedding blood with the sword, which was forbidden by the Scriptures. At the Battle of Bouvines, in 1214, Philip of Dreux, Bishop of Beauvais, 'holding by chance a club in his hand . . . forgot his calling and struck down the chief of the English and with him many others, breaking their limbs but shedding no blood . . .'

Machicolation: projecting part of the castle battlements, forming a platform or gallery, with holes in the floor through which the defenders could pour boiling liquid or hurl missiles on those attacking the walls. (See also *Crenellation* and *Merlon.*)

Mail: type of armour formed either from rings punched out of a sheet of metal or of individually-riveted hand-formed wire links with the ends flattened. There could be a hundred thousand of these links in a single mail shirt. Mail was flexible and comfortable enough – so much so that young knights 'breaking in' new mail shirts or harness turned somersaults in them – but was not an adequate defence against a spear-thrust, the smashing mace and the iron-tipped cloth-yard shaft from the long-bow. Mail was really a knitted garment made in metal, and much the

same technique was probably employed in making it, with the armourer working to a pattern and increasing or decreasing his rows according to the set instructions. A full wardrobe was obtainable in mail – hood, shirt, mittens, leg-defences, etc. It continued in use till roughly 1350, before it gave way to plate. (See *Plate Armour.*)

Though the term is in common use, it is inaccurate to talk about 'chain mail.' 'Mail' comes from Latin and French words meaning 'mesh' or 'net', and these give a much more accurate picture.

Main-gauche: the left-handed dagger, held in the left hand to parry or deflect blows, while the right hand was busy with the sword or rapier.

Malory, Sir Thomas (d. 1471): the Warwickshire knight who collected together all the stories he could find of King Arthur and his knights and turned them into the English of the common people, so that William Caxton, in *The Noble Histories of King Arthur and of Certain of His Knights*, (1485), was able to print one of the world's greatest collection of stories. Malory had been a member of Parliament for his county and also served in the French wars with one of the most illustrious English commanders, Richard de Beauchamp, Earl of Warwick (see *Warwick*), but in many ways he proved himself a sadly unknightly person. A document in the Public Record Office shows him to have been guilty of a whole list of crimes both against society and against the code of chivalry. He was a thief, a cattle-rustler, and had no regard for sacred things. He used battering-rams to smash down the doors of the Abbey of the Blessed Mary at Coombe, and stole its jewels and ornaments. He spent long years in prison. It was, in fact, while he was in prison that he wrote, or rewrote, many of the Arthurian stories that make up his book. At the end of one he refers to himself as 'a knyght presoner sir Thomas Malleorré'; and in another he invites his readers to pray that 'God sende hym good delyveraunce sone and hastely.'

Perhaps, in the end, Sir Thomas Malory, by giving generations of readers the heroic legends of the Round Table, recaptured some of his own lost knighthood, and brought back some lustre to his tarnished vows.

Maltese Cross: a cross with its four arms of equal length, widening from the centre out to the extremities, and with a V-shaped cut in them; the type of cross worn by the Knights Hospitallers and by the present Order of St. John of Jerusalem. (See *Knights Hospitallers*.)

Mamelukes: the mounted soldiers of Egypt encountered by the Crusaders. They were originally slaves brought in from the Caucasus as royal body-guards (*mamluc* is Arabic for 'slave'), and gradually rose to be the ruling class. They were annihilated in 1811 by Mejemet Ali.

It was the Mamelukes who crushed the Christian knights at Mansourah and captured the almost impregnable Krak-des-Chevaliers. (See separate entries for these.)

Mangon (Mangonel): a siege engine for hurling stones high into the air against a besieged place. Its main use was for breaching the walls so that a direct assault could take place. It worked by torsion (from the Latin verb meaning 'to twist'). A long flexible beam, fixed to twisted skeins of rope, was forced backwards and downwards and a heavy missile placed in a hollow at the free end. When released, the arm was sent upwards by the untwisting ropes and the stone flung against the target. (See also *Trebuchet*.) Sometimes lighted barrels of pitch, naphtha, etc., were used as missiles – these, of course, being hurled over the walls in the hope of starting a serious fire.

It was apparently possible to use the mangonel – perhaps a small variety – from the deck of a ship since, e.g., the chronicler Geoffrey de Villehardouin, in his recollections of the Crusades, writes: 'Meanwhile the Doge of Venice had not forgotten to do his part, but had ranged his ships and transports and vessels in line, and that line was well three cross-bow shots in length; and the Venetians began to draw near to the part of the shore that lay under the walls and the towers. Then might you have seen the mangonels shooting from the ships and transports, and the cross-bow bolts flying, and the bows letting fly their arrows deftly and well.' These catapult-type engines were obviously something very different from some of the giants used by the Moslems.

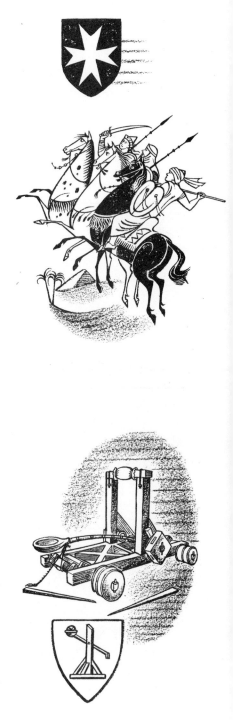

(See *Mansour the Victorious* for an example.)

We know, too, that these engines were used *inside* the besieged town as well as out, enabling the defenders to get some of their own back; e.g., Guillaume des Ormes, writing in 1240, says:

'Afterwards they set up a mangonel before our barbican, when we lost no time in opposing to it from within an excellent Turkish petrary [see *Petrary*], which played upon the mangonel and those about it; so that, when they essayed to cast upon us, and saw the beam of our petrary in motion, they fled, utterly abandoning their mangonel.'

In a great siege, against a place of importance, it was not unknown for two or three hundred missile-throwing engines to be in action.

Manny, Sir Walter (d. 1372): a Knight of the Garter and one of Edward III's most able commanders. He came to England as the squire of Philippa of Hainault when she was chosen as the bride of Edward III. Three years later he was knighted and distinguished himself in the Scottish wars.

He saw hard service in the French campaigns; along with the king and his company 'showed himself on that day a gallant knight' at the sea fight of Sluys in 1340 (see separate entry); was a leading spirit in the extraordinary bluff by which Henry of Lancaster captured La Réole, the strongest fortress in the Garonne valley (see *Henry of Lancaster*). In La Réole, Manny found the tomb of his father who, while Sir Walter was still an infant, had been murdered while on pilgrimage to St. James of Compostella. Edward III fought *incognito* under Manny's banner in 1348, when the king was twice beaten to his knees by Sir Eustace de Ribeaumont (see *Edward III*).

In 1371, Manny founded a house of Carthusian monks – the Charterhouse – in London, on the site of the present public school. A year later, at about the age of 62, he died and was buried with great pomp in the monastery he had just founded – 'for which all the barons and knights of England were much afflicted, on account of the loyalty and prudence they had always found in him.'

Mannyng of Brunne, Robert (flourished 1288–1338): a native of Brunne, or Bourne, Lincolnshire; a poet and 'the most skilful storyteller of his time.' Though he writes as a moralist and attacks, e.g., tournaments, religious plays performed on the highway, tyrannical lords, etc., he is a narrator of great charm and style. One of his most moving stories is that of 'The Merciful Knight.' This is a free rendering of the poem:

Between two knights there lay a great enmity, and each determined to kill the other. They met in mortal combat and one was slain. The dead knight had a son, a doughty young knight who resolved to avenge his father. He got together a great array and besieged his enemy who, when he knew of his coming, withdrew into his strongest castle. There for twelve months he was so closely invested that he could not set foot outside.

All this time he had been unable to go to church, neither to matins nor mass. And now it was the season of Lent, when men should put aside anger and pride. On Good Friday, the besieged knight looked out from his castle and saw men going to and from church. Barefoot they went to ask mercy for their sins.

'Ah!' thought the knight, 'it is a long time since I heard mass. Whatever God has in store for me, I will rise and go to the church.'

So he drew off his stockings and shoes, caused the gates to be unbarred, and made his way barefoot, as is the law, to church, to hear the holy service. His enemy met him in the way and said:

'Traitor! now you shall die and pay fully for my father's killing.'

The other knight fell at his feet and said:

'Have mercy on me, for the sake of Him who was born of the Virgin Mary and suffered death on the Cross this day to save both thee and me, and forgave them that spilt his blood. In the same way, forgive my guilt. I am your prisoner. Now grant me your grace, that God's grace may be on you at the day of Judgement.'

The young knight that was his enemy heard him plead so sorrowfully and said:

'Since you have besought me in the name of Jesus's blood that bought us dearly, and for his Mother's sake, for them I grant you my peace.'

He alighted quickly and in God's love kissed the knight.

'Now we are friends that formerly were angry. Let us go now to the church, in God's love and perfect charity, for the sake of Him who ordained peace.'

191

The older knight was overjoyed, as were all the company, that his misdeed had been forgiven. And both made their way to church, knelt down in the worship of Christ's passion to kiss the Cross, as is the custom in Christian law.

The rest of the story tells how a miracle occurred and, when the merciful young knight kissed the Cross, the figure on it stretched out His arms, clasped the knight and kissed him in blessing. The poem is written in a north midland dialect. Here is a short passage from the original, the lines where the besieged knight determines to go to church:

'Ey,' thoght the knyght, 'long ys gone,
That messe at the cherche herd y none.
what so ever God wyl for me werche,
y wyl ryse, and go to the cherche.'
He drogh of hys hosyn and hys shone,
And ded the gatys be on-done.
Bafere he yede, as ys the acuse,
To cherche, for to here Goddys servyse.

Manor: a term introduced into the English language by the Norman clerks of William the Conqueror. It did not necessarily mean an estate of any size, but only the residence of someone of local importance. It was not at first identified with a village; one village could, in fact, hold more than one manor. Later, 'manor' widened its meaning to include a knight's or landowner's whole estate, and the tenants that were bound to him.

Manwood, John (d. 1610): an Elizabethan lawyer who collected together and published many of the old forest laws of England, under the title 'A Brefe Collection of the Lawes of the Forest.' From them we get a good idea of the strictness with which the forests were controlled, for the benefit of the king and his court. They were a 'territorie of wooddy grounds and fruitful pastures, priviledged for wild beasts and foules of the forest, chase and warren, to rest and abide in the safe protection of the king for his princely delight and pleasure.' One early law says: 'If any one doe offer force to a Verderer, if he be a freeman, hee shall lose his freedome, and all that he hath. And if he be a villein, he shal lose his right hand.' Another offence could cost him his life. (See also *Deer*.)

Mansour the Victorious: a gigantic catapult or siege engine used by the Moslems against the Crusaders in the siege of Acre, 1291. With another, called Ghadban the Furious, it took two hundred wagons to carry the timbers necessary for their erection. They were part of an attack which lasted six weeks and saw the final victory of the infidel over this much-contested town, which was later levelled and its ground sowed with salt to discourage any further inhabitation.

Mansourah: see *Longsword, William*.

Mantlet (Mantelet): a tall rectangular shield of tough material used by archers for defensive purposes.

Mantling: see *Lambrequin*.

Marcher Lords (or Lords Marcher): the great Anglo-Norman barons who held the Welsh borders for the king, ruling despotically with aid of strong castles and mounted knights. They dominated the valleys and lowlands, but Welsh life continued largely undisturbed in the uplands and mountains, from which there were constant raids. The Marchers, though nominally subjects, lived by their own laws and were not readily brought to heel, though Edward I succeeded in disciplining them. Some of the great Marcher families were the Clares, the Mortimers, the Bohuns and Fitzalans.

Marches: the frontier, or debatable land, between two neighbouring countries, e.g., Wales and England (see *Marcher Lords*) or Scotland and England. The Scottish boundary country was divided into three Marches, the Eastern, the Western and the Middle, each under the jurisdiction of a warden whose duty it was to hold the borders. It was a countryside of incessant raids, plundering and bloodshed. Evidence of the sort of life can be found in the many castles, fortified monasteries, churches and pele towers (see separate entry) built to withstand the raiders, or reavers. For the most famous of the border forays see *Otterburn* and *Douglas, James, second Earl*.

The titles Marquis and Marchioness derive from the same source as March, i.e., Anglo-

Saxon *mearc*, a boundary, and indicate the ancient duty of a man holding such a rank.

Mareschal (or Marshal), William, Earl of Pembroke and Striguil (1146–1219): one of the finest of mediaeval knights and statesmen, whose chief characteristic was 'an uncompromising fidelity'. He was, in fact, a faithful servant and adviser to four English kings. He served his military apprenticeship in Normandy, was captured and ransomed by Queen Eleanor, wife of Henry II. From 1183–87 he was in the Holy Land, performing great exploits there. In an engagement against Prince Richard, later Richard I, he unhorsed him but spared his life. When Richard succeeded to the throne, he was one of the marshals at the coronation and held many high offices for another thirty years. On the death of King John, he was appointed regent for the nine-year-old Henry III and by his wisdom and statesmanship settled him securely on his throne. In his last illness, when the Great Council of the realm had gathered round his bedside to receive his resignation he said to the young king: 'Sire, I pray God if ever I have done anything pleasing to him, He will give you grace to be a gentleman.' Before he died he was admitted to the Order of the Knights Templars, the Master saying: 'In the world you have had more honour than any other knight for prowess, wisdom and loyalty.' He was buried in the Temple Church by Stephen Langton, Archbishop of Canterbury, with the words: 'Behold all that remains of the best knight who ever lived.'

We know a great deal about William Mareschal from the 19,000-line poetical biography of him, finished only six years after his death, *L'Histoire de Guillaume le Maréchal*. Mention of this, and of Mareschal's honeymoon, the first recorded in English literature, will be found in the entry for *D'Abernon, Sir John*.

Marshal: one of the greatest officers in the realm in the reigns of the Norman and Plantagenet kings. From being master of the horse, he became in time leader of the king's host. 'In time of war,' says an early document, 'with his Golden Staff he Marshalleth and ordereth Battles in the field, and hath the leading of the Vanguard.' He was also responsible for decisions on all questions relating to the laws and practice of chivalry. 'At Combats, Barriers, Tournaments, and Royal Jousts, the Earl Marshal is the chief Officer, to see those matters and actions of Honour and Arms accomplished.' He held his own Court, as head of the College of Heralds, 'either at Westminster, in the Painted Chamber adjoining to the Parliament House, or in his own house, where in the great hall he hath a large table or stage, four square, built with rails thereabout, and benches therein, and an half pace raised above the same; there the Earl sitteth in the midst thereof, being accompanied on either side with divers Noblemen, and sometimes Judges, according to the validity of the cause that is then to be handled, to the end that with their advice and council he may the more legally proceed.'

The title of Earl Marshal began to be used in the early 14th century. The Earl Marshal is still head of the College of Arms, the office being hereditary and held by the Dukes of Norfolk since 1672. Though his court no longer sits, the Earl Marshal's authority in matters of arms has never been withdrawn. The last great occasion when the Earl Marshal's responsibilities were seen at their most spectacular and colourful was at the coronation of Queen Elizabeth II, on June 2nd, 1953.

Martel-de-fer (= **Hammer of iron**): see *War Hammer.*

Martingale: part of a horse's harness; the long strap running from the headstall, down through the forelegs and fastened at the other end to the girth-strap. Its main object is to keep the horse's head down.

Maximilian Armour: the name given to a type of armour which originated in the period covered by the reign of the Emperor Maximilian (1493–1519). Its chief characteristic is its closely grouped channels or flutings. In the early 'Gothic' armour (see separate entry), these ridges and flutings often fanned out rather like Gothic arches. In the Maximilian armour they tended more to run in parallel lines. In use, it was found more in the tournament lists and in pageants. On the battle-field the plainer, undecorated style was preferred. Examples of the Maximilian style

are to be found in most of the major collections and museums of the world.

Meals: The details of the expenditure of knightly households make interesting reading. The earliest that have survived for a private house are those of Eleanor de Montfort, wife of Simon de Montfort (see *Montfort*), over a period of six months in 1265. The chief items are bread, wine, beer, fish, and oats and hay for the horses. There are other entries for various supplies such as apples, onions, almonds, poultry, eggs, peas, spices, sugar and milk.

The difference made to the amount of food and accommodation required when de Montfort himself turned up with his retinue may be judged from two entries:

'Wednesday (Feb. 25), for the Countess and the Abbot of Waverley: Grain, 1½ quarters, from stores [to make about 270 loaves]. Wine, 2½ sextaries [a sextary was 4 gallons]. Beer, previously reckoned. *Kitchen*, 400 herring. Fish, by purchase, 10s. 6d. Dishes, 15d. Pease, 23d. Napkins, 10½d. Onions, 6½d. Aples, 4½d. *Stables* Hay, from stores, for 32 horses. Oats, 2 quarters, from stores. Forge 12d.

Thursday (March 19), for the Earl and the Countess; Grain, 4 quarters bought, price 22s.; 1½ quarters from castle stores. Wine, 18¼ sextaries. Beer bought, 240 gallons, for 14s. *Kitchen* 1,000 herrings from castle stores and 700 herrings. Sea fish, 26s. ½d. Sea-wolves, 14s. 7½d. Fish from Stanes, 10s. Almonds, 36 lbs, for the aforesaid expenses. *Stables* Hay for 334 horses, from stores. Oats from store, 18¼ quarters; item, by purchase, for 9 quarters, 3 bushels; 18s 9d.'

It will be observed that the household had to provide for an extra 300 horses and that the consumption of wine was increased more than seven times. Wine was only for the nobles and gentlemen, the lower orders drinking vast quantities of spiced beer. Fish was an important item, for the Lenten fast was strictly observed and two or three days in every week were fish days. Herring and stockfish were the chief types, but such things as cod, ling, eels, lampreys, hake, and even whale and porpoise, figure in the de Montfort accounts. Most dishes were highly spiced to give them extra piquancy and to disguise the large amounts of salt in the preserved meat and fish. (Account details from Margaret Wade Labarge's *Simon de Montfort*, 1962.)

The Earl of Derby's 'Household Books' for 1561 show that, for a retinue of not less than 140, the ordinary weekly consumption of food and drink was 'one ox, a dozen calves, a score of sheep, fifteen hogsheads of ale, and plenty of bread, fish and poultry.'

For royal feasts, examples and details are more plentiful than for private households. 'The provisions for King Richard II and the Duke of Lancaster, when they dined with the Bishop of Durham in London in September, 1387, suggest the victualling of a town against a siege. What the number of their united retinues may have been I do not know, but they should have fared pretty well with 120 sheep, 14 salted and 2 fresh oxen, 140 pigs and 12 boars, 210 geese, 720 hens, besides 50 capons "of hie grece" and 8 dozen other capons, 50 swans and 100 dozen pigeons, a few odd scores of such things as rabbits and curlews, with corresponding quantities of accessories, as eleven thousand eggs, 120 gallons of milk and 12 gallons of cream.' (L. F. Salzman, *More Medieval Byways*, 1926.)

At a feast for 6,000 guests given at the installation of George Neville as Archbishop of York in 1467, a 'partial list of the food includes 300 quarters of wheat, 300 tuns of ale, 100 tuns of wine, 1 pipe of hippocras, a cordial of wine and spices, 104 oxen, 6 wild bulls, 1,000 sheep, 304 calves, 304 "porkes", 400 swans, 2,000 geese, 1,000 capons, 2,000 pigs, 104 peacocks, besides over 13,500 birds, large and small, of various kinds. In addition there were stags, bucks, and roes, five hundred and more, 1,500 hot pasties of venison, 608 pikes and breams, 12 porpoises and seals, besides 13,000 dishes of jelly, cold baked tarts, hot and cold custards, and "spices, sugered delicates and wafers plentie." ' (W. E. Mead, *The English Medieval Feast*, 1931.)

The Crusades increased the demand for fruits, sweetmeats and spices and, as early as the reign of Henry III (1207–72), there was already a wide variety of imports reaching London from the East.

Mediaeval Artillery: consisted mainly of

'petrariae' (the Latin word) or 'perriers' (from the French), both general terms for stone-throwing machines. They could also project other missiles at need, such as barrels of lighted pitch and naphtha. The structure of the various machines involved three principles, used either singly or in combination:

1. Tension. The long-bow with its arrow, and the cross-bow with its bolt, illustrate the principle, which was developed in machines like the *balista*. (See separate entry.)

2. Torsion. This comes from the Latin word 'to twist'. Engines based on this principle used great twisted skeins of rope to force a long flexible beam against a horizontal bar fixed to two massive uprights. When the beam was released, after being drawn right back and loaded, it sprang back and hit the horizontal beam with tremendous force, jerking the missile high into the air. The *mangon(el)* is the best example of this type. (See separate entry.)

3. Counterpoise. This involved the use of great counterweights and a long wooden arm with a sling at the far end. When the weights suddenly fell, the arm whipped through a quarter of a circle and caused the sling to discharge its contents with great force. See *Trebuchet* for this type of engine.

Distances are hard to find out about accurately. Sixty years ago an experimenter was able to hurl an 8 lb. stone nearly 500 yards with a far-from-perfect machine built on mediaeval principles; but this was a small weight compared with those actually used during sieges. Old writers give a range of 700–800 yards.

It is often said that the discovery of gunpowder, or its introduction in warfare, meant the end of the armoured knight. This, of course, is true, taking the long view. But it would be a mistake to think of it as a quick process. Edward III may have used his crakeys against the Scots in 1327, but, nearly 150 years later, at the Battle of Barnet, we can read of the one great bombard in Warwick's train keeping up a misdirected fire and doing no damage; and, 220 years after Crécy, Sir Philip Sidney was still fighting in armour and meeting his end because he was foolish enough to discard his leg armour.

Mêlée: a 'mix-up', or hand-to-hand fight in the lists between teams of knights. Though they were usually friendly contests, accidents were not uncommon. In a mêlée of the year 1240, 60 knights were killed, either crushed by their horses when they fell or choked by the dense clouds of dust raised during the struggle.

Sir Walter Scott gives a good picture of the mêlée in 'Ivanhoe':

'In fact, although the general tournament, in which all knights fought at once, was more dangerous than single encounters, they were, nevertheless, more frequented and practised by the chivalry of the age. Many knights, who had not sufficient confidence in their own skill to defy a single adversary of high reputation, were, nevertheless, desirous of displaying their valour in the general combat, where they might meet others with whom they were more upon an equality. . . .

'As yet, the knights held their long lances upright, their bright points glancing to the sun, and the streamers with which they were decorated fluttering over the plumage of the helmets. Thus they remained while the marshals of the field surveyed their ranks with the utmost exactness, lest either party had more or fewer than the appointed number . . . William de Wyvil, with a voice of thunder, pronounced the signal words – *Laissez aller*! The trumpets sounded as he spoke – the spears of the champions were at once lowered and placed in the rests – the spurs were dashed into the flanks of the horses, and the two foremost ranks of either party rushed upon each other in full gallop, and met in the middle of the lists with a shock, the sound of which was heard at a mile's distance . . .'

'Mercy Gramercy': see *Henry of Lancaster*.

Merlin: (i) the prince of magicians and enchanters, a familiar figure in the Arthurian legends. Though his origins are much earlier, Merlin makes his appearance in British romance in Geoffrey of Monmouth's *Histories of the Kings of Britain*, written about 1139, where he is met as a youth squabbling with another named Dalbutius

and, being summoned to the king's presence, begins his career of prophecy and spell-binding.

Merlin: (ii) the smallest of the British falcons, living chiefly in moorlands in the west and north. Dame Julia Berners, in the 14th century, described it as a fitting hawk for a lady to use.

Merlon: part of the castle battlements; the section of parapet between two embrasures.

Messengers: kept, before the days of a postal service, by wealthy households for carrying letters. Nobles, great knights, abbots, justices and, most of all, kings, kept them in regular employ. They took private letters, summonses to tournaments, to meetings of Knights of the Garter, to Parliament, etc. On occasion, they travelled to places abroad. These professional messengers were skilful, speedy people, knowing all the tricks of the road. They were known to cover the distance from London to Scotland in 6 days. If they were employed by the royal household or some powerful noble, few would dare to challenge their right of way. In the reign of Edward I, a messenger of the queen who was detained by the constable of Roxburgh Castle, claimed £10,000 for the insult to his sovereign, and £2,000 for himself.

There is still, in England, a group of about forty Queen's Messengers, or Queen's Foreign Service Messengers, mainly retired senior officers of the Army, Navy, and Air Force, employed on confidential diplomatic errands. They wear, hanging from a Garter-blue ribbon, a badge showing a silver greyhound.

Metals: one of the three groups of tinctures used in heraldry. There are only two 'metals', gold and silver, known as *or* and *argent*. (See *Hatching* for the way the metals are indicated in an uncoloured drawing.) It is one of the fixed rules of heraldry that a metal must never be charged upon a metal, nor a colour on a colour; e.g., you cannot have a golden lion on a silver background or field, nor a blue cross on a red field; but you would be quite correct in putting a blue lion on a silver field and a golden cross on a red field. (See also *Tinctures* and *Furs*.)

Mews: literally, a place to change or moult, especially a house for hawks. The Royal Mews (or stables) in London, are built on the site where the royal hawks were mewed. Frederick II of Germany (1194–1250), who wrote on the Art of Falconry, said: 'The mews chosen may be a tower somewhere in the country, or an isolated high building with no forest or trees nearby; for young falcons should be fed and raised in surroundings similar to those the parent birds would have selected, i.e., in some elevated spot far from dense forests and with large open spaces without many trees, similar to the open country they prefer for their hunting.'

Middle Ages: the period in history from the 5th to the 15th century, or, roughly, from 500 to 1500 A.D. What is called the High Middle Age extends over the 13th and 14th centuries, or from the reign of Edward I to that of Richard II, embracing the main age of chivalry.

Milan: the greatest centre of armour manufacture in Europe in the 15th and 16th centuries. (See *Italian Armour*.)

Military Orders: see *Knights Hospitallers, Knights Templars, Knights Teutonic.*

Milliner: = Milaner. *See Italian Armour.*

Mine, to: to burrow or dig into, for the purpose of causing a collapse. In the Middle Ages it was the most effective – and most guarded against – method of breaching a fortified place. The miners would tunnel under a tower or section of strategic importance, propping the excavation up with timber as they went. They then withdrew and set fire to the props. When they collapsed, if the job had been done thoroughly, down came the tower or wall as well. At a later stage, gunpowder was used by the miners. In one siege during the Hundred Years' War, the commander bluffed an important stronghold into surrendering, by pretending the walls were mined when, in fact, the engineers had found it impossible. (See *Henry of Lancaster*.)

As an example of the frightening scale that mining operations could attain, it was estimated that, during the Mameluke attack on Acre in

O

1291, the eleven outer towers were attacked by a thousand engineers simultaneously.

Minot, Laurence (1300?–1352?): an obscure poet, and probably a soldier, who wrote eleven martial and patriotic poems, preserved in the British Museum, mainly celebrating the great victories of Edward III over the period 1333–1352. He mentions his own name twice in the poems, otherwise we should not know even that. He writes of the king:

> *Now God, that es of mightes maste,*
> *Grant him grace of the Haly Gaste*
> *His heritage to win!*
> *And Mari moder, of mercy fre,*
> *Save oure king and his menye*
> *Fro sorow, and schame, and syn!*

We can render this:

> Now God, that is of greatest might,
> Grant him the grace of the Holy Ghost
> His heritage to win!
> And mother Mary, of mercy free,
> Save our king and his meinie (= retinue)
> From sorrow, and shame, and sin!

Of Edward's French opponent, he says impolitely:

> *Than the riche floure de lice*
> *Wan thare ful litill prise –*
> *Fast he fled for ferde.*
> *The right aire of that cuntre*
> *Es comen, with all his knightes fre,*
> *To schac him by the berd.*

Or:

> Then the rich fleurs-de-lys
> Won there but little prize –
> Fast he fled for fear.
> The rightful heir of that country
> Has come with all his knights free,
> To shake him by the beard.

Minstrels: (see also *Jongleurs*). The singers of war-songs and romantic stories who were an indispensable part of every mediaeval festivity. They were kept permanently in the employ of great households. Two of the most famous ministrels in English history are Taillefer and Blondel.

Taillefer, mounted on a swift horse, rode before the Norman host at Hastings, singing lustily of Charlemagne, Roland and Oliver. 'And when they drew nigh to the English:

202

"A boon, sire!" cried Taillefer. "I have long served you, and you owe me for all such service. To-day, so please you, you shall repay it. I ask as my guerdon and beseech you for it earnestly, that you will allow me to strike the first blow in the battle!"

And the Duke answered, "I grant it."

Then Taillefer put his horse to a gallop, charging before all the rest, and struck an Englishman dead, driving his lance below the breast into his body, and stretching him upon the ground. Then he drew his sword, and struck another, crying out:

"Come on, come on! What do ye, sirs? Lay on, lay on!"

At the second blow he struck, the English pushed forward, and surrounded and slew him.' (From Robert Wace's *Roman de Rou*.)

Blondin, Richard Coeur-de-Lion's minstrel, wandered through Europe trying to discover his master's whereabouts after the king had been captured by the Archduke of Austria and imprisoned in the castle of Durrenstein, Styria. Blondin adopted the ruse of singing a song the king knew well, which he would immediately associate with the minstrel and which, if he was within ear-shot, he could answer. Blondel's plan worked; but a ransom of 100,000 marks had to be raised before the king could be released.

Misericorde: literally, 'mercy'. A straight, thin-bladed dagger, to be found represented on a number of knightly effigies; apparently so-called because it was often used to give the final 'mercy' stroke to a fallen adversary.

Missaglia, Tomasso: see *Italian Armour*.

Moat: the defensive ditch round a castle. Though it is usually pictured filled with water, it was often dry. For the attackers seeking to mine or scale the walls it was necessary to fill in sections of the moat in order to make their approach.

Molay, Jacques de (1245?–1314): the 22nd and last Grand Master of the Order of Knights Templars. He was for a time Provincial Master in England. He described himself as a 'simple, unlearned warrior' and had no patience with book learning. He tightened up discipline in the

Order, and cared greatly for its glory, but he was a ruthless and arrogant leader. After the dissolution of the Order (see *Knights Templars*) he was tried and burnt at the stake, six and a half years after his arrest, after a courageous last speech in which he defended the Order.

Monmouth, Geoffrey of: see *Geoffrey of Monmouth*.

Monstrelet, Enguerrand de (d. 1453): born about 1390, probably in Picardy, of noble birth, and holder of several minor offices, such as Governor of Cambray. He is one of the principal chroniclers of chivalry, his writings conveniently forming a direct continuation of those of Froissart. (See separate entry.) His chief concern was to record the wars of his time, so that he gives us an account of the civil wars between Orleans and Burgundy, of the invasion of Normandy by Henry V and the career of Joan of Arc. In his prologue, Monstrelet tells us he took care 'to make every diligent enquiry as to the truth of different events, and questioned such persons as from their rank and birth would disdain to relate a falsehood.' Especially, he talked to 'kings-at-arms, heralds, pursuivants and lords resident on their estates, respecting the wars of France, who, from their offices or situations, ought to be well informed of facts.' The third part of the Chronicles attributed to him are probably by another, and less original, hand.

Montferrat, Conrad of: a principal leader of the Third Crusade. After the recapture of the Holy City by the Saracens in 1187, he saved Tyre by his resolute defence and many of the refugees crowded to his banner. In 1192 he was elected King of Jerusalem but, before his coronation, was murdered by an assassin's dagger.

Montfort, Simon de, Earl of Leicester (1208?–1265): one of the heroic figures of the 13th century. Born in Normandy, his claim to the earldom of Leicester came through an English grandmother. At first he appeared to be little more than one more foreign adventurer at the court of Henry III, but presently showed great personal qualities of courage and a sense of justice. After varied fortunes he became a popular leader against the influence of foreign favourites and the misrule of Henry. In the ensuing civil war he defeated and captured the king at Lewes and called a famous Parliament (1265) which included two citizens from each borough as well as the knights, nobles and ecclesiastics. Eight months later he was overwhelmed and killed by the royal forces at Evesham. His reputation stood high with the common people and he was credited with more than two hundred miracles.

His arms are carved in painted stone in the north aisle of the nave of Westminster Abbey – a white lion with a forked tail on a red field.

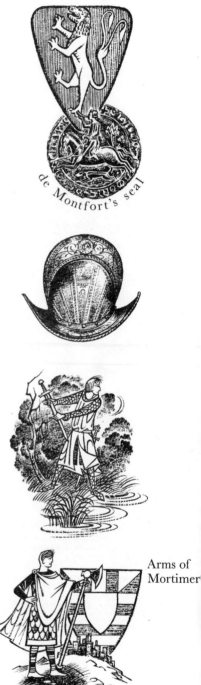

Arms at Westminster

de Montfort's seal

Montjoye St. Denis: the old national war-cry of France on the battle-field. It appears in the ancient royal arms of France.

Monumental Brass: see *Brass.*

Morgenstern: see *Mace.*

Morion: a late form of helmet (1570–1600), with strongly curved brim and a 'comb' at the top, sometimes as much as six inches high.

Morning Star: see *Mace.*

Morte d'Arthur: (i) the compilation of Arthurian stories made by Sir Thomas Malory (see *Malory, Sir Thomas*) and printed by William Caxton at Westminster in 1485. Though its full title is *The Noble Histories of King Arthur and of Certain of His Knights,* Caxton, in his epilogue, writes: 'Thus endeth thys noble and Joyous book entytled le morte Darthur.'

(ii) the poem by Tennyson describing the end of Arthur and the passing of the sword Excalibur when Sir Bedivere at last throws it into the lake. (See *Bedivere, Sir.*)

Mortimer, family of: one of the great families of Marcher Lords. (See separate entry.) The name is derived from Mortimer-en-Brai, in Normandy, from which came the first Roger de Mortimer, a relative of William the Conqueror, who gave him estates on the Welsh borders, including Wigmore, the future chief centre of the family's power. They fortified a number of great strongholds and played a dominant part in

Arms of Mortimer

English history, particularly in the 14th and 15th centuries.

An English Roll of Arms of 1270–1280 in the College of Heralds shows the arms of Mortimer as *barry of six, a chief paly, the corners gyronny azure and or, over all an escutcheon argent.* All of these heraldic terms are defined in various entries.

Mortimer's Cross, Battle of (February 2, 1461): fought between Edward, Duke of York (later Edward IV) and the Lancastrians, commanded by the Earl of Pembroke. On the morning of the all-day battle, Edward is said to have seen what seemed to him three suns, which suddenly joined together. He accepted this as a sign of good fortune – men in the Middle Ages were apt to seize on the slightest phenomenon as a promise of good or bad luck – and adopted the sun with rays as a badge.

The chronicler Holinshed records how the future king saw the sun 'like three sunnes, and suddenlie joined altogither in one; at which sight he took such courage that he, fiercelie setting on his enimies, put them to flight; and for this cause men imagined that he gave the sunne in his fulle brightnesse for his badge or cognisance.'

Edward certainly won a considerable victory, and went on to London to be proclaimed king; and his most famous badge was certainly the white rose in the sun. But, with deference to Holinshed, it was probably earlier in origin than Mortimer's Cross.

Motte-and-Bailey: the name given to the earliest type of Norman castle in England, made, not of stone, but of timber structures high on a motte, or mound. Sometimes this was a natural small hill or rock formation, but was often a great flat-topped mound raised by hard digging and the transport of immense quantities of soil. Much of the earth came from the ditch dug round the motte. The other unit, at a slightly lower level and surrounded by its own ramparts and defence ditch, was the bailey.

A 12th century French chronicler describes how the nobles in his part of France 'in order to defend themselves from their enemies . . . make a hill of earth, as high as they can, and encircle it with a ditch as broad and deep as possible.

206

They surround the upper edge of this hill with a very strong wall of hewn logs . . . Inside this wall they plant their house or keep.' The Bayeux Tapestry shows William I's soldiers throwing up this type of castle immediately after the Battle of Hastings.

Mottoes: are often considered an invariable accompaniment to a coat of arms, but, in fact, there are many without them. They are not part of grants of arms from the English College of Heralds, no one need have one and, unlike a coat of arms, no one needs any authority to adopt and use one. In Scotland, the position is different, since mottoes are registered, are granted as part of the arms and are hereditary.

Most family mottoes are of no antiquity. A few undoubtedly originated as war-cries in the Middle Ages, such as the Fitzgerald (Duke of Leinster) 'Croom-a-boo', which means 'Croom to victory!' and comes from the Castle of Croom in Co. Limerick. The same term appears in the motto of the Butler family (Marquess of Ormonde), 'Butler a boo.' The motto of the Percies (Duke of Northumberland), 'Esperance en Dieu', can probably be traced to the Percy war-cry of 'Esperance!' which Shakespeare puts into Hotspur's mouth in *Henry IV, Part I*. The English royal motto 'Dieu et Mon Droit' also probably began as a battle-cry.

Another small group commemorate historic events, such as 'Jour de ma Vie' taken by Sir Roger de la Warre after the Battle of Poitiers, in which he helped to capture King John of France. The motto is still carried by some of his descendants. The family of Kimberley display the single word 'Agincourt' as a motto, dating from an ancestor who was esquire of the body to Henry V, who granted him the arms and motto for his share in the great victory of 1415.

But most mottoes in England date no further back than the 18th century. No rules govern their adoption, their language, their number or their position. Some families have more than one. Some carry them beneath their arms, some above the crest. A browse through any volume such as a Burke's 'Peerage' – the short name by which this yearly publication is known – will reveal an astonishing range and complexity of mottoes – some terse, like 'Fight', 'Forward' and

'Thorough'; some long-winded, like 'Not for King and Country but for Both'; some daring, like 'Lead on' and 'Forward without Fear', others cautious, like 'Make haste slowly' and 'If I can'; some supremely arrogant, like 'Let Curzon hold what Curzon helde' and 'I Like my Choice'; some threatening, like 'Illingworth remembers' and 'Look out – I'm here'; and some extremely enigmatic and puzzling, one of the prizes going to Macpherson-Grant of Ballindalloch for 'Touch not the cat but a glove.'

Mowbray, family of: The holder of the Mowbray titles claims to be the Premier Baron of England, holding as one of them the Barony of Stourton, which is the oldest surviving barony created by Letters Patent, i.e., under the Great Seal of England. The long line produced many interesting characters, among them soldiers, knights, crusaders, benefactors and founders of churches, and holders of high office such as Earl Marshal. One, Thomas Mowbray, 12th Baron (1366?–1399), a Knight of the Garter and Warden of the Scottish marches, became involved in a quarrel with the Duke of Hereford, and a trial by combat was arranged before a great crowd at Coventry. But, doubtless to the disappointment of their supporters, Richard II stepped in at the last moment and stopped the fight, banishing both the would-be combatants for good measure.

Mufflers: mail mittens or fingerless gloves, enclosing the hand.

Mural Crown: in heraldry, a crown looking like a wall, with its top embattled like a castle.

Najera, Battle of (April 3, 1367): battle in Spain between the forces of Pedro 'the Cruel' of Castile and his half-brother Don Enrico (Henry) of Trastamara, who had driven him from his capital. It is remarkable for some of the personalities involved, for Enrico had secured the services of the great Bertrand du Guesclin (see separate entry); and Pedro, with his three dispossessed daughters, had played on the chivalric sympathies of the Black Prince at Bordeaux, with the result that the Prince came through the pass at Roncesvalles with famous captains like Knollys, Chandos and Calveley and with young John of Gaunt.

After several weeks of acute misery, in bitter weather, harried by dysentery and by marauding cavalry, while Enrico's army held an impregnable position and refused to be drawn into battle, the Black Prince managed to outflank them and presented himself in battle array at Najera in the Ebro plain.

Sir John Chandos was made knight-banneret that day, with Don Pedro himself cutting the tails of his pennant to make it square; and fought so lustily under his new banner that he drove ahead of his company and found himself unhorsed and surrounded. For some minutes he was in great peril of his life, till his friends broke through and rescued him. There was great gallantry on both sides, from the moment the Black Prince gave his great shout of 'Advance banners, in the name of God and St. George!' But, in the end, it was the same story that had been told on the battlefields of France at Crécy and Poitiers, with the English archers tumbling the chivalry of Spain till 16,000 knights and men-at-arms littered the plain. Among the captured was du Guesclin himself, taken by his old, and greatly esteemed, foe, Sir John Chandos.

The Prince of Wales had gained another great victory and, in the words of Froissart, 'was therefore the more honoured and renowned for it wherever true knighthood and deeds of enterprise were esteemed, particularly in the empire of Germany and England. The Germans, Flemings and English declared the prince of Wales was the mirror of knighthood, and that such a prince was worthy of governing the whole world.'

But it was a barren victory. Pedro the Cruel broke his promises of handsome payment, and dysentery and fever continued to prove more dreadful weapons than had the lances of Spain. One lustrous bauble survives to mark the dishonoured debts and the thousands of stout English yeomen who did not find their way back through Roncesvalles to their own country – the great ruby, called by the Black Prince's name and given to him by Don Pedro, that glows in the Imperial State Crown at the coronation of an English king or queen.

Naker: a kettle-drum; one of the array of musical instruments that often accompanied the mediaeval army and set it marching and singing. That musicians accompanied the army overseas we can see from Froissart's account of the battle of Les Espagnols-sur-Mer (see separate entry), when Edward III ordered them to strike up a dance and Sir John Chandos to sing.

Names: of people, and of things, provide us with many reminders of the Middle Ages, of the high days of chivalry and knighthood, and of all the trades and occupations that sustained them. Among surnames we have, of course, many a Squire and Knight, though it must be remembered that the original meaning of knight (Anglo-Saxon *cniht*) was a servant. This is not so incongruous as its sounds, since a knight was the servant of God, his lord and his lady.

There is the Frobisher (furbisher) who polished the knight's armour, and the Lorimer who made his bridles. Any telephone directory will have a list of the men who looked after his sporting activities, the Falconer (or Faulkner) and the Grosvenor (=*gros veneur*, great huntsman), while Messrs. Spark and Lennard tell us of the birds they flew (sparrowhawk and lanner).

Of the men who marched into battle (and won so many of them), none are more strongly represented than the archers and bowmen. A partial list of surnames shows:

Arrowsmith	maker of arrows
Fletcher	maker, or featherer, of arrows
Bower Bowyer }	maker of bows
Stringer	stringer of bows
Arblaster Ballister Bannister }	maker of cross-bows (arbalister = crossbow-man)

Boulter   maker of bolts for cross-bows.

The long, troubled story of the Crusades is with us in damask, the rich material with raised figures woven into the pattern that came originally from Damascus; and in the small damson, a plum from the same place. The Saracens ride again in another material, sarcenet, a thin, fine-textured silk.

Of all English words, there is none that takes us back so vividly and dramatically to those high adventures in the Holy Land as the humble codling, a kind of apple much used for baking. For the illustrious origin of this lowly word, see end of entry for *Richard I*.

Nasal: projecting piece of a helmet to protect the nose. It is best seen in Norman helmets, e.g., those on the Bayeux Tapestry. It was apparently either fixed or movable, since, at one point in the Battle of Hastings, when a rumour was circulating that Duke William was killed, he raised his nasal to show his face as proof that he was still very much alive.

National Flags: Early flags were almost always religious in their significance. Probably the earliest we know of in England was that borne by St. Augustine and his band of monks when he was sent to preach Christianity to the English nation. Bede tells us that they came into King Ethelbert's presence on the Isle of Thanet 'furnished with Divine, not with magic virtue, bearing a silver cross for their banner.'

Religious flags were given places of special honour in many early battles. A poem describing the capture of Rouen by the English in 1418 tells how they planted a number of banners to mark the victory:

> *To the Castelle firste he rode*
> *And sythen the citie all abrode,*
> *Lengthe and brede he it mette*
> *And riche baneres up he sette.*
> *Upon the Porte Seint Hillare*
> *A Baner of the Trynyte,*
> *And at Porte Kaux he sette evene*
> *A Baner of the Quene of Heven,*
> *And at Porte Martvile he upplyt*
> *Of Seint George a Baner breight.*

211

Only then, after he had set up the banners of the Trinity, the Queen of Heaven and St. George, did the captain:

> *. . . sette upon the Castelle to stonde*
> *The armys of Fraunce and Englond.*

At Agincourt, in 1415, Henry V displayed the banners of the Trinity, St. George and St. Edward as well as his own.

The chief banner under which English armies fought for centuries was that of St. George – a plain red cross on a white, or silver, field. When Richard II invaded Scotland an ordinance provided that 'every man of what estate, condition, or nation they be of, so that he be of our party, bear a sign of the arms of St. George, large, both before and behind.' (Spelling modernized.) In the reign of Henry V, John Talbot, Earl of Shrewsbury, issued the same instruction to the army going to France. Soldiers must 'beare a bande of Seint George sufficient large'. Strong attempts were made, too, to ensure that no enemy 'do bere the same token or crosse of Saint George.'

England, therefore, was fighting under the banner of its Patron Saint, just as the Scots fought under St. Andrew. The religious motive came first; and only later did the banner of St. George become identified with, and absorbed into, the arms of England or the national flag.

The national flag is now officially what is variously known as the Union Jack, the Union Flag and – the most correct, heraldically speaking – the Union Banner. It is 'the fighting emblem of the Sovereign', and may be flown on land by any British subject. It is a combination of:

The cross of St. George (argent, a cross gules)
The cross of St. Andrew (azure, a saltire argent)
The cross of St. Patrick (argent, a saltire gules)

Two refreshing modern writers on heraldry, Sir Christopher and Adrian Lynch-Robinson, describe it as giving 'equality to both Celtic peoples by the production of an ingenious composition, the official blazon of which, in its unintelligible complexity, is a serious rival to the best efforts of an income-tax official in one of his more lucid intervals.'

Naval Crown: heraldic crown, bearing on its rim the sails and sterns of old-time ships alternately.

212

Naval Engagements: see *Les Espagnols-sur-Mer* and *Sluys* for two great sea-fights in the days of chivalry.

Navarre: an ancient, and much fought over, province of Spain, sometimes independent, sometimes united with Aragon, sometimes with France. The 'Navarrery' was the war waged at one time by the kings of Navarre against France. Soldiers such as the Black Prince and Bertrand du Guesclin campaigned there.

Nebuly: one of the partition lines used to divide a shield. (See *Partition, Lines of.*)

Needle John: see *Hawkwood, Sir John.*

Negroli: one of the great families of armourmakers who settled in Milan and rose to fame and royal patronage. (See *Italian Armour.*)

Neville, family of: one of the greatest names in English history, from the early 14th century onwards. By creation, marriage and inheritance they acquired at various times, and for various periods, the earldoms of Westmorland, Salisbury and Warwick, as well as many baronies and other titles. Its greatest member was Richard Neville, Earl of Warwick (1428–71), called 'the King-maker' and 'the last of the Barons.' (See next entry for more details.) Nearly fifty others are found worth mentioning in the Dictionary of National Biography. Among them were many Knights of the Garter, Wardens of the Marches, Chancellors and Marshals of England. One of them, Anne, daughter of 'the King-maker', became Queen of England.

Its most famous badge was the bear and ragged staff, really a combination of two badges, which were often used separately.

Neville, Richard, Earl of Warwick (1428–71): called 'the King-maker'; owner of vaster estates than any subject had held before; a man of enormous wealth and innumerable retainers, popular with the crowd, magnificently dressed and capable of highly dramatic gestures, as when, at the Battle of Towton (see separate entry) in 1460, he rallied the Yorkist line by stabbing his horse before their eyes as a sign that he would not

fly, and swearing by the cross of his sword that he would not leave the field alive as a loser. He became a hero with the people by capturing five or six great Spanish and Genoese ships and bringing them into Calais. Writing to Margaret Paston on June 1, 1458, John Jernyngan wrote:

'Moreover, on Trinity Sunday in the morning, came tidings unto my Lord of Warwick, that there were 28 sail of Spaniards on the sea, and whereof there was sixteen great ships of forecastle; and then my lord went, and manned five ships of forecastle and three carvells and four spynnes; and on the Monday, in the morning after Trinity Sunday, we met together afore Calais at four at the clock in the morning, and fought together till ten at the clock; and there we took six of their ships, and they slew of our men about fourscore, and hurt a 200 of us right sore; and there were slain on their part about 120, and hurt a 500 of them.'

(The spelling has been modernized. A 'ship of forecastle' was one with the raised fighting-platform at the fore; a carvel or caravel was a lighter, smaller ship; and a spynne, or pinnace, was little more than a large rowing boat.)

According to one observer, Warwick always took care to owe the citizens of London 300,000 or 400,000 crowns, so that they were always anxious for his health and safety. A song of the time called him 'of Knighthode lodesterre, a guiding-star of knighthood borne of a stok that evyr schal be trewe.' But it was far from the truth. No-one could dispute his courage, but his loyalty was another matter. He was too arrogant and too touchy to remain faithful to one master.

He went down at the end to one of his former friends, Edward IV, at the Battle of Barnet (1471); was exposed to the public gaze of the Londoners, to prove there was no Warwick left to fight for, and was taken to Bisham Priory, Berkshire, for burial.

(See also *Warwick Roll*.)

Neville's Cross, Battle of (October 17, 1346): fought near Durham, between an invading army of Scots under David II, son of Robert the Bruce, and the northern levies led by Henry Percy, 2nd Baron, one of the Nevilles and William de la Zouche, Archbishop of York. (See *Zouche, William de la*.) The English archers were responsible for a complete victory. The Scottish king was taken prisoner and remained in captivity for eleven years, making a fortune for his captor, a young squire who was given the rank of banneret and a yearly pension of £500, which would be worth forty times as much today. Another disaster for Scotland was the capture of the celebrated Black Rood of Scotland, revered as a piece of the True Cross, set in an ebony figure of Our Lord, all enclosed in a small cross about nine inches long. The Rood, along with the royal banner, was taken to hang in St. Cuthbert's shrine at Durham, where nothing more seems to have been heard of it after the Reformation.

St. Cuthbert's banner was also present at the battle. It was:

'Suspended from a horizontal bar below a spear head, and was a yard or so in length and a little more than this in depth; the bottom edge had five deep indentations. The banner was of red velvet sumptuously enriched with gold embroidery, and in the centre was a piece of white velvet, half a yard square, having a cross of red velvet upon it. This central portion covered and protected a relic of the saint.' (Edward Hulme.)

Norfolk, Dukes of: hereditary Earls Marshal of England since 1672 and, by virtue of that office, heads of the College of Arms. Writing in 1873, Sir Bernard Burke, Ulster King of Arms, said:

'Just four centuries of ducal rank and just eight centuries of unsullied ancestry are associated with the name of Howard [the family name of the Dukes of Norfolk]. In the combination of antiquity of descent, and the possession of the highest peerage honours with the most brilliant public services and the most illustrious alliances, the family of the Duke of Norfolk is unrivalled. Next to the blood-royal, Norfolk is not only at the head of the titled ranks of this empire, but also, I maintain, at the head of European nobility.... No less than nineteen Howards [it is more now] have been Knights of the Garter – no other family can boast as many – and full twenty distinct peerages have at various times been conferred on this illustrious house.'

Another heraldic authority, earlier than Burke,

asks 'what other family pervades all our national annals with such frequent mention, and often involved in circumstances of such intense and brilliant interest? . . . heroes, poets, politicians, courtiers, patrons of literature, state victims to tyranny and revenge, and feudal chiefs.'

Our 19th century authors were perhaps a little carried away by their enthusiasm. There was, after all, a Tudor member of the family who 'for various selfish reasons changed his religion no fewer than five times' and was 'a monster of wickedness and hypocrisy' and another was deprived of the office of Lord High Treasurer of England for extortion and embezzlement. But these and other lapses in a thousand years of history do not dim the lustre of the innumerable achievements of this English family.

Norman Castle: see *Castle* and *Motte-and-Bailey.*

Normandy: in northern France, and easily accessible from England. A duchy since 911 and a fief of the French crown, it became some of the most contested and ravaged land in Europe. The Black Prince landed here for the Crécy campaign and Henry V conquered it in 1415. Duke William of Normandy, by his conquest of 1066, gave to England a new race of nobles, knights and landowners from whom sprang many of the most illustrious names in English chivalry.

Norroy King-at-Arms: see *Officers of Arms.*

Northallerton, Battle of: see *Battle of the Standard* and *Neville's Cross* (for St. Cuthbert's banner).

Northrop of Manningham, John: The City of Bradford, Yorkshire, includes in its coat of arms three horns and a well; and, for a crest, carries a tongueless boar's head with a sprig of oak tree behind it. The reason is a story told in *The Dalesman* for June, 1966:

'Some 500 years ago, it is said, there was a ravenous wild boar of enormous size which lived in Cliffe Wood . . . This boar infested the town and neighbouring districts, giving fear to the inhabitants. The Government offered a reward for the destruction of this beast. On

St. Martin's Day the king would present this to the deliverer.

A crafty woodsman hid himself in an oak tree to watch the habits of the boar, discovering that it frequented a particular well, today known as Boar's Well. In due course he shot the boar with his bow and arrow. It was too heavy for him to remove, so he cut out the tongue and placed it in his knapsack. . . .

When our hero had departed, another cunning young man came along, saw the boar lying defenceless and conceived the idea of claiming the reward. Again it was too heavy to remove, so he cut off the head. Later the same day he claimed the reward and was presented to the king. Closer inspection by the monarch revealed that the tongue had been removed and this man could not offer a suitable explanation.

Then the real hero, John Northrop, presented himself, unfolded the riddle of the missing tongue and was duly recognized and given title to a portion of land (which is now named Hunt Yard and is in Great Horton). There was a further provision that he should attend the market place in Bradford each St. Martin's Day holding a hunting dog while three blasts were blown on a "gelder's" horn.'

Northumberland, Earls of: a line of great northern landowners, of the Percy family, who for centuries played a great part in the martial history of England, especially along the borders, which they long guarded as Wardens of the Marches. So strong was their position, in such castles as Alnwick and Warkworth, that it was once a saying that 'the north knows no king but Percy.' Of the first six Earls (1377–1537), all were Wardens of one or other of the Marches and four were killed in battle.

The most famous early member of the family, Sir Henry Percy, called 'Hotspur' (see separate entry under this nick-name), son of the first Earl, did not succeed to the earldom because he was killed at the Battle of Shrewsbury in 1403.

(See also *Douglas, James, second Earl* and *Mottoes.*)

Nuremberg: One of the most famous centres of armour-making in Germany.

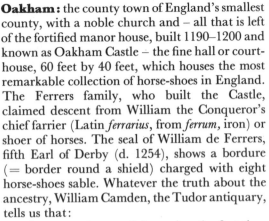

Oakham: the county town of England's smallest county, with a noble church and – all that is left of the fortified manor house, built 1190–1200 and known as Oakham Castle – the fine hall or court-house, 60 feet by 40 feet, which houses the most remarkable collection of horse-shoes in England. The Ferrers family, who built the Castle, claimed descent from William the Conqueror's chief farrier (Latin *ferrarius*, from *ferrum*, iron) or shoer of horses. The seal of William de Ferrers, fifth Earl of Derby (d. 1254), shows a bordure (= border round a shield) charged with eight horse-shoes sable. Whatever the truth about the ancestry, William Camden, the Tudor antiquary, tells us that:

'. . . every baron of the realm, the first time he comes through the town of Okeham where the Ferrers seat was, shall give a horse-shoe to nail on the Castle gate. If he refuse, the bailiff of the manor has power to stop his coach and take one off the horses' feet. But mainly they give five, ten or twenty shillings, more or less, as they please, and in proportion to the gift the shoe is made larger or smaller, with the name and title of the donor cut upon it. So it is nailed upon the gate.'

The custom is still kept up, but the horse-shoes have been transferred to the walls of the Castle hall.

Odo (d. 1097): Bishop of Bayeux and Earl of Kent; half-brother of William the Conqueror. Odo sent forty ships to help in the invasion of England and, despite the fact that he was a churchman, played a big part in the Battle of Hastings, where his weapon was the mace. (See *Mace*.)

'The varlets who were set to guard the harness began to abandon it as they saw the loss of the Frenchmen ... Being greatly alarmed at seeing the difficulty in restoring order, they began to quit the harness and sought around, not knowing where to find shelter. Then Duke William's brother Odo, the good priest, the bishop of Bayeux, galloped up and said to them, "Stand fast! Stand fast! be quiet and move not! Fear nothing, for, if God please, we shall conquer yet."

So they took courage, and rested where they were; and Odo returned galloping back to

218

where the battle was most fierce, and was of great service on that day. He had put a hauberk on, over a white aube [or alb, a white linen surplice]; wide in the body, with the sleeve tight; and sat on white horse, so that all might recognise him. In his hand he held a mace, and wherever he saw most need he held up and stationed the knights, and often urged them on to assault and strike the enemy.' (*Roman de Rou.*)

It will be clear that Odo, who had been made a bishop at about the age of fifteen, had his mind on other matters than holy ones. William, in fact, imprisoned him later for 'his overweening pride' and his tyranny as a ruler. He was banished in William II's reign and went on the First Crusade, dying in Sicily in 1097. Despite his great faults, he was a patron of learning and of the arts. There is a strong probability that it was he who commissioned the Bayeux Tapestry.

Officers of Arms: those who exercise official control over the granting, recording and display of arms; and who perform ceremonial duties on certain great state occasions, such as the proclamation of a new sovereign. Their origin may be found in the herald-messengers attached to all great households, wearing the arms of their master and, if necessary, able to recite his titles, his achievements and those of his ancestors. They later came to exercise control over such events as tournaments, and the king's own heralds gradually acquired special knowledge of the arms of his subjects and began to exert supervision over them, adjudicating in cases of dispute.

In 1484, Richard III formally constituted his body of royal heralds by special charter and thus founded the College of Heralds which, under the Sovereign and the Earl Marshal, exercises supreme control over all heraldic matters in England. (See *College of Heralds.*)

Many titles and offices have come and gone in the course of the centuries. Kings of Arms were, e.g., nominated at one time for such foreign territories as Anjou and Aquitaine; and we come across such forgotten offices as Falcon King of Arms, Leicester King of Arms, Marche Herald, Agincourt Herald, etc.

There are now thirteen officers attached to the College of Arms – three Kings of Arms, six

Heralds and four Pursuivants.

The Kings of Arms are Garter, Clarenceux and Norroy. (See *Kings of Arms*.)

The Heralds are Chester, Lancaster, Richmond, Somerset, Windsor and York.

The Pursuivants (i.e. originally 'followers' or attendants on the Heralds) are Bluemantle, Portcullis, Rouge Croix and Rouge Dragon. Bluemantle takes his name from the blue field of the French coat of arms assumed by Edward III when he claimed the title; Portcullis from the badge used by the Tudors; Rouge Croix (Red Cross) from the red cross of St. George; and Rouge Dragon from the red dragon of Wales, used as one of the supporters of the arms of Henry VII.

The official costume of the Officers of Arms is the tabard. (See separate entry.) Different materials are used for the three classes of Officer, Kings of Arms wearing velvet, Heralds satin, and Pursuivants damask silk. Kings of Arms and Heralds, but not Pursuivants, wear the collar of SS. (See separate entry.) There are also various differences in badges, batons, etc.

In Scotland, the principal Officer is the Lord Lyon King of Arms, assisted by three heralds and three pursuivants. In Ireland, Ulster King of Arms used to have two heralds and two pursuivants; but in 1943 the Government of Eire took over all the records and possessions of the Ulster Office and appointed its own Chief Herald and Genealogical Officer in Dublin. It was wished, however, that the ancient title and office of Ulster King of Arms should be somehow preserved, and Norroy King of Arms therefore combined the title with his own.

Most European countries have, or have had, their Officers of Arms in one form or another. It is a strange fact that, when the slaves in the West Indian island of Haiti rebelled against their French rulers and established a Negro kingdom, they established Officers of Arms. When Henri Christophe, an illiterate black slave, became king of Haiti in 1811, he created from his fellow slaves a body of nobles, a King of Arms and thirteen Heralds, each named after one of the island's townships – Cap Henri, Jacmel, Sans Souci, etc.

Old Man of the Mountains: Soon after the death of Mohammed, the prophet-founder of the faith against which the Crusaders fought, his followers split into two rival groups, each under its own Caliph (= 'successor' to Mohammed) and with separate chief cities, Baghdad and Cairo. The Christians called them all Saracens. The two great groups, which were dispersed and mixed-up in all the Mohammedan territories, were bitter enemies of each other, as well as being generally the foes of the Franks, which was the general name for all Christians, from whatever nation and country they were recruited. The sect that ruled from Cairo had a particularly violent and fanatical branch in Persia, where its chiefs got possession of several great mountain strongholds, the most important of which was Alamut. The members of this troublesome and dangerous branch were called the 'Assassins', derived from *Hashishiyun* (hasish), the drug they frequently took. 'Assassin' has now passed into our everyday language for a type of murderer.

The chief, or Sheik, of the Assassins received the name, the Old Man of the Mountains. The most famous of these leaders was Hasan-i-Sabbah, or Hassan-ben-Sabah, whose emissaries carried out many murders. See *Montferrat, Conrad of* for one Christian leader killed by the Old Man of the Mountains. An example of the other side of their activities, i.e., against other Mohammedans, is that the famous Saladin awoke in his tent one night to find on his pillow some cakes, still warm, of a kind baked only by the Assassins, a poisoned dagger and a warning letter. He was on his way to attack them, but, after this sharp warning, gave up the idea and made peace.

Oliferne, Agadinquor: Most European chroniclers, naturally, drew glowing pictures of Christian knights. But occasionally we get a vivid account of a Saracen. Here is one from Froissart:

'Among the Saracens was a young knight, called Agadinquor Oliferne, excellently mounted on a beautiful courser, which he managed as he willed, and which, when he galloped, seemed to fly with him. From his gallantry, he shewed he was a good man at arms; and, when he rode abroad, he had with him three javelins, well feathered, which he dexterously slung, according to the custom of his country. He was completely armed in black, and had a kind of white napkin wrapped about his head. His seat on horseback was

graceful . . . I heard that, during the siege [of a Tunisian town] he performed many handsome feats of arms . . . which the French knights saw with pleasure, and would willingly have surrounded him; but he rode with such activity and skill that all their efforts were vain.'

Oliver: in the *Song of Roland* (see separate entry) the great friend of Roland and, with him, chief of Charlemagne's paladins. Like Roland, he died in the battle at Roncesvalles, sung about by all the minstrels and troubadours of the Middle Ages. 'A Roland for his [your] Oliver' has become a proverbial saying, meaning to deal a blow of equal strength in return, to give as good as one gets.

Olwen: see *Kilhwch.*

Open Course: a joust between knights run in the open lists or field, without any barrier between.

Ordain, to: to enact the ceremony of making a knight; the *ordainer* was the one who performed the actual knighting.

Ordeal by Battle (or by Combat): see *Battle, Trial by.*

Orders of Chivalry: see *Knights, Various Orders of,* and separate entries for *Knights Hospitallers, Knights Templars, Knights Teutonic; Blue Garter, Order of; Golden Fleece; Royal Victorian Order; Thistle, Order of; St. Michael and St. George, Order of.* For Order of the Bath, see *Henry VII's Chapel* and *Knight.*

Ordinances for the Army: interesting examples have survived in the records of the College of Heralds and in the British Museum of the instructions drawn up for military expeditions in the Middle Ages. Two date from the reigns of Henry V and Henry VI, and cover in great detail the conduct, etc., demanded of the soldiers.

Henry V's Ordinance, dated 1419, is a general military code. The king is known to have hung a soldier on one occasion for robbing a church, and the opening clauses are devoted to offences of sacrilege: e.g.,

> 'Also that no maner of man be so hardey to robbe, ne [neither] to pille [pillage] Holy Church of no good ne ornament that longeth to the Churche, ne to slee [slay] no man of Holy Churche, religious, ne none other, but if he be armed, upon payne of deathe.'

One order forbids any man, also upon pain of death, to begin indiscriminate slaughter of the enemy by crying 'Havoc!' which explains why Shakespeare uses this expression in *Julius Caesar*, when Mark Antony says: 'Cry "Havoc!" and let slip the dogs of war.' Another lays down that every man shall pay a third of his 'winning by wars' to his captain, lord or master. No child of under fourteen years shall be taken prisoner, unless he is a lord's son or some other person of note. No man, whatever tidings or rumours he hears shall 'move him in disarray out of the battle; and – a very practical piece of economy – if any soldier finds any wine or food, he may help himself to as much as he wants, but he must save the rest for the benefit of others. A very humanitarian order forbids any man to take 'horse, mare, nor ox, nor none other beast' from any labourer going to the plough or harrow, or use his cart. In all there are more than forty ordinances.

The second set was drawn up by the famous soldier, John Talbot, Earl of Shrewsbury, probably for the army under his particular command. It includes some of the same sort of instructions for behaviour, but also gives valuable information about equipment; e.g.,

> 'Also that every Capitayne doe compelle ther yogmen [yeomen], every man in all haste, to make him a good substanciall stake of xi foote of lengthe.' These were pointed stakes stuck into the ground by the archers as a defence against the enemy cavalry.

> 'Also that every man make him a good substanciall fagott of xiii foote of length . . .' These were intended for screens against the enemy's shot, for filling in ditches during a siege, etc.

Other orders concern the making of scaling ladder of 15 rungs, and 'pavises' or tall shields, one to every pair of archers, so that one could hold it as defence, while the second shot his arrows.

Ordinaries: a group of charges upon a shield, many of which are defined separately in this book. There has been much argument and disagreement among experts as to why some charges should be called 'ordinaries', some 'sub-ordinaries' and some by completely different names. But the commonly accepted ordinaries are: the *Chief, Fess* (or *Fesse*), *Bend, Bar, Pale, Cross, Saltire, Chevron* and *Pile*. The sub-ordinaries are usually reckoned to be the *Inescutcheon, Bordure, Orle, Tressure, Canton, Flanches, Gyron, Lozenge, Fusil, Roundels, Annulet, Fret* and *Billet.*

Ordnance: heavy weapons of war, such as cannon and artillery.

Oriflamme: (see also *Arms of France*). The name of the ancient banner of France means 'gold' and 'flame'. It was always carried before the kings of France and, in times of peace, was kept in the treasure-house of the Abbey of Saint Denis. At first the banner seems to have been a plain red and was only later embroidered with golden flames or stars. It was reckoned a supreme honour to carry the oriflamme and its appearance on the field of battle was supposed to have an unnerving effect on the enemy ranks. An early French chronicle describes a French knight sitting on his great destrier, grasping a lance to which was attached the oriflamme, of red samite, with three tails and with green silken tassels between. The number of tails, however, varied.

Orle: in heraldry, a *bordure* is a frame right round the outside of a shield. An *orle* is a bordure inside the shield, some distance from the edge.

Orleans: see *Joan of Arc.*

Orleans, Maid of: see *Joan of Arc.*

Ormonde, John, sixth Earl of (d. 1478): an Irish nobleman, of whom Edward IV is reported to have said: 'If good breeding and liberal qualities were lost in the world, they might be all found in the Earl of Ormonde.'

Enguerrand de Monstrelet, in his Chronicles, tells us that, in the year 1449, 'the captain of Robert de Flocques, bailiff of Evreux, was sent with a certain number of men-at-arms to summon

224

the garrison and inhabitants of Vernon (Verneuil) to submit themselves to the king of France, by sending him the keys of the town. The governor, John Ormond, an esquire, son to the Earl of Ormond in Ireland, replied that he would willingly do so – and, by way of derision and mockery, sent for all the old keys he could from the locksmiths in the town, and presented them to the pursuivant who had brought the summons.'
In the attack on the town which followed, the English lost the bridge and Ormonde was pierced 'through both his cheeks' with an arrow. A parley then took place between besieged and besiegers. The French members of the garrison urged surrender to the king of France and, by weight of numbers, carried the decision. The English agreed only if letters were drawn up declaring the surrender had been arranged without their consent. With John Ormonde at their head, the 250 Englishmen were allowed to march away in safety with all their baggage.

Ormonde was a capable linguist and acted as ambassador to several European courts. In 1478, having (in what Burke calls 'a fit of devotion') gone on pilgrimage to Jerusalem, he died in the Holy Land.

Ostrevant, William de Hainault, Count of: a knight of whom we hear a good deal in the pages of Froissart, particularly at a great tournament held in London in 1390 by Richard II:

'Many knights and squires from foreign lands made preparations to attend it, some to see the manners of the English, others to take part in the tournaments. On the feast being made known in Hainault, Sir William de Hainault, Count d'Ostrevant, who was at that time young and gallant, and fond of tilting, determined in his own mind to be present, and to honour and make acquaintance with his cousin King Richard and his uncles, whom he had never seen.'

When the Count of Ostrevant informed his father of his plan, he met with much opposition on the grounds that the visit to England would incur the great displeasure of the king of France, to whom Ostrevant was connected by marriage. In the end, however, his father said: 'You are your own master. Act as you please.'

Ostrevant crossed the Channel with a great company of other knights and squires. He arrived too late for the opening of the tournament, which was called 'the feast of the challengers'; and a very pretty show it must have been, for there appeared 'sixty barded coursers ornamented for the tournament. On each was mounted a squire of honour that advanced only at a foot's pace.' Then came 'sixty ladies of rank mounted on palfreys most elegantly and richly dressed, following each other, every one leading a knight with a silver chain, completely armed for tilting.'

Count Ostrevant made up for lost time the next day when, the chronicler says, 'you would have seen . . . squires and varlets busily employed in different parts of London, furbishing and making ready armour and horses for their masters who were to engage in the jousts.'

At the end of the day the Count was awarded the prize for the best opponent (as distinct from the 'tenants' or challengers), having 'far eclipsed all who had tilted that day.'

After another three days of tournaments, King Richard entertained all the foreign knights and squires at a great banquet at Windsor Castle; and there the young Count received an even greater honour than the prize of the tournament. He was invited to become one of the members of the Order of the Blue Garter. He gladly accepted, and was admitted a knight-companion in the Chapel of St. George.

The sequel proved how right Ostrevant's father had been about the reaction of the king of France. There were plenty of jealous tongues to convey the news that the Count, by taking the oath of the Order of the Blue Garter, had made himself King Richard's man and could never in future bear arms against England. Ostrevant had some difficulty in persuading the king of France that he had been in no way disloyal to him. In the end, he went to Paris and did homage for his territories, the king having threatened to dispossess him if he did not.

Otterburn, Battle of (August 19, 1388): the foray on the Scottish border in which Hotspur was taken prisoner and James, second Earl Douglas, was killed. The Scots army was split into two forces, which came into England by different routes. It was the smaller division which, having harried the countryside as far south as Durham, doubled back to Otterburn in Northumberland, where they were surprised by two of the Percies, Ralph and Hotspur. Hotspur was the more anxious to seek out Douglas in that, a few weeks before, when the Scots were investing Newcastle, the two leaders had met in single combat outside the walls, and Hotspur had been unhorsed and stunned, losing his lance and pennon. Later, the captured pennon had been paraded outside the walls of Newcastle, Douglas saying:

'Sir, I shall bear this token of your prowess into Scotland, and shall set it high in my castle of Dalkeith, that it may be seen far off.'
Hotspur's reply was:

'Sir, ye may be sure ye shall not pass the bounds of the country till ye be met withal in such wise that ye shall make none avaunt [no boast] thereof.'
Hotspur fulfilled his promise at Otterburn where, though Douglas seems to have been waiting his appearance, the Scots were surprised by a sudden onslaught at dusk, when some were at supper and some already asleep. Froissart heard all about this moonlight battle from knights and squires on either side. He was particularly interested because, in his youth, he had travelled in Scotland and had stayed for a fortnight at the castle of Dalkeith with Douglas's father, when the second Earl was but a small boy. He says of Otterburn:

'Of all the battles that have been described in this history, great and small, this of which I am now speaking, was the best fought and the most severe; for there was not a man, knight or squire, who did not acquit himself gallantly, hand to hand with his enemy.'
It seems a just verdict. Douglas went down before three spear-thrusts, after performing prodigies of valour with his battle-axe. Mortally wounded, he cheered on his companions to the last, and asked them to raise his banner again from the place where it had fallen in the hands of his gallant young squire, David Collemine, who had refused knighthood from the hands of his lord that day till he had further proved himself. Sir Ralph Percy pressed so far ahead that he was cut off from his supporters and, badly

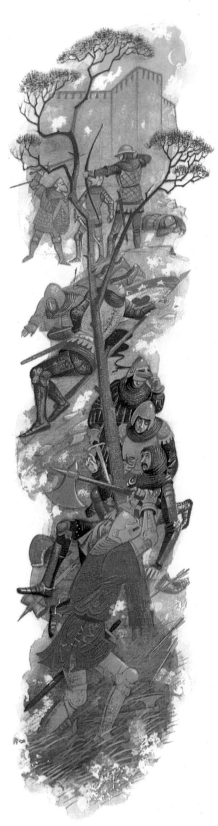

wounded, was taken by Sir John Maxwell, a Scottish knight, who saw to it that he was honourably treated and his wounds dressed. Hotspur had a long hand-to-hand struggle with a knight named Montgomery who, in the end, defeated and took him.

The final issue of the battle remains doubtful. The Scots claimed a decisive victory and, considering that they were the smaller force, certainly achieved great things; but the fact remains that they went back over the Cheviots without following up their advantage.

Montgomery was one of those who did well in more ways than one that day. Hotspur was ransomed for £3,000, Parliament voting £1,000 of it. One would like to know the fate of Hotspur's captured pennon. One account has it that Douglas gave it to one of his squires, in whose family it was treasured through the centuries. Bishop Percy, during a visit to Roxburghshire in 1774, was shown the 400-year-old tattered fabric that carried in its faded colours so much of border history. (See also *Douglas, James, second Earl of*.)

Ourique, Battle of (July 25, 1139): fought nearly 100 miles S.E. of Lisbon, Portugal, between Alfonso and a great army of Moors, including, it is said, five Saracen kings. Alfonso won a decisive victory and afterwards was crowned first King of Portugal.

Outlaws: favourite subjects for romantic song and story, though the reality usually provided a less agreeable picture. To be 'out of the law' meant that the man or woman concerned could no longer claim its protection or benefits. They were deemed to 'bear a wolf's head'; which meant that, at certain periods in our history, a man might kill an outlaw without fear of punishment, just as he would kill a dangerous wolf. Outlawry often meant the loss of all one's goods and lands, and the only life left was a wandering, hunted one in the all-sheltering forest, where pursuit was difficult and where, with a little luck and skill, a man could hide for years, occasionally breaking cover to visit his friends and kinsfolk.

One of the two best-known outlaws in English history and literature was Hereward (flourished about 1070), first called 'the Wake' by a writer about a hundred years afterwards. Hereward was a real person, but within fifty or sixty years of his death he was already a hero of song and story, so that it is almost impossible to disentangle fact and fiction. What is quite certain is that he carried out a heroic resistance to the Norman invaders in the marshes of Ely and gathered round him a resolute band of other outlaws. Hereward was gaining such a reputation that William I led an expedition in person to crush him. The king blocked every outlet on the eastern side and built a great bridge on the west. Hopelessly hemmed in, most of the outlaws surrendered, but Hereward contrived to escape. The rest is in doubt; and whether he continued his resistance elsewhere or made his peace, whether he was killed overseas in Maine or died at home in his bed, a reformed character, we shall probably never know.

Robin Hood, the other character, was more legendary, though there is a possibility that somewhere, at some time, there was an outlaw who provided the tiny kernel from which grew such a vast tree of stories. A number of counties claim him, including Yorkshire, Nottinghamshire, Cumberland and Huntingdon. 'Hood' derives from 'Hodeken', a forest elf, and this gives a good clue to the solidity of Robin and his merry men in the greenwood. But, for the comfort of those who are reluctant to banish him entirely to the realm of legend and fairy story, here is one fact to clutch at. In the year 1230, according to the records of the Exchequer, the sheriff of Yorkshire owed the sum of 32s. 6d., due from the sale of the goods of one Robin, an outlaw.

The most charming early 'outlaw' poem in the language is certainly *The Nut Brown Maid*, dating, probably, from the 15th century. In this, a gallant young squire has, apparently, to choose between a shameful death and escape to the greenwood. He comes to his betrothed, a great baron's daughter, and says:

> *I am the knyght; I come by nyght,*
> *As secret as I can;*
> *Saying, Alas! thus standeth the case,*
> *I am a banished man.*

His lady loyally wishes to follow him, to share his hardships, and the two have a long discussion, in delightfully musical and rhythmic language, with the squire describing all the difficulties and desperate dangers of the forest life, and the girl,

with great feminine firmness, insisting in accompanying him. Both have a little refrain, the squire always finishing his arguments, with slight variations, on the words:

> For I must to the grene wode go
> Alone, a banyshed man:

and the lady faithfully asserting:

> For in my mynde, of all mankynde
> I love but you alone.

Threats that their life would be without proper shelter in all weathers, that food would be coarse and scanty, that she would have to learn to draw a bow and cut off all her fine hair, these and all other dismal prophecies do not sway the nut-brown maid from her determination to live out her life with her young lord.

The ending is happy enough; for the shameful fellow has just been testing her out. He is neither a humble squire nor a banished man, but the son of the Earl of Westmorland.

> Nowe undyrstande, to Westmarlande,
> Which is myne herytage,
> I wyll you brynge; and with a rynge
> By way of maryage
> I wyll you take, and lady make,
> As shortely as I can:
> Thus have you won an erlys son,
> And not a banyshed man.

Outremer: literally 'overseas'; the general name for the territories, including Palestine, the Nile Delta, Cyprus and Cilicia, over which Mohammedans and Christians fought in the Crusades.

'Over-the-Barriers': see *Tilt*.

Oxford, John de Vere, thirteenth Earl of (1443–1513): an adventurous character who fought in the Wars of the Roses. After the Lancastrian defeat at Barnet (see separate entry), he escaped to France, got together a few ships and made a living by piracy. He then seized St. Michael's Mount, Cornwall, and was besieged there, 1473–4. He surrendered and, after a ten-year imprisonment at Hammes, Picardy, managed to persuade the governor of the castle to throw in his lot with Henry of Richmond, later Henry VII. Oxford fought at the Battle of Bosworth, which gave Henry the crown, and stood high in the king's favour. (See also *Livery and Maintenance, Statutes of*.)

Paladin: a knight-errant, a great champion.

Paladins of Charlemagne: the legendary company of knights that formed the élite of the Emperor's army. Of these, there was a special company of Twelve Paladins who were in his immediate entourage. (See *Charlemagne's Paladins* for some of their names.)

Pale: in heraldry, a vertical band running down the centre of the shield, occupying about a third of its width. One of the most famous examples of this in English history is not on a knightly shield, but on a sign outside a workshop. When William Caxton, the first English printer, set up his business in Westminster in 1476, he hung outside 'the sign of the Red Pale', so that his premises could be easily recognized. *Paly* is used to describe a shield divided into a number of vertical stripes, the number always being stated, e.g., *paly of six, or* and *azure*. Another way of dividing the field is *paly-bendy*, i.e., first by drawing vertical lines and then slanting, or *bendy* lines, the same width apart.

Palfrey: a horse of good breeding, used for travelling and hunting, and, because of its good disposition and ease of control, particularly valuable for occasions of display and ceremony. (See also *Horse* and *Jennet*.) The Monk in Chaucer's *Canterbury Tales*, who had 'ful many a deyntee hors' in his stable, chose a palfrey, 'broun as is a berye' on which to ride on his pilgrimage.

Palimpsest Brass: see *Brass* for a general account of these memorials. 'Palimpsest' really means 'scraped again'; and a palimpsest brass is one on which the original figure and lettering have been erased, and the brass re-used for a later figure. This was usually for reasons of economy. The same technique was used for documents when parchment and vellum were scarce and expensive. Sometimes, instead of erasing the earlier memorial, the brass was just turned over and the other side used.

The results could sometimes be amusing; e.g., in Waterperry Church, Oxfordshire, there is a brass to Walter Curzon. The brass tablet was first laid down in about 1450, when long, pointed shoes were in fashion. The brass was re-used in

1520, when toes were rounded. But the 1450 points were left, so that Curzon is shown wearing two pairs of shoes, one seventy years older than the other.

Pallisado Crown: in heraldry, a crown from the rim of which rise a number of 'palisades' or stakes, widening slightly from bottom to top, and each riveted separately.

Paris, Matthew (d. 1259): a Benedictine monk of St. Albans who became a distinguished historian and craftsman, a fine scribe and a worker in gold and silver. Henry III personally asked him to write a record of certain events 'lest in the future their memory be in any way lost to posterity.' His *Chronica Majora* is 'the first illustrated chronicle of current affairs.' His skilful pictures include a self-portrait. This is part of his description of the festivities at the marriage of Henry III with Eleanor of Provence in 1236:

'The whole city was ornamented with flags and banners, chaplets and hangings, candles and lamps, and with wonderful devices and extraordinary representations, and all the roads were cleansed from mud and dirt, sticks and everything offensive. The citizens, too, went out to meet the king and queen, dressed out in their best ornaments, and vied with each other in trying the speed of their horses. On the same day, when they left the city for Westminster, to perform the duties of butler to the king (which office belonged to them by right of old, at the coronation), they proceeded thither dressed in silk garments, with mantles worked in gold, and with costly changes of raiment, mounted on valuable horses, glittering with new bits and bridles, and riding in troops arranged in order. They carried with them three hundred and sixty gold and silver cups, preceded by the king's trumpeters and with horns sounding. . . . The nobles, too, performed the duties which, by ancient right and custom, pertained to them at the coronation of kings. . . . The grand marshal of England, the earl of Pembroke, carried a wand before the king and cleared the way before him both in the church and in the banquet-hall, and arranged the banquet and the guests at table.'

Parker, Sir James (d. 1492): the challenger in a famous joust in the reign of Henry VII (1457–1509), which is important because it shows the growing authority of the royal heralds. Parker had disputed the right of Hugh Vaughan, gentleman usher to Henry VII, to bear his coat of arms, and 'accused the sayd Hugh Vaughan to the king.' Vaughan produced as proof a grant of arms made by Garter King of Arms in 1491. Henry accepted this document, saying that since the grant was made by Garter it was as good as the king's own act. This was at Richmond, where jousts were being held. Hugh Vaughan thereupon ran a course with Sir James Parker, who was killed.

Parole: a word of honour, especially by a prisoner of war, promising either that he will not try to escape; or that, if released, he will return by a stated date. See *John II of France* for an example of a broken parole and how it was redeemed; and, for a story of a knight who kept his word and much impressed a Saracen chief, see *Hugo of Tabarie, Sir.*

Parrain: the knighter, the one conferring knighthood.

Partisan: large, spear-like weapon with a symmetrical head, about 30 inches long, broad at the base and tapering to a point. The blade was double-edged and usually had lugs of various designs at the bottom. This was one of the infantry weapons which, when developed in use, had a marked effect on the conduct of warfare, and, on several notable occasions, brought disaster to the ranks of steel-clad knights who had for so long dominated the battle-field. Here is a description from a modern novel (Jane Oliver, *Sunset at Noon*) of one of this group of weapons in use against the Scots at Flodden, in 1513. Perhaps the 'partisan' here described could more properly be called a halberd, though the various terms were, and are, used somewhat indiscriminately.

'Kicking off their shoes to grip the slimy turf, the Scots advanced down the slope in close formation, confidently presenting the enemy with a wall of spears. At Bannockburn such tactics had been triumphant. It was otherwise now. For

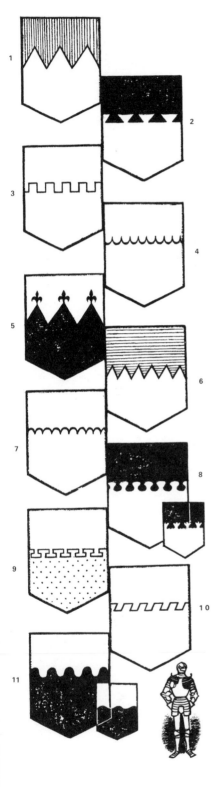

down the opposing slope the main body of their enemies advanced to meet them, armed with eight-foot bills, the terrible partisans which experience had evolved to meet the hedgehog of spears. The English bill combined a spear point with an axe-head which could be swung against the shafts of the Scottish spears, shearing their heads like ears of wheat, leaving the Scots with headless staves, as useless as the straw. Tossing them aside, the Scots drew swords and struggled on; slipping, falling, pushing themselves against the relentless surge of the harvesting English bill. Locked in a murderous grapple, they neither flinched nor broke, as the thundering assault on steel cap and plumed helmet, leather jack and plate of proof, sent the echoes rolling to the horizon hills.' (See also *Halberd*.)

Partition, Lines of: the lines used to divide a shield. They may be straight, but often are of various attractive forms, a number of which are defined elsewhere in this book. Here is an almost full list, numbered to correspond with the illustrations:

1. Dancetty.	7. Invected
2. Dovetailed.	8. Nebuly (which
3. Embattled.	can be deep or
4. Engrailed.	shallow).
5. Flory Counter-	9. Potenté.
Flory.	10. Raguly.
6. Indented.	11. Wavy.

Passage-at-Arms: a fight or encounter. One of the favourite forms adopted by a knight-errant was to pick a narrow place, such as a bridge or narrow patch between rocks, and 'hold the pass' against any other knight that came his way, sometimes camping out for weeks for this purpose. The romances of chivalry are full of this sort of exploit, but they happened in real life, too.

Of the fictional ones, one of the best, and most amusing, occurs in Conan Doyle's *Sir Nigel*.

Passant, Passant Guardant and Passant Regardant: see *Lion*.

Pauldron: armour, formed of several plates, to give special protection to the shoulder. Pauldrons for right and left shoulders were often different in size and pattern, the right being cut away, so

234

that the lance could be comfortably tucked under the arm, and the right enlarged till it defended the chest, too.

Pavilion: the gaily decorated tent used by the knight in the lists, to don his armour and wait his summons to the fight; or set up in hundreds on such ceremonial occasions as the Field of the Cloth of Gold. (See separate entry.) A typical 15th century pavilion is described as being of double blue satin, the valence embroidered with the knight's motto, his shield of arms fixed above, and eight other banners fluttering on it. The general effect can be judged from the fact that the word 'pavilion' comes from the French word for butterfly.

Special officers were employed by the king, with names such as Royal Pavilioner and Serjeant of the Tents, to look after the royal needs, though their duties usually embraced a much wider field than their title implies. (See *Tournament.*)

It was a profitable business for the merchants who got the coveted contracts for supplying the elaborate equipment and decorations for the lists. Edward III's pavilion-maker, a member of the Merchant Taylors Company or Guild, was able to buy a considerable mansion in London which became the Company Hall.

Pavise (Pavisse): tall, concave shield, often 'home-made', used by archers. (See also *Mantlet*, and *Ordinances for the Army*.)

Pay: Armies could be kept in the field only by a proper system of payments. Even the knight had to have his wages; though at some periods he owed the king, or his overlord, a fixed number of days' service for his lands, and though on some expeditions, such as the Crusades, the expenditure of personal fortunes was often involved, when kings wanted a standing army they had to meet the bill.

In 1170, a knight received about 8*d.* a day, and rather more if he was commanding foot soldiers. But prices rose sharply, and in another thirty years the knight could expect three or four times those amounts. Richard I paid his foot soldiers 2*d.* or 3*d.* a day, and a horse soldier 4*d.* or 6*d.* (It must be remembered that, in terms of value, all

these amounts need to be multiplied by at least 40.)

Edward III developed a system of making contracts with leaders to bring to the wars numbers of fighting men of stated types, at agreed rates of pay and for a fixed period. On one occasion, the Earl of Lancaster provided six knights-banneret, ninety knights, 423 mounted archers and 486 men-at-arms. Mounted archers at this time, if they supplied their own horses, were paid about 6*d.* a day, 3*d.* if one had to be found. An ordinary knight-bachelor earned about 2*s.* a day and a knight-banneret, 4*s.* (See separate entries for these terms.)

An actual figure that can be quoted is a contract of about 1340 to pay £76 every forty days to a company of six knights, twenty men-at-arms and twenty-four archers.

Here is a detailed account, showing what Henry V, in 1416, was paying the garrison of the Town of Calais. There were other garrisons for the Castle, etc. Spelling has been modernized, abbreviations extended, and amounts given in familiar forms rather than the more difficult mediaeval Roman numerals.

'The Captain at 6*s.* 8*d.* by the day, 3 knights every one at 2*s.*, 26 men of arms on horseback every one at 12*d.* by the day, 30 archers on horseback every one at 8*d.* And 200 archers on foot, every one at 6*d.* by the day.

'Also for the special reward of the Captain, a 100 marks by the quarter . . . £400 14*s.* 8*d.* by the year; and for special reward of the said 3 knights and 26 men on horseback, every one 5 marks by the quarter.

'Item, in the said Town, 40 arbalisters [cross-bowmen] . . . 18 at 10*d.* by the day and 22 every one at 8*d.* by the day; 20 carpenters, 15 masons, a plumber, a tiler, a yeoman artiller [gunner] every one at 12*d.* by the day and the said artiller's man at 6*d.* by the day . . .'

Paynim (Painim): a pagan, an infidel or Saracen; general term for an enemy of the Crusaders.

Pean: one of the heraldic furs. It is represented by gold spots on a black ground. (See *Furs* and *Ermine.*)

Pele Tower (or Castle): sometimes just referred to as a 'Pele'. Miniature castles, often consisting of just a strong tower, in which the inhabitants of a locality could take refuge against border raiders. Sometimes they took their cattle, too. The towers are most common in Northumberland, where they can be numbered in dozens. A common height was about thirty feet. Often, as at Corbridge, Elsdon and Embleton, they can be found forming part of the church or vicarage, and many were attached to large houses, not otherwise fortified. In 1791, Sir Walter Scott, writing to a friend in Edinburgh, said:

'Behold a letter from the mountains, for I am snugly settled here in a farmer's house about six miles from Wooler in the very centre of the Cheviot Hills in one of the wildest and most romantic situations which your imagination ever suggested. We are amidst places renowned by feats of former days; each hill is crowned with a tower, camp or cairn, and in no situation can you be near more fields of battle.'

The strength of the pele towers can be judged from the fact that when Earl Douglas reached Otterburn with his army, just before his battle with Hotspur (see *Otterburn, Battle of*) he tried to storm the Otterburn pele, but failed.

Many still stand, massive and indomitable; used as vicarages, forming part of some stately mansion or peaceful farm. One, near Newcastle airport, is now incorporated into an inn. (See also *Barmkin*.)

Pembridge, Sir Richard de (d. 1375): a knight who fought at Sluys and at Poitiers. (See separate entries for both of these.) His splendid armoured effigy is in the nave of Hereford Cathedral.

Pendragon: an ancient British title which means 'Chief leader in war'; someone appointed as supreme leader in time of emergency.

Pendragon, Uther: in legend, the father of King Arthur. When Uther saw a great star in the likeness of a dragon, Merlin foretold that he would be king of all Britain. 'And, remembering in what wise Merlin had interpreted the meaning of the star . . . [Uther] bade two dragons be

wrought in gold in the likeness of the dragon he had seen upon the ray of the star. And when that they had been wrought in marvellous cunning craftsmanship, he made offering of the one unto the chief church of the see of Winton [Winchester], but the other did he keep himself to carry about with him in the wars. From that day forth was he called Uther Pendragon . . .' (Geoffrey of Monmouth). (See also *Dragon*.)

Pennant: a long, narrow, streamer-like flag. Often spelt 'pendant' now, but pronounced the same.

Pennon: a small, pointed flag borne at the lance-head by knights, and sometimes by squires, if they commanded sufficient followers. Froissart, describing the French forces before the Battle of Poitiers, says: 'The Duke of Orleans commanded the first battalion, where there were thirty-six banners, and twice as many pennons.' The term is also used for the flag with one or two tails which were often cut off on the field of battle to convert it into the squarer banner of the knight-banneret, a more honourable rank.

Pennoncel: a small pennon.

Percival, Sir: One of the few knights of the Round Table who, because of the purity of his life and character, was able to catch sight of the Holy Grail. He had been in combat, and was immediately healed of his wounds.

Percy, Sir Henry: see *Hotspur* and *Otterburn, Battle of*.

Peregrine: one of the most powerful and speedy of falcons, reckoned by Dame Julia Berners as a fitting bird for an earl to use. Its chief haunts are cliffs and mountains. In colour it is slate-grey, barred with darker grey, above, with a buff tinge to the breast feathers; and white, barred with black, underneath.

Perilous Castle, the: see *Castle Dangerous*.

Perrier: general name for a stone-throwing machine in the Middle Ages. For various types see *Mediaeval Artillery*, *Balista*, *Mangon* and *Trebuchet*. See also *Petrary*.

Petard: a mine used to break down gates, draw-bridges, etc.; or a hand-bomb or pot filled with Greek fire thrown into the enemy ranks. A *petardier* was a soldier using such devices.

Petrary: a stone-throwing machine. *Perrier* (above) comes from the French for stone; *petrary*, from the Latin.

Peytrel (Peytral): armour covering a horse's chest.

Pheon: in heraldry, a broad arrow with teeth or notches on the inner edges of the barb. The most famous bearer of this device in English history was Sir Philip Sidney. His family arms are *or, a pheon azure.* (See *Sidney, Sir Philip.*)

Philip, Duke of Burgundy (1396–1467), called 'the Good': founder of the Order of the Golden Fleece. (See *Golden Fleece.*) He kept a brilliant court and aspired to be the leader of a stronghold of chivalry; but, if the events of 1453 are anything to go by, there were more dreams and words than hard action. In that year, Constantinople fell to the Turks, whose leader vowed that he would feed his horse on the altar of St. Peter, in Rome. A call went out for a crusade, and at Philip's court a great banquet was staged to publicize it. Olivier de la Marche, the contemporary chronicler, tells us that 'there came many lords accompanied by princes and knights, dames and maidens, who proceeded to survey the side dishes and were greatly edified thereby.' They had reason to be, for a fantastic variety of dishes had been set out, including one pie which 'contained twenty-six live people who played various instruments, each one in turn.' Each dish carried forty-eight different kinds of meat. But there was more to come:

'By the door through which all the side dishes were brought in and taken out entered a giant who, without the aid of art, was taller by a good foot than any man I had ever seen. He was attired in a long robe of green silk, striped in several places, and his head was adorned with a turban in the manner of the Moors of Granada. In his left hand he held a long and heavy sword of the old style, and in his right led an elephant draped with silk, on

whose back was erected a castle which contained a lady dressed in the fashion of a nun in white satin. . . .'

This was supposed to represent Holy Church coming to ask for the help of the knights of Burgundy. Shortly afterwards, the King of Arms of the Order of the Golden Fleece appeared, holding a pheasant with a collar of gold, pearls and precious stones; whereupon Duke Philip made a solemn vow to go and fight against the Turk. De La Marche does not explain the significance of the Vow of the Pheasant; but it seems to have had a stirring effect on the company, for:

'All those present followed his example and outbid each other; one vowed that he would not do less than take the Grand Turk alive or dead, another that he would never again wear armour on his right arm; this one swore never to sit down to table on Tuesdays, that one never to return home until he had thrown a Turk with his legs in the air.'

But, says Duruy, the French historian, 'each one carefully stipulated every ground that might excuse him from fulfilling his vow, and even if he had no excuse, his vow was not to be performed until the Duke had fulfilled his. But the Duke of Burgundy had sworn that he would march to the defence of the Christian faith only "provided that it was with the pleasure and consent of my lord the king, and that the land which God has committed to my care be in peace and security." In virtue of this prudent restriction the Duke of Burgundy did not go, no one went, no one had ever seriously intended to go.'

Philippa of Hainault (1314?–1369): queen of Edward III. There are few mediaeval people of whose physical appearance we have such exact details. An extremely careful observer recorded:

'. . . hair betwixt blue-black and brown. Her head is clean-shaped; her forehead high and broad, and standing somewhat forward. Her face narrows between the eyes, and the lower part of her face is still more narrow and slender than her forehead. Her eyes are blackish-brown and deep. Her nose is fairly smooth and even, save that it is somewhat broad at the tip and also flattened, and yet it is no snub-nose. Her nostrils are also broad and her mouth fairly wide. Her lips are somewhat full, and especially the lower lip. . . . The lower teeth project a little beyond the upper; yet this is little seen. Her ears and chin are comely enough . . . naught is amiss so far as a man may see.'

It was a bishop who wrote this catalogue – and he wrote it of an eight-year-old child. For he had been sent by Edward II to report on the suitability of Philippa of Hainault as a bride for the future Edward III. The report was apparently accounted satisfactory, for she married him six years afterwards. Over thirty years later, another observer said: she was 'tall and upright, wise, gay, humble, pious, liberal and courteous . . . beloved of God and of mankind.'

She was a great queen, a mother of knights (including the Black Prince and John of Gaunt), tough as a soldier herself at times, tender-hearted and merciful at others. It is of her that Froissart related the famous incident at Calais, when she interceded for the six burghers whose lives Edward III had demanded as a price for the trouble the town had caused him.

'When Sir Walter Manny had presented these six citizens to the king, they fell upon their knees and, with uplifted hands, said: "Most gallant king, see before you six citizens of Calais, who have been capital merchants, and who bring you the keys of the castle and of the town. We surrender ourselves to your absolute will and pleasure, in order to save the remainder of the inhabitants of Calais, who have suffered much distress and misery. Condescend, therefore, out of the nobleness of your mind, to have mercy and compassion upon us."

The king eyed them with angry looks (for he hated much the people of Calais for the great losses he had formerly suffered from them at sea) and ordered their heads to be stricken off. All present entreated the king that he would be more merciful to them, but he would not listen to them. . . . The queen of England, who at that time was very big with child, fell on her knees and, with tears, said:

"Ah, gentle sir, since I have crossed the sea with very great danger to see you, I have never asked you one favour. Now I most humbly ask you as a gift, for the sake of the Son of the

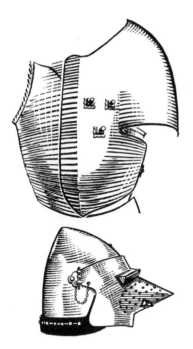

blessed Mary, and for your love to me, that you will be merciful to these six men."

The king looked at her for some time in silence, and then said: "Ah, lady, I wish you had been anywhere else than here. You have entreated in such a manner that I cannot refuse you. I therefore give them to you, to do as you please with them."

The queen conducted the six citizens to her apartments, and had the halters taken from round their necks, after which she new clothed them and served them with a plentiful dinner.'

The truth of this account has been disputed on the grounds that no other contemporary chronicler mentions it. But it is well in keeping with what we know of Philippa's character. In the same year (1347) she sought mercy from the king for some carpenters whose work had threatened the royal safety when some pavilions they had erected collapsed at a tournament in Cheapside.

Pieces of Advantage: extra pieces of armour added to the ordinary harness for special protection in the joust and tournament. At first, only the left side was reinforced, since this was most vulnerable to the lance, but other extras came along. They were a late production, appearing in about 1550.

Pig-faced Bascinet: see *Bascinet.*

Pilgrims, Castle of the: at Athlit, south of Carmel. One of the greatest of the Templar castles, so called because of the many pilgrims who gave a hand in its construction. It was immensely strong, guarded by the Mediterranean on three sides, with its own harbour and shipyard. Its battlements were ornamented with the sculptured heads of Templar knights. The castle was the last Christian stronghold to be abandoned on the mainland.

Plantagenet: the name usually given to the house of Anjou, or the Angevin kings of England, who reigned from 1154–1399. They included three of the greatest kings in the story of chivalry, Richard I, Edward I and Edward III. The list is:

Henry II	1154–1189	John	1199–1216
Richard I	1189–1199	Henry III	1216–1272

Edward I 1272–1307 Edward III 1327–1377
Edward II 1307–1327 Richard II   1377–1399
They took the name Plantagenet from the *planta genista*, the broom plant, a sprig of which Count Geoffrey of Anjou, father of Henry II, was fond of sticking in his cap. Once adopted as a royal badge, its use continued intermittently even after the house of Anjou had come to an end. Queen Elizabeth, for example, had a dress embroidered with the golden broom plant. Richard II was not, of course, the last of the family. Richard III, who died at the Battle of Bosworth eighty-six years later, was of Plantagenet descent.

They tell a strange story of the last of the Plantagenets in the village of Eastwell, Kent. In the early years of Queen Elizabeth's reign there lived in Eastwell Sir Thomas Moyle, knighted when the queen was four years old, a member of Parliament who was chosen Speaker in 1542. He was busy rebuilding Eastwell House when he noticed an elderly man, working as a bricklayer, who was called Richard and who seemed much better educated than the rest. Sir Thomas gained the workman's confidence and was told a story that must at first have strained his belief, but which apparently convinced him. As a boy, the old bricklayer had been brought up in the household of a schoolmaster, who had given him a good education. In August, 1485, he had been taken to a camp in Leicestershire where he had met a man of noble blood who told him he was his father, King Richard III of England; that a battle was to be fought that would either place him securely on his throne or else mean that he and his descendants would be hunted down and exterminated. If he lost the battle, the boy was to tell no one of his parentage. On August 22nd, the Battle of Bosworth was fought and Richard III was killed, leaving the way to the throne clear for his conqueror, Henry VII, the first of the Tudors.

The boy made his way south and eventually found himself at Eastwell, where he had sought work. In fact, he lived on there for sixty years, and near Eastwell House is a cottage which is said to have been built for the last of the Plantagenets by Sir Thomas Moyle, so that he could live out the rest of his days in peace and security.

Whatever the accuracy of that story, one thing is strangely true. The parish registers record the

death of an old man named Richard Plantagenet in 1550.

Plate Armour: armour made from flat plates of steel-like iron, as distinct from the mail that had preceded it. The thickness of the plates varied according to their position and the function they had to fulfil. The breast-plate, for example, had to be of great strength. The armourers brought their plates to a state of immense hardness and smoothness, so that the armour could not only prevent the penetration of blows, but make them glance off the surface. The period of plate continued for roughly three hundred years, starting about 1350. Back and breast defences were sometimes called a 'pair of plates'.

Points (on a shield): see *Honour Point*.

Poitiers, Battle of (September 19, 1356): the second of the Black Prince's great victories in France, surpassing even Crécy. After a year's campaigning in southern France, in which he had covered many hundreds of miles and captured, or recaptured, many towns and castles, the Prince marched north to the Loire, hoping to make contact with the Duke of Lancaster, who had been campaigning in Normandy. The Black Prince, with only 6,000–7,000 men, was running short of supplies, and a great French army, under the command of King John, who was very anxious to avenge his father's defeat at Crécy ten years before, had hurried south to meet him. The Prince ordered a retreat and for three or four days English and French marched south on more or less parallel lines, with King John trying to cut off his enemy.

The Black Prince was indeed in perilous plight, for John was at the head of one of the most splendid armies that ever took the field in France, mustering some 50,000 soldiers, headed by his four sons, more than two score dukes and counts, and 140 knights-banneret. The vast, steel-clad host, brave with thousands of banners and pennons, was an intimidating sight; and when at last the Prince took up a defensive position on a low ridge eight miles from Poitiers, it seemed to the French – and probably to the English – that they had their old foes in the hollow of their hands. Indeed, King John set almost contemptuous terms for surrender; and the Black Prince went so far as to offer to yield up all his booty and prisoners. But the French demanded unconditional capitulation and a hundred of the greatest English knights for ransom purposes. The Black Prince and his council of war decided to give battle.

Before it, Edward addressed his force in words very reminiscent of the words Shakespeare put into Henry V's mouth before Agincourt:

'What though we be a small body compared to the army of our enemies? Do not let us be cast down on that account, for victory does not always follow numbers, but where Almighty God pleases to bestow it. If, through good fortune, the day shall be ours, we will gain the greatest honour and glory in this world . . . I therefore entreat of you to exert yourselves, and combat manfully; for, if it please God and St. George, you shall see me this day act like a true knight.'

To the archers, he said:

'Follow the standards, obey implicitly in body and mind the commands of your leaders. If victory shall see us still alive, we shall always continue in firm friendship together, being of one heart and mind.'

They obeyed their instructions superbly. The French vanguard, after making some headway, was thrown into abject confusion by the ruthless, disciplined onslaught of the archers. The Dauphin's division did little better, though it reached the thick hedge behind which the Black Prince had stationed two of his main divisions, under Warwick and Salisbury, and some desperate hand-to-hand fighting took place before the French fell back. Then the main French host, under King John, moved down from the other side of the valley, massive, menacing in their glittering ranks, eager for battle. The weary English watched its advance in dismay, for this surely was the end. There was only one answer, and the Black Prince made it. The order was given for attack along the whole front. Every man with a horse climbed into the saddle, a detachment was sent to outflank the French and take them in the rear; then, ordering his banner-bearer, Sir Walter Woodland, to advance his banner in the name of God and St. George, the

Black Prince thundered into the attack at the head of his close-knit ranks, with the archers casting aside their bows and taking to the sword. At a critical moment, the outflanking cavalry crashed into the French rear.

By mid-day it was all over. The broken French were pursued to the walls of Poitiers, leaving behind them in English hands the French king, one of his sons, and more than two thousand nobles and knights. Thousands more lay dead on the field.

It is said that such a prospect of ransom money had never appeared before at one time. Indeed, the number of prisoners was an embarrassment and large numbers were set free immediately, having given their parole to come to Bordeaux before Christmas and pay their ransom. To add to the money, there were 'the quantities of gold and silver plate, rich jewels, and trunks stuffed full of belts that were weighty from their gold and silver ornaments, and furred mantles . . . for the French had come as magnificently and richly dressed as if they had been sure of gaining the victory.'

(For other episodes in the battle, see *Audley, Sir James* and *John II of France*.)

Polder, or Polder Mitten: see *Epaule de Mouton.*

Pole-axe: a weapon often used by knights, its name correctly describing it. The axe, often of beautiful craftsmanship, was set on a four to six-foot wooden pole, the shaft being sometimes partly sheathed in iron. Its length meant that it must be wielded with both hands, for parrying blows as well as for attack. The head was really a combination of weapons – a cutting edge to the blade, a hammer-head or miniature sort of mace on the other side and, for good measure, a long spike on top. (See *Howel-y-Fwyall* for a notable exponent of this weapon.)

Poleyn: piece of plate armour, separately fashioned, to enclose the knee cap and also protect the side and back of the knee.

Pommel (Pummel): the large knob, often richly decorated, at the top of a sword handle; or the high front part of a saddle.

Portcullis: strong framework or grating of heavy wood or metal, looking like a farmer's harrow, which slid down in grooves to seal the castle gateway. The name means 'sliding door'. In Tudor times there was a coin called a portcullis from the design in the reverse; and one of the present Officers of Arms (see separate entry) is Portcullis Pursuivant.

Postern: a small rear or back gate, often spoken of in connection with castles.

Pourpoint: quilted or padded doublet worn in the 14th and 15th centuries. (See also *Gambeson.*) It was often reinforced by metal studs or discs.

Prick (Pryck) Spur: the type in common use till the end of the 13th century, with a spike, short or long, behind the heel with which to urge on the horse. (See *Spur.*)

Proverbs of Hendyng: a collection of proverbs, popular in mediaeval households, put together in verse form in the 13th century, and containing wise words still quoted today in one form or another; e.g., 'Brend child fur dredeth' – 'a burned child fears the fire'; and 'fer from eye, fer from herte' – 'far from eye, far from heart', or, 'out of sight, out of mind'. Here is one full verse (out of forty), difficult to read, but with its catchy rhythm plain to see:

> *Wis mon halt is wordes ynne;*
> *For he nul no gle bygynne,*
> > *Er he have tempred is pype.*
> *Sot is sot, & that is sene;*
> *For he wol speke wordes grene,*
> > *Er then hue buen rype.*
> *'Sottes bolt is sone shote;'*
> > ..   *Quoth Hendyng.*

To paraphrase this roughly, 'A wise man holds his words, since he doesn't want to start any trouble before he's ready. A fool's a fool, it's plain to see, because he lets fly before things are ripe. "Fool's bolt is soon shot", says Hendyng.'

It is easy to see where the moralist was drawing his picture from in this verse. An American officer in the War of Independence, Israel Putnam, is credited with having said at Bunker's Hill, 'Don't fire till you see the whites of their eyes'; and, obviously, mediaeval commanders were known

to say much the same sort of thing. An archer who let fly his arrows or bolts before he was sure of his target was asking for trouble. A good example occurred at the Battle of Towton (see separate entry) at the end of March, 1461. Thick snow was drifting down when the Lancastrians met the Yorkists there. As the Lancastrian soldiers peered through the drift, they saw the first of the Yorkist troops appearing. Flight after flight of arrows was loosed against the oncoming army they could not see, till someone grew suspicious and halted the fire – not before it was time. The Yorkists had deliberately thrown out a thin skirmishing line to draw their fire. The Lancastrian arrows had been fired into thin air and presently, when the Yorkist bowmen advanced, they picked up the fallen arrows and used them back.

Psalters: The growing interest in books and learning in the Middle Ages led to many more manuscripts appearing, and being bought by nobles and knights. Among the most prized possessions were the great psalters and books of hours, used for prayers and in church services. The Luttrell Psalter has already been described in the entry for *Luttrell, Sir Geoffrey.* Another was the *Tenison Psalter,* ordered by Edward I for a wedding present to his eldest son. The *Bedford Missal,* in the British Museum, was written and painted in between 1423 and 1430, for John, Duke of Bedford, son of Henry IV, and Anne his wife. It was given to Henry VI and later was owned by Henry II of France. Its illuminations are among the finest known. Such stirring legends as St. Michael slaying the dragon were favourite subjects for illumination. A typical Book of Hours in the Bodleian Library shows the saint in a red cloak with a green lining. His armour is steel-blue. His spear is plunged almost casually into a dragon which looks as if it had monkeys among its ancestors, while his left hand steadies on the ground a curiously impracticable shield with the cross of St. Michael. The background is a fine network of red and blue diamonds decorated with fleurs-de-lys. In the margin of trailing ivy-leaves, a soul is being weighed in the balance. It is grotesque, naïve, amusing, moving and superb. Nothing was too commonplace, too ordinary, too everyday, to be incorporated and ennobled in these great manuscripts. Lions, monkeys, elephants, pigs, cats, peacocks, rabbits, snails, cockle-shells, horses, ploughs, harrows, mermaids and dragons riot and glow in the company of saints and martyrs. This is the full zest of mediaeval life finding expression, just as it did in its churches and cathedrals and, in another sphere, in the trappings and display of chivalry.

Pursuivants: see *Officers of Arms*.

Q

Quarrel: the short bolt or arrow discharged from the cross-bow. The word comes from the French *carré*, meaning square, and is a reminder that the bolt-heads were usually four-sided.

Quarry: a term in falconry: the prey carried off by the hawk.

Quarter, Giving of: sparing the life of a defeated enemy or prisoner. No special rules seem to have been observed on the subject, especially when the ordinary soldier was concerned. The higher ranks always stood a better chance because of their ability to find a handsome sum in ransom. 'No quarter!' or 'Havoc!' (the signal for indiscriminate slaughter) were terrible cries to hear on the battle-field, and, though their contemporaries apparently looked on it as something all in the day's work, the names of some of the greatest commanders are sullied with barbarous acts of slaughter of this kind.

After the capture of Acre in 1191, Richard Coeur-de-Lion, on the thinnest of excuses that Saladin had not properly observed the terms of a treaty made with him, massacred 2,700 of the captured garrison.

The courtly victor of Poitiers, who could kneel before the captured king of France and wait on him at the table, brought his thirty years of campaigning, in which he had deservedly won such glory, to a dismal end in the ruthless sack of Limoges (1370), in which he slaughtered men, women and children.

The heroic Henry V hanged eight gunners in 1418, because a cannon-ball struck his tent. At Agincourt, three years before, he ordered the slaughter of prisoners when it was reported that a fresh body of French troops was attacking from the rear and pillaging the baggage. It was stopped, over-late, when the rumour turned out to be false.

The French chronicler Philip de Commines records how King Edward IV changed his views on the subject of giving quarter:

'It is the custom in England, when a battle in won, to give quarter, and no man is killed, especially of the common soldiers. . . . King Edward told me that, in all the battles which he had gained, his way was, when the victory was on his side, to mount on horseback and cry out to save the common people and put the gentlemen to the sword, by which means none, or very few of them, escaped.'

That was when he was younger. After he had been temporarily overthrown and exiled, his attitude was different:

'King Edward had resolved, at his departure from Flanders, to call out no more to spare the common soldiers, and only kill the gentlemen; for he had conceived a mortal hatred against the commons of England for having favoured the Earl of Warwick so much, and for other reasons besides, so that he spared none of them at that time.' (i.e., at the Battle of Barnet).

Quarters: the sections of the field of a shield obtained by dividing it into four approximately equal parts by a vertical and a horizontal line. When this happens, it is divided *quarterly*, and arms charged on the quarters are called *quarterings*. Mathematics and heraldic terminology have little to do with each other; e.g., a shield can be divided into more than four quarters, but they still retain the name. Thus, a shield divided into eight sections by means of vertical and horizontal lines has eight quarters and is described as *quarterly of eight.*

There is another complication in this difficult, but important, branch of the science of heraldry. Any quarter of a shield may itself be quartered. When this happens, the original four main sections are called *grand quarters*. Quarters are numbered in this sequence:

$$1 \quad 2$$
$$3 \quad 4$$

Suppose the 1st and 4th quarters of a shield are themselves each divided into quarters, and the 2nd and 3rd are left as they are. We then have a shield in which we have four *grand quarters*, two of which (1st and 4th) are *quarterly quartered.*

It is theoretically possible to divide a shield into thousands of quarters. The Duke of Northumberland is said, because of all the family alliances and marriages through the centuries, to be able to claim more than 500 quarterings. But the highest number registered at the College of Heralds is for a family in Shropshire, whose blazon begins: *quarterly of three hundred and twenty-three.*

251

Quarterstaff: a long, stout pole, carried for offence and defence, and often used in robust sports and competitions where cracked pates and bruised limbs were not objected to. It frequently features in the greenwood stories of Robin Hood and similar heroes.

'The Miller pressed furiously forward, dealing blows with either end of his weapon alternately, and striving to come to half-staff distance, while Gurth defended himself against the attack, keeping his hands about a yard asunder, and covering himself by shifting his weapon with great celerity, so as to protect his head and body. Thus did he maintain the defensive, making his eye, foot, and hand keep true time, until, observing his antagonist to lose wind, he darted the staff at his face with his left hand; and, as the Miller endeavoured to parry the thrust, he slid his right hand down to his left, and with the full swing of the weapon struck his opponent on the left side of the head, who instantly measured his length upon the green sward.' (*Ivanhoe.*)

Quatrefoil: see *Cinquefoil.*

Queen Elizabeth's Armoury: the old name for the collection of arms and armour in the Tower of London. A collection dating from the Middle Ages, surviving from such occasions as royal tournaments and gifts from foreign princes, had long been maintained, but it was not well displayed and, until the 1830's, a fairly high charge had been levied for admission so that it had not been much seen by the general public.

In 1826, Samuel Meyrick (afterwards knighted) an authority on armour, was asked to advise on the better maintenance and display of the collection. As a result, new accommodation was provided at the Tower and a space nearly 150 feet long devoted to a glittering array of twenty equestrian figures topped by crimson banners bearing name and date, and surrounded by other armour and weapons, all in magnificently restored condition. In 1837, the year of Queen Victoria's coronation, the entrance fee was lowered and thousands of visitors crowded in, extra Beefeaters being drafted in to cope with them. The Tower Armouries remain one of the most popular sights of London. The old royal armoury has been steadily added to, so that the Tower now holds the national collection of European arms and armour. It can also fairly claim to be the oldest museum in England.

Queen of the Tournament: or Queen of Beauty; the lady chosen, or elected, to preside over the festivities, and to award the prize to the victorious knight. Sir Walter Scott, in *Ivanhoe* describes one way of appointing her:

' "Sir Disinherited Knight," said Prince John, "since that is the only title by which we can address you, it is now your duty, as well as privilege, to name the fair lady who, as Queen of Honour and of Love, is to preside over the next day's festival . . . it is your undoubted prerogative to confer on whom you please this crown, by the delivery of which to the lady of your choice, the election of tomorrow's Queen will be formal and complete. Raise your lance."

The Knight obeyed; and Prince John placed upon its point a coronet of green satin, having around its edge a circlet of gold, the upper edge of which was relieved by arrow points and hearts placed interchangeably.'

Much to the discontent of some of the Norman ladies, who were accustomed to occupying the position, the Disinherited Knight dropped the point of his lance and placed the coronet at the feet of the Saxon Rowena, who was immediately proclaimed Queen of Love and Beauty for the next day. When it arrived, Rowena was conducted to her seat of honour by Prince John himself and was given a temporary retinue of maids of honour. When the same knight had again put up the best performance of the day, John said:

'. . . we a second time award you the honours of this tournament, and announce to you your right to claim and receive from the hands of the Queen of Love and Beauty, the Chaplet of Honour which your valour has justly deserved.'

Queen's College: Both the Oxford and the Cambridge college of this name have connections with the days of chivalry. Queen's College, Oxford, was founded in 1340 by Robert de Eglesfield, who named it in honour of Queen

Philippa (see *Philippa of Hainault*), wife of Edward III and heroine of the story of the Burghers of Calais. Queen's College, Cambridge, was founded in 1448 by Margaret of Anjou (1430–1482), wife of Henry VI. She had a stormy and adventurous career, devotedly championing the cause of her husband and son in the Wars of the Roses, when necessary raising and organizing armies herself. In one dramatic episode in Northumberland, after the defeat of her troops, she was escaping across country with her young son Edward when she was confronted by a robber in the depths of a wood. She had plenty of shortcomings, but cowardice was not one of them. She confronted the robber boldly and revealed her identity, appealing to him to safeguard the young prince. Luck was with her. He was a former Lancastrian who had lost all his possessions. He took her to a cave and sheltered her for several days till she was able to join some of her supporters and take ship for France.

Queens, Four: Raymond Berenger IV, Count of Provence, set up something of a record by having four daughters, Margaret, Eleanor, Sancha and Beatrice, all of whom married kings.

Margaret married the crusading king, Louis IX of France (St. Louis), and acquired one of the worst mothers-in-law on record. The chronicler Jounville tells us that she would not let husband and wife be in each other's company. At their favourite palace, at Pontoise, the king's chamber was above the queen's, and the unfortunate pair used to meet on the twisting stairs connecting the two rooms. If Blanche, the queen-mother, was seen approaching her son's room, the ushers struck the door with their rods as a signal to Louis, so that he could rush up the stairway and be in the room when she arrived. Margaret's ushers did the same when Blanche was seen heading for her hated daughter-in-law's chamber.

Eleanor became Queen of England as the wife of Henry III. She probably did rather better in mothers-in-law and, as the mother of Edward I and ancestress of Edward III, the Black Prince and Henry V, may be said to have played an important role in the history of chivalry. (For a description of her marriage, see *Paris, Matthew*.) Her life was far from tranquil – on one occasion the London mob wanted her drowned as a witch

– but she found peace at last as a nun at Amesbury, Wiltshire.

Sancha married Henry III's brother Richard, Earl of Cornwall, who was elected King of the Romans in 1256. He was an able prince, who led a crusade in 1240, but high hopes of his early career were not fulfilled and he died an embittered man.

The fourth sister, Beatrice, married Charles of Anjou, brother of Louis IX. Charles is described as 'cold, cruel, and inordinately ambitious.' Beatrice, with three queens for sisters, was not without ambitions herself; and they were realized when her husband, in 1265, marched into Italy, killed Manfred of Sicily and became King in his place. He went on crusade and was on the disastrous expedition in which Louis died before the walls of Tunis.

Quest: the act of seeking, of going in search, especially in the days of chivalry. Sometimes the object of the search or enterprise was itself called the quest.

The most famous legendary quest was that of the Holy Grail. (See *Grail.*) Another in the Arthurian stories was that of the Questing Beast. 'Questing' here means baying, as hounds do. The Questing Beast was so called because, wherever he went, he made a noise like sixty hounds giving tongue. It had a serpent's head, the body of a leopard, the hind-quarters of a lion and the feet of a hart. King Pellinore pursued it vainly for twelve months, and after his death Sir Palomides took up the quest. The monster's other name was Glatisaunt.

Queue: a bracket or bar of iron to help take the weight of the lance. The first sort of support provided was a curving arm or rest bolted to the right of the breast-plate. Then an even better idea was introduced in about 1460 – a 'queue', meaning a tail or stem, sticking out from the back-plate. This was provided at the end with a down-curving arm, under which the butt of the lance could be lodged securely to counteract the upward thrust. The result was that, resting in front and held down behind, most of the weight of the lance was transferred to the body. These devices are found mainly on tilting armours.

Queue-fourchée: a forked tail, as found sometimes in heraldic beasts. (See *Lion.*) Note that this is different from *double-queued*, which means two-tailed. A forked tail starts from the base as one tail, but divides into two further up.

Quillons: the cross-guards of a sword.

Quintain (Quentain, etc.): a popular game in the Middle Ages, but serving serious purposes of training in knightly accomplishments. A dummy or figure of some sort was rigged up on a pivot, and the rider charged at it with lance or spear. Sometimes a weighted sand-bag was attached to the other end of the beam, so that it would swing round and buffet the rider who was too slow in getting away.

Quiver: a sheath or case for arrows, slung on belt or baldric.

Quixote, Don: the hero of the Spanish mock-romance by Miguel de Cervantes (1547–1616), published in 1605. Don Quixote de la Mancha was a middle-aged knight of about 50, 'tall, meagre, lantern-jawed, hawk-nosed, long-limbed . . . with a pair of black whiskers' and styling himself 'The Knight of the Woeful Countenance.' He had filled his library and his brain with romances, 'selling many a good acre of tillage-land to buy books of chivalry.' His niece complained:

> 'It was often my uncle's way to stay two days and nights poring over these unholy books of misadventures, after which he would fling the books away and snatch up his sword and fall to slashing the walls; and when he was tired out he would say he had killed four giants like towers; and the sweat that flowed from him when he was weary he said was the blood of the wounds he had received in battle.'

Eventually, the fevered imagination of the knight led him to set out as a knight-errant himself, on a scarecrow of a horse and attended by an ignorant peasant named Sancho Panza as his squire. His most famous exploit was to tilt at a group of windmills, believing them, with their flailing arms, to be giants. Inns in his sight became castles; grazing sheep, armies. In the end, Don Quixote was restored to his right mind.

Cervantes was mocking the fantastic romances of chivalry; and hundreds of thousands of readers laughed with him.

When he was twenty-four Cervantes fought at the Battle of Lepanto (see separate entry) and was wounded. Four years later, returning to Spain from a military expedition he was captured by Moorish pirates and imprisoned at Algiers, where he had to wait for five years before he was ransomed.

'To tilt at windmills' has passed into our everyday language, meaning to misguidedly take on some powerful opponent or situation with stupidly ineffective weapons. We have 'quixotic,' too, to describe a well-intentioned and chivalrous action that is hopelessly impractical or extravagantly idealistic.

Quo Warranto, Inquest of (1278–79): an enquiry set on foot by Edward I into the private powers and privileges exercised by the barons. The chronicler Walter of Hemingford, writing in about 1300, tells us:

'Shortly afterwards the king disturbed some of the nobles of the realm by wishing to know, through his justices, on what warrant they held their lands; and if they had no good warrant to show, he immediately seized their estates. Among the others, Earl Warenne was summoned before the king's justices, and was asked by what warrant he held. He thereupon produced in court an ancient rusty sword and said:

"See, sirs, see, here is my warrant. For my ancestors came across with William the Norman, and conquered their lands with the sword, and with the sword shall I defend them against whoever wishes to take them from me." '

John de Warenne, Earl of Surrey (1231?–1304) campaigned in France, Spain, Wales and Scotland, and was present at many battles and sieges.

Raby Castle: in county Durham, was one of the great northern strongholds of the family of Neville (see separate entry). It is a good example of the transition between the bare, utilitarian military castle and the spacious and more comfortable dwelling of a great household. The embattled walls enclosed about two acres of land, and the upper hall, ninety feet long, could accommodate a small army of retainers.

Seven hundred knights, retainers all
Of Neville, at their master's call,
Together sat in Raby's Hall.

Raby, Rose of: Cecily, daughter of Ralph Neville of Raby, 1st Earl of Westmorland. She was the mother of Richard III (see separate entry).

Railway Knight, The: in the Eglington Tournament of 1839 (see *Eglington Tournament* and *Tournament*) the 'knights' in training used a dummy knight on wheels, which cavorted down a track towards the central barrier or 'tilt', which was erected in a large garden behind the Eyre Arms, near Regents Park, London. The wooden horse was christened the 'Railway Knight.' Though the onlookers applauded it as a clever modern device, something like it was, in fact, in use at the end of the age of chivalry.

Rampant, Rampant Guardant and Rampant Regardant: see *Lion.*

Ramparts: the embankment piled up round the edge of the *motte*, or mound, in early castles. Usually timber stockades were added or, later, a low wall.

Randolph, Sir Thomas, first Earl of Moray (d. 1332): a good example of a coward and betrayer making good and redeeming his knighthood. After the defeat of Robert Bruce at Methven in 1306, he saved his skin by renouncing his leader and joining in the hunt for him. Two years later he was himself captured by one of Bruce's lieutenants and made his submission to his old master, who let bygones be bygones, and raised him to a position of great trust. This time he did not betray it, but became Bruce's most valued friend and adviser. He performed many great feats of arms in Bruce's service, including the capture of Edinburgh Castle, then in English hands, by escalade, i.e., by scaling the walls. It was a castle of great natural strength and strongly garrisoned, so that Randolph's siege seemed hopeless. But luck came his way in the shape of a man named William Frank who, in his younger days, had been one of the castle garrison and who had often used a precipitous route down into the city in order to see his sweetheart. He thought he could remember the ancient path and volunteered to lead a party up it to the bottom of the castle walls.

Randolph chose thirty men, took along a scaling ladder, and entrusted himself to Frank.

'Having clambered with great difficulty and exertion about half way up the rock, the adventurous party reached a broad projection, or shelf, on which they rested some time to recover breath. While in this position, they heard above them the guard . . . of the garrison making their rounds . . . Randolph and his men having waited till they had gone to a distance again got up, and at the imminent peril of their lives, fairly succeeded in clambering up the remaining part of the rock to the foot of the wall, to which they affixed their ladder. Frank, the guide, was the first to mount the walls; Sir Andrew Gray was the next; Randolph himself was the third. Before the whole could reach the summit of the wall, the alarm was given, and the garrison rushed to arms. A fierce encounter took place; but the governor having been slain, the English surrendered themselves to mercy.' (Robert Chambers).

Randolph commanded one of Bruce's divisions at Bannockburn (see separate entry) and, upon the death of Bruce, became Regent of Scotland.

Ransom: the sum of money, or the equivalent in valuables, paid to secure the release of a prisoner. Ransom money was one of the high hopes of the soldier in the Middle Ages. The more noble the rank, the greater the sum that could be demanded, and a lucky few minutes' encounter in battle could provide a fortune for the capturer. This explains the undignified squabbles that sometimes occurred as to who had really taken a distinguished prisoner. King John, at the Battle of Poitiers (see separate entry) provides a good example. Froissart tells us:

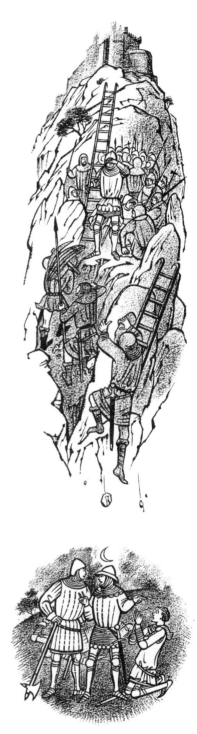

259

'There was much pressing at this time, through eagerness to take the king; and those who were nearest to him, and knew him, cried out: "Surrender yourself, surrender yourself, or you are a dead man." In that part of the field was a young knight from St. Omer, who was engaged by a salary in the service of the king of England. His name was Denys de Morbeque; who for five years had attached himself to the English, on account of having been banished in his younger days from France for a murder committed in an affray at St. Omer. It fortunately happened for this knight that he was at the time near to the king of France, when he was so much pulled about. He, by dint of force, for he was very strong and robust, pushed through the crowd, and said to the king in good French: "Sire, sire, surrender yourself." The king, who found himself very disagreeably situated, turning to him, asked: "To whom shall I surrender myself? To whom? Where is my cousin the prince of Wales? If I could see him, I would speak with him." "Sire," replied Sir Denys, "he is not here; but surrender yourself to me, and I will lead you to him." "Who are you?" said the king. "Sire, I am Denys de Morbeque, a knight from Artois; but I serve the king of England, because I cannot belong to France, having forfeited all I possessed there." The king then gave him his right-hand glove, and said, "I surrender myself to you." There was much crowding and pushing about, for every one was eager to cry out, "I have taken him!"

Later, the Black Prince sent the Earl of Warwick and Lord Cobham to ride over the battlefield to see if they could discover what had happened to the French king. They met him in the centre of a jostling crowd.

'The king of France was in the midst of them, and in great danger; for the English and Gascons had taken him from Sir Denys de Morbeque, and were disputing who should have him, the stoutest bawling out, "It is I that have got him!" "No, no," replied the others, "we have him." The king, to escape from this peril, said, "Gentlemen, gentlemen, I pray you conduct me and my son in a courteous manner to my cousin the prince; and do not make such a riot about my capture, for I am so great a lord that I can make you all sufficiently rich".'

The two lords rescued the king and brought him safely to the Black Prince. About ten knights and squires were by this time claiming the capture. When the matter eventually came to be settled, these were narrowed down to two, de Morbeque and another Gascon, Bernard de Trouttes. They arranged to fight each other, but the prince put them under arrest till they were back in England. The king of France, however, supported de Morbeque's claim, and the Prince of Wales therefore ordered him to be paid privately the sum of 2,000 nobles.

Froissart records many other examples. Also after Poitiers, a Gascon squire named John de Helennes seriously wounded a young English knight, Lord Berkeley, 'who for the first time that day displayed his banner.' Berkeley surrendered and gave him his word that he would remain his prisoner, rescued or not. John de Helennes bound up Berkeley's wounds, placed him on his horse and led him to Châtelherault, where he stayed with him over a fortnight seeing that he had proper medical treatment. When Berkeley had sufficiently recovered, de Helennes put him in a litter and had him carried to his own house in Picardy, where Berkeley remained more than a year before he was cured and was able to return home. In the end, the English knight paid a ransom of 6,000 nobles.

For another Poitiers prisoner, Charles of Blois, Sir Thomas Dagworth was offered the huge sum for those days of £4,900. For other examples of ransoms see *Holland, Sir Thomas* and *Neville's Cross, Battle of.*

Rapier: a late type of sword, slender and finely pointed; used for thrusting and parrying, instead of cutting and hewing with the edge.

Ravenspur: near Spurn Head, in Yorkshire. In early times it was an important port on the River Humber, and saw the beginning of a number of momentous events. Edward IV landed here in 1471 after his temporary exile, and went on to win, a month later, the decisive battle of Barnet, in which Warwick the Kingmaker was killed. Earlier, Henry IV had landed at Ravenspur to claim the crown from Richard II.

Record Office, Public: the chief repository in England of original documents, brought together from the courts of law and various government departments, and dating from the Norman Conquest. The Office is in Chancery Lane, W.C.2, but, since the total number of records runs into many millions, they cannot all be stored there. There is a large provincial repository at Ashridge, Hertfordshire. At Chancery Lane, there are three Search Rooms, called the Round Room, the Rolls Room and the Long Room. In all, there are seats for 140 readers and searchers, who may be investigating anything from eleventh century manorial documents to modern legal records.

All English counties, and a number of cities and county boroughs have their own officially approved record offices containing mainly, but not exclusively, material of local importance and interest. These records have often been collected in from large numbers of ancient parishes and therefore contain much information about great local families. To quote one example, the Record Office for the county of Essex has records for nearly 400 parishes out of a total of 410.

Red Cross: see *National Flags.*

Red Cross Knight: the knight, representing St. George of England, who plays an important part in Edmund Spenser's *Faerie Queene*, a long metrical romance, in six books, the first three of which were published in 1590 and were dedicated to Queen Elizabeth. Spenser intended to extend the work to twelve books, but did not live long enough.

In Book 1, Una comes to Gloriana's court to seek the aid of a true knight to slay the terrible dragon that keeps her mother and father prisoner. This part of the poem is concerned with their adventures, the knight's ultimate triumph and his marriage with Una. The Red Cross Knight is thus described:

A gentle Knight was pricking on the plaine,
Ycladd in mightie armes and silver shielde,
Wherein old dints of deepe woundes did remaine,
The cruell markes of many a bloody fielde;
Yet armes till that time did he never wield.
His angry steede did chide his foming bitt,
As much disdayning to the curbe to yield:

Full jolly knight he seemd, and faire did sitt,
As one of knightly giusts and fierce encounters fitt.
   (*Ycladd* = clad, clothed; *giusts* = jousts)
Una, descended from ancient kings and queens,
but driven from her inheritance by the 'infernall
feend', rode meekly beside him on a donkey.
A lovely Ladie rode him faire beside,
Upon a lowly Asse more white than snow,
Yet she much whiter; but the same did hide
Under a vele, that wimpled was full low;
And over all a blacke stole shee did throw:
As one that inly mournd, so was she sad,
And heavie sate upon her palfrey slow;
Seemed in heart some hidden care she had,
And by her in a line a milkewhite lambe she lad.
   (*vele* = veil; *inly* = inwardly; *lad* = led)

Regalia: strictly speaking, things regal, apper-
taining to the king, but now used over a much
wider field; the symbols, emblems, insignia and
decorations of royalty, especially those used at
coronations and on great occasions of state; more
loosely applied to the insignia of orders of
chivalry, civic authorities, church dignitaries, etc.
   The regalia of the English sovereigns is kept
in the Tower of London. Most of it dates from the
seventeenth century, since the old symbols and
trappings of six hundred years of kingship were
sold or melted down during the Protectorate of
Oliver Cromwell (1653–1658). At the restoration
of Charles II in 1660, as much as possible was
recovered, repaired and reinstated; where the
originals had disappeared, replicas were made,
if possible to the old designs. The chief items in
the magnificent collection are:

   St. Edward's Crown: named after Edward the
    Confessor's Crown, and used only at corona-
    tions. It is made of gold, decorated with
    jewels and pearls, and weighs about 5 lb.
    Above the slender pearl-encrusted arches
    rises the orb of sovereignty, surmounted by a
    superb cross, symbolic of the source of all
    kingship, power and dignity.
   The Imperial State Crown: made for the
    coronation of Queen Victoria in 1838, and
    containing the ancient jewel, known as the
    Black Prince's Ruby, given to Edward, the
    Black Prince by Pedro the Cruel in 1367,
    and worn on Henry V's helm at Agincourt.
    The crown is set with more than 3,000

precious stones. Two other noteworthy gems are the great Stuart sapphire from the crown of Charles II, and, set high above them all in the surmounting cross, what is reputed to be the oldest of the crown jewels – the sapphire from the ring of Edward the Confessor.

The earliest queen's crown in the regalia is that made for Mary of Modena, queen of James II. There are a number of other crowns.

The Orbs: two golden globes, each surmounted by the cross of Christianity. The larger was made for Charles II, the smaller for William III and Mary.

The Sceptres: the symbols of royal authority. There are five in the regalia, including St. Edward's staff of gold, 4 feet 7 inches long; the King's Royal Sceptre, 3 feet long, richly jewelled and surmounted by a cross. It contains the largest cut diamond in the world – the 'Star of Africa.' This sceptre, the ensign of kingly power and justice', is placed in the sovereign's right hand at the coronation. The King's Sceptre with the Dove is placed in the left hand. Above the golden orb at the top is a cross on which rests a dove with outstretched wings, symbolic of peace.

The Spurs: the golden spurs of St. George are the emblem of knighthood and chivalry. They were formerly buckled on at the coronation.

The Rings: among these is 'The Wedding Ring of England' – the ring set with a sapphire with the Cross of St. George inset in rubies, which is placed on the sovereign's finger after the sceptres are received.

The Anointing Spoon: one of the two ancient items which survived the Commonwealth destruction. It dates from about 1200 and was probably made for the coronation of King John. The bowl was repaired for Charles II.

The Ampulla: the vessel containing the holy oil used for anointing the new sovereign. This is the other ancient piece, probably dating from the reign of Henry IV (1399–1413). The Ampulla is in the form of a golden eagle, with a wing-span of seven inches, through whose beak the oil is poured into the Anointing Spoon.

The Swords: Of the five swords, one is girded on the sovereign by the Archbishop, with the words: 'With this sword do justice, stop the growth of iniquity, protect the holy Church of God, help and defend widows, orphans. . . .' The rest are carried in the procession, including the great State Sword seen at the opening of Parliament, and the blunted Curtana, Sword of Mercy.

It will be seen that the royal regalia and the ceremony of coronation are full of the symbols and the innermost aspirations of chivalry, with the sovereign, under God, as the fount of it all.

The wanton destruction during the Commonwealth was carried out in the hope that with the disappearance of the symbols would go the old veneration for royalty and its semi-mystical powers. The Anointing Spoon and Ampulla probably escaped because they were not so obviously the insignia of kingship. When, in 1649, Parliament ordered the King's Jewel House to be forced open, a poet named George Withers dressed up in the crown and royal robes, thus, 'with a thousand ridiculous and apish actions', inviting the contempt of the crowd for all the ancient ritual. The officers recorded details of some of the items, and one would like to have seen 'King Alfred's crowne of goulde wyer worke, set with slight stones and 2 little bells' (valued by them at £248 10s.) and 'the Imperiall crowne of masy gould, £1,110.' The sum received from the sale of the gold and jewels was £3,650. At the Restoration, the new regalia cost £31,978. All these amounts must, of course, be multiplied many times over to get any idea of the value in modern times.

Reins: see *Bridle*.

René of Anjou (1409–1480): called 'the Good'; Duke of Anjou, Count of Provence, King of Sicily. In 1448 he founded the Order of the Crescent. About the same time, he compiled one of the earliest and most detailed books on the tournament, with the title *Traité de la forme et devis d'un Tournoi* – Treatise on the form and particulars of a Tournament. Among the interesting ceremonies it describes are the display

Girding Sword   State Sword   Curtana Sword of Mercy

of the crested helms of all the combatants, for the double purpose of allowing the chief spectators and judges to identify them and giving an opportunity to eject any knight with an unworthy record; and the election of a specially privileged knight to carry on his lance the *couvre-chef de mercy*. (See separate entry.)

Rerebrace: armour for the upper arm.

Resistance of Armour: the development of armour is the story of the endless battle between the armourer and the manufacturer of weapons and missiles, the one striving to make defences that nothing can penetrate, the other intent on producing something that cannot be resisted. Probably, the armourer may be said to have had the best of the contest, for, at the height of his craft, he produced plate armour that was practically impenetrable, either because of the extreme strength of the plate, or because it was so skilfully rounded and polished that the most powerful blows glanced harmlessly off. Only blows of extreme strength from mace, axe or sword were able to smash or cut through armour of this quality. It is commonly assumed that the introduction of fire-arms meant the end of armour's effectiveness. This is not so. The 17th century saw the production of a good deal of armour described as pistol- and musket-proof. Sometimes soldiers wore two breastplates, one on top of the other. The trouble was that, in order to maintain the effectiveness of the armour, the armourer had to make it of ever heavier plate till, in the end, the soldiers refused to wear it. On occasion, they even demanded extra pay for the wearisome task of wearing it on long marches.

Interestingly enough, though the fact is not always realized, the armoured soldier is with us again, and even the civilian, wearing his crash-helmet on a motor-cycle, has his links with the armies of the past. The so-called 'bullet-proof' vest is familiar equipment with many soldiers. It is estimated that 80 per cent of casualties come, not from direct hits, but from fragments of explosive shell travelling at a diminished speed, and against these modern light-weight armour is very effective protection. As the curator of the Department of Arms and Armour in the Metropolitan Museum of Art, New York, has written:

'These workaday helmets and body armour cast no bronze gleam across a plain, nor do they light up the sky, but they have won the respect of their wearers, and they can share in the glory of the helms and suits of armour once worn by kings and emperors, glistening with precious metals and glittering with jewels.'

Rest, Lance: see *Lance*.

Retinue: the body of retainers (retinue really means 'retained' or engaged) or attendants following a king, prince or great lord. They incurred great enmity from the common people because of their extravagance and ill-behaviour. There is a poem written as early as about 1310 attacking them. The writer of 'A Song against the Retinues of the Great People' complains bitterly of their pride, their idle fashions and loud behaviour, and asks the pertinent question:

> *Whil God wes on erthe*
> *And wondrede wyde,*
> *Whet we the resoun*
> *Why he nolde ryde?*

That is, while God himself was on earth, wandering wide, what was the reason he would not ride [in such state]? It finishes with some straight-from-the-shoulder lines:

> *Herkneth hideward, horemen,*
> *A tidyng ich ou telle,*
> *That ye shulen hongen*
> *Ant herbarewen in helle!*

– which can roughly be translated: 'Listen here, you horsemen! I've got news for you – you can all go hang and find your resting-place in hell!'
(See also *Livery* and *Livery and Maintenance*.)

Rheims (Reims): the ancient and historic city nearly 100 miles from Paris, on the River Vesle, where the kings of France were crowned, a custom probably originating with the baptism there of Clovis, the founder of the French monarchy, in the year 496.

In 1359, Edward III, to assert his overlordship of France, arrogantly decided to march on the city and have himself crowned in the cathedral. One of the greatest armies England ever mustered in the Middle Ages left in October, with nearly every great name in the annals of chivalry of the period represented. Froissart gives a list that

sounds like a roll of drums and a din of trumpets:

'Henry, duke of Lancaster; John, earl of March, constable of England; the earls of Warwick and Suffolk, marshals of England; the earls of Hereford, Northampton, Salisbury, Stamford, Oxford; the bishops of Lincoln and Durham; the lords Percy, Neville, Despenser, Roos, Manny, Reginald Cobham, Mowbray, Delawarre; sir John Chandos, sir Richard Pembridge, the lord Maine, the lord Willoughby, the lord Felton, the lord Basset, the lord Charlton, the lord Silvancier; sir James Audley, sir Bartholomew de Burghersh, the lord Scales, sir Stephen Cossington, sir Hugh Hastings, sir John Lisle, sir Nesle Loring, and a great many others . . .'

And a brave show they made of it, as, having disembarked at Calais, they began their march:

'First marched five hundred knights, well armed, and a thousand archers, in the van of the king's battalion, which was composed of three thousand men at arms and five thousand archers; himself and attendants riding among them in close order after the constable. In the rear of the king's battalion was the immense baggage-train, which occupied two leagues in length. It consisted of upwards of five thousand carriages, with a sufficiency of horses to carry the provision for the army, and those utensils never before accustomed to be carried after an army, such as handmills to grind corn, ovens to bake their bread, and a variety of other necessary articles.

'Next marched the strong battalion of the prince of Wales. He was accompanied by his brothers. It was composed of full two thousand men at arms, most excellently mounted and richly dressed. Both the men at arms and archers marched in close order, so that they were ready instantly to engage, should there be occasion.' There were also 'five hundred pioneers with spades and axes, to level the roads, and cut down trees and hedges.'

They progressed in easy stages through a devastated countryside, their finery and bright steel soaked and dimmed by constant rain. When at length they reached Rheims after a month's dispiriting march, they found the gates barred and the garrison ready for a prolonged siege. After many weeks, Edward gave it up and brought his great host to Paris. Here, too, he was met with silence and stillness. No army sallied out, no challenges were answered. All round him was the bitterness and barrenness of one of the longest winters on record. Edward gave it up again. The crowning disaster was the terror of 'Black Monday' (see separate entry).

In contrast to Edward III's ignominious failure to be crowned in Rheims may be put the triumphant day when Joan of Arc fulfilled her promise to bring Charles VII of France there for his crowning. On July 17, 1429, she came with him through the great west door, with its series of soaring arches and its sculptured ranks of saints and sovereigns, and saw him anointed.

When the Archbishop had crowned him, the trumpets had shrilled and the congregation had shouted their acclamations, the Maid knelt before Charles and said:

'Now is finished the pleasure of God, who willed that you should come to Rheims and receive your crown, proving that you are truly the King, and no other, to whom belongs this land of France.'

There are many stories of Rheims, and not all of martial display, ceremony and dignity. Ten years after Charles VII's coronation, when peace terms were being discussed near Calais, the Archbishop of Rheims was unable to attend one of the conferences because he had injured himself playing football!

Rhodes, Knights of: see *Knights of St. John of Jerusalem.*

Rhodes, Dragon of: one of the best of the early 'dragon' stories, set in the island when it was in the occupation of the Knights of St. John. Part of the island was held in a state of terror by a particularly unpleasant dragon which lurked in a mountain cave and preyed continually on the country folk, on their cattle and sheep, and on pilgrims who came to visit a nearby shrine. Many knights of the Order of St. John of Jerusalem went to do battle with the beast, but when time-after-time they failed to return, the Grand Master forbade any other knight to attempt the mission.

Theodore, a young knight of Provence, who had only recently been recruited to the Order, determined, despite his oath of obedience, to

ignore the Grand Master's ruling and bring great glory to himself and the brotherhood. Obtaining leave to return to France, he spent several months having a wooden dragon constructed, exactly like the terror of Rhodes, and equipped it with a mechanism that could cause it to rise in the air, exposing its vulnerable under-belly, which was not protected by thick scales. Theodore then trained two war-like bulldogs to attack the model dragon. At the same time, he would bear down on it with his horse, aiming his lance-point at the stomach. For a time the fearsome model scared both horse and dogs, but they were induced to overcome their fears – though the story says nothing about the continual frustration experienced by the bulldogs in attempting to sink their teeth into hard wood.

With the training satisfactorily completed, Theodore took ship again for Rhodes, accompanied by his dogs and his squires. Immediately after landing, he made his way to the shrine near the dragon's lair, and there kept his vigil, praying for success on the morrow. At dawn, armed cap-à-pie, he rode to where the dragon lay coiled in sleep in the mouth of its cave. The dogs bayed their displeasure, the monster stirred and added its cacophony to the discord ringing round the rocks. Theodore waded in with spear and sword. The spear sprang back from the adamantine scales and fell harmlessly to the ground. The horse, despite all the practice, swerved out of course, and would not face the fire-spitting jaws. Theodore leapt to the ground and plied his blade, but the swishing dragon's tail lifted him from his feet and crashed him to the ground.

Now it was up to the dogs. Fortunately, they had been apt pupils. They plunged their teeth into the roaring dragon, which obligingly reared up in its pain and presented the right target for the battered Theodore, who rushed up to the monstrous shape looming above him and plunged in his sword to the hilt. The dragon's last desperate scream made men tremble for miles around.

But Theodore had another dragon to face – the austere figure of the Grand Master of his Order, whose command he had disobeyed. The old man did not spare him. Courage was not enough. Obedience and humility were more than mere bravery, and without them he was unworthy to bear the cross of the Order. Sorrowfully the young knight acknowledged his fault, put off his proud armour and laid it, with his sword, at the Grand Master's feet.

He moved towards the door but, before he crossed the threshold, the raised voice of the old knight called him back. By his meek submission, Theodore had shown himself to be worthy after all. Let him return and receive the honour that was his due.

It need hardly be added that, in the fullness of years, with wisdom added to his youthful courage, Theodore sat in the Grand Master's seat, and, doubtless, gave young knights the dressing-down any worth-while aspirant deserves from time-to-time.

Rhuddlan Castle: one of the great castles erected by Edward I, near the site of an earlier one, during the conquest of Wales. It occupied a commanding position in the north and was of considerable strategic importance. The Welsh prince Llewelyn (d. 1282), 'the last champion of Welsh liberty', swore fealty to Edward there in 1277, and one of the king's assemblies of barons was held in the castle. Rhuddlan was one of the places where Edward encouraged new settlers to move in, by allowing them to use wood from the royal forests for their houses and forgoing his rents for several years.

Rhymer, Thomas the: see *Thomas the Rhymer*.

Rhys ap Gruffydd (1132?–1197): a Welsh prince and soldier who was a considerable trouble to Henry II before he eventually acknowledged his overlordship. He is perhaps best remembered, however, not for any military exploits, but for the fact that he held the first recorded *eistedfodd* (= a sitting) or meeting of bards who competed in music, poetry and minstrelsy. At the feast of Christmas in 1176, the prince staged an encounter in Cardigan Castle.

'At Christmas in that year the Lord Rhys ap Gruffud held court in splendour at Cardigan, in the castle. And he set two kinds of contests there: one between bards and poets, another between harpists and crowders [fiddlers] and pipers and various classes of music craft. And he had two chairs set for the victors. And he honoured those with ample gifts. And of the harpists, a young man from Rhys's court won the victory. As between the bards, those of Gwynedd prevailed. Each of the suitors obtained from Rhys that which he sought, so that no one was refused. And that feast, before it was held, was announced for a year through all Wales and England and Scotland and Ireland and the other islands.' (*The Chronicle of the Princes.*)

Ricasso: the thicker section of a sword between the quillons, or cross-guards, and the actual cutting blade, giving additional strength to the blade.

Richard I (1157–1199): called *Coeur-de-Lion*, the Lion-hearted. One historian sums him up as 'a bad son, a bad husband and a bad king, but a gallant and splendid soldier.' It is as the last that history has chosen chiefly to remember him. He is described as:

'Lofty of stature, of shapely build, his hair halfway between red and yellow, his limbs straight and supple. His arms were somewhat long and, therefore, better fitted than those of most folk to draw or wield a sword . . . His features showed him to be a ruler, while his manners and bearing added not a little to his general presence. He could claim the highest position and the praise, not only by reason of his noble birth, but because of his virtues. He far surpassed other men in courtesy and the greatness of his strength.'

His coronation on September 3, 1189, was a splendid affair and set a pattern followed for centuries. He came in procession from the Palace of Westminster to the Abbey, with his lords bearing the royal cap of maintenance, the golden sceptre and the knightly spurs. On head, shoulders and chest was placed the consecrated oil of anointing; then he was gorgeously robed in tunic, dalmatic, stole and mantle; on his feet were gold-laced sandals and the golden spurs; on his red-gold head the cap of maintenance and the crown of England. With ring on finger and golden sceptre in hand he came to his throne amid the soaring notes of the *Te Deum laudamus*.

If England thought a truly kingly figure had come to rule her, she was right. But she was to see little of him. Little more than three months after that stately coronation, he was gone. He was in England only once more, from March to May, 1194. The kingdom he so shamefully neglected was only a source of income to finance his interminable fighting. He said he would sell London itself if he could find a buyer.

Judged by the standards of the battle-field, however, he was another sort of being, indomitable in courage, terrible in strength, superb as a leader of men.

A curious story of him is told by the Tudor antiquary William Camden:

'When it was signified unto King Richard the First, son to . . . King Henry, sitting at supper in his Palace of Westminster . . . that the French King besieged his town of Vernoil [Verneuil] in Normandy, he, in greatness of courage, protested in these words: "I will never turn my back till I have confronted the French."

For performance of which his princely word, he caused the wall in his palace at Westminster to be broken down directly towards the south, posted to the coast, and immediately into Normandy, where the very report of his sudden arrival so terrified the French that they raised the siege and retired themselves.' (*Remains Concerning Britain*.)

His mere name seems to have been enough to strike fear. Jean, Sire de Joinville, the great chronicler of the Crusades (see *Joinville*), gives us a vivid impression:

'So soon as Acre was taken, King Philip returned to France, for which he was greatly blamed; but King Richard remained in the Holy Land, and did there such mighty deeds that the Saracens stood in great fear of him; so much so, as it is written in the book of the Holy Land, that when the Saracen children cried, their mothers called out, "Whisht! here is King Richard!" in order to keep them quiet. And when the horses of the Saracens and Bedouins started at tree or bush, their masters said to the horses, "Do you think that is King Richard?" '

Much has been written about Richard, both by his contemporaries and by later historians. Other pictures and glimpses of him in this book may be found under *Chalus; Gisors, Battle of; Jaffa; Long-bow; Minstrels; Quarter, Giving of; Richard of Devizes;* and *Saladin*. We can catch him

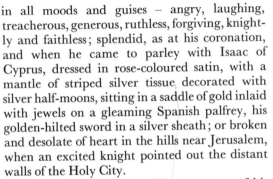

in all moods and guises – angry, laughing, treacherous, generous, ruthless, forgiving, knightly and faithless; splendid, as at his coronation, and when he came to parley with Isaac of Cyprus, dressed in rose-coloured satin, with a mantle of striped silver tissue decorated with silver half-moons, sitting in a saddle of gold inlaid with jewels on a gleaming Spanish palfrey, his golden-hilted sword in a silver sheath; or broken and desolate of heart in the hills near Jerusalem, when an excited knight pointed out the distant walls of the Holy City.

'While they were speaking . . . one of his knights cried: "Sire, sire, come so far hither, and I will show you Jerusalem!" And when the king heard this he threw his coat-armour [i.e., probably, his shield] before his eyes, all in tears, and said to our Saviour: "Fair Lord God, I pray Thee suffer me not to see Thy Holy City, since I cannot deliver it from the hands of Thine enemies." '

Another chronicler gives us an equally moving picture of Richard on the star-lit deck of the ship bearing him away from the arid land to which he had given the best of his aspirations and strength:

'And all night long the vessel sped on by star-light, till, as the morning broke, the king, after long reflection broke out into prayer:

"O Holy Land, to God do I entrust thee. May He, of His mercy, only grant me such span of life that, by His good will, I may bring thee aid. For it is my hope and purpose to aid thee at some future time."

And with this prayer, he pressed his sailors to set all sail . . .'

By his own wish, Richard I was buried at Fontevrault beside his mother, Eleanor of Aquitaine, and at the feet of his father, Henry II. The most impressive memorial in England is the great equestrian statue at Westminster. But the most curious tribute to him, and to the way this indifferent king and high-hearted warrior became enshrined in the memories of the common people, is a humble English apple called a 'codling.' The name can be traced back in successive stages through the centuries; from *codling* or *codlin* to *quodling*; from *quodling* to *querdling*; from *querdling* to *querdelyoun*; and thence to *Coeur-de-Lion*.

Richard II (1367–1400): called 'of Bordeaux', from the place of his birth. Richard of Bordeaux has little place in the annals of chivalry, since he was unmilitary by nature and had a pronounced feminine streak. But one or two things are worthy of note. His coat of arms showed three crowns. This was because he was born on the Feast of the Epiphany, or manifestation of the infant Christ to the Three Kings or Wise Men.

His coronation in 1377 produced, apart from the usual splendid pageantry and ceremony, one spectacular innovation – the appearance of the King's Champion at the Coronation Banquet. (See *Champion of England.*)

An interesting document that has survived from his reign, in the possession of the College of Heralds, is a set of ordinances, or rules, for jousts, drawn up by the Constable of England, Thomas, Duke of Gloucester. At the head of the document is a sketch showing Richard II receiving it from the Constable.

Richard III (1452–1485): the son of Richard, Duke of York and Cecily Neville, 'The Rose of Raby.' Though physically not as deformed and ugly as some early historians painted him, he was an unscrupulous and violent man who was probably responsible for the murder of the two little princes Edward and Richard, sons of Edward IV. The best that can be said about him is that he was a courageous soldier. He led the van at Edward IV's victories of Tewkesbury and Barnet, and his end at the Battle of Bosworth (1485), which put the Tudors on the throne of England, was almost heroic in its desperate valour.

'Richard rose in his stirrups so that all might hear. "We ride to seek Henry Tudor." Their faces showed that they understood, and awaited only his command. One of his squires put the battle-axe in his grip. He raised his gauntleted arm to signal his trumpeters. For the last time there sounded in the ears of men the battle-call of the fierce and valiant Plantagenets. . . .

The steel ranks of Henry Tudor's guard surged forward. A mighty figure loomed up in Richard's path – Sir John Cheyney, noted for his girth and height. With a shock they crashed together, the giant and the frail King,

Richard swinging his battle-axe in a flashing arc. The giant reeled, fell to the ground. Richard drove onward, cutting a path with his terrible axe . . . hewing his way towards the standard of the red dragon, borne by the stalwart William Brandon. . . .

Down went the dragon of Cadwaller, and Brandon rolled dead in the dust. In a tight arc about Richard his men were slashing their way forward. Only a few more yards now to Henry Tudor . . . But as he hewed his way he became aware that all about him his men were falling, overcome by masses of weapons. "Treason!" he shouted suddenly. "Treason! Treason!" Swinging his battle-axe he thrust onward.

He heard yells . . . a shock of steel. Stanley's cavalry had crashed against his tiny fellowship. "Treason!" he cried again, even as he struck with his axe . . . None of his Household remained at his side. He was beating about him against a thicket of spears and swords, rocked by blows he could not feel. And still on his helmet shone – through the dust, through the flailing steel – the golden circlet of his crown. "Treason!" he shouted, swinging his axe –

A dozen weapons smashed through his armour. In the midst of his foes, alone, he was beaten lifeless to the ground, leaving his kingdom and his fame to the hands of Henry Tudor.'

(Abbreviated from Paul Murray Kendall, *Richard the Third*. This account of the battle is largely based on the description by the historian Polydore Vergil, who was asked by Henry VII to write the history of England.)

Richard of Cornwall: see *Queens, Four*.

Richard of Devizes (flourished about 1190): a monk of Winchester who wrote a chronicle of the deeds of Richard I. Here is an example of his colourful writing, describing the king before Messina:

'The terrible standard of the dragon is borne in front unfurled, while behind the king the sound of the trumpets excites the army. The sun shone brightly on the golden shields.

The ships which the king found already prepared on the shore were one hundred in number, and fourteen busses, vessels of very

great magnitude and admirable swiftness, strong vessels and very sound, whereof this was the equipage and appointment. The first of the ships had three spare rudders, thirteen anchors, thirty oars, two sails, three sets of ropes of all kinds, and besides these double whatever a ship can want, except the mast and the ship's boat. There is appointed to the ship's command a most experienced steersman, and fourteen subordinate attendants picked for the service are assigned to him. The ship is freighted with forty horses of value, trained to arms, and with arms of all kinds for as many horsemen, and forty foot, and fifteen sailors. . . .

So great was the splendour of the approaching armament, such the clashing and brilliancy of their arms, so noble the sound of the trumpets and clarions, that the city quaked and was greatly astounded, and there came to meet the king a multitude of all ages, people without number, wondering and proclaiming with what exceeding glory and magnificence the king had arrived, surpassing the King of France, who, with his forces, had arrived seven days before . . . The armies cheered one another with mutual applause and intercourse, as if so many thousand men had been all of one heart and one mind.'

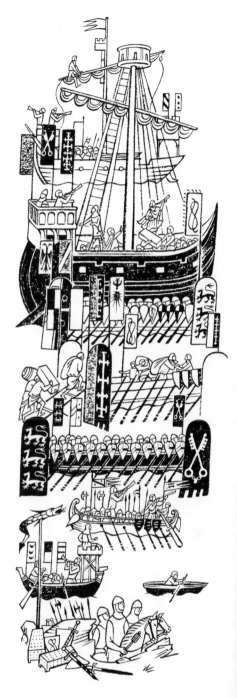

Richmond Herald: see *Officers of Arms.*

Ring: see *Annulet.*

Ripon: an ancient town and bishopric in the West Riding of Yorkshire. It suffered periodically from the hands of Danes, Normans and Scots. In 1318, e.g., Robert Bruce brought his raiders over the border almost as far south as York, and Ripon, after its citizens had withstood a siege in the minster itself, escaped only by paying over a ransom of £1,000.

Ripon once had a great reputation for the making of spurs, and 'true as Ripon steel' was an enviable compliment. According to Doctor Brewer, the spikes of a Ripon spur would strike through a shilling piece without turning the point.

Rivers, Anthony Woodville, second Earl: see *Woodville, Anthony.*

Rivets, Almayne or Almain: see *Almain Rivets.*

Roan: a horse of dark colour with a marked tinge of red, with grey or white markings interspersed. Richard II had a famous horse called Roan Barbary, to which Shakespeare makes reference in *Richard II.* At Pomfret Castle, one of Richard's grooms, who has seen Henry IV riding the deposed king's horse, says:

> *I was a poor groom of thy stable, king,*
> *When thou wert king; who, travelling towards York,*
> *With much ado at length have gotten leave*
> *To look upon my sometimes royal master's face.*
> *O, how it yearn'd my heart when I beheld*
> *In London streets, that coronation-day,*
> *When Bolingbroke rode on roan Barbary,*
> *That horse that thou so often hast bestrid,*
> *That horse that I so carefully have dress'd!*

(Act V, sc. iv).

Robert I (de Bruce) (1274–1339): King of Scotland, called 'the Liberator'. Scotland's greatest warrior-king and one of the greatest national leaders in history, despite the fact that he never commanded a large army and was for long periods a hunted outlaw. Sir Arthur Bryant calls him 'this king in the heather, this mountain fox with the mist in his beard.' He had his black times – one of his enemies, 'Red' Comyn, was murdered in the sanctuary of a church, either by Bruce himself or his followers – but he brought his little country, ravaged and disunited, to the greatest victory in its long story, by means of an iron will, indomitable courage, humour and, above all, that gift for leadership which is given only to the few, which defies exact analysis, and which has little to do with physical strength or a handsome presence.

He had paid homage to Edward I as King of Scotland in 1296 but, when the opportunity came in 1306, had himself crowned at Scone. Not long after he was defeated at Methven and took to the hills, where he led a wandering life of much hardship, later crossing to Ireland. Back in Scotland, outlawed, excommunicated and sometimes desperately sick, he survived a series of adventures in which fact and fiction have now become so interwoven that it is difficult to separate them. One of the most noteworthy was his single-handed defence of a ford against a troop of two hundred or more soldiers from Galloway, hunting the small band of fugitives with bloodhounds. Bruce had found a spot for his exhausted men to rest, and, with only two followers, came down to the ford to see if the pursuers were on his track. When he heard the hounds giving tongue, he sent back his two companions to warn the rest of the company. Then, seeing the narrowness of the ford over which the soldiers must pass to take him, he stationed himself where only one could pass at a time, and proceeded to tackle them. By the time his company came rushing to the rescue, he had accounted for fourteen men.

The triumph that paid for all came in 1314, nearly seven years after his old enemy Edward I, the Hammer of the Scots, had died on his way north to crush him. Edward II was a sorry successor to the old war-lord, and Bannockburn, fought on June 24, 1314, was the crowning disaster of a reign of ineptitude. Edward's army, aided by Welsh and Irish auxiliaries, may well have numbered 25,000 men. 'So vast,' wrote John Barbour, the Scots poet who talked with men who were at Bannockburn, and who indulged his poetic fancy a little, 'was the army which was now collected that nothing nearly so numerous had ever before been arrayed by England, and no force that Scotland could produce might possibly have been able to withstand it in the open field.' Robert Bruce had about a quarter of the English numbers.

The four Scots 'battles' or divisions straddled the Roman road running straight northward to Stirling castle, about three miles away. The English had marched from Falkirk that morning and, believing that an easy victory was at hand, determined to attack without delay.

The battle began dramatically enough. A group of English knights thrust forward across the Bannock Burn. One of them suddenly saw before him a Scottish horseman out reconnoitring in front of his outposts. Round his helmet was the circlet of kingship, and the young English knight realized it was Bruce in person. Here indeed was an early chance for glory. He put spurs to his horse and bore down triumphantly on the weatherbeaten, wiry figure on a small grey palfrey. He was an elusive target. As the Englishman reached him, he side-stepped, rose high in

the saddle and smashed his axe down on to the passing helmet. The knight crashed to the ground, his feet freeing themselves awkwardly from the twisting stirrups of his plunging destrier.

The early skirmishes brought no success to Edward's forces. It was decided to wait until the next day. Meanwhile, the English king laid the foundations of major disaster by moving his army down into the marshy valley of the meandering burn, where they passed an uneasy night, their morale already lowered by the reverses suffered.

Next day, June 24th, was Midsummer Day. In the summer dawn, the Abbot of Inchaffrey celebrated mass on high ground in view of the whole Scottish army; after which the Scots knelt to receive his blessing, and he passed among them exhorting them to fight for their rights and liberties. Edward II saw this and wondered if the little army was kneeling to ask mercy.

'You say truly,' said one of his knights, 'they ask mercy, but it is not of you, but of God. Yon men will win the field or die.'

Bruce had had to make the difficult decision whether he should pursue his old disconcerting tactics of withdrawing into the heather and harrying the English with flying raids, or risk the whole of his little army, and the whole fate of his stout-hearted country, on one desperate throw. He was doubtless helped to make up his mind by the fact that Edward had placed his army in such a vulnerable position; and he is said to have received encouragement from a deserter from the English ranks who reported on the poor spirits of Edward's host.

With his mind made up, he wasted no time. Before the English had finished arming, and before their battle-plan had time to be put into action, the Scottish spears were on the move down the slope in three bristling divisions. The English archers, who should have been smashing these masses of foot-soldiers with a rain of arrows, were still in the rear of Edward's forces, out of position, with jostling ranks of knights and horsemen in between them and the enemy. The English knights, gallantly enough, and some incompletely armed, flung themselves onto the close ranks of moving spears, and went down. Slowly, relentlessly, Bruce's 'battles' herded the unorganized English host into an ever-shrinking area bounded by marsh, bog, river and gorge. At a critical moment, Bruce flung in his five hundred horsemen to break the body of English archers, who had at length managed to get into position and were beginning belatedly to justify their reputation. Finally, Bruce called on his reserve, the body of men under his own command from Carrick, the Isles and the western Highlands. The last straw for the wavering, struggling English ranks was the sight of yet another close-packed company moving out from a wood to add their weight to a struggle that was already a one-sided nightmare. In point of fact, it was only Bruce's camp-followers moving in intent on plunder. But it was enough.

Seven hundred knights, many great nobles and thousands of humbler folk lay where they had fallen in the mire, in the Bannock Burn, in the broader waters of the Forth. Half a thousand, worth high ransom, were taken prisoner. By horse and by boat, bleating an oath that he would found a college of friars if only heaven allowed him to get away, Edward II escaped to England by a circuitous route, leaving behind the royal baggage-train and a treasure in jewels and money.

Bruce went on to other triumphs before he made his peace with Edward III and, after a year or two of unaccustomed peace and security at Cardross Castle, died a leper.

(For other information see *Camp-followers; D'Argentine, Sir Giles; Douglas, Sir James* (1286?–1330); and *Inverurie, Battle of.*)

Robert (d. 1103): a crusader and valiant knight about whom too little is known. He went to the Holy Land on the First Crusade, when Jerusalem fell and the kingdom of Jerusalem was established. He was taken prisoner at Ramlah, refused to deny Christ and was martyred for his faith.

Robert, Duke of Normandy (1054?–1134): known as 'Curthose'. He was the eldest son of William the Conqueror and came within reach of being king of England. A turbulent and brave soldier, he quarrelled with his father, raised troops against him and wounded him by mischance at Gerberoi in 1077. Later, he took his energy and his courage to Palestine, having pledged his duchy of Normandy for five years for

the sum of 10,000 marks in order to finance the expedition. He saw distinguished service, particularly at Antioch in 1098, when he was largely responsible for a victory under the walls of the city.

Three years later, keeping up his talent for quarrelling with his own family, he invaded England in an effort to take the throne from Henry I. The two brothers made peace at Alton, Hampshire, but were soon at each other's throats again in Normandy. This time, Henry made a thorough job of it. He captured Robert at Tinchebray in 1106, brought him back to England and kept him in prison for the next twenty-eight years, well-treated but highly indignant. He appears on the Bayeux Tapestry, and there is a wooden effigy of him in Gloucester Cathedral in crusading armour.

Robert de Stuteville (d. 1186): justiciar and sheriff of Yorkshire; took a leading part in the capture of William the Lion of Scotland. (See *William the Lion*.)

Robert of Gloucester (flourished 1260–1300): historian and compiler of a metrical chronicle of England to the year 1270. Probably it was composed in the Abbey of Gloucester, and it seems equally probable that Robert either saw some of the events or was able to talk with eyewitnesses. But more than one hand can be traced in *Robert of Gloucester's Chronicle*, the longest version of which runs to over 12,000 lines. At the end of his description of the Battle of Evesham (1265), in which Simon de Montfort was killed, the poet writes:

Suich was the morthre of evesham: vor bataile non it nas.

(Such was the murder of Evesham: for battle none it was!)

and, a few lines further on:

... this isei roberd
That verst this boc made: & was wel sore aferd.

(I, Robert, saw this, that first made this book, and was very sore afraid.)

Robert of Brunne: see *Mannyng of Brunne, Robert*.

Robert of Averbury (flourished about 1356): historian. Compiled a chronicle of the achievements of Edward III, down to 1356.

Robes: In the Middle Ages, the king's court and his most important followers received many payments in 'kind' as well as in money. Among the rewards 'robes' played a noteworthy part and they are frequently mentioned in accounts. Doris Mary Stenton says: 'These robes were all-enveloping garments of thick cloth suitable to protect their wearers from the draughts in contemporary halls and churches.' The quality of the robes was nicely graduated according to the status of the wearer. Knights, for example, expected robes with squirrel's fur, lesser men making do with rabbit. In the reign of Edward II (1307–27) a household ordinance was drawn up, going into the matter of robes in some detail. 'A banneret received 16 marks a year in two equal portions for his robes, a simple knight received 8 marks. The two clerks who sat at the accounting table received 2 robes a year in cloth or 46 shillings and eight pence. Grooms in the various departments received one cloth robe a year or one mark, that is 13 shillings and 4 pence.'

Robin Hood: see *Outlaws* and *Ivanhoe*.

Robin of Redesdale (flourished about 1470): the name adopted by a rebel leader – probably Sir John Conyers or his brother Sir William – against Edward IV. Taking advantage of a great wave of unrest and discontent in the north, Robin of Redesdale collected a force of perhaps 60,000 men in support of the house of Lancaster. (See *Roses, Wars of the*.) The rebels won a notable success at the Battle of Edgecote, July 26, 1469. For a time it seemed likely that Edward's army, which had hurried north to crush the revolt, would crush them; then occurred one of the lucky chances that were apt to turn the tide in mediaeval combats, when the confused conditions of hand-to-hand fighting often made it impossible for troops to know the general state of the battle. The incident illustrates, incidentally, two other things – the way in which personal badges and devices were widely known, and the effect that the name of a great leader could have on the fortunes of a battle.

At a critical moment, when the issue was in the balance, a rebel officer climbed to the crest of a small rise, displaying to all the surrounding combatants the badge of the bear. Everyone recognized it as the device of Warwick the King-maker (see *Neville, Richard, Earl of Warwick*) and the shout arose and spread like the ripples in a lake, 'A Warwick! A Warwick!' Convinced that Warwick himself was joining the battle, with a host of reinforcements, the royal forces broke. Among the casualties on Edward's side, either during or after the battle, were the Earl of Pembroke and the father and brother of Elizabeth Woodville, Edward IV's queen. (See *Woodville, Sir John* and *Woodville, Richard, 1st Earl Rivers.*)

Roches, Peter des (d. 1238): one of the warrior-churchmen of the Middle Ages, attempting, as so many did, the irreconcilable tasks of professing a religion of peace, splitting heads, founding churches and indulging in very shady political manoeuvring. He served Richard I as clerk, knight and chamberlain; continued in King John's service and was appointed Bishop of Winchester. In the next reign he acted as Henry III's tutor, played a leading part in defeating Prince Louis of France's forces at Lincoln in 1217, and went on Frederick II's crusade in 1227. After another period in England he fell from favour and went into exile, where he kept his hand in by helping Pope Gregory IX defeat the Romans at Viterbo. He died in England three years later at Farnham, the manor of the Bishops of Winchester.

Rochester Castle: one of the finest examples of Norman military architecture in England, noteworthy for its great square tower keep, with its four floors and twelve-foot-thick walls, rising 120 feet. Among its sieges was one by King John, who demonstrated the effectiveness of the art of mining with his engineers. (See *Mine, to.*) By tunnelling under the keep, enormously strong though it was, he brought down one of the corners in ruins.

Roebuck: very swift and graceful deer, prefering high ground and mountainous country.

Roland, Count: the supposed nephew of Charlemagne, and the hero of one of the greatest cycles of song and legend of the Middle Ages. As with so many of the greatest figures in romance, there may have been a real person on whom the whole structure was built. There was, for example, a 'Prefect of the Marshes' called, by an early historian, Hruodlandus, who was killed in the Battle of Roncesvalles, the encounter upon which the most famous of the Roland stories was based.

Roland's legendary sword was Durandal, his horse, Veillantif. The other immortal piece of equipment in the story is the horn of Roland (see next entry). The enduring popularity of the Roland story may be judged from the fact that we can connect one of the standard sizes of modern paper with this hero of chivalry. This is 'post', a sheet about 16 inches by 20 inches of a quality suitable for writing paper, etc. The early paper makers introduced designs into their sheets of paper which are called paper-marks or, more commonly, water-marks. They were the personal trade-marks of the manufacturer, and were formed by twisting the design in wire into the bottom of the mould in which the pulp lay. Modern writing paper is often still marked in this way, and the water-mark can be seen by holding the paper up to the light.

One of the popular early water-marks was the horn of Roland in various shapes and sizes. Sometimes Roland appeared as well, seated on his horse, in the act of blowing it. Later, Roland's horn became corrupted into a post-horn of the type carried by stage-coaches, etc.; hence, our term 'post' for a paper size.

Roland, Song of: the story and song told, recited and sung by innumerable story-tellers and minstrels through the length and breadth of Europe, always being altered and added to, according to the choice or flight of fancy of the individual. It was a story that, in the hands of a practised minstrel, could be relied on to draw the breathless attention, the ringing applause and the unashamed tears of the audience. This was the song that the minstrel Taillefer (see separate entry) sang before the Norman host at Hastings, encouraging the Conqueror's knights to deeds of hardihood.

The song was developed about a minor battle

that took place in the pass of Roncesvalles, in the Pyrenees, in A.D. 778. When Charlemagne was returning from a campaign against the Moors of Spain, a band of brigands fell on the rear-guard in the pass and plundered the baggage-train. It was not the first time such an ambush had been staged, and it was certainly not the last.

In the story built on this slender foundation, the Saracen king Marsilius was desperately anxious for Charlemagne and the Christian host to leave his ravaged land and sent an emissary, Blancandrin, to seek terms. Blancandrin, bearing the olive branch of peace and with a baggage-train of treasure for the Emperor, assured him that if he returned to France with his army, Marsilius would follow to Charlemagne's court, embrace the Christian faith and thenceforth hold his lands as the vassal of France.

Of Charlemagne's lords, Roland was strongly against trusting the infidel king; but the treacherous Ganelon, backed by some of the oldest and wisest advisers, counselled that the offer should be accepted, and, in the end, Ganelon was sent back to Marsilius to arrange the terms of peace. Arrived at the Saracen court, Ganelon indulged in the piece of double-dealing that was going to make his name pass into the colloquial speech of the Middle Ages as synonymous with traitor. He advised Marsilius to appear to accept Charlemagne's terms, then, when the main army had passed through Roncesvalles, to fall on the rear-guard, which, Marsilius could rest assured, would be commanded by the Saracens' arch-enemy, Roland. Ganelon came back with Saracen gold and jewels as a reward for this sweet treason.

Things went as Ganelon planned. When the question of the command of the rear-guard arose, Ganelon, with false flattery about his courage, said no one was better fitted for the task than Roland. Roland's intimate friend Oliver and the best of Charlemagne's chivalry asked to share the duty.

Charlemagne's great host marched homeward to the France they had not seen for seven long years and wound through the pass of Roncesvalles, the long cavalcade of knights and foot-soldiers, with their polished armour and horse-harness, their banners and pennons, making a ribbon of light and colour in the grey fastnesses of the mountains. In the rear came Roland and his rear-guard, always casting wary eyes back to where the Saracen king and his host lurked. With the dawn, Oliver saw and heard them.

> *Resplendent shines the sun upon that host,*
> *That moves like some strange brightly coloured snake*
> *Along the valley in unending line.*
> *A hundred thousand Saracens are there,*
> *Each rider filled with pride and lust for blood.*
> *The steel of sabres flashes in the light.*
> *The flaunting banners ripple in the breeze*
> *And wake the darkened scene to vivid life.*
> *Behold these hundred thousand marching men;*
> *A wondrous sight they make, a deadly too!*
> *For how can Roland with his few stand firm*
> *Against such overwhelming odds as this?*
> *The bugles sound a carillon of notes*
> *And from the hills a thousand echoes ring.*
> *The air is vibrant like a restless sea;*
> *It seems the heavens and earth reverberate*
> *To this defiant call from pagan throats.*

(trans. Hilda Cumings Price.)

Oliver wanted Roland to sound his horn at once, to summon back Charlemagne before it was too late. But Roland said it would bring disgrace on France and the name of his family if he appeared to be lacking in courage and unwilling to fight against odds. So the hopeless battle was joined and, fighting with unexampled courage, the peers of France went down one by one. Only with almost his last gasp did Roland blow his horn, falteringly at first, then louder, stronger, till the notes reached the ear of Charlemagne. Ganelon tried to convince the Emperor that Roland was sounding the horn only in jest or while he hunted. Suspicion began to dawn in Charlemagne's mind, then came conviction that there had been treachery. He angrily delivered Ganelon into the hands of his chief cook to hold till his return; then the orders rang out, the army turned and pressed back through the mountain ravines to the rescue of Roland. Far in the distance the Saracens heard the din of ten thousand trumpets, then the tramp and jingle of the approaching army and, finally, the battle-cries of 'Montjoie!'

The Saracens turned in retreat, leaving every foot of ground covered with dead and dying, ten infidels for every Frenchman. Roland's last act was to stand upright in a desperate surge of strength and, to prevent it falling into Saracen

hands, try to dash his sword Durandal to pieces against a rock. But the blade was so true it would not splinter. Instead, the rock split from top to bottom.

The avenging host of Charlemagne wreaked terrible vengeance, destroying the Saracen strongholds, killing Marsilius and every Moor who would not be baptised. It was the end, too, for Ganelon. On Charlemagne's return he sat in state with the remaining chivalry of France around him and invited them to pronounce judgement on the traitor. Stripped of armour, shield, and sword, every last vestige of the knighthood he had so dishonoured, he was dragged out to be torn in pieces by wild horses.

Rolls of Arms: the records made by skilled observers, usually heralds, of the coats of arms displayed by nobles, barons and knights. Though they are now sometimes separated, they were once literally 'rolls', small sheets stitched together and then rolled up into one bundle.

The English College of Heralds has some splendid examples, probably the finest being one dating from 1270–80, giving 195 shields in rows of five. After seven hundred years, the colours still glow and the great names of chivalry speak in the proud devices. There are the red chief and saltire of Bruce; the silver orle on red of Balliol; the blue, gold and silver of Mortimer; the horseshoes of Ferrers; the silver and red quarters, with a black bend over all, of Despenser. These are the coats that went into battle and tournament in the reign of Edward I, brave in new paint and embroidery at the onset, streaked, muddied and bloodstained by evening, only to be refurbished and carried again by generation after generation.

Another type is the one-family roll, the chronicle of a particular household, great or small. Again, the College of Heralds can show the finest examples, notably the great Warwick or Rous Roll, painted between 1477 and 1485 by John Rous, chantry priest at Guy's Cliffe, Warwick, and devoted to the history of the Earls of Warwick. This is a vellum roll 11 inches wide and 24 feet 6 inches long. Here is all the blaze of heraldry of one of the greatest families in English history with all the quarterings brought to them by their various illustrious marriages – the crosslets of the Beauchamps, the gold and blue chequers of Newburgh, the silver saltire on red of Neville, and all the rest. This roll has, too, 63 skilfully painted figures, mainly of the Earls of Warwick, but also of royal, and other, benefactors of the town of Warwick. Among them is Guy of Warwick (see separate entry) carrying an enormous pole-axe, with which he has accounted for a whole menagerie of monsters at his feet; Felice, in the same story, receiving the ring sent by Sir Guy just before he died; King Alfred's daughter, Ethelfleda, delicately balancing the town of Warwick in her mediaeval hand, and William the Conqueror, three golden lions on his shield, with the prostrate Harold at his feet, the arrow in his eye and the kingly circlet of England still round his helmet.

Romances of Chivalry: for various famous stories and characters see *Amadis of Gaul; Angarad of the Golden Hand; Archalaus the Enchanter; Arundel; Balan; Bedivere; Camelot; Charlemagne* and *Charlemagne's Paladins; Excalibur; Galahad; Gawaine, George, St.; Geraint; Giants; Grail; Guinevere; Guy of Warwick; Hugo of Tabarie; Idylls of the King; Isumbras; Jehan de Saintre; Joyous Garde; Kay; Kilhwch; King Cole; Launcelot; Lyonesse; Mabinogion; Malory; Mannyng of Brunne; Merlin; Oliver; Pendragon; Percival; Quixote, Don; Red Cross Knight; Rhodes, Dragon of; Roland* and *Roland, Song of; Round Table; Seven Champions of Christendom; Siege Perilous; Tintagel.*

Roncesvalles, Battle of: see *Charlemagne* and *Roland, Song of.*

Rondel Dagger: military dagger with the pommel and hand-guard formed of roundels or rondels – flat discs or small plates of various shapes set horizontally to the blade.

Rose: The rose occurs very early in heraldry, and is always shown as 'displaying' five petals. It is, in fact, the common wild rose of the English hedgerows. In Tudor times, the rose is often shown with a double row of petals.

It is worth noting that there is at least one real Tudor rose – a cultivated one – still left in England. The archivist of Canterbury Cathedral found it crushed in the folds of a Tudor document, where it had lain undisturbed for nearly four centuries.

Rose of England: the golden rose, originally a royal badge brought in by Henry III's queen, Eleanor of Provence.

Rose of Lancaster: the red rose. When John of Gaunt, fourth son of Edward III, married Blanche of Lancaster he incorporated the red rose in his arms and it became the badge of the Lancastrian kings who descended from him.

Rose of York: the white rose. (See also *Rose of Lancaster*.) The origins of the rose of York are rather more difficult to establish. Roger Mortimer, second Earl of March (1327?–1360), used the white rose as a badge. From him descended Richard Plantagenet, Duke of York, who unsuccessfully claimed the throne, Edward IV and Richard III, all three of whom used the white rose among their badges, so that this is a probable explanation.

Rose Noble: an early English gold coin carrying the device of the wild rose.

Roses, Wars of the: name given to the struggle for the throne of England between the two great rival families of Lancaster and York; usually considered as beginning with the first Battle of St. Albans (1455) and ending with the Battle of Bosworth (1485).

For some personalities involved see *Edward IV; Jockey of Norfolk; Neville, Richard, Earl of Warwick; Richard III; Robin of Redesdale; Woodville, Anthony, 2nd Earl Rivers; Woodville, Sir John; Woodville, Richard, 1st Earl Rivers.* For information about some of the battles see *Long-bow* (for Battle of Towton); *Mortimer's Cross; Mediaeval Artillery, Liveries* and *Neville, Richard, Earl of Warwick* (for Battle of Barnet); *Proverbs of Hendyng* (for Battle of Towton); *Richard III* (for Battle of Bosworth); *Robin of Redesdale* (for Battle of Edgecote); *St. Albans; Tewkesbury* and *Wakefield.*

One historian, C. A. J. Armstrong, has collected together a number of examples of how fast news travelled during the troubled period of the Wars of the Roses. These are some:

Battle of Wakefield: fought December 30,

1460. News received in London, January 2, 1461. Distance, 182 miles.

Return of Edward IV after temporary exile: landed at Ravenspur, March 14, 1471. News received in Bury St. Edmunds, March 19. Distance, 245 miles.

Battle of Barnet: fought April 14, 1471. News received in Cerne Abbas (Dorset) the next day. Distance, 130 miles.

Death of Edward IV: April 9, 1483, in London. News received in Calais the next day. Distance, 92 miles. (Cross-Channel communication was good that day, with no interception by Easterling pirates, etc.)

Battle of Bosworth: fought August 22, 1485. News received in York the next day. Distance, 120 miles.

Rouen: city in northern France on the River Seine; the capital of Normandy and the chief residence of its Dukes since the 10th century; held by the English kings till 1204, when it was captured by Philip Augustus of France; retaken after a long siege by Henry V in January, 1419. Joan of Arc was tried and burned there in 1431.

We have an eye-witness account of Henry V's siege, from July 29, 1418 to January 13, 1419. He describes how, by the time Christmas was at hand, the inhabitants had been reduced to sore straits, with no bread, ale or wine, meat or fish. Their sustenance was water and vinegar, horse-flesh, dogs, mice, cats and rats, and so desperate did they become in their scramble for food that 'love and hearty kindness was then from them passed.' They kept up a brave show of manning and patrolling the battlements, unwilling to let Henry V know in what sorry condition they were, but some of the citizens were taken prisoner and revealed the truth. Many of the poorer people, man, woman and child, were thrust outside the gates and told to fare for themselves as best they could. These came to the English, went on their knees and cried: 'Have mercy on us, ye good Christian and worthy Englishmen.' It is pleasant to record that Henry V took pity on them and gave them food and drink, though he would not keep them in the camp and many died of exposure outside the walls of Rouen.

Henry V seems to have done even better at the feast of Christmas when, 'in reverence of that

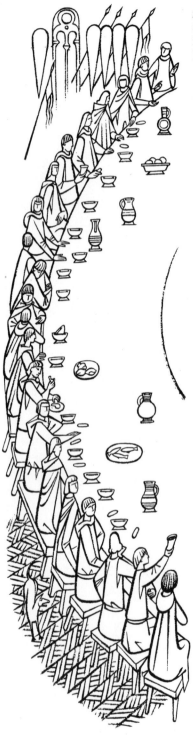

glorious feast of the birth of our lord Jesu Christ and of his mother saint Mary', he sent out heralds inviting those within and without the city to have meat and drink, and safe-conduct to come and go. His charity may have had something to do with the surrender of the city soon after, for the chronicler says the citizens exclaimed that 'these Englishmen be of good and tender heart...' with 'more pity and compassion by a thousand than hath our own nation.'

They had less pity and compassion twelve years later when Joan of Arc was barbarously tried and burned in the market-place. Bound to the stake with a chain, she looked her last on the France she had served with such devotion, at the huddled timber houses and the cathedral spire soaring nearly 500 feet above them, at the jostling crowd of onlookers, and said: 'O Rouen, Rouen! must I die here?'

Rouge-Croix Pursuivant: see *Officers of Arms.*

Rouge-Dragon Pursuivant: see *Officers of Arms.*

Round Table: the table made by Merlin for Uther Pendragon and given by him to King Leodegrance, whose daughter Guinevere became King Arthur's wife. Leodegrance gave the Round Table to Arthur as a marriage gift.

'... he hath lands enough, but I shall send him a gift shall please him much more, for I shall give him the Table Round, the which Uther Pendragon gave me, and when it is full complete there is an hundred knights and fifty.'

With it Leodegrance sent a hundred good knights, and with these Arthur began his famous fellowship of the Round Table. One of the seats was the Siege Perilous, always left empty for the one predestined knight who was fit to occupy it. (See *Siege Perilous.*)

There were several actual Round Tables made in imitation of the legendary one. In Edward I's reign, Roger Mortimer is said to have established one at Kenilworth Castle for 'the encouragement of military pastimes.' In 1344, Edward III founded the Order of the Blue Garter as a revival of Arthur's company of knights and 'immediately after these first martial exercises were over [i.e., the preliminary tournaments] (to the end better accommodation might be had for the knights that should afterwards come thither) the King caused carpenters, masons and carriages to be imprest for the erecting the foresaid building of the Round-Table in the Castle.' (*The History of that Most Victorious Monarch Edward III*, 1688.)

Roundels: in heraldry, plain circular figures of colour or metal. The chief ones are:

Name	Metal or Colour
Bezant	Gold
Plate	Silver
Torteau	Gules (red)
Hurt	Azure (blue)
Ogress or Pellet	Sable (black)
Pomeis	Vert (green)
Golpe	Purpure (purple)

The bezant and plate are always flat and the torteau is usually so. The rest are shown as solid and are shaded to give them a rounded appearance. One common and attractive roundel is the Fountain, which is a roundel divided into wavy bands of silver and blue. The family of Stourton carries six 'fountains' on its shield. They took their name from the manor of Stourton, which, in turn, took its name from the River Stour. The source of the river is a group of six wells, or, in the words of Leland, the Tudor antiquary, 'six fountaynes or springes . . . The Lorde Stourton giveth these 6 fountaynes yn his Armes.'

Rounsey (Rouncy): a strong horse of no special breeding used mainly by men-at-arms and travellers. Chaucer's Shipman 'rood upon a rouncy as he kouthe [could].'

Rous Roll: see *Rolls of Arms.*

Rowel: spiked wheel or disc on a spur, instead of the plain 'prick'. The rowel was introduced towards the end of the 13th century. At first the neck was short and the number of points on the wheel only five or six. Later the number grew to as many as two or three dozen, delicately arranged like a flower, and the neck was much longer. A famous equestrian figure of a knight in the Wallace Collection, Hertford House, London, has spurs with slightly curving necks ten inches long. (See *Spurs.*)

Royal Arms of England: see *Arms of England.*

see 'Hatching' for meaning of shading

Royal Arms of France: see *Arms of France*.

Royal Arms of Scotland: see *Scotland, Arms of*.

Royal Badges: the successive reigning houses of England, and individual members of them, adopted a large variety of badges. Some examples are:

Henry II: broom-cod (planta genista).

Richard I: crescent and star (used also by John and Henry).

Edward III: golden tree-stump, falcon, gryphon, boar.

Richard II: white hart, sun-in-splendour.

Henry VI: red rose, swan, fox's brush.

Edward IV: rose-en-soleil (a combination of the blazing sun of York and the white rose of York).

Richard III: white boar.

Henry VII: portcullis, 'sun-burst'.

Catherine of Arragon (Queen of Henry VIII): bundle of arrows; a red rose joined to a pomegranate.

Jane Seymour (Queen of Henry VIII): green hill with tree and flowers, girded about with castle walls.

Royal Banner: a common error is to refer to the Royal Banner as the Royal Standard. A standard (see separate entry) is, properly speaking, a long tapering flag of the type used by the nobles and captains on the battle-field to rally their troops around. These standards did not display the arms of the bearer. A banner should display the full arms. The flag that flies above a palace or castle displaying the royal arms is, therefore, the Royal Banner. The flags of the various Orders of Chivalry – the Garter, the Bath, etc. – are always, quite correctly, called banners.

Royal Standard: see *Royal Banner*.

Royal Victorian Order: an Order of Chivalry instituted on April 21st, 1896, entirely in the gift of the Sovereign, to reward personal service. There is also a Royal Victorian Chain which is not part of the Victorian Order but which is granted by the Sovereign as a special mark of esteem and of distinction.

Running Vine Pattern: see *Etched Decoration (on armour)*.

Sabatons (Sabbatons): foot-armour consisting of overlapping plates; often broad-toed, sometimes rounded, occasionally completely square. In the Wallace Collection, London, as part of a Maximilian harness of 1535, there are some fine examples of the so-called 'bear's paw' pattern, from the fancied resemblance to a clawed bear's foot.

Saddle: an all-important part of the knight's equipment. The most popular type used in western Europe in the Middle Ages probably originated from the kind the Crusaders found in general use by the Arabs. This gave the rider some protection almost from waist to knee. (See *Henry V* for a surviving war-saddle.) The main parts of the saddle were the wooden framework, well glued and riveted, and the various straps and metal fittings. The frame was covered with fibre and the whole, inside and out, finished with various materials – sheepskin, leather, velvet, etc. – for the purposes of comfort, of decoration and, much more important, of preventing the horse's sweat from damaging the 'sinews' or fibre. An order of Henry VII's, in 1499, signed by the king himself, shows the care that had to be taken in the supply of saddles and horse furniture:

'We will and charge you that ye deliver . . . first, for two hobbies two saddles covered with crimson velvet bordered about with cloth of gold and lined with buckram, two pair of stirrup leathers doubled, two pair of stirrups, two girths of twine and two coverings of black leather for the said saddles; two horse harnesses of crimson velvet bordered about with cloth of gold garnished with beckets [loops], two leading reins of red leather, two halters double reined, two crinets [neck coverings]. For a palfrey, a covering with scarlet engrailed about with black velvet, with buttons and tassels of silk and gold of our colours and lined with canvas; a headstall covered with black velvet and a pair of broad reins garnished with beckets pendant and buttons of copper and gilt, a bit gilted, a pair of gilt bosses and surcingle [belt or girth] of twine, a leading rein of red leather, a halter double reined, a crinet, three horse-clothes of white and green, three surcingles of twine, three headstalls, three pair of broad reins, three bits. . . .'

(Spelling modernized.)

The war-saddle, though very carefully made, was naturally a tougher and less ornate affair than the types used for travelling, hunting and parade purposes. These used the same techniques, but showed more magnificent craftsmanship. The design was somewhat different, too, since they did not need to give the same measure of protection to the user. Richard I had one parade saddle which, we are told:

'Glittered with red and gold spangles, and had on the hinder part two small lions of gold turned towards each other, with their mouths open, and each stretching out one of its forelegs, as if to attack and devour the other.'

There is a beautiful example of the parade saddle, dating from about 1400, in the Metropolitan Museum of Art, New York. The wooden frame is covered with staghorn, carved with court lords and ladies and St. George killing the dragon.

Saddle-tree: the wooden framework of the saddle. See *Saddle*.

St. Albans, Battle of: name of two battles in the Wars of the Roses.

1. May 22, 1455. The opening battle of the Wars, in which the Lancastrians were defeated, Henry VI being wounded and a number of his nobles killed.

2. February 17, 1461. This time the Lancastrians were victorious, but completely threw away their advantage. Within a fortnight, the Yorkists had taken London, and Edward IV was proclaimed king.

Writing about the first battle, John Crane, in a letter to John Paston, said: '. . . there was, as we can tell, . . . at most slain six score; and as for the lords that were with the king, they and their men were pilled [pillaged] and spoiled out of all their harness and horses; and as for what rule we shall have yet I weet [know] not.'

St. Andrew's Cross: (see *National Flags*). The national flag of Scotland, a silver saltire on a blue field. (See *Saltire*.)

St. Denis, Abbey Church of: the church, in the suburbs of Paris, of which is has been said that 'no other church in Christendom shone with such

magnificence and splendour.' This was the great
abbey church of the kings of France, where, for
more than a thousand years, sixty-three abbots
had ruled, till the desecration and wanton
destruction of the French Revolution broke its
glory and pride. It has been partially restored;
but other forces than those of the eighteenth-
century mob keep it a faded shell of what it once
was, for it is surrounded by slums, poverty and
industrial ugliness.

Roger Payne, in 'The Splendour of France',
gives us a vivid picture of St. Denis in its prime:

'In the twelfth century the Abbey Church
of St. Denis was a jewel casket of blinding
colours. The doors were of bronze sheeted with
hammered gold; the altar and all the holy
vessels were of purest gold; the windows
blazed with coloured glass. The relics of the
martyrs were enclosed in jewel-studded reli-
quaries of a blinding brilliance, befitting the
presence of the patron saint of France, who
according to the legend had received com-
munion from the hands of Christ. There was
no holier place in France than this shrine to
St. Denis. For this reason the French kings
were buried here, and here they came in time
of war to receive from the abbot the sacred
banner of the kingdom, the *oriflamme*, with its
golden flames on a scarlet ground, which was
displayed in the sanctuary in time of peace.
Here Joan of Arc, wounded in battle, came to
offer up the mysterious sword she received from
St. Catherine and the pure white banner
emblazoned with the fleur-de-lys and the
figure of the Saviour.'

The Abbey Church was largely the creation of
the great Abbot Suger of whom the same author
says:

'Almost single-handedly Abbot Suger, the
son of a serf, brought Gothic art into existence.
He it was who filled the churches with light
and sent the slender columns spinning so high
they seem to be reaching to the foothills of
heaven. He shattered the walls to let the light
in, and gilded the altar so that it should shine
like the sun. For him all light was heavenly,
being God's breath made visible, and the
radiance of the angels. So he built a church
like a cascade of jewels, a fountain of emeralds
and rubies, a lake of silver and gold, to bring

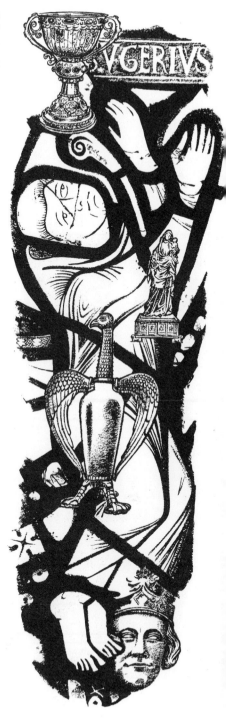

U

people nearer the heart of the glowing mystery of light.'

(See also *Oriflamme*.)

St. George's Chapel: the magnificent Chapel in Windsor Castle, begun by Edward IV in June, 1475 and finished, except for the stone vaulting over the organ, 34 years later. It is the home of the greatest Order of Chivalry in the world, the Order of the (Blue) Garter, founded by Edward III. (See *Blue Garter, Order of the*.)

The building, one of the most beautiful in Christendom, contains so much fine craftsmanship that it is as much a memorial to the workmen that fashioned it as to the proud line of knights who are honoured there. We know the names of many of the craftsmen, including John Tresilian, master in metalwork; Henry Jenyns, master mason; Robert Ellis and John Hills, carvers of the choir stalls; William Berkeley, John Hylmer and William Vertue, who worked up aloft on the choir ceiling. It is sometimes difficult to believe that these men were working with such tough materials as wood and stone, so fine and delicate is the intricate tracery.

But, in terms of history and of chivalry, the most precious survivals are the stall-plates of the Knights of the Garter, the metal plates, fastened to the backs of the choir stalls, carrying the arms of the men who, through the centuries, have occupied the stalls and worshipped in the Chapel of the Order. For some three hundred years these plates were enamelled on gilt or silvered copper; then, till the early years of the 20th century, the arms were painted on the copper. After that, the plates were again enamelled. If all the stall-plates were there, they would number more than 900; but some have been lost, stolen, or removed when a knight was degraded. There are now nearer 700. The earliest plate is that of Ralph, Lord Bassett, and dates from about 1390. It shows his arms, *or, three piles gules and a quarter ermine* and, with them, his crest of a black boar's head, with gold tusks, and collared with a jewelled crown.

One interesting point about many of the plates is that, in order to emphasize the religious aspect of membership of the Order, one of the usual rules of heraldry is deliberately broken and the helms and crests face right, towards the altar, instead of left.

It is not always realized that St. George's Chapel contains a number of smaller chapels or chantries, each with a separate name and history. One of the most interesting is the Bray Chapel, commemorating Sir Reginald Bray, the knight who is reputed to have recovered the crown from the hawthorn bush where it had rolled from the helm of Richard III when he fell at Bosworth. (See *Richard III.*) Bray had a curious heraldic badge – a pun on his name – the bray or comb-like tool used by weavers for crushing and fining hemp. This device appears, it has been estimated, 175 times in stone, wood and metal in the Chapel.

The Knights of the Order of the Garter cannot often attend services in St. George's Chapel. But they have their resident representatives in the persons of the Military Knights of Windsor. These are usually distinguished army officers who are given a small income and quarters within the Castle. Each Sunday a number of the Military Knights take their seats in St. George's, dressed in scarlet, with white shoulder-belts. In former years, instead of a uniform, they wore a cloak of Garter blue. The name has changed, too. They used to be the 'Poor Knights', and their illustrious line has included many famous soldiers, including some who fought on the fields of France in the Hundred Years' War.

St. George's Cross: (see *National Flags*). The national flag of England, a red cross on a silver field.

Saint Grail: see *Grail*.

St. James of Compostella: see *James of Compostella, Saint*.

St. John of Jerusalem, Knights of: see *Knights of St. John of Jerusalem*.

St. John's Cathedral: the cathedral of Valetta, in the island of Malta, 'with all the chivalry of Europe within its walls.' It contains twenty-four tombs of Grand Masters of the Order of St. John of Jerusalem, and its paving has been described as 'one huge carpet or tapestry of inlaid heraldic floor-slabs of the Knights.'

St. Louis of France: see *Louis IX*.

St. Michael and St. George, Order of: instituted April 27th, 1818, by the Prince Regent on behalf of George III. It has usually been awarded to subjects who have held high and confidential office in Britain's colonial possessions or given distinguished service to the Empire and Commonwealth. There are three ranks, Knights Grand Cross, Knights Commanders and Companions.

St. Patrick's Cross: the national flag of Ireland, a red saltire on a silver field. (See *Saltire*.)

Saker: (1) a type of large falcon used in hawking. The *Sakeret* is the male, a smaller bird than the female. (2) a small piece of artillery.

Salade Helmet: spelt also *Sallet*. Type of helmet popular between about 1450 and 1510. It rested entirely on the head and was not attached to the body armour. In many examples the top has a ridge or crest which sweeps down into a long tail at the back. Sometimes the helmet measured as much as eighteen inches from back to back. The later types had a movable visor. Examples of salade helmets can be found in the paintings of such artists as Albrecht Dürer.

Saladin: the common name of Salah ad-Din Yusuf (1137–1193), Sultan of Egypt and Syria, the most famous of the Saracen chiefs and opponent of the Crusaders. He performed many acts of generosity and true chivalry, e.g., when he sent fresh horses to the dismounted Richard I in the midst of a battle (see *Jaffa*) in recognition of his bravery; and, when the same king lay tossing with fever in his tent, sent him peaches, pears, and snow from Mount Ascalon to cool him. In fact, in many ways he was a truer knight than numbers of the Christians who rode against him. Sir Steven Runciman, the great modern historian of the Crusades, says of him:

'Of all the great figures of the Crusading era Saladin is the most attractive. He had his faults. In his rise to power he showed a cunning and a ruthlessness that fitted ill with his later reputation . . . But when he was severe it was for the sake of his people and his faith . . . Unlike the Crusader potentates, he never broke his word when it was pledged to anyone, whatever his religion. For all his fervour, he was always courteous and generous, merciful as a conqueror and a judge, as a master considerate and tolerant.'

In direct contrast to his greatest opponent, Richard Coeur-de-Lion, with his great stature, his fondness for display, his bursts of boisterous good humour, Saladin was a slight figure of a man, shunning ostentation, modest and scholarly.

Sallet: see *Salade*.

Saltire: a cross in the form of an X. The common name for this type of cross is a St. Andrew's Cross, though St. Patrick's Cross is also a saltire. (See both these entries.) These two saltires are combined with the Cross of St. George to form the Union Flag or Union Jack. If a shield is divided *per saltire*, the partition lines are in the form of a St. Andrew's Cross.

Sangreal: see *Grail*.

Saracens: the general name given by crusaders and Christians to all infidels – Arabs, Moors, Moslems, etc. To the Saracens, all Christians were 'Franks'. James Elroy Flecker (1884–1915) wrote a well-known poem called 'The War Song of the Saracens', some lines in which indicate the extent of their conquests:

*From the lands where the elephants are, to the
    forts of Merou and Balghar,
Our steel have we brought and our star to shine
    on the ruins of Rum.
We have marched from the Indus to Spain, and by
    God we will go there again;
We have stood on the shore of the plain where
    the Waters of Destiny boom. . . .*

A reminder of these warlike peoples, of leaders like Saladin, and of the Crusaders, can be found in many English villages and towns in the inn-sign of the 'Saracen's Head'.

Sarcenet (Sarsenet): a fine soft-textured silk, chiefly used for linings, ribbons, etc. The name is derived from 'Saracen' and probably goes back to a material introduced to England by the Crusaders.

Scabbard: the case or sheath holding the blade of sword or dagger. Scabbards were made in

endless variety, from those of plain, workmanlike leather or tough parchment to ornate examples like that worn by Richard I at a meeting with the Emperor of Cyprus, made of silver scales; or the scabbard of the sword used at the coronations of English kings and queens, studded with diamonds, emeralds and rubies forming the rose of England, the thistle of Scotland and the shamrock of Ireland.

In battle or tournament, a scabbard was often a useless encumbrance, and the knight slipped his sword through a belt-ring, from which it could be instantly wrenched.

Scaling-fork: military weapon with a particularly long shaft and prominent hooks, sometimes carried on scaling-ladders to drag defenders from the battlements.

Scaling-ladders: long ladders reared against the walls of castles, fortified towns, etc., by the attackers. It is clear that these were often improvised from whatever materials could be found in the area of battle, for John Talbot, Earl of Shrewsbury's orders to his army in the reign of Henry VI instruct 'every seven gentlemen or men-at-arms' to 'make them a good sufficient ladder and a strong of 15 rungs.'

(See *Escalade*; and, for a noteworthy example of the use of a scaling-ladder, *Randolph, Sir Thomas*.)

Schallern: see *Salade Helmet*. This is the German word for this type of helmet.

Schiltrons: the dense groups of close-packed spearmen used, e.g., by Wallace at Falkirk and Bruce at Bannockburn (see separate entries for these battles).

'Knowing that he would again have to defeat armoured cavalry with infantry ... he [Wallace] had trained his men to fight in dense oblongs called schiltrons or shield-troops, with triple tiers of twelve-foot spears facing outwards which it was almost impossible for cavalry to break ... a schiltron resembled a vast steel hedgehog.' (Sir Arthur Bryant)

Scimitar: curving sword, commonly broadening towards the point, with a single cutting edge

302

on the convex side.

Scotland, Royal Arms of: a red lion on a golden field, within a tressure of fleur-de-lys. The correct heraldic description is *or, a lion rampant within a double tressure flory counter-flory gules*. See *Tressure* for an explanation of this term.

Scrope-Grosvenor Controversy: see *Chaucer, Geoffrey*.

Scutage: derived from Latin *scutum*, a shield. Money paid to the king by a knight or other tenant instead of performing military service in the field.

Seals: (1) stamps, usually of metal or wood, carrying devices for making impressions in wax, lead or other material, attached to documents as a proof that they are authentic.

(2) the pieces of wax, lead, etc., themselves.

Seals are important sources of historical information, and particularly in connection with early coats of arms, badges and devices. Mediaeval seals on documents, in England, were always of wax – made of about two-thirds beeswax and one-third resin. Three colours are found – natural dark yellow, red (obtained by adding vermilion) and green (by adding verdigris). Seals were either hung onto the document by means of a strip of material or, later, applied to the surface itself. Where large numbers of people were involved in an agreement, it is possible to find dozens of wax seals appended to the same document, hanging almost like dense clusters of multi-coloured fruit. An agreement between Ranulph, Earl of Chester and Lincoln, and the men of Frieston and Butterwick, preserved in the Public Record Office, has 50 different seals. Two shapes are commonly found – either roughly round or 'vesica', i.e., oval, or a shape made by two arcs of circles, giving a point at each end. The latter were often used by great ladies, and by religious institutions, churchmen, etc. One of the chief reasons for using seals at all was that so many of the people involved in various transactions could neither read nor write.

Numberless examples could be quoted of interesting seals, shedding light on mediaeval people, or the organization of the king's or baron's

household, the administration of affairs and the despatch of official and private business. But a few random examples must suffice here.

Royal seals show how early the lions or leopards became the badge of the kings of England; e.g., they are represented on the seals of Prince John (later King) and of Richard I.

A Barons' Letter of the year 1310 in the Public Record Office carries no less than 96 seals used by the lords of the realm at that time.

A particularly magnificent and well-known seal is one of John de Warenne, Earl of Surrey and Sussex (1286–1347). This is in dark green wax, a little over four inches across, attached to a document by plaited laces of red and lilac silk. One side shows the Earl in his robes on a throne or chair of state, against the background of a 'warren', with rabbits, a deer, etc.; the other shows him armoured and on horseback at full gallop. The Earl's shield and the trappings of the horse show plainly the chequers that were the arms of the family. His Great Seal displays an interesting crest above the helmet, a delicate eight-armed affair rather like a frost-crystal in form.

Other fine crests appear on the seals of Humphrey de Bohun, Earl of Hereford, 1301; Edward of Carnarvon, Prince of Wales, 1305; Henry de Beaumont, Earl of Buchan, 1322; and, on a 13th century example, of Hugh le Despenser. The last has a helm charged with his arms, *quarterly plain and fretty, over all a bend charged with three pierced mullets of six points.*

Semée: in heraldry, scattered all over or powdered with small charges, e.g., flowers. The arms of the family of Courtown, of Wexford, in Ireland, are *azure, semée of crosses crosslet, three lozenges, or.*

Seneschal: an important officer in the households of princes and high-ranking dignitaries in the Middle Ages, often with responsibilities for the supervision of feasts and other great domestic occasions. In King Arthur's court, Sir Kay was the seneschal.

Sergeant (Serjeant): apart from certain specialized meanings (e.g., in legal and official circles) this nowadays means a non-commissioned officer in the armed forces. It has changed its meaning since the Middle Ages, when it meant simply a non-knightly man-at-arms or trooper. In some of the Military Orders it also seems to have been used for esquires aspiring to knight-hood. Thus, early 14th century documents show the Knights Hospitallers in England to have been divided into three classes, Knights, Chaplains and Esquires or Serjeants-at-Arms.

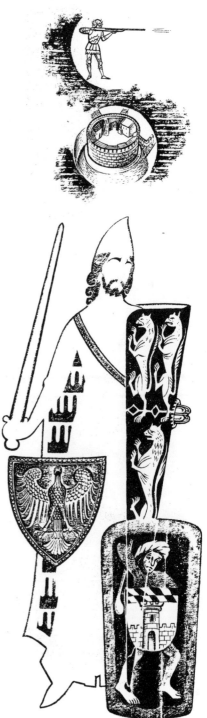

Serpentin (Serpentine): a type of hand-gun, introduced in about 1500. The slow-burning fuse, formerly held in the hand, was fixed to a twisted or serpent-shaped lever, which brought the ignited fuse or 'match' down onto the priming powder.

Seven Champions of Christendom, The:
 St. Andrew for Scotland
 St. Anthony for Italy
 St. David for Wales
 St. Denys for France
 St. George for England
 St. James for Spain
 St. Patrick for Ireland.
 Richard Johnson's *The Famous Historie of the Seven Champions of Christendom* appeared in England in 1596–97.

Sharp Lance Running: a joust with unblunted lances. (See *Coronel, Lance of Courtesy, Joust à Plaisance* and *Joust à l'Outrance*.)

Shell Keep: the strong circular stone wall round the top of the *motte* or mound of early castles. It replaced the old palisade and gave better protec-tion to the buildings within. (See *Motte-and-Bailey*.) There is a fine example of the shell keep at Restormel in Cornwall and perhaps half-a-dozen other well-preserved specimens in other parts of England.

Shield: for various types see *Buckler, Heater Shield, Kite-shaped Shield, Mantlet* and *Pavise*; and for some of the accessories see *Enarmes* and *Guige*. Many examples of shields from the 13th, 14th and 15th centuries have survived. The best were made using a technique we are apt to consider modern – sticking together several layers of close-grained wood, with the grain of each layer running at right angles to the one above and

below it. This gave a shield which would not easily get out of shape and which it was almost impossible to split. The outside surface was usually covered with leather or some other tough material, painted with the owner's device or coat of arms, and perhaps decorated with metal studs, etc.

A type which did not follow what we now regard as the conventional 'shield shape' appeared in the 14th century – a near-rectangular affair with rounded corners and a notch in the top left-hand corner (from the onlooker's point of view) for the lance. One occurs on the tomb of Sir Richard Pembridge, in Hereford Cathedral (*c.* 1375). Most shields curved round the body, but Sir Richard's, and a number of the same pattern, are concave.

Shield of Peace and Shield of War: see *Edward the Black Prince.*

Ships, Mediaeval: The war-ship of the Middle Ages was the galley, a long, lightly built craft of shallow draught, driven by oars and equipped with sharp, iron-shod ram. They were fast and could move in any direction. But they were built for conditions such as are found in the Mediterranean and not for the tough conditions of the Atlantic. For this reason, among others, England never used the galley, but the round ship for both the peaceful purposes of trade and for war. The round ship, as its name implies, had no beautiful lines. It was almost as broad as long, was a wretched sailer and could move only down-wind with any certainty, so that it was extremely difficult to grapple the enemy's ships and let the knights and soldiers get to grips. It was the round ship that was used in such sea fights as *Les-Espagnols-sur-Mer* and Sluys. (See separate entries for these battles.)

Mediaeval ships seem to have put up a brave display of heraldry, if one can judge from early seals and the many painted illustrations of them in early chronicles and other manuscripts. Thus, an early seal of Faversham shows a ship with a pendant at the masthead, the banner of St. George at the forecastle and two other banners aft; and a Hastings seal has the banner of England on the after-castle, as well as other flags. A ship of Henry VIII's time in a British Museum

Mediaeval round-ships

manuscript has a huge streamer of St. George, the royal arms and various royal badges displayed including the rose and crown, the fleur-de-lys, the portcullis and the ostrich feather.

A detailed roll has survived from the year 1350, showing the flags manufactured for the king's ships. Some of the items are:

2 penoncels $3\frac{1}{4}$ yards long and 3 cloths wide, charged with a shield of the royal arms surrounded by a blue garter.

2 streamers for the 'Jerusalem', one 32 yards long and 5 cloths wide with the royal arms in chief and striped red and white fly; the other 30 yards long, of red worsted, charged with white dragons, green lozenges and leopards' heads.

A streamer of the 'Marye', 32 yards long, with the figure of St. Mary in chief, and the royal arms quarterly in the fly.

3 streamers 5, 10, and 30 yards long with the royal arms in chief and fly chequered green and white, powdered with green and red roses.

Another Exchequer Roll, in the reign of Henry V, contains items such as the following:

For the 'Trinity Royal'

A banner of council of the royal arms and St. George; gittons [guidons] of the Holy Trinity, St. Mary, St. Edward, the royal arms, St. George, the ostrich feather, swan; and Standards of St. Mary, St. George, the ostrich feather and royal arms.

['Gittons', as distinct from Standards, were small swallow-tailed flags.]

For the 'Holy Ghost'

A streamer of the 'Holy Ghost'.

Gittons of the Holy Ghost, antelope, royal arms, swan, and St. Edward.

Standards of the Holy Ghost, St. George, antelope and swan.

Henry VIII's great ship 'Henri Grâce à Dieu' had the banners of England, England and Spain, Castile, Guienne, Wales, Cornwall, the pomegranate and rose, the rose of white and green, and St. Edward; streamers 'with a dragon' 45 and 42 yards long; one with a lion 36 yards long; one with a greyhound; and various streamers up to 45 yards long, decorated with a dragon, a greyhound, a lion, etc. (These examples, with many others, can be found in W. G. Perrin, *British Flags*, 1922.)

Carrack, 1497

Henri Grâce a Dieu (Great Harry), 1514

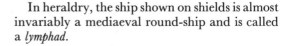

In heraldry, the ship shown on shields is almost invariably a mediaeval round-ship and is called a *lymphad*.

Short-wings: see *Hawk* and *Hawks of the Fist*.

Sidney, Sir Philip (1554–1586): rather late to be considered as belonging to the age of chivalry, but remembered always for the manner of his death when, with a gesture straight from the knightly chronicles, he refused a drink of water in favour of a common soldier who needed it more.

Sidney was taking part in a skirmish outside the town of Zutphen, which was held by a Spanish garrison, when he was struck by a musket-ball above the left knee. He was carried back to the English camp, and his friend Sir Fulke Greville later wrote the story.

'In which sad progress, passing along by the rest of the army, where his uncle the general was, and being thirsty with excess of bleeding, he called for drink, which was presently brought him; but as he was putting the bottle to his mouth he saw a poor soldier carried along who had eaten his last at the same feast, ghastly casting up his eyes at the bottle; which Sir Philip, perceiving, took it from his head before he drank, and delivered it to the poor man with these words: "Thy necessity is yet greater than mine." And when he had pledged this poor soldier, he was presently carried to Arnhem.'

The sad thing is that, had it not been for a foolish act, Sidney might have lived to fight another day and, doubtless, bring greater lustre to his name and glory to his country. When the English rode to attack the food-train that was the object of the skirmish at Zutphen, Sir William Pelham, marshal of the forces, dashed off without his leg armour. Sidney, not to be outdone, threw off his as well and left undefended the upper leg which received the musket-ball. But he was a great and gallant man, who bore his subsequent pain with fortitude for sixteen days before he died.

He was poet as well as soldier. The entry for *Douglas, James, second Earl* tells of a remark he made about the popular ballad of 'Chevy Chase', written about the Battle of Otterburn.

His friend Fulke Greville, who was another poet as well as a statesman, was proud of three things in his life, and had them written on his tomb. He said he was the servant of Elizabeth, the counsellor of James I, and the friend of Sir Philip Sidney.

(See near *Genealogy* for an illustration of part of the Sidney family tree.)

Siege: the process of sitting an army or strong force around or in front of a fortified place, with the object of compelling the garrison or inhabitants to surrender. Sometimes this was attempted by direct attack, sometimes by the slow process of preventing supplies reaching those inside and so starving the besieged place into submission.

For various methods, machines, etc., used in sieges, see *Balista, Battering-ram, Belfry, Breach, Catapult, Escalade, Mangon, Mansour the Victorious, Mine, Perrier, Petrary, Scaling-fork, Scaling-Ladder, Siege Towers, Siege Train, Trebuchet.*

For some incidents connected with sieges see *du Guesclin, Bertrand; Henry of Lancaster; Isabella; Joan of Arc; Philippa of Hainault; Randolph, Sir Thomas; Rouen; Sidney, Sir Philip.*

One of the best detailed accounts of a mediaeval siege is given by William of Malmesbury (d. 1143?) in his Chronicle of the Kings of England. He is describing the siege of Jerusalem during the First Crusade:

'As they saw, therefore, that the city was difficult to carry on account of the steep precipices, the strength of the walls, and the fierceness of the enemy, they ordered engines to be constructed. But before this, indeed, on the seventh day of the siege, they had tried their fortune by erecting ladders, and hurling swift arrows against their opponents: but, as the ladders were few, and perilous to those who mounted them, since they were exposed on all sides and nowhere protected from wounds, they changed their design. There was one engine which we call the Sow . . .; because the machine, which is constructed of slight timbers, the roof covered with boards and wickerwork, and the sides defended with undressed hides, protects those who are within it, who, after the manner of a sow, proceed to undermine the foundations of the walls. There was another, which, for want of timber was but

a moderate sized tower, constructed after the manner of houses: . . . this was intended to equal the walls in height. The making of this machine delayed the siege, on account of the unskilfulness of the workmen and the scarcity of the wood.

'And now the fourteenth day of July arrived, when some began to undermine the wall with the sows, others to move forward the tower. To do this more conveniently, they took it towards the works in separate pieces, and, putting it together again at such a distance as to be out of bowshot, advanced it on wheels nearly close to the wall. In the meantime, the slingers with stones, the archers with arrows, and the cross-bow-men with bolts, each intent on his own department, began to press forward and dislodge their opponents from the ramparts; soldiers, too, unmatched in courage, ascended the tower . . . Nor, indeed, were our foes at all remiss; but trusting their whole security to their valour, they poured down grease and burning oil upon the tower, and slung stones on the soldiers . . . During the whole of that day the battle was such that neither party seemed to think they had been worsted; on the following, which was the fifteenth of July, the business was decided.

'For the Franks, becoming more experienced from the event of the attack of the preceding day, threw faggots flaming with oil on a tower adjoining the wall, and on the party who defended it, which, blazing by the action of the wind, first seized the timber, then the stones, and drove off the garrison. Moreover the beams which the Turks had left hanging down the walls in order that, being forcibly drawn back, they might, by their recoil, batter the tower in pieces in case it should advance too near, were by the Franks dragged to them, by cutting away the ropes; and being placed from the engine to the wall, and covered with hurdles, they formed a bridge of communication from the ramparts to the tower. Thus what the infidels had contrived for their defence became the means of their destruction.'

Siege Perilous: the seat at King Arthur's Round Table always kept empty for the one knight fit to occupy it. No one else could occupy it on pain of death. Neither the King nor his knights knew who the chosen knight would be, though the truth was revealed to a hermit who came to Arthur's court one Whit Sunday.

'And when the hermit saw the siege perilous, he asked the king and all the knights why that siege was void. Sir Arthur and all the knights answered, "There shall never none sit in that siege but one . . ." Then said the hermit, "Wot ye what is he?" "Nay," said Arthur and all the knights, "we wot not who is he that shall sit therein." "Then wot I," said the hermit, "for he that shall sit there is unborn, and this same year he shall be born that shall sit there in that siege perilous, and he shall win the Sangreal." ' (*Morte d'Arthur*.)

The knight who later occupied the seat was Sir Galahad, who was led to it in 'a coat of red sandel, with a mantel upon his shoulder furred with fine ermines.' As the hermit had foretold, Galahad also achieved the quest of the Holy Grail. (See *Galahad* and *Grail*.)

The word 'siege' used in this story and the 'siege' of a town or fortress are really the same. To besiege a place means to sit down in front of it as if occupying a seat.

Siege Towers: wooden movable towers (see also *Belfry*), knocked up on the spot, as high as the walls or higher, from which the archers could fire more effectively on the defenders of town or castle.

Siege Train: that part of the army bringing along the engines, artillery, etc., needed for siege work and forming part of the permanent equipment rather than capable of being constructed on the spot.

Sigismund (1368–1437), Emperor of Germany: grandson of the blind John of Bohemia (see separate entry) killed at Crécy. Despite early promise as a ruler, and being capable of bursts of energy, he lacked resolution and trustworthiness. He was a visitor to England in 1416, when he made pilgrimage to Thomas à Becket's shrine at Canterbury. An interesting story is recorded of Sigismund. He was present one day in the Paris Parliament when a number of legal cases were being heard and judgment delivered.

One man, not of noble or knightly rank, was clearly going to lose his case simply because he belonged to the common people. Sigismund had one of the quick-witted flashes that made him likeable; he rose from his seat, touched the man with his sword and made him a knight. It is a sad comment on justice at the time, but a good mark to Sigismund.

Silken Thomas: see *Kildare, Thomas, 10th Earl of*.

Sinclair, William (d. 1337): Bishop of Dunkeld, Scotland, and known as 'the King's bishop' from his share in a battle at Donibristle, 1317. The English had sent an army by sea, the ships anchoring off Inverkeithing in the Firth of Forth. The landing took the Scots by surprise, and a hastily-mustered force of about 500, under the command of the Earl of Fife, turned tail. They were met, however, by Bishop Sinclair, galloping at the head of sixty horsemen to help repel the invader. He reined in his horse and poured scorn on the retreating men, telling the knights in the company that they deserved to have their gilt spurs hacked off. Then, throwing off his bishop's vestment, he seized a spear and, shouting 'Who loves his king, or his country, follow me!' spurred off shorewards, followed by his sixty. The rest of the force, their panic overcome by Sinclair's example, rallied in support.

The English were driven back to their boats with heavy losses. When Robert Bruce heard of the encounter he declared that Sinclair should always thereafter be his own bishop; and his countrymen gave him the honourable title of 'the King's bishop'.

Sluys, Battle of: the first of the three important sea-fights of the Hundred Years' War, fought on June 24, 1340. The others were *Les-Espagnols-sur-Mer*, 1350 (see separate entry) and La Rochelle, 1372. They were battles fought, not by trained seamen forming a royal navy, but by land forces fighting at sea. The first two were resounding victories for the English; the third a dismal defeat, the decisive weapon being the great stones and bars of iron dropped on the lighter English vessels by the higher-built ships of Castile fighting on the side of France.

At Sluys, Edward III was in command. He adopted land tactics by pretending to be in retreat and then turning on the enemy. The result was an action fought by ships in a packed mass without any pretence at manoeuvre. As on the battle-fields of France, it was the knights and the archers who won the day. The strategy is made clear by Froissart:

'The king then drew up all his vessels, placing the strongest in the front, and on the wings his archers. Between every two vessels with archers there was one of men at arms. He stationed some detached vessels as a reserve, full of archers, to assist and help such as might be damaged.

'There were in this fleet a great many ladies from England, countesses, baronesses, and knights and gentlemen's wives, who were going to attend on the queen at Ghent: these the king had guarded most carefully by three hundred men at arms and five hundred archers. . . .

'The battle then began very fiercely; archers and cross-bowmen shot with all their might at each other, and the men at arms engaged hand to hand: in order to be more successful, they had large grapnels, and iron hooks with chains, which they slung from ship to ship, to moor them to each other. There were many valiant deeds performed, many prisoners made, and many rescues. . . .

'The king, who was in the flower of his youth, showed himself on that day a gallant knight, as did the earls of Derby, Pembroke, Hereford, Huntingdon, Northampton, and Gloucester; the lord Reginald Cobham, lord Felton, lord Bradestan, sir Richard Stafford, the lord Percy, sir Walter Manny, sir Henry de Flanders, sir John Beauchamp, sir John Chandos, the lord Delaware, Lucie lord Malton, and the lord Robert d'Artois, now called earl of Richmond. I cannot recall all the names of those who behaved so valiantly in the combat. . .

'After the king had gained this victory, which was on the eve of St. John's day, he remained all that night on board of his ship before Sluys, and there were great noises with trumpets and all kinds of other instruments.'

Smithfield: district of central London, north of

the river and just outside the old city walls, which was a favourite tournament ground in the Middle Ages. (See *Tournament*.)

Solerets (Solerets): flexible foot armour made of steel plates or *cuir-bouilli*. (See separate entry.) Often they were fastened on by straps which could be cut if the knight was fighting on foot, so that the projecting point was removed to permit easier walking.

Somerset Herald: one of the heralds attached to the English College of Arms. See *Officers of Arms*.

Song of Roland: see *Roland, Song of*.

Sortie: from the French *sortir*, to go out; a sudden raid from a besieged place, usually of only a small force, to harry the besiegers.

Souvenance, Flower of: see *Flower of Souvenance*.

Sow: a type of siege engine. For description, see William of Malmesbury's account of the siege of Jerusalem, under *Siege*.

Spanish Morion: see *Morion*.

Spaulder: small series of overlapping plates of armour to protect the shoulder.

Spear: general term for a weapon with a pointed head on a long shaft. The knight's spear was the lance. (See separate entry.) Another name for a joust was a 'spear running'.

Splinted Armour: see *Studded and Splinted Armour*.

Spurs: see *Prick Spur* and *Rowel* for the two main types of this necessary part of the knight's horse equipment. Fairly simple as the spur may seem in basic design, there was plenty of room for variety, and it often displayed superb craftsmanship in the Middle Ages. As many as ten or a dozen parts of a spur may be distinguished, including the strap-plate, for holding the strap or straps round the front of the ankle; the heel plate round the back; the neck, between the side arms and the prick or rowel; the ridge, which is the highest part of the neck; and the jingle, often attached to the hub of the rowel, giving a dainty tinkling sound when the rider is in motion.

Squire: see *Knight* and *Chaucer, Geoffrey.*

Squire of the Body: an attendant on knight, noble or king, with special responsibilities for helping them to arm, leading their horses and attending them in battle.

Squire of Low Degree, The: a poem dating from the early part of the 15th century and concerned with the ever-popular theme (then, as now) of the lowly squire winning the hand of a high-born lady. For two real-life examples, see *Holland, Thomas,* and *Woodville, Richard.* The king, in typical style, tries to turn the princess's thoughts away from her humble squire with a variety of alternative attractions, but she, stout lass, will have nothing to do with them. These are some of the things she scorned in favour of her 'Squyr of Lowe Degre':

> *To morowe ye shall on hunting fare,*
> *And ryde, my doughter, in a chare,*
> *It shalbe covered with velvet reede,*
> *And clothes of fyne golde al about your hed,*
> *With damske, white, and asure blewe,*
> *Wel dyapred with lyllyes newe;*
> *Your pomelles shalbe ended with gold,*
> *Your chaynes enameled many a folde. . . .*
> *Jennettes of spayne, that ben so wyght,*
> *Trapped to the ground with velvet bright.*

(reede = red; damske = damask; asure blewe = azure blue; dyapred = diapered; lyllyes = lilies; pomelles = pommels; chaynes = chains; Jennettes of spayne = jennets of Spain.)

Stag: see *Deer.*

Stall-plate: see *St. George's Chapel.*

Standard: a word which has had several meanings through the centuries. The most important are (1) a pole or staff supporting some device or symbol that was not, properly speaking, a flag; (2) a framework or scaffolding on wheels, sup-

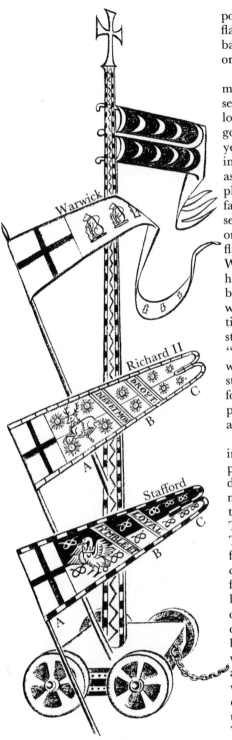

Warwick

Richard II

DROYT

OBLYATHON

C

B

A

Stafford

LOYAL

HVMBLEE

C

B

A

porting a variety of objects, including banners or flags; (3) a long tapering flag displaying the badges and, sometimes, the motto of king, noble or knight.

Under (1) we hear, e.g., of Robert of Normandy, in the attack on Jerusalem of 1099, seizing from one of the Saracen commanders a long pole, silvered over and crowned with a golden apple or ball. Under (2), nearly a hundred years later, there is a record of Richard I going into battle with what a contemporary describes as 'a very long beam, like the mast of a ship, placed upon four wheels in a frame very solidly fastened together and bound with iron, so that it seems incapable of yielding either to sword, axe or fire. Affixed to the very top of this, the royal flag commonly called banner, flies in the wind . . . While that standard remained erect the people had a sure place of refuge. Hither the sick were brought to be cured, hither were brought the wounded, and even the famous or illustrious man tired out in the fighting. Whence, because it stands fast as a sign to all people, it is called the "Standard". It is placed upon four wheels, not without reason, in order that, according to the state of the battle, it may be either brought forward as the enemy yield or drawn back as they press on.' (See also *Battle of the Standard* for another example.)

From the point of view of chivalry, the most interesting study is the third development – the personal standards of knights, which come to be distinguished from banners. The banner remains more of a rallying point and carries the arms of the owner; it is square or rectangular in shape. The standard is long, narrow and split at the end. There are many examples of commanders on the field of battle cutting off the tails of a standard to convert it into a temporary banner in token of the fact that the owner, because of his gallantry, has been raised to a higher rank. The standard never carried the whole arms, or achievement, of its owner – only his badges and devices. Because the banner became a symbol of higher status, there were many more standards than banners in an army. But it must be understood that the banner was not a substitute for the standard. The man entitled to display a banner could also go on using a standard, or a number of them, as well. The distinction is that those authorized to carry

316

a banner were also entitled to standards; but those of lower rank, entitled only to a standard, could not adopt a banner.

A manuscript in the British Museum gives details of some of the royal standards, as distinct from banners. If they were displayed in front of the king's tent or pavilion, they were apparently about six feet long; but if carried, with the wind fluttering and streaming them, they could be as long as thirty feet. The section of the standard nearest to the staff carried the red cross of St. George. The rest was divided into three or four parts, divided by stripes or *bends* on which mottoes could be placed. Sometimes the upper and lower sections of the standard were of different colours. In the descriptions below, these colours are given first. The badges or devices carried in the various sections are lettered A, B, C, etc. Reference to the drawing in the margin on p. 316, lettered in the same way, will show exactly where the badges were placed on each standard.

EDWARD IV
Azure and gules.
A. A lion passant guardant or, armed azure, langued gules, on his head the crown of England proper, between in chief three red roses, and in base three white roses, all encircled by rays of gold.
B. A red and white rose.
C. Two red and two white roses, as in A.
   Motto: Dieu et mon Droyt.

HENRY VII (i)
Argent and vert.
A. A dragon statant wings endorsed gules, vomiting flames proper between four flames of fire also proper.
B. Two similar flames.
C. Five similar flames.
   Motto: Dieu et mon Droyt.

HENRY VII (ii)
Argent and vert.
A. A greyhound statant argent, collared gules, between four red roses barbed and seeded proper.
B. Two similar roses.
C. Five similar roses.
   Motto: Dieu et mon Droyt.

SIR WILLIAM COURTENAY
Gules.

A. A boar passant argent, armed and hoofed or, charged with a crescent sable on the shoulder; in dexter chief and base a dolphin embowed argent.

B. Two dolphins charged with a crescent.

C. Two more dolphins.

Motto: Passes bien Devant.

The College of Heralds has a similar manuscript, dating from about 1532. Two examples from it are described below:

LORD WILLOUGHBY
Azure and gules.

A. A moor's head, without the neck, proper, full-faced and ducally crowned and charged with a crescent for difference, and three ships' rudders or.

B. Two similar ships' rudders.

C. Four similar ships' rudders.

No motto. (On another standard of Lord Willoughby's it is given as Verite est sens pere.)

SIR JOHN DIGBY (Knight Marshal of the King's Household)
Azure.

A. An ostrich argent, beaked, membered and vorant a horseshoe or, with three cyphers of J.D., connected by a knot gules.

B. Two similar cyphers.

C. Four similar cyphers.

Motto: As God be plesid.

The British Museum document directs that every standard is 'to have in the chiefe the Crosse of St. George, to be slitte at the ende, and to conteyne the crest or supporter, with the poesy, worde, and devise of the owner.' Detailed directions are also given in more than one document of this time (reign of Henry VIII) for the length of the standards, which decreased in length down the social scale, e.g.:

Duke's Standard	7 yards
Earl's Standard	6 yards
Baron's Standard	5 yards
Knight Banneret's Standard	4½ yards
Knight's Standard	4 yards

With standards blowing over, approximately, every hundred men, in addition to the banners, guidons, pennons, pennoncels and streamers, the

318

mediaeval army on the march, and at the charge, must have been as brave a sight as the chroniclers loved to paint it.

Statant, Statant Guardant and Statant Regardant: see *Lion.*

Stephen (1097?–1154), King of England: a brave knight and soldier who was crowned king in 1135 and spent much of his reign under arms. We have a vivid word-picture of him at the Battle of Lincoln, where he was captured by some of the barons in 1141, fighting desperately till his sword broke, then taking an immense axe and holding off for a while the whole pack of enemies closing in on him. He was the first English king to allow and encourage tournaments. But, despite his personal courage, he was a weak and ineffective king, under whom the country suffered grievous cruelty and hardship. For a description of the miserable conditions see *Castle.*

Stoke d'Abernon: see *D'Abernon, Sir John.*

Stone-throwing Machines: see *Balista, Catapult, Mangon, Perrier, Petrary* and *Trebuchet.*

Strapwork Decoration (of Armour): see *Etched Decoration.*

Streamers: long and narrow flags, particularly used at sea. In the early 14th century, they seem to have been from about 15 to over 30 yards in length and about a yard wide. Drake's squadron sailing in search of Spanish treasure had, in addition to the larger flags, 3 streamers with the Queen's badges in silver and gold, and 80 other streamers.

Street of the Armourers: see *Italian Armour.*

Studded and Splinted Armour: the name sometimes given to the type of armour worn in the period roughly from 1335–1360. It was, in fact, a transitional period between the hey-day of mail and that of plate, and many different, and mixed, styles were worn.

Sub-ordinaries: see *Ordinaries.*

319

Supporters: in heraldry, the human figures, animals, etc., which are placed on either side of a shield, as though holding it up. The best-known supporters in England are the Lion and the Unicorn, so familiar on royal achievements of arms. Supporters occur in great variety, as the following small sample shows:

Aberconway: wyverns.

Aberdeen: an earl, and a doctor of law, both in robes.

Abingdon: a friar and a savage.

Amherst: Canadian war-Indians.

Berners: a falcon and a greyhound.

Coleridge: an otter and a black lion.

De L'Isle and Dudley: porcupine and lion.

Hart: Chinese dragon and peacock.

Rowallen: a salmon and a seal.

Scarborough: parrots.

Wittenham: wild boars.

(Note: no details of tinctures, positions, etc., have been given in the above examples. These are often elaborately detailed.)

Surcoat: a garment worn over armour from about 1190–1420. It varied greatly in length at different periods, from almost heel-length early on to the shorter, more closely fitting jupon of later times. The longer types were slit back and front to make riding easier. They had two or three uses. They kept a certain amount of rain and dirt off the armour. They were a slight protection against heat. And, at a later period, they made a showy background for the display of the wearer's device or coat of arms. (See also *Alwyte Armour.*)

Surnames: see *Names.*

Swan: a bird which, through the centuries, has had close connections with royalty and with chivalry. It was used as a badge by, e.g., Henry IV and Henry V, and it appears in the achievements of, among others, the Mandevilles, the Nevilles, the Staffords, the Buckinghams and the Bourchiers. For one of his tournaments Edward III had tunic and shield worked with the motto:

Hay, Hay the white swan,
By God's soul, I am thy man.

This is thought to have been a gesture of courtesy or a compliment to the Queen of Beauty

320

of the tournament, either because she was of
swan-like grace or because she herself used the
white swan as a personal badge. A famous hero of
legend was Lohengrin, the Knight of the Swan,
who came to Brabant in a ship drawn by a white
swan, and married a duchess he delivered from
captivity without revealing his name. When,
troubled by the amusement of her friends at this
odd position, she began to press for information
about his name and parentage, the swan re-
appeared and the knight sailed away again.
Wagner made an opera out of the story.

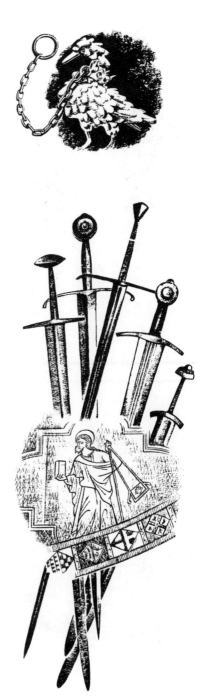

In July, 1955, a student working on the excavation of a mediaeval friary at Dunstable, Bedford-
shire, found a remarkable jewel now known as
the Dunstable Swan Jewel and kept in the
British Museum. The jewel is about an inch long
and an inch-and-a-half high, of gold covered
with white enamel to represent the feathers.
There is a gold coronet round the neck. It may
have originally been worn by a member of some
knightly order named after the Knight of the
Swan, or by a member of some noble family
whose badge it was.

Sword: for some types, see *Falchion, Flamberge,
Rapier, Scimitar, Two-handed*; for some parts,
Pommel, Quillons, Ricasso, Scabbard, Tang; and for
two famous swords of legend, *Excalibur* and
Roland, Song of (for Durandal). See also *Regalia*
for some royal swords.

Syon (Sion) Cope: a magnificent example of the
mediaeval English embroidery famous throughout Europe, often worked by nuns. The cope is
an elaborate sleeveless vestment worn by churchmen at solemn ceremonies and festivals, but not
all their embroidery and decoration are on religious themes. The Syon Cope, e.g., now in the
Victoria and Albert Museum, London, contains
many representations of secular coats of arms in
the Middle Ages.

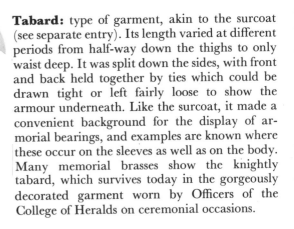

Tabard: type of garment, akin to the surcoat (see separate entry). Its length varied at different periods from half-way down the thighs to only waist deep. It was split down the sides, with front and back held together by ties which could be drawn tight or left fairly loose to show the armour underneath. Like the surcoat, it made a convenient background for the display of armorial bearings, and examples are known where these occur on the sleeves as well as on the body. Many memorial brasses show the knightly tabard, which survives today in the gorgeously decorated garment worn by Officers of the College of Heralds on ceremonial occasions.

Tabard Period: the name sometimes given to the period of armour between 1430 and 1500.

Taillefer (d. 1066): the Norman minstrel who, before the Battle of Hastings, sang to hearten the Conqueror's troops, struck the first blow in the battle and was the first Norman casualty.

'Then Taillefer, who sang right well, rode mounted on a swift horse, before the duke, singing of Charlemagne, and of Roland, of Oliver, and the Peers who died in Roncesvalles. And when they drew nigh to the English, "A boon, sire!" cried Taillefer; "I have long served you, and you owe me for all such service. To-day, so please you, you shall repay it. I ask as my guerdon and beseech you for it earnestly, that you will allow me to strike the first blow in the battle!" And the duke answered, "I grant it." Then Taillefer put his horse to a gallop, charging before all the rest, and struck an Englishman dead, driving his lance below the breast into his body, and stretching him upon the ground. Then he drew his sword and struck another, crying out, "Come on, come on! What do ye, sirs? Lay on, lay on!" At the second blow he struck, the English pushed forward, and surrounded and slew him.'

(Robert Wace, *Roman de Rou, c.* 1170.)

Talbot, John, 1st Earl of Shrewsbury (1388?–1453): one of the most dashing and gallant of the commanders of the Hundred Years' War, present at innumerable battles and sieges and occupying many high offices. With his death at Castillon in

1453, the English claims to French territory came to an end, Calais alone remaining of all their conquests. Talbot was called 'the English Achilles'.

Talisman, The: a novel by Sir Walter Scott (1825), reckoned among the best of his historical stories. It is concerned with the Third Crusade and its chief characters, including Richard I and Saladin. One of the real events included is the overthrow of the banner of Leopold, Duke of Austria, at the head of the German forces. Claiming a position equal to that of Richard of England and Philip of France, he set up his banner with theirs, only to have it hurled into the ditch by the English. Leopold never forgot the insult, and Richard paid for it dearly; for eighteen months later, when travelling back from the Holy Land disguised as a Knight Templar, the English king was recognized at an inn near Vienna and taken before Duke Leopold, who first imprisoned him, then handed him over to the Emperor Henry VI, who, in turn, held him in captivity till a huge ransom of 100,000 marks had been raised.

Tang: the narrow iron tongue at the top of a sword, making one piece with the blade. The tang forms the centre of handle or grip, and goes through the pommel at the top, where it is hammered over to rivet the whole sword securely.

Tassets: overlapping plates of armour protecting the thighs.

Templars: see *Knights Templars*.

Temple Church, London: the great church of the Knights Templar, made circular in form like the Church of the Holy Sepulchre in Jerusalem. It contains fine memorials to the knights of the Order. (See *Knights Templars*.) In 1917 when, for the first time for nearly 700 years, a Christian army entered Jerusalem under General Allenby, the effigies of the knights in the Temple Church were crowned with laurel in acknowledgement that the object for which they had striven so mightily had been at last achieved.

Tennyson, Alfred, Lord: see *Idylls of the King*;

and quotations in *Bedivere, Sir*; *Code of Chivalry* and *Lyonnesse*.

Tenure: the right of holding property, or the manner and conditions of holding it. The rendering of military service has been mentioned under *Knight's Fee*. Sometimes this service was only local; e.g., the tenant of the manor of Ruardin in Gloucestershire held it by payment of £1 3s. annually and the obligation to attend the Constable of the Castle of St. Briavel, with horse and coat of mail, within the bounds of the forest. But much stranger payments and methods of service were sometimes required, some a formality, some in the nature of courtly gestures, some with a practical basis. The following list gives examples. Some are only part of the service due, and some (e.g., the first one) could doubtless be got out of on payment of money instead.

Place	Method of Tenure
Brooke House, Penistone, Yorkshire.	A snowball at midsummer and a rose at Christmas. (Kept up as late as the 18th century.)
Dunton and Kettleston, Norfolk.	Keeping one of the king's falcons.
Land in Southampton.	100 barbed arrows to the king annually.
Middleton, Wiltshire.	Keeping two wolf-dogs at the king's expense – 4½d. daily.
Coumnevill.	One hazel bow and five feathered arrows annually.
Hame, Surrey. (Land held from the men of Kingston.)	To the men of Kingston, three clove gilliflowers at the King's coronation.
Wynfred Neuburgh, Dorsetshire.	Holding the basin at the washing of the King's hands on the day of his coronation.
Lympstone, Dartmoor.	Three arrows, feathered of peacocks, stuck into an oaten loaf worth half a farthing, when the King came to hunt on Dartmoor.
Hook Norton (held by Ela, Countess of Warwick).	The Countess to carve for Edward I on Christmas Day.
Shrivenham, Berkshire.	When the King crossed Shrivenham Bridge, a neighbouring landowner brought two white capons, with the words: 'Behold my lord these two white capons, which you shall have another time, but not now.'

Teutonic Knights: see *Knights, Teutonic*.

Tewkesbury Abbey: in the flat meadows at the junction of the Severn and Avon where Lancastrians and Yorkists fought in 1471. It is one of the most splendid parish churches in southern England and contains some fine monuments from the days of chivalry. Sir Guy de Brian, who carried Edward III's dragon banner at Crécy, is there; so is Hugh Despenser, who led the advance guard in the same battle.

Tewkesbury, Battle of: not counting Bosworth (1485), the last battle of the Wars of the Roses, fought on May 4, 1471. It saw the total defeat of the Lancastrians, headed by Queen Margaret, who was captured, the death of Prince Edward, and the secure establishment of Edward IV on the throne.

Thistle, Order of the: the ancient Order of Scottish chivalry, by legend dating from the early 10th century, when, on the eve of a battle against Athelstane, king of the English, a bright cross, in the form of that on which St. Andrew suffered martyrdom, appeared in the heavens. On gaining the victory, the Scots vowed that this cross should always be borne on their banners and those of their descendants. Whatever the origins of the Order, it fell out of favour until it was revived by James II in 1687. By a statute of 1827 the Order was to consist of the Sovereign and sixteen knights. The Star of the Order is a silver St. Andrew's Cross, in the centre of which is a green thistle, surrounded by the motto of the Order, *Nemo Me Impune Lacessit* – No one wounds me with impunity.

Thomas the Rhymer (1220?–1297): known also as Thomas of Erceldoune, a village in Berwickshire. He was credited with powers of prophecy, and foretold among other events the Battle of Bannockburn. He was also a poet of some note, though some of the verse about knights and ladies attributed to him probably came from other sources.

Tiercel: male falcon, especially of the peregrine and goshawk. (See separate entries for these and for *Falcon*.)

Tilt: (1) the verb, meaning to run a course with a lance in joust or tournament. We still say that someone rushing at top speed is going 'full tilt'.
    (2) the noun, meaning the long barrier erected

down the lists from the early 15th century onwards. See *Italian Course*. The tilt was usually of wood covered with cloth and lessened the danger of collision.

Tilting Spear: see *Bourdonass* and *Lance*.

Tinctures: in heraldry, a word used generally to cover 'colours', 'metals' and 'furs', the three ways of providing colours and textures on a shield. (See separate entries for *Metals* and *Furs*.) There are five main 'colours', often abbreviated in the way shown:

Blue	called Azure	(Az.)
Black	called Sable	(Sa.)
Green	called Vert	(not abbreviated)
Purple	called Purpure	(Purp.)
Red	called Gules	(Gu.)

If an object is shown in its natural colouring, e.g., a flower or an animal, it is described as 'proper', abbreviated ppr. It is also possible, when colours cannot be used, for the various tinctures to be shown by types of shading. For these, see *Hatching*. A third method is to sketch the arms in pen and ink and indicate the tinctures in words. This is showing them 'in trick'.

Tournament: the chief sport and most important school of the age of chivalry; the training ground of the great warrior, the opportunity for the unknown and fortuneless, the career of the landless, the favourite spectacle of the masses. They began as real encounters with dangerous weapons, in which a man hazarded life and limb, and finished as more-or-less harmless pageants.

Many efforts were made to ban or severely limit tournaments for religious and political reasons. The Church objected on moral grounds; the king because it was a wasteful way of losing fine soldiers and leaders, and because it was always a dangerous thing in troublous times to have large numbers of belligerent nobles and knights assembled in one place. Richard I, as one of his innumerable devices for raising money, licensed tournaments and appointed five 'steads' or fields for them in the country. Combatants paid their fees in advance according to rank, e.g., twenty marks for an earl and, at the other end of the scale, two marks for a landless knight. But efforts such as these were short-lived. Tournament grounds were attached to many towns, castles and even domestic dwellings, and the encounters even took place in streets and market squares. Tournaments were often widely advertised, and became great social occasions rather like a fair, with all the attendant side-shows and collection of petty crooks intent on rich pickings among the crowd.

Interesting details of the costs and intricate detail of royal tournaments are furnished in such records as the Wardrobe Accounts. Those kept by William de la Zouche (see *Zouche*) in the reign of Edward III show that John Skelton, a London armourer, provided armour, banners, standards, coats-of-arms, etc. The King's armourer, Peter of Bruges, received one payment of £106 18s. for gold and silver foil, silk fringes, etc., for the manufacture of harness, banners, crests and all the rest of the glittering display which seems to have become inseparable from the mediaeval tournament. Velvets, silks, buckram, taffeta and other materials were used lavishly for the trappings of horses. (See *Caparison* for some examples from the reign of Edward IV.) As well, there were the special costumes of the royal household. For a tournament in the year 1342, Edward III had a velvet tunic, sprinkled with small Saracens of gold and silver, each with a jewelled royal motto, and with two Saracens holding shields showing the King's arms.

For a good deal of additional information about the tournament, its weapons, customs, area, personalities, etc., see *A l'Outrance; Baston Course; Bataille Français, Bourdonass; Brandon, Charles; Brocas Helm; Caparison; Coronel; Course; Eltham Palace; Eglinton Tournament; Field of the Cloth of Gold; Free Course; German Course; Helm; Henry II of France; Italian Course; Ivanhoe; Joust; Joust à Plaisance; Jousting Cheques; Lance; Lance of Courtesy; Lists; Mêlée; Ostrevant, Count of; Pavilion; Pieces of Advantage; Queue; Quintain; Railway Knight; René of Anjou; Smithfield; Unknown Knight; Westminster Tournament Roll; Woodville, Anthony; Woodville, Sir John; Yaxley, John; Zouche, William de la.*

A distinction must be made between the ordinary tournament and the duel of chivalry, arranged to settle a quarrel, a point of honour or a legal dispute. Both took place in similar circumstances, with a good deal of fuss and

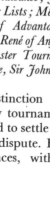

pageantry and with crowds of onlookers; and both were governed by much the same set of rules. But the duel's cause was different; anger and rancour were often its mainspring, rather than the desire for knightly fame and entertainment; and its end was more often fatal, for the expected end of the duel of chivalry was frequently the *coup-de-grâce*, the finishing stroke with dagger or sword. An example of the duel or combat of chivalry will be found under *Parker, Sir James*, which is thought to have been the last case in England.

A famous example, happily without fatal result, took place in 1390, on Old London Bridge. A quarrel occurred at a banquet in Scotland as to whether the Scots or the English were more courageous, and the English ambassador to the Scottish court, Lord Welles, issued a challenge to mortal combat to any Scottish knight. Sir David Lindsay (1365?–1407) accepted the challenge in defence of the honour of Scotland.

The fight took place on May 6, 1390, in the presence of Richard II and his queen, and a vast crowd. The two knights thundered over Old London Bridge in the first encounter and met fairly and squarely, breaking their spears; but while Welles reeled in the saddle from the shock, Sir David sat so still and rock-like that he was accused of being fastened in the saddle. By way of convincing proof that this was not so, he knelt before the king and then vaulted straight back into the saddle. Spears were again shattered in the second course, but both knights kept their seats. In the third, Welles was knocked clean out of the saddle, and Lindsay swung himself from his horse and knelt by his fallen opponent. The challenge had been to mortal combat and he was entitled to the final stroke; but, instead, he gently removed Welles's helm and cradled him in his arms till he could be removed to have his wounds dressed.

There have been many attempts to re-create the tournament in modern times. In the 18th and 19th centuries they were staged in Germany, Italy, Sweden, Denmark, Austria, Spain and Malta. America had its share. In 1778, a young officer named Lord Cathart organized one in Philadelphia in honour of General Sir William Howe when he retired, and many were held in the southern states between 1830 and 1860.

The most ambitious and elaborate revival took place in England in August, 1839, when the 13th Earl of Eglington arranged a much-publicized tournament at Eglington Castle, Ayrshire. The ancient rules governing the tournament were studiously hunted out. Some 150 would-be knights attended the preliminary meetings; about 40 decided to participate. Many were frightened off by the expense, for those who had no ancestral armour at home and could not borrow had to have a harness specially made. The man entrusted with most of this work was Samuel Luke Pratt, a dealer in armour with premises in Bond Street, London. At the first talks, it was calculated that about £40 would be needed to equip a combatant satisfactorily – the equivalent of about four times that sum today – but in the end it worked out at nearer £400. Some of the items in Lord Glenlyon's account were a knight's harness of polished steel for £105; a set of horse caparisons, with horse armour and tilting saddle, for £42 10s.; a mail hauberk for £12 12s.; an emblazoned shield and gonfalon banner for £11 11s. and a pair of gilt spurs for £3 3s.

In the end, the roll of knights was reduced to 19, among them the Earl of Eglington, the Earl of Cassillis, the Earl of Craven, the Marquess of Waterford, Viscount Alford and Viscount Glenlyon.

The scale of events when the tournament actually took place seems to have taken everybody by surprise. Spectators swarmed to Eglington by train, by road and by sea, in their tens of thousands; and with them came a choice assortment of the underworld with objectives rather less than knightly. There were people in trees, on carriage roofs, on every slope and vantage point. Four thousand crowded the stands. A total of 100,000 is thought to be a conservative estimate.

Just as the opening half-mile cavalcade of knights, ladies, squires, heralds, officials, musicians and the rest were setting out to the lists, the rain came down in icy squalls. Most of the magnificent ceremonial had to be dispensed with, and the Queen of Beauty arrived at her stand in a carriage and went in from the back. Roofs began leaking and the royal box and grandstand were flooded. The soaked crowds were in need of high drama to warm their hearts

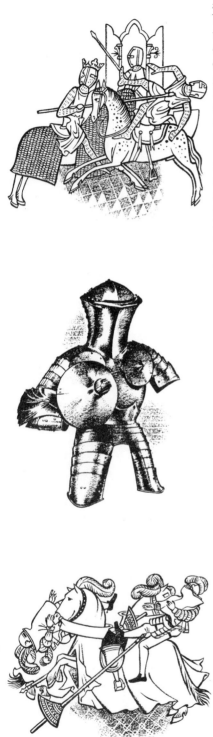

and rekindle some of the preliminary excitement. What they got when the first two knights spurred towards each other was absurdity. The horsemen completely missed each other and one of them dropped his spear, with his wife's kerchief gallantly tied to it. The rest of the combatants had little better luck. Only Lord Eglington himself, jousting with Lord Waterford, produced anything like the real thing, splintering his lance perfectly on the centre of his opponent's shield. The day's misfortunes were not over. Slithering through the rain and mud, Eglington came to the dripping grandstand to tell two thousand special guests that the mediaeval banquet arranged for the evening, and the following ball, had had to be cancelled because the great marquee was flooded. In the words of Ian Anstruther, who has graphically described the whole affair from its first conception to its miserable end in 'The Knight and the Umbrella':

'Then began a confused exodus which truly defied description. As one hundred thousand spectators began to make their way from the Lists, forced to head for home on foot, the rain pouring, the wind howling and the mud pulling their shoes from their feet, young and old, rich and poor, jostled together like cattle at a fair and behaved with as little civility.'

*   *   *

In the early autumn of 1966, the staff of the Kent and Sussex Hospital, Tunbridge Wells, received a shock; for men arrived in the casualty department carrying a knight in armour. He had been taking part in the celebrations commemmorating the Battle of Hastings nine hundred years before and had become badly entangled with his opponent. It turned out that he was left-handed and had insisted on fighting that way, with dire results.

This raises the whole question of the left-handed knight. Was there, or could there be, such a thing? What happened to a man whose right hand was so badly damaged that he could no longer use it in the tournament?

Mr. Ewart Oakeshott, a profound student of these matters and of all things connected with the knight of chivalry, has kindly instructed the present writer on this point; and, while there is no simple answer, it seems certain that any boy born left-handed would be taught to joust right-handed. Horses were carefully schooled to lead with the right foot and receive an adversary's horse on the near side. While less conventional movements were sometimes necessary in the open mêlée, the joust proper was a carefully regulated business, played according to fixed rules. Mr. Oakeshott believes that a knight with a badly maimed right hand could fight, or learn to fight, as well as ever with his left; but that he would give up jousting.

Tourney: another name for Tournament.

Tours, Battle of: an early battle between the Cross and the Crescent, fought on October 10, 732, between the Franks under Charles Martel (= the Hammer) and the Saracens under Abderrahman. The armies met in the plains between Tours and Poitiers, and the Saracen conquests in Western Europe received a decisive check. We have accounts not only from the Christian side but, what is more rare, from the Arab chroniclers. One says:

'The hearts of Abderrahman, his captains and his men were filled with wrath and pride, and they were the first to begin the fight. The Moslem horsemen dashed fierce and frequent forward against the battalions of the Franks, who resisted manfully, and many fell dead on either side, until the going down of the sun. Night parted the two armies: but in the grey of the morning the Moslems returned to the battle. Their cavaliers had soon hewn their way into the centre of the Christian host. But many of the Moslems were fearful for the safety of the spoil which they had stored in their tents, and a false cry arose in their ranks that some of the enemy were plundering the camp; whereupon several squadrons of the Moslem horsemen rode off to protect their tents . . . And while Abderrahman strove to check their tumult, and to lead them back to battle, the warriors of the Franks came around him, and he was pierced through with many spears, so that he died.'

Tower of London: the fortress built by William the Conqueror to protect – and intimidate – the city. Part of the buildings are Norman, but many later styles are also represented. The oldest

and most important part is the White Tower, the name given to the Keep or Great Tower. At one period in its history the Tower was really white, for Henry III had the whole building, inside and out, whitewashed. The Tower was occupied as a palace by all English kings and queens down to James I, and it has also served as a prison, as the royal mint, as the Public Records repository and, for centuries, as the arsenal for small arms. The Tower is still garrisoned. Among the interesting prisoners held here were the Burghers of Calais. (See *Philippa of Hainault*.)

For some account of the history of the collection of armour see *Queen Elizabeth's Armoury*. For some exhibits see *Brocas Helm; Brandon, Charles* and *Greenwich Armour*. Among the last is a harness of Henry VIII's for fighting on foot, weighing 93 lbs. There is a notable difference between the armour made for the king as a young man and in his later years, when he had put on a great deal of weight. The Sword Room contains some exhibits of extreme rarity – some English longbows, brought up from the wreck of the *Mary Rose*, which sank in 1545. The Tower also houses the Crown Jewels. (See *Regalia*.)

Towton, Battle of: perhaps the most important battle of the Wars of the Roses, fought on March 29, 1461. It was a decisive victory for the Yorkists, won after a ten-hour fight. It was in this battle that Warwick stabbed his horse before a wavering Yorkist line as a sign that he would not retreat.

Trapper: cover for a horse, a caparison. See *Caparison* for some examples.

Trebuchet: one of the stone-throwing machines used in siege warfare. See *Mediaeval Artillery* for a description of its action. It was usually constructed on the spot from readily available materials, and dismantled after the siege. Once the range was secured, it was a fairly accurate weapon owing to its uniform action.

Tressure: see *Orle*. A tressure is a very narrow orle, and almost never appears singly on a shield. Instead, the double tressure is used, with a very small gap between the two. It is ornamented with fleurs-de-lys, whose heads can either all point outwards or else alternately outward and inward. If the former, the tressure is *flory*; if the latter, *flory counter-flory*. The best known tressure is on the Royal Arms of Scotland, whose charge is *or, a lion rampant within a double tressure flory counter-flory gules.*

Trick, in: see *Tinctures.*

Troubadours: the poets and minstrels who flourished in southern France, especially Provence, and in northern Italy, from the 11th to the 13th centuries.

Trouvères: the troubadours of northern France, from the 12th to 14th centuries.

Two-handed Sword: type of great sword which became popular in the 15th century. Its size and weight made it necessary to use two hands to wield it and it could not therefore be used in close formations, where wide cutting sweeps were impossible. The grip was long in proportion to the blade. The average total length was something over five feet – a foot in the grip and the rest blade; but some larger specimens went up to six feet or more. One from the Edinburgh Castle collection is four feet three inches in the blade and one foot nine inches in the handle.

Uber die Pallia: see *Italian Course.*

Ulster King of Arms: see *Officers of Arms.*

Unicorn: one of the favourite fabulous beasts of the Middle Ages, probably compounded from various travellers' accounts of the rhinoceros, the narwhal (the 'sea unicorn'), etc. It first took a prominent place in heraldry when unicorns were adopted as supporters for the royal arms of Scotland. When James VI of Scotland became James I of England, he took one of the Scottish unicorns as supporter for the English royal arms to symbolize the union of the crowns, and there it remains to this day on the *sinister* or left side. The royal arms displayed in Scotland reverse the positions of the lion and the unicorn and give the unicorn pride of place on the *dexter* or right side.

Various reminders of the ancient rivalry between the two countries can be found in literature, symbolized by the lion and the unicorn. Edmund Spenser, in the *Faerie Queene*, uses the simile:

> *Like as a Lyon, whose imperiall powre*
> *A proud rebellious Unicorn defies . . .;*

and the old nursery rhyme (doubtless never repeated in Scotland) runs:

> *The lion and the unicorn*
> *Were fighting for the crown:*
> *The lion beat the unicorn*
> *All around the town.*
> *Some gave them white bread,*
> *And some gave them brown;*
> *Some gave them plum cake*
> *And sent them out of town.*

Unknown Knight: a favourite character of the romances of the Middle Ages, and sometimes occurring in real life. There was always an irresistible appeal about the nameless champion overthrowing the mighty, revealing himself as the young hero at the end, or riding away as mysteriously as he had come. Ivanhoe, in Scott's novel of the name, is a good example. (See *Ivanhoe* for an extract.) Bertrand du Guesclin (see *Du Guesclin*) is a case of the real thing. Bertrand, because of his uncouthness and ugliness, as well as his youth, was not allowed to take part in a great tournament at Rennes, at which his father was one of the leading contestants. Bertrand, however, managed to borrow some armour from his cousin and presented himself in the lists as an unknown esquire.

'. . . the heralds, after a glance at heels, breast and shield for signs of rank and family, could do no more than announce "an esquire unknown"; for there were only plain steel spurs at the heels, the shield bore no device, and over the polished armour was no blazoned surcoat. Now a jouster who refuses to disclose his name and rank may well be a very noble person indeed; or he may be some great lover riding thus masked in the service of his lady. In any case, he is mystery, he is romance, and pretty, bored eyes brighten at the sight of him.

'The newcomer rode forward into the lists, and had not long to wait for an opponent. A knight couched his lance, and thundered down upon him. The unknown met him firmly – so firmly indeed that horse and rider went crashing down . . . Another knight rode at him, and another; and ever the heralds announced their decision, "*Victoire a cel aventurier venu novellement!*" [Victory to the newly-arrived venturer!] Fourteen times the cry rang out, after fourteen courses, each run with the same battering-ram strength and smooth perfection of technique; and fourteen times the unknown wheeled his mount at the end of the lists and awaited further victims.'

(M. Coryn, *Black Mastiff*)

In the end, Bertrand's father, Reynaud du Guesclin, himself took lance and bore down on the challenger. But this time there was no crash of encounter. The unknown squire had recognized his father and would not run the risk of unhorsing him. For a few minutes there was a danger that the fickle crowd would turn against the knight they thought might be deliberately avoiding meeting the toughest opponent of the day; then another horseman came at him with the deliberate intention of knocking off Bertrand's helm, and he sat revealed to all the spectators, his sudden refusal explained.

After that, Bertrand du Guesclin was properly armed and equipped by his father.

Upper Cannon: pair of plates of armour enclosing the upper arm. The pair for the forearm were the Lower Cannon.

Uther Pendragon: see *Pendragon, Uther* and *Round Table*.

V

Vair: one of the heraldic 'furs' (see separate entry). *Vair* is supposed to imitate the coat of a squirrel, with a blue back and white (silver) belly and is represented by curious little shapes like lamp-shades or bells, placed alternately the right way up and upside-down; those the right way up are azure (blue) and the others argent (silver). Other tinctures can be used for this fur, but in this case they are termed *vairé* and the tinctures named, e.g., *vairé, or and vert* (gold and green).

An interesting case of mistranslation, or mis-hearing, has occurred in connection with *vair*. Cinderella originally had fur slippers; but at some point a scribe wrote the French word not as 'vair' but 'verre', which sounds the same but means 'glass' instead; so that the princess-to-be acquired some extremely uncomfortable and impracticable glass slippers.

Valet: a word which has changed its meaning in the course of the centuries. Nowadays it is used only for a man's personal servant concerned with his clothes. In the Middle Ages, it could mean a squire of the body, responsible for the knight's armour, etc.

Vallée-aux-Clercs: literally, the 'valley of the clerks' – the name still held by the valley where the English clerks went out to count the French dead after the Battle of Crécy. (See *Crécy*.)

Vallery, Crown: in heraldry, a crown the spokes of which are shouldered where they meet the rim and come to a point at the top.

Vambrace: armour for the arms. Originally the term applied only to the forearm, but later covered the whole arm defences.

Vamplate: round disc to protect the hand on the shaft of a lance. It did not appear until about 1430.

Venery: the art or practice of hunting.

Verneuil: an important town of Normandy, several times taken by the English. (See *Richard I*.) In 1356 it was taken by Henry, Duke of Lancaster and in 1424 by the Duke of Bedford. Fighting in the latter siege was a French knight named Jean de Bueil who wrote a novel called *Le Jouvencel*, based on his experiences as a soldier. It gives a vivid picture of the author passing through a countryside which should be gay with the bursting of spring, but which is desolated by the interminable wars – a place 'more like the dens of savage beasts than the habitation of people.' A tale coming at the end of the age of chivalry, it gives a truer picture than many of the conditions of knighthood at the time, with the empty glitter and display stripped away and, in its place, 'great pain and harshness' which must be endured and triumphed over for true valour to be displayed.

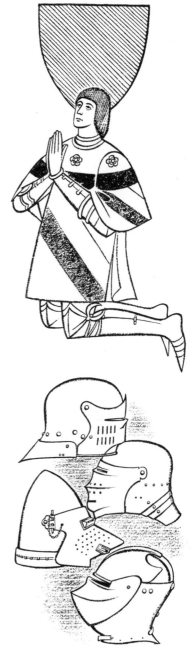

Vert: the heraldic green.

Vigil: the all-night watch sometimes kept by the candidate for knighthood, kneeling before the altar where his arms are laid, as a sign that they are to be devoted to Christian service.

Visitation: among its various meanings, a visit to, or tour in, an area by an Officer of Arms, acting under Royal Commission, to record the arms and pedigrees of those entitled to bear arms. These records are some of the most important possessions of the College of Heralds. The earliest Commission was issued to Clarenceux Herald in 1530 to visit the Counties of Berkshire, Gloucester, Oxford, Stafford, Wiltshire and Worcester.

Visor: covering of the face-opening of a helmet. There were many varieties, some being permanent fixtures, others removable simply by taking the pins out of the side hinges.

Vows: solemn promises or pledges. Some singularly stupid ones were made in the name of chivalry as well as many very sincere and admirable ones. Some of the stupid variety are mentioned in the entry for *Philip, Duke of Burgundy* and another under *Isabella*. Among the highest vows were those taken by knights on their initiation into the Orders of Knighthood. While these varied from Order to Order, their basic principles were much the same. The heart of them can be found under *Code of Chivalry*.

Wakefield, Battle of: a Lancastrian victory in the Wars of the Roses, December 31, 1460. Among the chief casualties was Richard, Duke of York, the father of Edward IV and Richard III. York's forces were not at full strength and he was advised to delay a little; but he rode recklessly straight into an ambush and went down 'like a fish in a net or a deere in a buckestall.'

Wallace, Sir William (1272–1305): the Scottish national leader and patriot. He was a man of great stature and strength, able to withstand hardship and privation, and filled with a fiery spirit of independence that infected his followers. He won a series of notable victories and drove the English out of most of Scotland; but suffered a severe reverse at Falkirk in 1298 (see separate entry), after which he was limited to sporadic guerilla warfare, with a large price on his head. He was betrayed by one of his own countrymen, Sir John Menteith, and taken prisoner on August 5, 1305. On August 23 he was tried in Westminster Hall on a charge of treason, and was mockingly crowned with laurel because he had aspired to the crown of Scotland. Wallace stoutly maintained that he could not be a traitor to the king of England, since he was never his subject and had never sworn allegiance to him. He was dragged at the tails of horses to a gallows in Smithfield and there barbarously executed.

One of the things that spread Wallace's fame and surrounded his name with many stories was a long poem by Blind Harry, or Henry the Minstrel (flourished 1470–1492).

Wallace Collection: a famous collection left to the nation in 1897 by the widow of Sir Richard Wallace. It is housed in Hertford House, Manchester Square, London, W.1, and includes among its many treasures some fine specimens of armour.

War-cries: one of the inevitable accompaniments of the battles of the Middle Ages. They fall into two main classes, the personal or family battle-cries and the national cries. Some of the former are noted under *Mottoes*. Among other recorded examples are:

Dex Aie! (God help us!)	The Normans at Hastings.
Holy Cross!	The English at Hastings.
St. Iago! Charge, Spain!	Spanish armies.
Montjoye St. Denys!	France.
St. George! St. George for Guienne!	England.

War hammers

Wardrobe Accounts: see *Tournaments* and *Zouche, William de la.*

War Hammer: a weapon much like the modern craftman's claw-hammer in general outline, but with a handle at least twice as long, and, often, a thrusting point at the top. Sometimes the handle was plain, sometimes bound, with the hand protected by a small disc above the grip.

Warwick, Earls of: see (1) *Beauchamp, Richard, Earl of Warwick;* (2) *Neville, Richard, Earl of Warwick;* (3) *Rous Roll;* (4) *Guy of Warwick,* for a story with close Warwick associations.

Westminster Abbey: see *Edward I; Eleanor of Castile; Henry V; Henry VII's Chapel; Jerusalem Chamber; Montfort, Simon de; Regalia; Richard II; Sanctuary; White Hart.*

Westminster Tournament Roll: a well-known pictorial record, in the possession of the College of Heralds, of the jousts held by Henry VIII at Westminster in February, 1511, in honour of Queen Catherine of Arragon and the birth of their son, Henry Duke of Cornwall. It is nearly 60 ft. long by 14¾ in. wide, made up of 35 sheets of vellum illuminated in gold, silver and various colours. The roll shows the whole panorama of the event, the procession to the lists, the tournament and the return to court. One of the most splendid portions of the Roll shows the Officers of Arms – four heralds and two pursuivants – leading in the four 'tenants', or knights who were to hold the lists. These were the King himself, Sir Edward Nevill, William Earl of Devon and Sir Thomas Knyvet. The four champions ride in armour under striped tents carried by thirty-eight attendants. The King's tent is of gold and red brocade, with blue stripes; the other tents are striped red and blue and 'powdered' or sprinkled with golden K's.

(See also *Brandon, Charles, 1st Duke of Suffolk.*)

Effigy of Richard Beauchamp, Earl of Warwick

The Tilt Yard at Westminster was on the site of the present Horse Guards, near Downing Street.

Wey, William (1407?–1476): an early travel writer who not only made pilgrimages himself but also gave most useful guidance to others. He was at Compostella in 1456 (see *James of Compostella, St.*) and in Palestine 1457–58 and 1462. He recommended the pilgrim to acquire a bed, a mattress, two pillows, two pairs of sheets and a quilt in Venice and, on the homeward journey, to sell them all back to the same merchant who sold them! This was apparently a well-established practice. All the features of a good modern guide-book were included – a vocabulary of useful phrases and sentences, rates of exchange, suggestions for places to visit, routes to follow, a map, etc. He also has wisdom to offer on travel by sea, recommending a berth in the highest part of the ship, because those in the lowest are 'ryght smolderyng hote and stynkynge.' Not more than 40 ducats should be charged from Venice to the port of Jaffa, and this should include hot meat twice a day, good wine and pure water. The careful pilgrim lays in a stock of private provisions, too, for 'though you shall be at the table with your patron [i.e., the captain's table] notwithstanding you shall oft-time have need to your victuals, bread, cheese, eggs, fruit, and bacon, wine, and other, to make your collation.' (Spelling modernized.)

Once arrived in Palestine, the traveller must keep an eye open for thieves and robbers. 'Also take good heed of your knives and other small things that you bear upon you, for the Saracens will go talking with you and make good cheer, but they will steal from you that you have.' The pilgrim is specially advised to be quick off the mark at Jaffa in order to get the best donkey to ride on. The donkey played an important part in pilgrimages, and even knights did not disdain this lowly form of transport when they were on peaceful journeys.

White Armour: see *Alwyte Armour*.

White Company: see *Free Companies*.

White Cross Knights: another name for the

Knights Hospitallers, or Knights of St. John of Jerusalem (see separate entry), from the white cross on a black habit worn by them.

William I (the Conqueror): see *Gonfalon* and *Taillefer*.

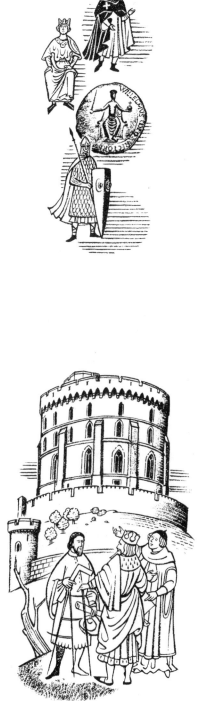

William the Lion (1143–1214): king of Scotland. He supported a revolt against Henry II of England in the hope of getting back Northumberland for Scotland, but he was captured near Alnwick Castle and brought ignominiously to Henry at Northampton, from where he was sent to imprisonment in the Castle of Falaise, Normandy. Jordan Fantosme, in his 'Chronicle of the Scottish Wars', gives an account of Henry II's reception of the news of the capture, including the lines:

> *And the King is so merry and joyful that night*
> *That he went to his knights and awoke them all.*

By the subsequent Treaty of Falaise, the Scottish king was released, but had to surrender many of his greatest castles and be subject to England. He was able to buy the lot back for 15,000 marks from Richard I in 1189, the year in which Coeur-de-Lion succeeded to the throne and immediately began making preparations for his Crusade.

Winchomb, John: see *Jack of Newbury*.

Windsor Castle: one of the chief residences of the sovereigns of England. William the Conqueror began the building, or added to an existing one. There is clear evidence of its original *motte-and-bailey* form. Edward III demolished a good deal of it and carried out a rebuilding programme under the direction of the great William of Wykeham (1324–1404), later Bishop of Winchester and Chancellor of England. Edward sent for workmen from all over the country. The sheriff of Norfolk and Suffolk, for example, received an order to send William of Wykeham eighty masons 'with the tools belonging to their trade', who were to remain in the king's employment as long as was necessary. Later monarchs carried out other alterations and additions. For the greatest addition see *St. George's Chapel*.

Windsor Herald: see *Officers of Arms*.

Woeful Countenance, Knight of the: Don Quixote de la Mancha. (See *Quixote, Don.*)

Wolfs of Landshut, The: a famous family of German armourers. A particularly famous harness called the Burgundy Cross armour was made by a Landshut armourer for Philip II of Spain. It is decorated with bands of natural steel colour, on which are gilded figures, etched alternately, of the Cross of Burgundy and the emblems of the Golden Fleece.

Woodville, Anthony, 2nd Earl Rivers (1442?–1483): one of the most accomplished knights and noblemen of the 15th century, soldier, jouster, translator, poet. (See *Flower of Souvenance* and *Caxton, William.*) The first book printed in England was a translation made by him of a French manuscript of the sayings of the ancient philosophers. It was originally lent to him by a Gascon knight when the two men were on board ship to make pilgrimage to the shrine of St. James of Compostella. (See *James of Compostella, St.*)

Anthony Woodville's most famous exploit was his two-day tournament with Anthony of Burgundy at Smithfield in 1467, as a result of the incident of the *Flower of Souvenance* (see entry), and the challenge to the Burgundian knight. It was two years before the latter was able to arrive in England to meet his opponent.

The encounters of the first day were on horseback. In the first course, the horses were so fresh and unruly that they veered and there was no score. For the second course, the lances were discarded and the two knights used swords. This time they met fair and square in the middle of the lists. The shock of the encounter was such that Anthony of Burgundy's horse reared up and toppled over backwards, pinning his rider to the ground. When he was released he was so angry that he accused Woodville of having some unfair weapon, such as a spike in the trappings of his horse, which had caused the accident. Woodville's answer was to ride before the king (Edward IV) and to show the accoutrements of his steed. The king sent them off to their lodgings. A French knight has recorded that Anthony of Burgundy's parting words that day were: 'Doubt not. He has fought a beast today, but tomorrow he shall fight a man.'

On the second day the two knights fought with axes and, after a tremendous struggle in which many great blows were exchanged, Anthony of Burgundy came within peril of his life when Woodville's axe sliced through the side of his visor. The king did not wish the bout to end in the guest being killed and sent his staff soaring into the lists as a sign that the fight should stop. The two men were so blinded with sweat and flying sand, and so preoccupied with their struggle, that they did not notice the royal command and one of the officers of the lists thrust his stave between them. The stave was shattered, but it brought the knights to a halt. They came before Edward, who complimented them on their courage and hardihood, and ordered them now to go their ways in peace. The two knights left the lists with their axes in their hands to show that they had not been disarmed. 'And soo were they departid,' wrote the chronicler of the tournament, 'to the honour of the Lord Scalys for both dayes.' Lord Scales was another of Anthony Woodville's titles. (For other details of this fight see *Battle-axe*.)

Soon after his friend and brother-in-law Edward IV died, Woodville was arrested on a flimsy charge of high treason and executed. One of his last acts was to write a poem on the sudden cruel change of fortune that had come to him, a change that he met with as much courage as he had shown in battle and tournament. His will directed that his body armour and horse harness should be sold to buy shirts and smocks for the poor.

He was a Knight of the Garter, and his stall-plate can be seen in St. George's Chapel, Windsor. (See separate entry.)

Woodville, Sir John (d. 1469): brother to Anthony Woodville, above. He was an accomplished jouster and, at the nine-day celebrations in Bruges when Margaret, sister of Edward IV, married Charles, Duke of Burgundy, in 1468, he was awarded the prize of the tournament. Anthony broke eleven lances in the same jousts. Only a year later Sir John was taken prisoner at the Battle of Edgecote and, at the age of twenty-four, was executed with his father (see below) at Kenilworth, without trial.

Woodville, Richard, 1st Earl Rivers (d. 1469): father of Anthony and John Woodville, above, and of Elizabeth, queen of Edward IV. His was one of the real-life cases of the 'squire of low degree' marrying the princess; for, as a courageous but humble knight, he had secretly married Jacquetta, widow of the great Duke of Bedford, brother to Henry V. The newly married couple had to seek the royal pardon from Henry VI and were fined a thousand pounds. Thereafter his rise was rapid, and within fifteen years he was created Baron Rivers and a Knight of the Garter. He set the seal on his fortunes when his daughter Elizabeth, widow of a Lancastrian knight, married the Yorkist Edward IV. Woodville became High Constable of England in 1467, but two years later was taken prisoner at Edgecote with his son John (see above) and summarily executed at Kenilworth.

Worship: a word which has narrowed in meaning since the Middle Ages. It is frequently met with in the days of chivalry in its older senses; e.g., Chaucer describes a man as being 'of worship and honour', i.e., worth-ship or worth; and Spenser another man as of much 'worship in his native land', i.e., accorded honour and respect. To have the 'worship' of an encounter was to have the merit or victory.

Wreath: see *Achievement*. Part of the total heraldic composition of a person's arms; the twisted, two-coloured circle fitting round the top of the helmet and the base of the crest. The tinctures are usually those of the chief colour and 'metal' of the arms. (See *Metals*.)

Yaxley, John (flourished 1325–57): the first known Royal Pavilioner, or official in charge of the royal tents, an office maintained by English monarchs for more than five centuries, Yaxley served Edward II and Edward III. The importance of the appointment grew with the increasing popularity of tournaments, and the Pavilioner was concerned not only with the maintenance and pitching of tents, but with the erection of special stands, etc., for the more privileged spectators. The extent of his responsibilities may be judged from occasions like Edward III's invasion of France in 1346 when, outside Calais, there were whole streets and squares of tents for the troops, the king's entourage and the accompanying officials; so that it seemed to one observer as if London had been transported to the other side of the Channel. (See *Pavilion* for the origin of the name.)

York Herald: see *Officers of Arms*.

York, House of: the most short-lived of the royal houses of England. It began with the proclamation of Edward IV in March, 1461 and finished when his brother Richard III fell at Bosworth in August, 1485. The Yorkist kings were:

Edward IV	1460–1483
Edward V	11 weeks in 1483
Richard III	1483–1485

For some of the events, military and peaceable, of this troubled period, see *Caxton, William; Edward IV; Roses, Wars of* (and entries for various battles); *St. George's Chapel;* and *Woodville, Anthony.*

York, White Rose of: the best-known of the Yorkist badges. See *Rose of York*.

Z

Ziska, John (1360–1424): one of the most remarkable leaders of the Middle Ages, a nobleman who led the peasants of Bohemia to a series of victories in defence of the Protestant religion. At first their chief weapon was the flail, and Ziska developed a system of manoeuvres with armoured wagons – which can fairly claim to have been the origin of the modern tank – which baffled some of the finest conventional troops in Europe. By means of strict training and discipline, he taught his peasant troops to handle their wagons with such speed and skill that at the shortest notice they could wheel them into a solid defensive ring; or they would lure the enemy to attack a few apparently helpless wagons in front, then suddenly sweep the rest round, completely enclosing the attackers. The terrible flails, wielded by the brawny arms of the countrymen, did the rest. Each wagon had a driver, two men to protect him, and seventeen others armed, as time went on, with a variety of weapons, including pike, bow, mace and hand-gun. Every thousand men was made up of a hundred cavalry, nine hundred foot soldiers, and fifty wagons. Ziska is also credited with being the first European captain to make full use of the artillery arm.

The secret of his extraordinary success, apart from his fertile mind, was the unwavering discipline that held his troops. 'He who disobeys orders,' Ziska said, 'shall be punished in body and goods be he prince, knight, noble, burgher, craftsman or peasant.' Games, dancing, music, revelling, were condemned. Not for them the lively rhythm of drum and fife. Their only battle-music was the Ziska psalm, roared as they swung into action with their terrible flails.

Zouche, William de la (d. 1352): archbishop of York and holder of a number of other ecclesiastical appointments. He took part in the Battle of Neville's Cross (see *Neville's Cross*): but the most interesting feature of his career is that he was clerk and, later, keeper of the king's wardrobe, and his detailed accounts give us a great deal of information about the cost of tournaments, etc., in Edward III's reign. (See *Tournaments* for some of the items.)

Zutphen, Battle of: the skirmish of September 22, 1586, in which Sir Philip Sidney was mortally wounded. (See *Sidney, Sir Philip.*) Zutphen is in the Gelderland province of Holland.

And if it should seem as though the chivalry of our own times is reduced to something less noble than of old, when men risked life, and things dearer than life, in defending the weak and attacking the oppressor in his stronghold – when the hardness of the actual fight against evil-doers was not exaggerated in the romances which pictured the knights contending with dragons and enchanters and giants – we must remember that our . . . world is yet far from cleared of the monstrous powers of evil, which still oppress and devour the weak; and that a battle, not really less resolute, nor, if need be, less desperate, than those of old, is still carried on by those who, under the modest guise of common life, are fighting in the true spirit of chivalry . . .

But whether we are content with the chivalry of manners, or aspire to a place in the brotherhood of the chivalry of action, our principles, our maxims, and our examples have come down to us as an inheritance from the past – an inheritance common to all who care to claim it; and won for us by the old knights, fighting in the name of God and of their ladies.

Sir Edward Strachey, Introduction to *Le Morte d'Arthur*, 1868.

SUBJECT INDEX

This index reproduces the most important heavy-type entries in the Dictionary, but arranged under main subject headings. It will sometimes be necessary, in order to arrive at the main entry, to follow through a cross-reference.

350

Vigil
Vows
White Cross Knights

Legends, Stories and Poems
Amadis of Gaul
Angarad of the Golden Hand
Archalaus the Enchanter
Arthur, King
Arundel
Balan, Sir
Balin, Sir
Bard
Bedivere, Sir
Caerleon-upon-Usk
Camelot
Chanson de Roland
Chansons de Geste
Charlemagne's Paladins (or
    Peers)
Dagonet
Enid
Excalibur
Galahad, Sir
Gawaine (Gawayne), Sir
Geraint, Sir
Geste
Giants
Grail, The
Guinivere (Guinevere)
Holy Grail
Hugo of Tabarie, Sir
Idylls of the King
Isumbras (Isenbras, etc.), Sir
Ivanhoe
Jehan de Saintré
Jongleurs
Joyous Gard (Joyeuse Garde,
    etc.)
Kay, Sir
Kilhwch
King Cole
Knight of the Leopard
Knight of the Tower
Launcelot (Lancelot), Sir
Lyonesse
Mabinogion, The
Mannyng of Brunne, Robert
Merlin
Minot, Lawrence
Minstrels
Morte d'Arthur
Oliver
Outlaws
Paladins of Charlemagne
Pendragon, Uther
Percival, Sir
Proverbs of Hendyng
Quixote, Don
Red Cross Knight
Rhodes, Dragon of
Robin Hood
Roland, Count
Romances of Chivalry
Round Table
Seven Champions of
    Christendom
Siege Perilous
Squire of Low Degree, The

Talisman, The
Tennyson, Alfred, Lord
Thomas the Rhymer
Troubadours
Trouvères
Unknown Knight
Uther Pendragon
Woeful Countenance, Knight
    of the

Men and Women
Athelstane
Audley, Sir James
Baldwin of Flanders
Bayard, Pierre du Terrail
Beauchamp, Richard, Earl of
    Warwick
Berchlingen, Götz von
Bernard, Saint (Bernard of
    Clairvaux)
Black Prince
Bohemund of Tarantum (or
    Otranto)
Brandon, Charles, 1st Duke of
    Suffolk
Brian, Sir Guy de
Buch, Captal de
Calveley, Sir Hugh
Captain, the Great
Caxton, William
Chandos, Sir John
Charlemagne (Charles the
    Great)
Chaucer, Alice
Chaucer, Geoffrey
Cid, The
Clisson, Sir Oliver de
Coddrington, Sir John
D'Abernon (D'Aubernon,
    D'Aubernoun), Sir John
D'Argentine, Sir Giles
Defender of the Holy Sepulchre
Delves of Doddington
Denys (or Denis), Saint
Douglas, Sir James ('The Good')
Douglas, James, 2nd Earl of
Du Guesclin, Bertrand
Dutton of Dutton
Edward I
Edward III
Edward IV
Edward, Prince of Wales
Eleanor of Castile
Erpingham, Sir Thomas
Fastolf, Sir John
Frederick I (Barbarossa)
Froissart, Sir John
Fulleshurst, Sir Robert
Geoffrey of Monmouth
George, Saint
Gloucester, Humphrey, Duke of
Godfrey of Bouillon
Götz of the Iron Hand
Grey, Thomas, 2nd Marquis of
    Dorset
Guildford, Sir Henry
Guillim, John
Guy, Earl of Warwick
Hawkestone of Wrinehill

Hawkwood, Sir John
Henry II of France
Henry V
Henry VIII
Henry of Lancaster, Duke of
    Lancaster
Holland, Thomas, 1st Earl of
    Kent
Hotspur
Howel-y-Fwyall, Sir
Howell of the Horse Shoes
Ibn Jubayr
Infidels
Ironside, Edmund
Isabella
Jack of Newbury
James IV of Scotland
James of Compostella, St.
James of St. George
Joan of Arc
Joan of Kent
Jockey of Norfolk
John of Bohemia, King
John II of France
John of Austria, Don
John of Gaunt, Duke of
    Lancaster
Joinville, Jean de
Kildare, John FitzThomas, 1st
    Earl of
Kildare, Thomas, 10th Earl of
King-maker, The
Knevynton, Sir Ralph de
Knollys (Knolles), Sir Robert
Knyvet, Sir Thomas
La Hire
Lancaster, House of
Lannoy, Gilbert de
La Tour Landry, Geoffroi de
Leybourne (Leyburn), William
    de
Lindsay (Lyndsay), Sir David
Longespée, William
Longsword, William
Louis IX
Luttrell (Luterel), Sir Geoffrey
Malory, Sir Thomas
Manny, Sir Walter
Mannyng of Brunne, Robert
Manwood, John
Mareschal (Marshal), William,
    Earl of Pembroke
Minot, Laurence
Molay, Jacques de
Monstrelet, Enguerrand de
Montferrat, Conrad of
Montfort, Simon de, Earl of
    Leicester
Mortimer, family of
Mowbray, family of
Negroli
Neville, family of
Neville, Richard, Earl of
    Warwick ('The King-maker')
Norfolk, Dukes of
Northrop of Manningham, John
Northumberland, Earls of
Odo
Old Man of the Mountains

351

Oliferne, Agadinquor
Ormonde, John, 6th Earl of
Ostrevant, William de, Count
   of Hainault
Oxford, John de Vere, 13th
   Earl of
Paris, Matthew of
Parker, Sir James
Pembridge, Sir Richard de
Philip, Duke of Burgundy
   ('the Good')
Philippa of Hainault
Plantagenet
Queens, Four
Raby, Rose of
Randolph, Sir Thomas, 1st
   Earl of Moray
René of Anjou
Rhys ap Gruffyd
Richard I ('Coeur-de-Lion')
Richard II
Richard III
Richard of Cornwall
Richard of Devizes
Rivers, Anthony, 2nd Earl
Robert I (de Bruce)
Robert (the Crusader)
Robert, Duke of Normandy
Robert de Stuteville
Robert of Gloucester
Robert of Avebury
Robin of Redesdale
Robin Hood
Roches, Peter des
St. James of Compostella
St. Louis of France
Saladin (Salah ad-Din Yusuf)
Seven Champions of
   Christendom
Sidney, Sir Philip
Sigismund, Emperor
Sinclair, William, Bishop
Stephen, King
Taillefer
Talbot, John, 1st Earl of
   Shrewsbury
Thomas the Rhymer
Wallace, Sir William
Warwick, Earls of
Wey, William
William I
William the Lion
Winchcomb, John
Wolfs of Landshut
Woodville, Anthony, 2nd Earl
   Rivers
Woodville, Sir John
Woodville, Richard, 1st Earl
   Rivers
Yaxlee, John

York, House of
Ziska, John
Zouche, William de la

Places (other than Battlefields
   and Castles, listed separately)
Caerleon-upon-Usk
Canterbury
Christendom
Cordova
Eltham Palace
Flanders
Granada
Holy Land
Jaffa
Jerusalem
Ludlow
Marches
Milan
Navarre
Normandy
Nuremberg
Oakham
Orleans
Outremer
Queen's College
Ravenspur
Record Office, Public
Rheims (Reims)
Ripon
Rouen
St. Denis, Abbey of
St. George's Chapel, Windsor
St. John, Cathedral of, Valetta
Smithfield
Stoke d'Abernon
Temple Church, London
Tewkesbury Abbey
Tower of London
Vallée-aux-Clercs
Verneuil
Westminster Abbey

Sieges, Siege Equipment, etc.
Balista
Battering-ram
Belfry
Bore
Breach
Cat
Catapult
Escalade
Fire-pot
Greek Fire
Mangon (Mangonel)
Mansour the Victorious
Mine, to
Perrier
Petard
Petrary

Scaling-fork
Scaling-ladders
Siege
Siege Towers
Siege Train
Sortie
Sow
Stone-throwing Machines
Trebuchet

Sports and Pastimes
Austringer
Bells
Buzzard
Creanse
Deer
Eyass
Falcon
Falcon Gentle
Gerfalcon (Gyrfalcon)
Golden Eagle
Goshawk
Hawk
Hawks of the Fist
Hawks of the Lure
Hobby
Hood
Jesses
Jongleurs
Joust
Jugglers
Kestrel
Lanner
Leash
Lure
Merlin
Mews
Peregrine
Quarry
Quarterstaff
Quintain (Quentain, etc.)
Roebuck
Saker
Stag
Tiercel
Tilt
Tournament
Venery

Tournaments
   See Jousts and Tournaments

Warfare
   See Battles and Warfare
   and Sieges

Weapons
   See Arms